The **Rough Guide** to

Toronto

written and researched by

Phil Lee and Helen Lovekin

NEW YORK • LONDON • DELHI

www.roughguides.com

Introduction to
Toronto

The economic and cultural focus of English-speaking Canada, Toronto is the country's largest metropolis. In recent decades, the city has thrown itself into a spate of serious image-building, with millions of dollars lavished on glitzy architecture, slick museums, an excellent public transport system and the redevelopment of its waterfront. As a result, Toronto has become one of North America's most likeable cities, an eminently liveable place with a proud sense of itself.

The city sprawls along the northern shore of Lake Ontario, its bustling, vibrant centre surrounded by a jingle and jangle of satellite townships and industrial zones. As "Greater Toronto", these areas cover no less than 600 square kilometres. In the centre, huge new shopping malls and skyrise office blocks reflect the economic successes of the last two or three decades. This recent period of growth has attracted immigrants from all over the world, transforming an overwhelmingly Anglophone city into a cosmopolitan megalopolis of some seventy significant minorities. Indeed, getting the feel for Toronto's diversity is one of the city's great pleasures. Nowhere is this better experienced than in its myriad cafés and restaurants, where standards are high and prices low. Toronto also boasts a pulsating club scene, not to mention a classy programme of performing arts, from dance to theatre and beyond.

Toronto also has its share of attention-grabbing sights, largely conve-

iii

Fact file

• The **Hurons** settled the northern shore of Lake Ontario long before the Europeans arrived, naming the site of the city "Toronto", meaning "place of meeting".

• The **American military** occupied Toronto twice during the War of 1812.

• Toronto is just 140km from the **American border** at Niagara Falls, in New York State.

• Toronto has a **population** of around 2.3 million, making it the largest city in Canada by a long chalk – its nearest rival is Montréal, with some 1,800,000 inhabitants.

• The city achieved its **present dimensions** in 1998 when, much to the chagrin of many locals, the six semi-independent boroughs of what had been Metropolitan Toronto were merged into one megacity.

• Toronto is the **provincial capital** of Ontario, one of ten provinces and three territories that make up Canada. The bicameral federal government meets at the nation's capital, Ottawa, on the Ontario/Québec border.

niently clustered in the city centre. The most celebrated of these is the CN Tower, the world's tallest free-standing structure. Much more enjoyable are the pick of the city's museums – for starters, there's the outstanding Art Gallery of Ontario and the delightful Gardiner Museum of Ceramic Art – and a brace of Victorian mansions. Though these sights illustrate different facets of Toronto, in no way do they crystallize its identity. The city remains opaque: too big and diverse to allow for a defining personality and too metamorphic to permit rigid definition. This, however, adds an air of excitement and unpredictability to the place. In fact, for many it's the surging vitality of the city that provides the most abiding memories.

What to see

Toronto's centre is readily divided into three main areas, the most diverse of which is **Downtown**, bounded by Front Street to the south, Gerrard Street to the north, Spadina Avenue to the west and Jarvis Street to the east. Here you'll find the city's most visited attractions, kicking off with the famous **CN Tower** and the humpy **SkyDome** sports stadium next door. These two structures abut the **Banking District**, whose assorted skyscrapers display some of the city's most striking architecture, especially in the quartet of hulking black blocks that comprise the **Toronto Dominion Centre**. One of the four blocks holds the delightful **Gallery of Inuit Art**, an exemplary collection of Inuit sculpture gathered together from the remote settlements of the Arctic north in the 1960s. Close by, **St Andrew's Presbyterian Church** is a proud reminder of the nineteenth-century city, its handsome neo-Romanesque stonework overlooking the home of the Toronto Symphony Orchestra, **Roy Thompson Hall**.

The Banking District fizzles out at Queen Street, giving way to **Nathan Phillips Square**, site of both the old and new City Halls, and the sprawling **Eaton Centre**, Toronto's main shopping mall, which extends along Yonge as far as Dundas. Next door, the Bay department store holds the charming **Hudson's Bay Company Gallery**, where there's an excellent sample of Canadian paintings. If this whets your appetite, you can move on to the **Art Gallery of Ontario** (AGO), home to a first-rate selection of

Tom Thomson

In May of 1912, **Tom Thomson** (1877–1917) ventured north from Toronto bound for Algonquin Park, where he spent the summer travelling around by canoe and painting the wilderness. Upon his return to Toronto, Thomson's friends – who were to become the nucleus of the Group of Seven (see p.57) – took a long look at his sketches and paintings and agreed that the wilds of northern Ontario were, as Arthur Lismer expressed it, "a painter's country". Over the next few years, the Group went on to develop a distinctive Canadian aesthetic in their paintings of the outback. Sadly, Thomson himself, who drowned in a freak accident, only saw the beginnings. There are examples of Thomson's work in all of the major art galleries, but his quintessential canvas, the striking *West Wind*, can be found at the Art Gallery of Ontario (see p.55).

Toronto's neighbourhoods

Peppered throughout Toronto are a dozen or so distinct **neighbourhoods**. Though many consist of just a few streets, these enclaves still sustain a flavour all their own. Street signs identify some of the neighbourhoods, but architecturally one is often indistinguishable from the next. The following rundown will help you get the most from the city's demographic mosaic, whether you want to shop, eat or just take in the atmosphere. Bear in mind that there is a certain artificiality to the nomenclature – Chinatown, for example, has hundreds of Vietnamese residents, while Little Italy is home to a large contingent of Portuguese.

The Annex, bounded east–west by Bathurst Street and Avenue Road, and north–south by Bloor and Dupont streets, was, in its heyday (1890–1910), the most fashionable part of town. Since then, this residential district has lost much of its allure, though it's still dotted with stately old mansions.

The Beaches (see p.83), lying south of Queen Street East between Woodbine and Victoria Park avenues, is a prosperous and particularly appealing district with chic boutiques, leafy streets and a sandy beach trimmed by a popular boardwalk. Pianist Glenn Gould was born here.

Cabbagetown (see p.71), east of Jarvis Street and roughly bounded by Gerrard Street East on its south side, Wellesley Street East to the north and the Don River to the east, is renowned for its Victorian houses. Its name comes from the district's nineteenth-century immigrants, whose tiny front gardens were filled with cabbages.

Chinatown (see p.59) is concentrated along Dundas Street West between Bay Street and Spadina Avenue. This is one of Toronto's most distinctive neighbourhoods, with busy restaurants and stores selling anything from porcelain and jade to herbs and pickled seaweed.

The Gay Village (see p.163), with its plethora of bars, restaurants and bookshops, is centred on the intersection of Church and Wellesley streets.

Greektown, a burgeoning neighbourhood along Danforth Avenue, is located between Pape and Woodbine avenues. With scores of authentic restaurants, this is the place to go for Greek food.

High Park (see p.91) takes its name from the park that overlooks the Gardiner Expressway to the west of Downtown. Its main drag, Roncesvalles Avenue, is the heart of Toronto's large Polish community.

Kensington Market (see p.59), just north of Dundas Street West between Spadina and Augusta avenues, is the most ethnically diverse part of town, combining Portuguese, West Indian and Jewish Canadians, who pack the streets with many tiny shops and open-air stalls.

both European and Canadian works. Spare a thought also for **Fort York**, the colonial settlement where Toronto began; it's now stranded on the western edge of Downtown in the shadow of the Gardiner Expressway. In the opposite direction, the **St Lawrence** neighbourhood is one of the city's more distinctive, its main claim to fame being a clutch of fine old stone buildings. From here, it's another short hop east to the **Distillery**

Little India is along Gerrard Street East, running one block west from Coxwell Avenue. Visually, it's not too appealing, but the area does have a number of fine Indian restaurants.

Little Italy – the so-called Corso Italia – runs along College Street between Bathurst and Clinton, and is one of Toronto's liveliest neighbourhoods.

Little Portugal, a crowded, vital area packed with shops and neighbourhood food joints, is focused on Dundas Street West, west of Bathurst Street as far as Dovercourt Road.

Queen Street West (see p.55), between University and Spadina, has one of the highest retail rents in the city and is home to all things trendy and expensive. The students and punks who once hung around here have moved on to what is known as **West Queen West**, between Bathurst Street and Ossington Avenue.

Rosedale is a byword for prosperity, a well-heeled neighbourhood whose leafy streets and old mansions have traditionally been home to the city's elite. Its boundaries are Yonge Street to the west, the Don Valley Parkway to the east, St Clair Avenue to the north and Bloor Street East to the south.

Yorkville (see p.70), just above Bloor Street West between Bay and Avenue Road, was "alternative" in the 1960s, with appearances by figureheads of the counterculture like Gordon Lightfoot and Joni Mitchell. Today, the alternative vibe of the place is long gone, and the district holds some of Toronto's most expensive clothing shops and art galleries, as well as several good bars and restaurants.

District, not actually a district at all, but rather Toronto's brightest arts and entertainment complex, which occupies a sprawling former distillery dating from the nineteenth century.

Moving north, **Uptown** runs from Gerrard as far as Dupont Street. With the exception of the **Ontario Legislative Assembly Building**, a whopping sandstone pile on University Avenue, the principal attrac-

The Distillery District

In 1832, James Worts and William Gooderham, two immigrants from England, built a windmill beside Lake Ontario, in Toronto. Five years later, Gooderham added a distillery to produce whisky from Ontario grain. The distillery was a great commercial success. By the 1860s it was producing two and a half million gallons of whisky from a quarter of a million bushels of grain. In 1869, a fire destroyed most of the original works, but its replacement – a series of tidy brick buildings – survives to this day, on Mill Street, just east of the foot of Parliament Street. The distillery closed in 1990, but the old works remains the best-preserved Victorian industrial complex in Canada. The complex has recently been revamped as the **Distillery District** (see p.49 for more information), which now holds, amongst much else, over twenty art galleries, independent designers, bakeries, shops, a microbrewery and no less than three performance venues – all without a multi-national chain in sight.

tions here are the museums, beginning with the wide-ranging applied art of the **Royal Ontario Museum** (ROM), where pride of place goes to the Chinese collection. Smaller and more engaging are both the **Gardiner Museum of Ceramic Art**, which holds a connoisseur's collection of ceramics, and the fascinating range of footwear displayed at the **Bata Shoe Museum**. Also of interest are a pair of intriguing old houses: **Casa Loma**, a mock-Gothic extravagance dating from 1911, and **Spadina House**, whose studied charms are the epitome of Victorian gentility.

The third part of the city centre is the Lake Ontario **waterfront**. Formerly a grimy industrial strip of wharves and warehouses, it's now flanked by deluxe condominiums and bright office blocks. This is one of the smartest parts of the city and it comes complete with open-air performance areas, bars, restaurants, shops and a couple of art galleries, including the enterprising **Power Plant Contemporary Art Gallery**. The waterfront is also where ferries leave for the **Toronto Islands**, the low-lying, crescent-shaped sandbanks that shelter the harbour and provide opportunities for city folk to go walking, swimming and sailing.

To get the real flavour of Toronto's core, it's best to **explore on foot**, a perfectly feasible option as distances are quite manageable. However, visiting some of the more peripheral attractions – like Casa Loma and Spadina House – can be a bit of a trek, especially in the summer when the city is often unbearably humid. Fortunately, Toronto's **public transport** system is excellent, consisting of a comprehensive, safe and inexpensive network of streetcars, buses and subways that delves into every nook and cranny of the city. This system also brings most of the city's **suburbs** within easy striking distance. By and large they are of limited interest, though, the main exception being **The Beaches**, a delightful neighbourhood bordering Lake Ontario, just a twenty-minute streetcar ride east of Downtown.

Finally, Toronto is a convenient base for exploring **southwest Ontario**, a triangular tract of land that lies sandwiched between lakes Huron and Erie. Significant parts of the region are blotched by heavy industry, but there's also mile upon mile of rolling farmland and a series of excellent attractions, the best of which are within a two- to three-hour drive of Downtown. These excursions include Canada's premier tourist spot, **Niagara Falls**, as well as nearby **Niagara-on-the-Lake**, a beguiling town of leafy streets and charming colonial houses. There's also **Goderich** and **Bayfield**, two lovely little towns tucked against the bluffs of the Lake Huron shoreline, and **Severn Sound**, home to a pair of top-notch historical reconstructions, Discovery Harbour and Sainte-Marie among the Hurons. The sound is also the front door to the beautiful **Georgian Bay Islands National Park**. Beyond southwest Ontario, the most obvious target is **Kingston**, an appealing mid-sized town with a clutch of old stone buildings, about 260km east along the lake from Toronto.

When to go

Toronto has a harsh **climate**. In the winter, it's often bitterly cold, with sub-zero temperatures and heavy snowfalls. January and February are usually the coldest months, though real winter conditions can begin in early November and drag on into late March. Summers, on the other hand, are hot and humid. July and August are consistently the hottest months, sometimes uncomfortably so. Spring and autumn offer the city's most enjoyable weather, with lots of warm, sunny days and balmy nights.

Climate and weather

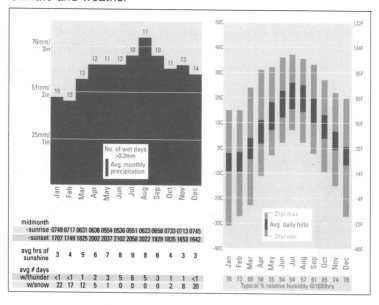

This box adapted from *The Rough Guide to Weather*, by Bob Henson.

22

things not to miss

It's not possible to see everything Toronto has to offer in one trip – and we don't suggest you try. What follows is a selective taste of the city's highlights; outstanding museums, lively neighbourhoods and great things to eat and drink. Arranged in five colour-coded categories, you can browse through to find the very best things to see, do and experience. All highlights have a page reference to take you straight into the guide, where you can find out more.

01 Kensington Market Page **59** ● Once the market for Toronto's Jewish community, Kensington Market is probably the pick of the city's open-air street markets, for everything from food to clothes.

02 The Mulberry Tree B&B

Page **122** • Set in lovely old premises, this is quite simply the best B&B in town, a charming and perfectly balanced mix of home comforts and efficiency.

03 The Hockey Hall of Fame

Page **45** • Canada's Holy Grail is ice hockey's Stanley Cup, and the very first is displayed here in this ice-hockey-mad attraction.

04 The Art Gallery of Ontario (AGO)

Page **55** • This prestigious gallery has a fabulous collection of Canadian art, a wealth of works by Dutch Golden Age painters and the world's largest assemblage of Henry Moore sculptures.

05 Walking the Beaches Boardwalk

Page **83** • Toronto's lakeshore setting is seen to fine advantage on the 3km-long boardwalk in The Beaches neighbourhood.

06 CN Tower

Page **35** • Like it or lump it, the CN Tower is Toronto's mascot – and one of the world's best-known buildings.

07

Cabbage-town Page 71
•This fashionable neighbourhood, with its trim Victorian terraces, is named after its first occupants' habit of planting cabbages in the gardens.

08 Bata Shoe Museum Page 70 •

This inventive, creative museum – housed in a structure built to resemble a shoe box – is dedicated to footwear from Ottoman platforms through to French chestnut-crushing clogs.

09 Exploring Chinatown

Page **59** • The focus of Toronto's sizeable Chinese community is Chinatown, where scores of stalls line the streets, selling every Asian delicacy you can imagine.

10 St Lawrence Market neighbourhood Page 46 • Great
architecture – some of the city's oldest buildings are here – plus a lively market, bar and restaurant scene make this neighbourhood a real pull.

11 Royal Ontario Museum (ROM) Page 65 • Dinosaurs are
one of the ROM's most popular attractions, though there's daintier stuff too, especially in the Chinese galleries.

12

Yorkville shopping Page **70** • Chi-chi shopping at its most deluxe – from antique furniture to fururistic fashion, gaudy jewellery to Gaelic music – is Yorkville's main appeal.

13 Toronto International Film Festival

Page **161** • The city's International Film Festival, the largest of its kind in North America, is a star-studded, ten-day cinematic knees-up.

14 Toronto Symphony Orchestra

Page **158** • The much-lauded Toronto Symphony Orchestra perform Downtown at the Roy Thompson Hall.

15

High Park Page **91** • Perhaps the pick of the city's parks, High Park is a rolling expanse of lawn, lake, wood and garden; in its midst is a delightful outdoor theatre.

16 **The Toronto Islands** Page **79** • The balmy breezes that ripple across the low-slung Toronto Islands make this the spot to come in the height of the summer – and, even better, cars are forbidden.

17

The University of Toronto Page **64** • The campus of the U of T, one of North America's most respected universities, is a laid-back affair with a string of good-looking old stone buildings; in one of these, insulin was invented.

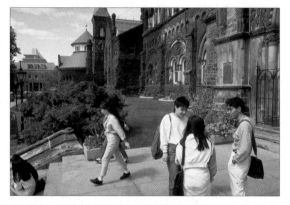

18

Casa Loma Page **72** • Casa Loma is the nearest thing Toronto has to a castle, a behemoth of a building conceived by the incorrigibly eccentric Henry Pellatt.

19
Queen Street West
Page **55** • The grooviest place in town, awash with cafés, restaurants and designer shops grabbing your attention – though it's the streetlife that really turns heads.

20
Ice skating at New City Hall
Page **183** • When they built the New City Hall in the 1960s, the wintertime ice rink in front of its main doors was a real brainwave.

21
A game at SkyDome
Page **38** • Looking something like a giant armadillo, SkyDome is a great place to watch baseball and football.

22
Theatre Page **154** • Toronto offers a superb range of theatre; the Royal Alexandra dabbles in everything from classical repertory to glitzy musicals.

Contents

Using this Rough Guide

We've tried to make this Rough Guide a good read and easy to use. The book is divided into seven main sections, and you should be able to find whatever you want in one of them.

Front section

The front **colour section** offers a quick tour of Toronto. The **introduction** aims to give you a feel for the city and tells you the best times to visit. Next, we round up our favourite aspects of Toronto in the **things not to miss** section – whether it's a bustling market, a thrilling sporting event or a stimulating museum. After this comes the Rough Guide's full **contents** list.

Basics

The **Basics** section covers all the **pre-departure** nitty-gritty to help you plan your trip, and the practicalities you'll want to know once you're there. This is where to find out about money and costs, city transportation and local media – in fact just about every piece of **general practical information** you might need.

The City

This is the heart of the Rough Guide, divided into user-friendly chapters, each of which covers a major portion of Toronto or the surrounding area. Every chapter begins with an **introduction** that helps you decide where to go, followed by a chapter map and an extensive tour of the sights.

Listings

Listings contains all the consumer information you need to make the most of your stay in Toronto, with chapters on **accommodation**, places to **eat and drink**, **music venues**, **performing arts** and **festivals**. Specialized information for families travelling with children, as well as for gay visitors, is also provided.

Contexts

Read **Contexts** to get a deeper understanding of Toronto's engaging **history**, from the First Nations to the rise of the British, and on into the city's transformation into a major megalopolis. We also cover Toronto's rich **literary tradition**, and survey some of the best **books** concerning or set in Toronto.

Index + small print

Apart from a **full index**, which includes maps as well as places, this section covers publishing information, credits and acknowledgements, and also has our contact details in case you want to send us updates, corrections or suggestions for improving the guide.

Colour maps

The back-of-book colour section has five **detailed maps** to help you get around and explore Toronto easily, locate every sight discussed in the guide and make your way around the wider Southwest Ontario region.

Map and chapter list

Contents

Contexts

Index + small print

Colour maps at back of book

Southwest Ontario
Greater Toronto
Downtown Toronto and the waterfront

Uptown Toronto
Toronto subway and rapid transit

Map symbols

maps are listed in the full index using coloured text

-----	International boundary	ⓘ	Information office
=✦=	Canadian highway	⊠	Post office
=⑤=	US interstate highway	◉	Accommodation
=⑤=	US highway	⚠	Campsite
=⑤=	Provincial highway	✈	Airport
═══	Major road	⚲	Lighthouse
═══	Minor road	⚑	Church (regional maps)
-----	Path	▬	Building
═══	Railway	⊞	Church (town maps)
—◉—	Metro line	⬭	Stadium
───	Coastline/river	⊡	Cemetery
— —	Ferry	▦	Park

Basics

Basics

Getting there

As Canada's commercial hub, Toronto is not at all difficult to reach. Flying is the most popular, time-effective option, unless you're already somewhat close by the city, in which case there are plenty of road and rail links to get you there. From outside of North America, flying is of course pretty much your only option. The main airport is Pearson International, northwest of the city (see "Arrival" for more).

Airfares from the UK, Australia and New Zealand to Toronto depend on the **season**, with the highest prices applying from around mid-June to early September, the peak tourist season. You'll get the best prices during the low season, mid-November through to April (excluding Christmas and New Year, when seats are at a premium and prices are hiked up). Note also that flying on the weekend is generally more expensive. If you're flying from the US or from anywhere else in Canada, the same general strictures apply, though the market is more unpredictable, with airlines constantly moving their prices up and down.

Airfare costs can often be cut by going through a **specialist flight agent** rather than an airline. These agents come in two main flavours: there are **consolidators**, who buy up blocks of tickets from the airlines and sell them at a discount, and **discount agents**, who in addition to dealing with discounted flights may also offer special student and youth fares, plus a range of other travel-related services such as travel insurance, car rentals and the like. Some agents specialize in **charter flights**, which may be cheaper than anything available on a scheduled flight – though be aware that departure dates are fixed and withdrawal penalties high.

Package deals from **tour operators** are rarely going to save you money in getting to Toronto. That said, several of the best provide excellent city breaks at competitive prices, putting you up in good-quality accommodation.

Booking flights online

Many airlines and discount travel websites offer you the opportunity to **book tickets online**, cutting out the costs of agents and middlemen. Good deals can also often be found through **discount or auction sites**, as well as through the airlines' own websites.

Travel and booking websites

ⓦ **travel.yahoo.com** Incorporates a lot of Rough Guide material in its coverage of destination countries and cities across the world, with information about places to eat, sleep and etc.

ⓦ **www.cheapflights.co.uk** Bookings from the UK and Ireland only (for US, use ⓦ www.cheapflights .com; for Canada, ⓦ www.cheapflights.ca; for Australia, ⓦ www.cheapflights.com.au). Flight deals and travel agents, plus links to other travel sites.

ⓦ **www.aircanadascanada.com** Canadian holiday packages for US travellers.

ⓦ **www.airgorrilla.com** Easy-to-use site posts the most economical, direct flights from major US cities to Canadian destinations, including Toronto.

ⓦ **www.cheaptickets.com** Discount flight specialists.

ⓦ **www.etn.nl/discount.htm** A hub of consolidator and discount agent Web links, maintained by the non-profit European Travel Network.

ⓦ **www.expedia.com** Discount airfares, all-airline search engine and daily deals (US only; for the UK, use ⓦ www.expedia.co.uk; for Canada, ⓦ www.expedia.ca).

ⓦ **www.flyaow.com** Online air travel info and reservations site.

ⓦ **www.gaytravel.com** Gay online travel agent, offering accommodation, cruises, tours and more.

ⓦ **www.hotwire.com** Bookings from the US only. Last-minute savings of up to forty percent on regular published fares. Travellers must be at least 18 and there are no refunds, transfers or changes allowed.

ⓦ **www.lastminute.com** Offers good last-minute holiday package and flight-only deals (UK only; for Australia, use ⓦ www.lastminute.com.au).

ⓦ**www.priceline.com** Name-your-own-price website that has deals at around forty percent off standard fares. You cannot specify flight times (although you do specify dates) and the tickets are non-refundable, non-transferable and non-changeable (US only; for the UK, use ⓦwww.priceline.co.uk).

ⓦ**www.skyauction.com** Bookings from the US only. Auctions tickets and travel packages using a "second bid" scheme. The best strategy is to bid the maximum you're willing to pay, since if you win you'll pay just enough to beat the runner-up, regardless of your maximum bid.

ⓦ**www.smilinjack.com/airlines.htm** Lists an up-to-date compilation of airline Web addresses.

ⓦ**www.travelocity.com** Destination guides, hot Web fares and best deals for car rental, accommodation and lodging. Provides access to the travel agent system SABRE, the most comprehensive central reservations system in the US.

ⓦ**www.travelshop.com.au** Australian website offering discounted flights, packages, insurance and online bookings.

From North America

For those coming **from the northern / northeastern US**, Toronto is eminently accessible – it's just a couple of hours' drive from the US / Canadian border at Niagara Falls (near Buffalo, New York) and only four hours' or so drive from Detroit, Michigan. Consequently, many American visitors, especially those from New York state, Ohio, Illinois and Michigan, choose to drive when visiting Toronto. **From further afield**, almost all major US cities have **direct flights** to the city, and services are characteristically frequent.

A much less popular option for getting to Toronto from the US is **via bus or train**, which can be taken from a variety of northeastern US cities. **Canadians visiting Toronto** usually choose to drive or fly, though there are of course similar mass ground transit options.

By plane

The greatest number of daily flights between major US cities and Toronto occur on weekdays, reflecting the high volume of business travel. All seven major US carriers fly to Toronto, so be sure to look around for the most direct routing.

At over 500 flights a day from 50 US cities, Canada's national carrier by far is **Air Canada**. **United Airlines** code-shares with Air Canada on major transporter routes to Toronto, such as those from New York, Chicago, Los Angeles and other major US cities. **Delta Airlines** and **American Airlines** have parallel route structures.

Fare structures on all major airlines are extremely fluid, and travellers should consult airline websites for the best deals. As a rule, direct, non-stop flights on Air Canada are at a premium, with a standard return fare from New York, Chicago, or Los Angeles in the area of (presented in low season–high season format) US$280–800, US$300–480 and US$330–890, respectively. A rough range of flight costs between Toronto and Montréal, Ottawa, Halifax or Vancouver under the same criteria is Can$200–500, Can$120–280, Can$400–1200 and Can$480–1200, respectively.

Booking at least two weeks ahead is an immediate way to save money. If your travel dates include a weekend, you will also realize savings. Air Canada offers two discount air travel alternatives, **Tango** and **Air Canada Jazz**. Jazz is for short-haul US and Canadian regional flights, on smaller aircraft. Tango has limited, consolidator-type routes to US cities and offers dedicated routes from Calgary, Edmonton, Montréal, Ottawa and Vancouver (as well as seven other provincial capitals) to Toronto. The difference in cost between these no-frills Air Canada brands and the regular service is anywhere between twenty to forty percent.

The motive behind Air Canada's new-found interest in discount air service is the scrappy, Calgary-based **WestJet** (ⓦwww.westjet.com), which innovated the paperless ticket, no-frills, book-online airline in Canada. Their speciality, servicing the western part of Canada, makes it a particularly good choice for Toronto/ Vancouver flights. Prices with WestJet, Tango and Jazz are highly competitive, and both offer specials on major routes that can go as low as Can$99 one-way from Vancouver. Various taxes are added to the price.

Airlines and routings

Air Canada ☎1-888/247-2262, ⓦwww.aircanada.ca. 500 flights a day from 53 US cities, all year long.

Air Canada Jazz ☎1-888/247-2262,
🌐ww.airnova.com. Air Canada's regional carriers
have all been collected under the Jazz banner. Best
for intra-Canadian flight deals. Daily non-stop
departures from Vancouver, Calgary, Montreal and
Ottawa.
American Airlines ☎1-800/433-7300,
🌐www.aa.com. Four one-stop flights daily from LA,
via Chicago; four direct flights daily from Chicago;
and five from New York City.
Continental Airlines domestic ☎1-800/523-
3273, international ☎1-800/231-0856,
🌐www.continental.com. Daily stop-over flights
from Los Angeles, Chicago and New York City.
Delta Air Lines domestic ☎1-800/221-1212,
international ☎1-800/241-4141,
🌐www.delta.com. One direct daily flight from JFK
in New York City; eight daily flights from O'Hare in
Chicago, via Cincinatti; and four daily flights from LA
via New York City or Atlanta.
Northwest / KLM Airlines domestic ☎1-
800/225-2525, international ☎1-800/447-4747,
🌐www.nwa.com, 🌐www.klm.com. Fifteen flights
daily from Los Angeles, via Minneapolis or Detroit.
United Airlines domestic ☎1-800/241-6522,
international ☎1-800/538-2929, 🌐www.ual.com.
Air Canada's code-share partner in the US, United
has ten direct daily flights from New York City; ten
from Chicago; and one from Los Angeles (with two
transfers, in Denver and Chicago).
US Airways domestic ☎1-800/428-4322,
international ☎1-800/622-1015,
🌐www.usair.com. Six flights daily from Los
Angeles,Chicago and New York City, none of which
are direct; via Washington, Philadelphia, Pittsburg,
Boston and Cleveland.

By bus

As with air travel, Toronto is a major transportation hub for continental **bus travel**.
Taking the bus is inexpensive compared to
both rail and air, it's timely, and your bus
arrives in the city centre, rather than a
good twenty-seven kilometres (sixteen
miles) outside of town at the airport. It
goes without saying, though, that travelling
by bus is pretty much the slowest way one
can go.

Toronto is served from the United States
and Canada by **Greyhound** (US ☎1-
800/229-9424, Canada ☎1-800/661-8747,
🌐www.greyhound.com). Trips to Toronto
from New York, Detroit, Chicago and
Montreal take 11, 6, 15 and 8 hours,

respectively. It takes about two and a half
days to travel to Toronto from Los Angeles
by bus, so budget and time constraints are
the determining factors here.

By rail

Rail travel is for people who believe that half
the fun is getting there. For example, a trip
from New York City to Toronto will take
almost thirteen hours including the wait at the
border, or about fifteen hours from Chicago.
Of course you can structure your trip to stop
off at cities along the way or you can simply
enjoy the leisurely pace and the view.

If you are coming from a US city to Toronto
you will be aboard one of Canada's **VIA Rail
Canada** (☎1-888/842-7245, 🌐www.viarail
.com) passenger trains. **Fares** are roughly parallel to airfare unless you don't book ahead.
The best economy fares – which can save you
over thirty percent – are obtainable two to
three weeks in advance. There are deals in
place for students and seniors that offer fifty
percent off a second fare. You can book tickets either through Via Rail or **AMTRAK** (which
you'll take for your return trip; ☎1-800/872-
7245, 🌐www.amtrak.com). Keep in mind that
for US passengers booking Via tickets, these
must be booked at least six days in advance,
as paper tickets will be mailed.

By car

Getting to Toronto **by car** is easy enough –
if, that is, you're starting out from somewhere in northeastern Canada or the US.
Beyond this area, driving to Toronto will simply take a prohibitively long time. See p.15
for information on what's needed to cross
the US/Canadian border.

From New York to Toronto, you're looking at approximately 790 kilometres (490
miles), which, not counting time waiting at
the border, translates to about eight hours'
driving time. **From Detroit**, it's approximately 370 kilometres (230 miles), or roughly four
hours' drive. **From Montréal**, it's about 540
kilometres (335 miles), and driving will take
you about five and a half hours.

You can of course **drive your own vehicle**, or you can **rent a car**. If you rent a car
in the US, inform whoever helps you that

you intend to take the car into Canada – just to be on the safe side, though this usually makes no difference. A few major North American **car rental agencies** are **Alamo** (℡1-800-522-9696, ✆www.alamo.com), **Avis** (US ℡1-800/331-1084, Canada ℡1-800/272-5871, ✆www.avis.com), and **Hertz** (US ℡1-800/654-3001, Canada ℡1-800/263-0600, ✆www.hertz.com). Keep in mind that prices for car rental are not cheap; unless you really want to drive, you might be better off – time-, money- and convenience-wise – getting to Toronto by plane.

Discount travel companies

Airtech ℡212/219-7000, ✆www.airtech.com. Standby seat broker; also deals in consolidator fares and courier flights.

Council Travel ℡1-800/2COUNCIL, ✆www.counciltravel.com. Nationwide organization that mostly specializes in student/budget travel. Flights from the US only. Owned by STA Travel (see below).

Educational Travel Center ℡1-800/747-5551 or 608/256-5551, ✆www.edtrav.com. Student/youth discount agent.

SkyLink US ℡1-800/AIR-ONLY or 212/573-8980, Canada ℡1-800/SKY-LINK, ✆www.skylinkus.com. Consolidator.

STA Travel US ℡1-800/781-4040, Canada ℡1-888/427-5639, ✆www.sta-travel.com. Worldwide specialists in independent travel; STA also does student IDs, travel insurance, car rental, rail passes, etc.

Student Flights ℡1-800/255-8000 or 480/951-1177, ✆www.isecard.com. Student/youth fares, student IDs.

TFI Tours ℡1-800/745-8000 or 212/736-1140, ✆www.lowestairprice.com. Consolidator.

Travac ℡1-800/TRAV-800, ✆www.thetravelsite.com. Consolidator and charter broker with offices in New York City and Orlando.

Travel Cuts Canada ℡1-800/667-2887, US ℡1-866/246-9762, ✆www.travelcuts.com. Canadian student-travel organization.

Worldtek Travel ℡1-800/243-1723, ✆www.worldtek.com. Discount travel agency for worldwide travel.

Tour operators

Air Canada's Canada ℡1-800/254-1000, ✆www.aircanadascanada.com. Inclusive travel packages.

American Express Vacations ℡1-800/241-1700, ✆www.americanexpress.com/travel. Hotels, packages, transportation, weekend getaways and last-minute deals.

Brewster Tours Canada ℡1-800/661-1152, ✆www.brewster.ca. Vancouver-based rail tour specialists offer packages to or from Toronto on VIA Rail's famed *Canadian*.

Collette Vacations US ℡1-800/321-8684, ✆www.collettevacations.com. Independent as well as escorted tours with a choice between Toronto proper or Toronto and Niagara.

Destinations Canada Canada ℡1-888/475-4226 or 416/488-1169, ✆www .destinationscanada.com. Air-inclusive packages for both Toronto and surrounding area, with hotel upgrade options and air add-ons for US departures.

Escape Tours Canada ℡1-866/607-4567, ✆www.escapetours.org. Toronto-based central Canada speciaists run small (up to six people), flexible tours of Toronto and the surrounding area, including Algonquin Park and the Niagara Region.

Fresh Tracks Canada Canada ℡1-800/667-4744, ✆www.freshtracks.ca. Specializes in train-travel packages, with Toronto as a hub. Includes sightseeing tours in Toronto and other major cities. Some packages are train/plane affairs with side trips to Niagara.

Great Adventures Canada ℡1-800/638-3945, ✆www.greatadventuretours.com. Specializes in groups and conventions with step-on guides, wholesale hotels, discount attractions and full transportation serving Chicago, Detroit, Windsor, Niagara and Toronto.

Gray Line ℡1-800/667-0882, ✆www.grayline.ca/tours. The Gray Line (Greyhound in the US) offers both day-trips and tour packages of Toronto and the surrounding area. The packages are three-day/two-night affairs with attractions passes available at time of booking. Gray Line also has a Discovery Pass that allows for travel all over North America.

Keytours Toronto Canada ℡416/361/1113, ✆www.keytours.com. Toronto package specialists offer wide variety of experiences: sightseeing, attractions, theatre and so on. They are open twenty-four hours a day and their Key Concierge service is a boon for those who can think for themselves but don't want to engage in details.

Odyssey Learning Adventures Canada ℡1-800/263-0050, ✆www.odysseylearningadventures .ca. Odyssey offers a trip on VIA's transcontinental *Silver & Blue* passsenger train, departing from Montréal and stopping in Toronto, with an accompanying guide/historian to bring it all to life.

Toronto Tours ☎416/869-1372, ⊚www
.torontotours.com. Toronto-based day-tour
specialists offering tours of the city sights, Niagara
and Toronto Harbour – perhaps the most original of
the offerings. Harbour cruises can be on motorized
cruisers or on masted tall ships, meals included.
Yankee Holidays US ☎1-800/225-2550,
⊚www.yankeeholidays.com. Strong showing of
two- to five-day packages that feature Toronto's
theatres, restaurants, cultural attractions and
neighbourhoods. Tours of nearby Niagara region also
available.

From the UK and Ireland

Toronto is accessible **from the UK mainland** by either charter or scheduled flight.
The majority of flights leave from London
Heathrow, with other airports offering a slim
to slender range of choices; Manchester and
Glasgow have the most. **From Ireland –**
north or south – there is only seasonal
scheduled direct service to Toronto; the
main options are either charter flights or
routings via the UK mainland or a US hub
airport. Keep in mind that direct, non-stop
flights can often – but certainly not always –
be at a premium when compared with one-
stop flights.

A standard return **fare** from London
Heathrow direct to Toronto with Air Canada,
the principal carrier, can range from
£400–1200 (low season–high season). With
restrictions, though, this can easily be
trimmed to a very affordable £250–300.
From **Ireland**, Air Canada's direct flights
from Dublin and Shannon to Toronto
(June–Sept only) can cost as little as €345,
but without restrictions can weigh in at
around €1650.

Airlines and routings

Aer Lingus UK ☎0845/084 4444, Republic of
Ireland ☎0818/365 000, ⊚www.aerlingus.ie.
Dublin to Boston; Boston to Toronto.
Air Canada UK ☎0870/5247 226, Republic of
Ireland ☎01/679 3958, ⊚www.aircanada.com.
London Heathrow to Toronto; Manchester and
Glasgow to Toronto (April–Oct only); Dublin and
Shannon to Toronto (June–Sept only).
American Airlines UK ☎0845/7789 789 or
020/8572 5555, Republic of Ireland ☎01/602
0550, ⊚www.aa.com. London Heathrow to Toronto
via Boston or Chicago.

British Airways UK ☎0845/77 333 77, Republic
of Ireland ☎1800/626 747, ⊚www.ba.com.
London Heathrow to Toronto; Irish flight connections
to Toronto via London Heathrow.
British Midland UK ☎0870/607 0555, Republic
of Ireland ☎01/407 3036, ⊚www.flybmi.com. In
conjunction with Air Canada, British Midland have
flights from London Heathrow to Toronto and from
Manchester to Toronto (April–Oct only).
Continental Airlines UK ☎0800/776 464 or
01293/776 464, ⊚www.continental.com/uk,
Republic of Ireland ☎1890/925 252,
⊚www.continental.com/ie. From London Gatwick,
Manchester, Birmingham, Glasgow, Dublin and
Shannon to Toronto via Newark, New Jersey.
Delta UK ☎0800/414 767, Republic of Ireland
☎01/407 3165, ⊚www.delta.com. London Gatwick
to Toronto via Cincinnati; Dublin to Toronto via
Brussels.
KLM/Northwest Airlines UK ☎0870/507 4074,
⊚www.klmuk.com. Aberdeen, Birmingham,
Edinburgh, Glasgow, Humberside, Leeds-Bradford,
London City, London Heathrow, Manchester, Norwich
to Amsterdam; Amsterdam to Toronto; Aer Lingus
connection from Dublin to Amsterdam, then
Amsterdam to Toronto.
Lufthansa UK ☎0845/7737 747, Republic of
Ireland ☎01/844 5544, ⊚www.lufthansa.co.uk.
Frankfurt to Toronto with connections from several
UK airports.
United Airlines UK ☎0845/8444 777,
⊚www.unitedairlines.co.uk. London Heathrow to
Toronto via Chicago or Washington, DC.

Flight and travel agents

Apex Travel Republic of Ireland ☎01/241 8000,
⊚www.apextravel.ie. Specialists in flights to
Australia, Africa, the Far East, the USA and Canada.
Aran Travel International Republic of Ireland
☎091/562 595, ⊚homepages.iol.ie/~arantvl
/aranmain.htm. Good-value flights to all parts of the
world.
Bridge the World UK ☎0870/444 7474,
⊚www.bridgetheworld.com. Specializing in round-
the-world tickets, with good deals aimed at the
backpacker market.
CIE Tours International Republic of Ireland
☎01/703 1888, ⊚www.cietours.ie. General flight
and travel agent.
Co-op Travel Care UK ☎0870/112 0099,
⊚www.travelcareonline.com. Flights and holidays
around the world.
Destination Group UK ☎020/7400 7045,
⊚www.destination-group.com. Good discount
airfares.

Flightbookers UK ☎0870/010 7000, ⓦwww.ebookers.com. Low fares on an extensive selection of scheduled flights.

Go Holidays Republic of Ireland ☎01/874 4126, ⓦwww.goholidays.ie. Package tour specialists.

Joe Walsh Tours Republic of Ireland ☎01/676 0991, ⓦwww.joewalshtours.ie. General budget fares agent.

Lee Travel Republic of Ireland ☎021/277 111, ⓦwww.leetravel.ie. Flights and holidays worldwide.

McCarthy's Travel Republic of Ireland ☎021/427 0127, ⓦwww.mccarthystravel.ie. General flight agent.

North South Travel UK ☎01245/608 291, ⓦwww.northsouthtravel.co.uk. Friendly, competitive travel agency, offering discounted fares worldwide – profits are used to support projects in the developing world, especially the promotion of sustainable tourism.

Premier Travel Northern Ireland ☎028/7126 3333, ⓦwww.premiertravel.uk.com. Discount flight specialists.

Quest Travel UK ☎0870/442 3542, ⓦwww.questtravel.com. Specialists in round-the-world and Australasian discount fares.

Rosetta Travel Northern Ireland ☎028/9064 4996, ⓦwww.rosettatravel.com. Flight and holiday agent.

STA Travel UK ☎0870/1600 599, ⓦwww.statravel.co.uk. Worldwide specialists in low-cost flights and tours for students and under-26s, though other customers welcome.

Top Deck UK ☎020/7244 8000, ⓦwww.topdecktravel.co.uk. Long-established agent dealing in discount flights.

Trailfinders UK ☎020/7628 7628, ⓦwww.trailfinders.co.uk, Republic of Ireland ☎01/677 7888, ⓦwww.trailfinders.ie. One of the best-informed and most efficient agents for independent travellers; produces a very useful quarterly magazine worth scrutinizing for round-the-world routes.

Travel Cuts UK ☎020/7255 2082 or 7255 1944, ⓦwww.travelcuts.co.uk. Canadian company specializing in budget, student and youth travel and round-the-world tickets.

usit NOW Republic of Ireland ☎01/602 1600, Northern Ireland ☎028/9032 7111, ⓦwww.usitnow.ie. Student and youth specialists for flights and trains.

Tour operators

Airtours UK ☎0870/238 7788, ⓦwww.uk.mytravel.com. Large tour company offering trips worldwide.

All Canada Travel & Holidays ⓦwww.titanserver.co.uk/all-canada. Comprehensive Canada agent. Runs everything from escorted coach tours to adventure holidays and city breaks. Bookings through appointed travel agents.

AmeriCan Adventures UK ☎01295/756 200, ⓦwww.americanadventures.com. Small group camping adventure trips throughout the US and Canada.

American Holidays Belfast ☎028/9023 8762, Dublin ☎01/433 1009, ⓦwww.american-holidays.com. Specialists in travel to the USA and Canada.

British Airways Holidays UK ☎0870/442 3820, ⓦwww.baholidays.co.uk. Using British Airways and other international airlines, offers an exhaustive range of package and tailor made holidays around the world including Ontario.

Canada's Best UK ☎01502/565648, ⓦwww.best-in-travel.com. Canada specialist offering a wide range of holiday options. Deals in Ontario cottages, resorts and inns, as well as Toronto hotels. Package and tailor-made holidays.

Thomas Cook UK ☎0870/5666 222, ⓦwww.thomascook.co.uk. Long established one-stop twenty-four-hour travel agency for package holidays or scheduled flights, with bureau de change issuing Thomas Cook traveller's cheques, travel insurance and car rental.

Thomas Cook Holidays UK ☎0173/3417 100, ⓦwww.thomascook.com. Range of flight and board deals and tours worldwide.

From Australia and New Zealand

There are no direct, non-stop flights **from Australia and New Zealand** to Toronto; the main variation is really where you break your journey – either an Asian city, like Hong Kong, or in North America, usually Los Angeles or Vancouver; the same applies to charter flights. **Fares** vary considerably, but not so much with the time of year, as fares remain fairly consistent whatever date you travel. Rather, price differences have more to do with the restrictions attached to your ticket. There are, for example, discounts for mid-week travel and advance booking. As illustrations, the standard return fare from Sydney to Toronto (via Vancouver) with Air Canada costs around Aus$3200, whereas Air New Zealand charges in the region of NZ$2300 for their Auckland to Toronto (via Honolulu or Los Angeles) return flight.

Airlines and routings

Air Canada Australia ☎1300/655 747 or 02/9286 8900, New Zealand ☎09/379 3371, ✇www.aircanada.com. Canada's principal domestic carrier. Sydney to Toronto via Vancouver; Auckland to Toronto via Honolulu or Los Angeles, with Air New Zealand.

Air New Zealand Australia ☎13 24 76, ✇www.airnz.com.au, New Zealand ☎0800/737 000, ✇www.airnz.co.nz. Auckland and Wellington to Toronto via Los Angeles or Honolulu, with Air Canada.

Cathay Pacific Australia ☎13 17 47, ✇www.cathaypacific.com/au, New Zealand ☎09/379 0861 or 0508/800 454, ✇www.cathaypacific.com/nz. Adelaide, Auckland, Brisbane, Melbourne and Sydney to Toronto via Hong Kong.

Japan Airlines Australia ☎02/9272 1111, New Zealand ☎09/379 9906, ✇www.japanair.com. Auckland, Brisbane, Cairns, Christchurch, Melbourne and Sydney to Toronto, via Tokyo or Osaka.

Singapore Airlines Australia ☎13 10 11, New Zealand ☎0800/808 909, ✇www.singaporeair.com. Adelaide, Auckland, Brisbane, Christchurch, Melbourne, Perth, Sydney to Toronto, via Singapore.

United Airlines Australia ☎13 17 77, ✇www.unitedairlines.com.au, New Zealand ☎09/379 3800 or 0800/508 648, ✇www.unitedairlines.co.nz. Sydney to Toronto via San Francisco and Chicago.

Flight and travel agents

Flight Centre Australia ☎13 31 33 or 02/9235 3522, ✇www.flightcentre.com.au, New Zealand ☎0800 243 544 or 09/358 4310, ✇www.flightcentre.co.nz.

New Zealand Destinations Unlimited New Zealand ☎09/414 1685 ✇www.holiday.co.nz.

Northern Gateway Australia ☎1800/174 800, ✇www.northerngateway.com.au.

STA Travel Australia ☎1300/733 035, ✇www.statravel.com.au, New Zealand ☎0508/782 872, ✇www.statravel.co.nz.

Student Uni Travel Australia ☎02/9232 8444, ✇www.sut.com.au, New Zealand ☎09/379 4224, ✇www.sut.co.nz.

Trailfinders Australia ☎02/9247 7666, ✇www.trailfinders.com.au.

Tour operators

Adventure World Australia ☎02/8913 0755, ✇www.adventureworld.com.au, New Zealand ☎09/524 5118, ✇www.adventureworld.co.nz. Agents for a vast array of international adventure travel companies that operate trips to every continent.

Canada & America Travel Specialists Australia ☎02/9922 4600, ✇www.canada-americatravel.com.au. Wholesalers of Greyhound Ameripasses, plus flights and accommodation in North America.

Connections Australia ☎1800/077 251 or 07/3839 7877, New Zealand ☎0800 376 780, ✇www.connections1835.com.au. Package and tailored group adventure tours in the US and Canada for the 18–35 age bracket.

Silke's Travel Australia ☎1800 807 860, or 02/8347 2000, ✇www.silkes.com.au. Gay and lesbian specialist travel agent.

Sydney Travel ☎02/9220 9230, ✇www.sydneytravel.com. US and Canadian flights, accommodation, city stays and car rental.

Viator Australia ☎02/8219 5400, ✇www.viator.com. Bookings for hundreds of travel suppliers worldwide, including countries throughout Europe, North America, the Caribbean, Asia and the Pacific region.

Red tape and visas

Citizens of the EU, non-EU Scandinavia and most Commonwealth countries travelling to Canada do not need an entry visa – all that is required is a valid passport. United States citizens simply need some form of photo identification plus proof of US citizenship. This can be a valid US passport, an original US birth certificate (or certified copy thereof), or original US naturalization papers. Note that a US driver's licence alone is insufficient proof of citizenship.

All visitors to Canada have to complete a **customs declaration form**, which you'll be given on the plane or at the US/Canadian border. On the form you'll have to give details of where you intend to stay during your trip. If you don't know, write "touring", but be prepared to give an idea of your schedule and destinations to the immigration officer.

At point of entry, the Canadian immigration officer decides the **length of stay permitted**, up to a maximum of six months, but not usually more than three. The officers rarely refuse entry, but they may launch into an impromptu investigation, asking how much money you have and what job you do; they may also ask to see a return or onward ticket. If they ask where you're staying and you give the name and address of friends, don't be surprised if they check. Note also that although passing overland between the US and Canada is usually straightforward, there can sometimes be long delays.

For visits of **more than six months**, **study trips** and stints of temporary **employment**, contact the nearest Canadian embassy, consulate or high commission for authorization prior to departure (see opposite for contact details). Once inside Canada, if an extension of stay is desired, written application must be made to the nearest Canada Immigration Centre well before the expiry of the authorized visit.

Australia Canberra High Commission, Commonwealth Ave, Canberra, ACT 2600 ☎02/6273 3285, ✆www.dfait-maeci.gc.ca /australia; Perth Consulate, 267 St George's Terrace, Third Floor, Perth, 6000 Australia ☎08/9322 7930 ✆www.dfait-maeci.gc.ca /australia; Sydney Consulate General, Level 5, Quay West Building, 111 Harrington St, Sydney, NSW 2000 ☎02/9364 3000, ✆www.dfait-maeci .gc.ca/australia.
Ireland Embassy, 65 St Stephen's Green, Dublin 2 ☎01/417 4100, ✆www.canadaeuropa.gc .ca/ireland.
New Zealand Auckland Consulate 48 Emily Place, Auckland ☎09/309 3690, ✆www.dfait-maeci.gc .ca/newzealand; Wellington High Commission, PO Box 12049, Thorndon, Wellington ☎04/473 9577, ✆www.wellington.gc.ca.
UK High Commission, Macdonald House, 1 Grosvenor Square, London W1X 4AB ☎020/7258 6600, ✆www.dfait-maeci.gc.ca/london. Also consular representation in Belfast, Birmingham, Cardiff and Edinburgh.
USA Embassy, 501 Pennsylvania Ave NW, Washington DC 20001 ☎202/682 7726, ✆www.can-am.gc.ca/washington. Also consular representation in Atlanta, Boston, Buffalo, Chicago, Dallas, Detroit, Los Angeles, Miami, Minneapolis, New York, San Francisco, San Jose, Seattle.

Insurance

Prior to travelling, you should take out an insurance policy to cover against theft, loss and illness or injury. Before paying for a new policy, however, it's worth checking whether you already have some degree of coverage: some all-risks home insurance policies may cover your possessions when overseas; many private medical schemes include cover when abroad; and bank and credit cards often have certain levels of medical or other insurance included if you use one of them to pay for your trip. In addition, holders of official student/teacher/youth cards in the US may be entitled to meagre accident coverage and hospital in-patient benefits. Students will often find that their student health coverage extends during vacations and for one term beyond the date of last enrolment.

Rough Guides travel insurance

Rough Guide offers its own low-cost travel insurance, especially customized for our statistically low-risk readers by a leading British broker, provided by the American International Group (AIG) and registered with the British regulatory body, GISC (the General Insurance Standards Council). There are five main Rough Guides insurance plans: **No Frills** for the bare minimum for secure travel; **Essential**, which provides decent all-round cover; **Premier** for comprehensive cover with a wide range of benefits; **Extended Stay** for cover lasting two months to a year; and **Annual multi-trip**, a cost-effective way of getting Premier cover if you travel more than once a year. Premier, Annual Multi-Trip and Extended Stay policies can be supplemented by a "Hazardous Pursuits Extension" if you plan to indulge in sports considered dangerous, such as scuba-diving or trekking. For a policy quote, call the Rough Guide Insurance Line: toll-free in the UK ☎0800/015 09 06 or ☎+44 1392 314 665 from elsewhere. Alternatively, get an online quote at ⓦwww.roughguides.com/insurance.

After exhausting the possibilities above, you might want to contact a specialist travel insurance company. A typical travel insurance policy usually provides cover for the loss of baggage, tickets and – up to a certain limit – cash or cheques, as well as cancellation or curtailment of your journey. Most of them exclude so-called **dangerous sports** – white-water rafting, mountain climbing and so forth – unless an extra premium is paid. Many policies can be chopped and changed to exclude coverage you don't need – for example, sickness and accident benefits can often be excluded or included at will. If you do take medical coverage, ascertain whether benefits will be paid as treatment proceeds or only after your return home, and whether there is a twenty-four-hour medical emergency number. When securing baggage cover, make sure that the per-article limit – typically under £500/US$750 – will cover your most valuable possession. If you need to make a claim, you should keep receipts for medicines and medical treatment, and in the event you have anything stolen, you must obtain a crime report statement or number. Call ☎416/808-2222 to report your loss.

Health

It is vital to have travel insurance (see "Insurance" above) against potential medical expenses. Canada has an excellent health service, but non-residents are not entitled to free health care, and medical costs can be astronomical, depending on the treatment. If you have an accident, medical services will get to you quickly and charge you later.

Doctors and pharmacies

Doctors and **dentists** can be found listed in the *Yellow Pages*, though for **medical emergencies** call ☎911. If you are bringing medicine prescribed by your doctor, bring a copy of the prescription; first, to avoid problems at customs and immigration, and second, for renewing medication with Canadian doctors, if needed.

As you would expect, Toronto has scores of **pharmacies**, which can advise on minor ailments and distinguish between unfamiliar brand names for the visitor. Shopper's Drug Mart has two central pharmacy locations, at

17

700 Bay St (open 24hrs; ☎416/979-2424) and 722 Yonge St (open 9am–midnight; ☎416/920-0098). For a **holistic apothecary**, try The Big Carrot, at 348 Danforth Ave (☎416/466-2129, ⊛www.thebigcarrot.ca), a large whole-foods co-op with a wide selection of herbal remedies and health products.

Specific health problems

Canada requires no specific vaccinations – but problems can arise when you're walking or camping in the backcountry; Algonquin Park (see p.113) is a case in point. Here, although tap water is generally safe to drink, it's always prudent to ask. You should also always **boil backcountry water** for at least ten minutes to protect against the **Giardia** parasite (or "beaver fever"). The parasite thrives in warm water, so be careful about swimming in hot springs – if possible, keep nose, eyes and mouth above water. Symptoms are intestinal cramps, flatulence, fatigue, weight loss and vomiting, all of which can appear up to a week after infection. If left untreated, more unpleasant complications can arise, so see a doctor immediately if you think you've contracted it.

Blackfly and **mosquitoes** are notorious for the problems they cause walkers and campers, and are especially bad in areas near standing water and throughout most of northern and much of central Ontario. Horseflies are another pest. Late April to June is the blackfly season, and the mosquito season is from June until about October. If you're planning an expedition into the wilderness, you'd be well-advised to take three times the recommended daily dosage of vitamin B complex for two weeks before you go, and to take the recommended dosage while you're in Canada; this cuts down bites by up to seventy-five percent.

Once you're there, **repellent creams** and **sprays** may help: the best are those containing DEET. The ointment version of Deep-Woods Off is the best brand, with 95 percent DEET. If you're camping or picnicking you'll find that burning coils or candles containing allethrin or citronella can help. If you're walking in an area that's rife with pests, it's well worth taking a gauze mask to protect your head and neck; wearing white clothes and no perfumed products also makes you less attractive to the insects. Once bitten, an **antihistamine cream** like phenergan is the best antidote. On no account go anywhere near an area marked as a blackfly mating ground – people have died from bites sustained when the creatures are in heat. Also dangerous, and newly arrived in Ontario, is **West Nile virus**, a mosquito-born affliction with life-threatening properties; the virus has appeared in a couple of places in Ontario and will probably spread – so pay attention to local advice.

If you develop a large rash and flu-like symptoms, you may have been bitten by a tick carrying lyme borreliosis (or "**lyme tick disease**"). This is easily curable, but if left untreated can lead to nasty complications, so see a doctor as soon as possible. It's spreading in Canada, especially in the more southerly and wooded parts of the country; you should check on its prevalence with the local tourist authority. It also may be advisable to buy a strong **tick repellent** and to wear long socks, trousers and sleeved shirts when walking.

In backcountry areas, look out for **poison ivy**, which grows in most places, but particularly in a belt across southern Ontario. If you're likely to be walking in affected areas, ask at tourist offices for tips on where it is and how to recognize the plant, which causes itchy open blisters and lumpy sores up to ten days after contact. If you do come into contact with it, wash your body and clothes as soon as possible, smother yourself in calamine lotion and try not to scratch. In serious cases, hospital emergency rooms can give antihistamine or adrenalin jabs.

Information, websites and maps

Information on Toronto is easy to get hold of, either via the Internet, or, after arrival, from downtown's Ontario Tourism Travel Information Centre. Maps are widely available from bookshops and newsagents.

Visitor information

The excellent **Ontario Tourism Travel Information Centre**, on Level 1 of the Eaton shopping centre at the corner of Yonge and Dundas sts (Mon–Fri 10am–9pm, Sat 9.30am–7pm & Sun noon–5pm; ☎1-800/ONTARIO, or within Toronto ☎905/282 1721), stocks a comprehensive range of information on all the major attractions in Toronto and throughout Ontario. Of particular interest here are the **free city maps**, the *Ride Guide* to the city's transport system, and **entertainment details** in the monthly, free magazine *Where*. The centre will also book hotel accommodation on your behalf both in Toronto and across all of Ontario; for more on Accommodation, see Chapter 6. Ontario Tourism also operates an all-encompassing **website**, ⓦ www.ontariotravel.net, which is particularly strong on practical information.

Alternatively, visit the **Info TO visitor information centre** (daily 9am–5pm), located in the city's Convention Centre at 255 Front St West, a couple of minutes' walk west from Union Station (daily 9am–5pm). Privately run, the TO centre is more geared-up for selling tour tickets than providing information, though they do have a reasonable supply of free literature on the city and its environs. They are not, however, nearly as good as the Ontario Tourism Travel Information Centre.

Finally, **Tourism Toronto**, the city's official visitor and convention bureau, operates a telephone information line, whose operators can handle most city queries and will make hotel reservations for you, as well (Mon–Fri 8.30am–5pm, Sat 9am–5pm, Sun 10am–5pm; ☎1-800/499-2514 or 416/203-2500). At time of writing, they are also planning to introduce an online accommodation booking service via their website, ⓦ www.torontotourism.com.

Websites

ⓦ **www.ago.net** The Art Gallery of Toronto's comprehensive site provides high-quality reproductions of the gallery's key paintings and details of its temporary exhibitions. Plus, there's information regarding the museum's many programmes, including lectures, guided tours and art courses.

ⓦ **www.canadianhockey.ca** Proof positive that Canadians are passionate about their national sport, ice hockey; operated by Hockey Canada.

ⓦ **www.city.toronto.on.ca** Official municipal site covering everything from living in Toronto through to tourist attractions. Has links to a series of city maps which you can use to pinpoint local amenities, and carries a guide to events and concerts.

ⓦ **www.gaytoronto.com** Gay Toronto is a useful starting point if you're looking to find out what's on where and when on the male scene – but it has no information for women. There's a useful bulletin board service, which has an accommodation section.

ⓦ **www.infoniagara.com** Official municipal website, with details of Niagara Falls' attractions, accommodation and restaurants.

ⓦ **www.martiniboys.com** Perhaps the best online guide of Toronto's hottest, coolest, must-be-seen-at bars and clubs, as well as intelligent, well-written restaurant reviews. The Martini Boys are invaluable in a town that takes eating and drinking so seriously.

ⓦ **www.moltencore.com/club.html** Molten Core, an admittedly partisan guide to the city's drinking, eating and more especially club and live music scene, features entertaining, provocative and well-informed reviews.

ⓦ **www.niagaraparks.com** This is the official website of the Niagara Parks Commission. It provides information on all the major attractions in and around Niagara Falls. Has a link to a "falls cam", which provides live pictures of the natural wonder.

ⓦ **www.ontariotravel.net** Whether you're planning a trip to Toronto or a more wide-ranging holiday in the province of Ontario, this official site of Ontario Tourism is an excellent, regularly updated website with all sorts of ideas, information and options. Has an events calendar, accommodation details, maps, a travel tips section and weather forecasts. The accommodation feature allows you to build a very specific request, and then returns choices of inns, hotels and B&Bs, from which you can make reservations.

ⓦ **www.theatreintoronto.com** This useful site ties together ⓦ www.torontoperforms.com, the only site for updated show listings and information in a searchable database, and ⓦ www.totix.ca, which offers half-price, same-day tickets for purchase online or at the booth.

ⓦ **www.thestar.com** The *Toronto Star* is the city's best newspaper; its website is strong on news, sports and weather updates. There's also a regularly updated "what's on" section covering local music, film and TV schedules.

ⓦ **www.toronto.com** The city's first comprehensive sounds/sights/attractions site remains one of its best. Designed for people who live in Toronto and want to enjoy it, the site features plenty of good insider perspective. The online hotel reservations are handy for visitors, and if you decide you like the city well enough you can always surf apartment availability.

ⓦ **www.tribemagazine.com** This free magazine, focusing on the dance music scene in Canada, is available online in full, and gives frequently updated details on Toronto's clubland.

Maps

The **city maps** contained within the guide will be adequate for most purposes, but you might also consider investing in the *Rough Guide Toronto Map* (Can$13.50/US$8.95/ UK£4.99), designed to be used in conjunction with this book. Full-colour, non-tearable, weatherproof and pocket-sized, it details attractions, places to shop, eat, drink and sleep as well as the city streets, and includes transport routes and a "time map" of opening hours. Upon publication (Feb 2004 in the UK, March 2004 in the US and Canada), it will be available from bookshops worldwide (for information on bookstores in Toronto, see p.169). If you plan to venture further out into Ontario, MapArt (ⓦ www .mapart.com) produces a very clear, accurate map of the province, for Can$4, as well as an excellent *Ontario Road Atlas*, for Can$22.

Arrival

Located 27 kilometres (sixteen miles) northwest of the city centre, Toronto's Pearson International Airport is linked to almost every major city in the world, with flights from every corner of Canada arriving all the time as well. In fact, the majority of visitors to Toronto arrive by plane.

Toronto's **bus and train stations**, conveniently located downtown, link the city to many other Canadian and American cities. Those coming in **by car** will find the city encircled by a number of efficient motorways – and although traffic congestion can be a problem, delays are not usually as severe as in many other large cities.

By air

Coming in by air, you'll almost certainly land at Pearson International, about forty minutes by car from downtown. The airport is currently being expanded with the addition of a flashy new terminal, which will replace the oldest of the three existing terminals. Two terminals will be devoted to international flights, and one to domestic. Each terminal has – or will have – a full range of facilities, including money-exchange offices, ATMs and free hotel hotlines. A free airport coach shuttle connects the terminals.

The **Airport Express bus service** (daily: one every thirty minutes 5am–1am, with an additional 3am departure; ☎905/564-6333, ⓦ www.torontoairportexpress.com) picks up passengers outside all the terminals and heads toward downtown, taking between forty and sixty minutes to get there – though heavy traffic can make the journey considerably longer. The bus drops off passengers at the coach station (see below for details) and seven of Toronto's major hotels: the *Westin Harbour Castle*, *Royal York*, *Crowne Plaza*, *Sheraton Centre*, *Colony*, the *Holiday Inn* on King and the *Delta Chelsea*. **Connector minibuses** take passengers to most of the other downtown hotels.

Tickets for the airport bus can be purchased either at the kiosks next to the bus stop outside the terminal buildings or from the driver. A one-way fare is Can$14.95, round-trip Can$25.75; the minibus service that goes on from the seven downtown hotels mentioned above costs an extra Can$3.30 (round-trip Can$5.50).

Much less expensive, if rather more time-consuming, are the several **bus services** linking the airport with the city's subway network. The two fastest are operated by the **TTC** (the Toronto Transit Commission), which runs all of the city's public transport – for more on which see p.22. The TTC's **Airport Rocket** (#192; daily 5.30am–2am, every 20–30mins; Can$2.25 one-way), takes about twenty minutes to reach Kipling subway station, at the west end of the subway network. From there, it takes another 20mins or so by subway (which operates Mon–Sat 6am–1am, Sun 9am–1am) to get downtown. The Rocket is supplemented by a night bus (#300A; hourly 2am–5am), which leaves the airport to run downtown along Bloor Street. The second option, TTC bus **#58A**, links the airport with Lawrence West subway station, to the north of downtown (daily 5am–1am; 45mins; Can$2.25 one-way). Buses leave from designated **stops** outside each of the terminal buildings (though currently Terminal 1 is excluded) and payment can be made to the driver.

In addition to these options, **GO Transit**, which runs the suburban rail network in co-operation with the TTC, operates a **bus service** from the airport to Yorkdale and York Mills subway stations, to the north of downtown (hourly: Mon–Sat 6am–1am, Sun 9am–1am; Can$3.50 one-way). The journey time is around forty minutes to Yorkdale, and fifty to York Mills.

There's an airport **limo service** (a shared taxi system) next to each terminal's bus platform; limos cost about Can$40 per person for the journey from the airport to downtown.

Unlike taxis, the price is fixed, an important consideration if you arrive (or leave) during rush hour; the disadvantage is that they mostly only leave when they're full. Individual **taxis** charge about the same – $40 from the airport to the city centre – but fares are metered.

Finally, Air Canada (☎1-888/247-2262) operates flights from Montréal, Ottawa and London, Ontario, into the much smaller **Toronto City Centre Airport**, which is on Hanlan's Point in Toronto's harbour, close to downtown. From the airport, there's a free **minibus service** to the *Royal York Hotel*, on the corner of Front Street West and York Street.

By bus

Toronto's **coach station** is located at 610 Bay St, metres from Dundas Street West and a five-minute walk from the subway stop at the corner of Yonge and Dundas. If you're arriving late at night, note that the bus station's immediate environs are unsavoury – though it only takes a couple of minutes to reach more reassuring parts of downtown. Nonetheless, if you're travelling alone and late at night, it's probably best to take a taxi to your ultimate destination.

By train

All incoming trains arrive at **Union Railway Station**, at the junction of Bay Street and Front Street West. The station complex, which is the hub of the city's public transportation system, includes a subway station and also holds the main terminal for the **GO trains and buses** (www.gotransit.com) that service the city's suburbs. Details of GO services are available at their station ticket offices, or by calling toll-free ☎1-888/438-6646 (within Toronto ☎416/869-3200).

By car

From Niagara Falls and points west along Lake Ontario, most traffic arrives via the **QEW** (Queen Elizabeth Way), which funnels into the **Gardiner Expressway**, an elevated motorway that cuts across the southern side of downtown, just south of Front Street. The Gardiner is notorious for delays.

From the east, most drivers opt for the equally busy **Hwy-401**, which sweeps along Lake Ontario before veering off to slice through the city's suburbs north of downtown. Driving in from the north, take **Hwy-400**, which intersects with Hwy-401 northwest of the centre, or **Hwy-404**, which meets Hwy-401 northeast of the centre. Note that on all routes you can expect delays during rush hours (roughly 7.30–9.30am and 4.30–6.30pm).

To relieve congestion on Hwy-401, an alternative motorway, **Hwy-407ETR**, has been built further north on the city's edge. It was North America's first all-electronic toll highway: instead of toll booths, each vehicle is identified by an electronic tag (a transponder), and the invoice is posted later. Toll charges are fixed at 11.5¢ per kilometre and there's also a small supplementary charge per trip for any vehicle without a transponder – these vehicles are identified by licence plate photos. If you rent a car, be aware that rental companies slap on an extra administration charge (of around $15) if you take their vehicles on this road.

City transportation and tours

Fast, frequent and efficient, Toronto's public transportation is operated by the Toronto Transit Commission, or the TTC (☎416/393-4636 daily 8am–6pm, ⊛www.ttc.ca), whose integrated network of subways, buses and streetcars serves virtually every corner of the city.

With the exception of downtown, where all the major sights are within easy walking distance of one another, your best option is to use public transport to hop between attractions – especially in the cold of winter or the sultry summertime. Much to its credit, the TTC has gone to great lengths to assure the safety of its passengers: all subway stations have DWAs (Designated Waiting Areas), which are well-lit, have an intercom connection with TTC staff and are monitored by closed-circuit TV. In addition, TTC buses operate a Request Stop Program, which allows women travelling alone late at night (9pm–5am) to get off buses wherever they want, and not just at regular TTC stops. A similarly positive approach has been adopted for passengers with disabilities, who can use a dedicated service, Wheel-Trans (see p.22 for more on this). Many TTC buses are handicap-accessible as well, and more are on order – though as yet not all the stops have been retrofitted for disabled persons.

On every part of the TTC system, a single journey costs Can$2.25 (local students and seniors Can$1.50; children under two travel free). **Tickets** are available at all subway stations and from bus and streetcar drivers. Metallic **tokens** can also be used, issued at

(see p.22

Subterranean Toronto

Toronto has the world's largest **underground shopping complex**, over one thousand shops and stores spread out along a seemingly endless network of subterranean pedestrian walkways and mall basements. The network links forty-eight office towers and six major hotels and, most of all, keeps city folk well away from the extremes of their climate. The network stretches north from Union Station to the Eaton Centre and the coach terminal, and west–east from the CBC Broadcasting Centre to the King Street subway; access points – of which there are many – sport a multi-coloured sign inscribed "**PATH**".

subway stations, but are impossibly small and difficult to keep track of. More economically, a batch of five tickets or tokens can be bought for Can$9.50, or Can$17 for ten, at any station and at most convenience stores and newsstands. Each ticket or token entitles passengers to one complete journey of any length on the TTC system. If this involves more than one type of transport, it is necessary to get a paper **transfer** at your point of entry. Streetcar and bus drivers issue them, as do the automatic machines located at every subway station. A **day pass** costs Can$7.75 and provides one adult with unlimited TTC travel all day on Saturdays and after 9.30am on weekdays. On Sundays, the same pass becomes a terrific deal for families: it covers up to six people (though only two can be adults).

The subway

Toronto's **subway**, the core of the city's public transportation network, is a simple, two-line system (see our map at the back of the book). The Bloor–Danforth line cuts east to west along Bloor Street, while the Yonge–University–Spadina line forms a loop with Union Station at its head; north of Union, this subway line runs along University Avenue and Yonge Street. Transferring between the two lines is possible at three stations only: Spadina, St George and Bloor–Yonge. The subway operates Mon–Sat 6am–1 or 2am, Sun 9am–1 or 2am.

Buses and streetcars

The subway provides the backbone of the TTC system, but its services are faithfully supplemented by **buses and streetcars**. The system couldn't be simpler, as a bus and/or streetcar station adjoins every major subway stop. Hours of operation vary with the route, but are comparable with subway

times; there is also a limited network of **night buses** running along key routes hourly or so between 1am and 6am.

Commuter lines

In addition to subways and buses, the TTC runs several **commuter lines**. The most useful is the **Scarborough Rapid Transit**, a streetcar service that picks up passengers at the eastern terminus of the Bloor–Danforth subway line and makes a five-stop trek to the heart of Scarborough, a Toronto suburb (see p.86). Transfers from the rest of the TTC network are valid on the Scarborough Rapid Transit. Finally, **GO trains** (☎416/869 3200, ⓦwww.gotransit.com) arrive and depart from Union Station, and link the city's various suburbs and neighbouring towns. There are no free transfers from the TTC system to GO train lines – though these are primarily used by commuters and are of little use for tourists based in the city.

Taxis

Taxis cruise the city in abundance and can be hailed from any street corner. Give the driver your destination and ask the approximate price before you start. **Fares** are generally reasonable, based on a fixed tariff of Can$2.50 for the first .235km and 25¢ for every .235km thereafter. As an example, a ride from Union Station to the far side of Cabbagetown should cost around $10. Of the multitude of cab companies to choose from, the most reliable tend to be **Co-op Cabs** (☎416/504-2667) or **Diamond Taxicab** (☎416/366-6868). Toronto taxi drivers anticipate a tip of ten to fifteen percent on the total fare.

Organized tours

Organized tours are big business in Toronto and the range of what's on offer is exemplary

Orientation and street numbers

Yonge Street is Toronto's principal north–south artery. Main drags perpendicular to Yonge use this intersection to change from **west to east** – Queen Street West, for example, becomes Queen Street East when it crosses Yonge. Note, therefore, that 1000 Queen Street West is a long way from 1000 Queen Street East.

– from ghost walks and boat cruises through to the more predictable coach tours. Of the latter, **Gray Line** (☎1-800/594-3310 or 416/594-3310, ◐www.grayline.ca) operates fairly enjoyable city bus tours, the most inexpensive of which is a two-hour zip round the main attractions for Can$32 (mid-April to mid-Oct; three daily). They also run ten-hour coach trips to Niagara Falls (mid-May to mid-Sept; two daily; Can$125) and twelve-hour excursions to Georgian Bay (see p.107), including an island cruise (mid-May to mid-Oct; one daily; Can$60).

Perhaps of more appeal, Gray Line also operates hop-on, hop-off **tours of the city** in double-decker buses and vintage streetcars. These vehicles shuttle around the city centre from March to November, appearing at regular intervals (thirty mintues to an hour) at about twenty major attractions. A ticket, valid for two days, costs Can$34. The best place to join the tour is the stop on the corner of York and Front streets, near the CN Tower. On all Gray Line trips, there are concessionary fares for seniors (age 60+) and children (ages 5–11). Rather more intimate –

and a good deal more economical – is **Travel Express** (☎905/855 5252), who operate guided minibus tours of Niagara Falls (Can$70) and three-hour minibus excursions round Toronto (Can$50).

More inventively, **A Taste of the World** (☎416/923-6813, ◐www.torontowalksbikes.com) offers a creative programme of guided walks – Literary (2.5hrs; Can$15), Foodies (3.5hrs; Can$35) and Ghost (2hrs; Can$15) – throughout the year. These come highly recommended and advance booking is advised. If you'd like to take a boat trip, the **Mariposa Cruise Line** (☎416/203-0178; ◐www.mariposacruises.com) offers a good range of lake and harbour tours from the jetty on Queens Quay West. Alternatively, **Toronto Boat Cruises** (☎416/203-2322; ◐www.greatlakesschooner.com) features genuine sailing trips on a three-master, the *Kajama* (May Sat & Sun three daily, June–Aug three to four daily; Can$20). There are lots of **other options** – and the annual *Visitor Guide*, available at either of the city's tourist offices (see p.19), outlines most of them.

Costs, money and banks

By western European standards, Toronto is very reasonably priced, with most basic items – from maps through to food and clothing – costing significantly less than back home. US residents and Australians, on the other hand, will find prices about the same; maybe a little higher, but not by much. As for dining and drinking, the sheer plethora of restaurants and bars keeps prices down. Less positively, accommodation, almost certainly your major outlay, is generally more expensive than in the rest of Canada, though there are plenty of bargains to be had. Throughout the guide, standard prices are given in Canadian dollars ($); where there might be any confusion between that and American dollars, especially in the Basics section, we distinguish between the two (Can$ vs US$).

Daily costs

If you're prepared to buy your own picnic lunch, stay in hostels, and stick to the least expensive bars and restaurants, you could scrape by on around **Can$60/US$40/£25 per day**. Staying in a good B&B, eating out

in medium-range restaurants most nights and drinking often in bars, you'll go through at least **Can$150/US$100/£65 per day**, with the main variable being the cost of your room. On **Can$240/$160/£100 per day** and upwards, you'll be limited only by your energy reserves – though if you're planning to stay in the best hotels and to have a big night out pretty much every night, this still won't be enough. As always, if you're travelling alone you'll spend much more on accommodation than you would in a group of two or more: most hotels do have single rooms, but they're fixed at about 65 percent (ie, not half) of the price of a double.

Restaurants don't come cheap, but costs remain manageable if you avoid the extras and concentrate on the main courses, which start at around Can$12/US$8/£5 – though you can, of course, pay a lot more. **Tipping** at a restaurant is expected – between ten and fifteen percent – unless the service has been dire; taxi drivers expect a tip too, in the same amount. **Museum admission prices** are mostly in the Can$7/US$5/£3 range, but discounts of at least fifty percent are routinely available for children, seniors and students; indeed, **concessionary fares and rates** are offered on all sorts of things, including public transport (which is already fairly inexpensive, at Can$2.25 a ride).

Finally, a word about **taxation**. Virtually all prices in Canada for everything from bubblegum to hotel rooms are quoted without tax, which means that the price you see quoted is not the price you'll end up being required to pay. Across the province of Ontario, which includes Toronto, there's a **Provincial Sales Tax** (PST) of eight percent on most goods and services, including hotel and restaurant bills; this is supplemented by the nationwide **Goods and Services Tax** (GST), a seven percent levy equivalent to VAT in Europe. As a small mercy, visitors can claim a **GST rebate** on certain goods and short-term accommodation over the value of Can$50 and up to Can$200 per night. Claim forms are available at many hotels, shops and airports, or from any Canadian embassy. Return them, with **all original receipts**, to the address given on the form. Those returning overland to the US can claim their rebate at selected border duty-free shops. For more information, call either ☎902/432-5608 (outside Canada) or ☎1-800/668-4748 (within Canada), or consult ⓦwww.ccra.gc.ca/visitors.

Currency

Canadian **currency** is the dollar ($), made up of 100 cents (¢) to the dollar. Coins are issued in 1¢ (penny), 5¢ (nickel), 10¢ (dime), 25¢ (quarter), $1 and $2 denominations: the $1 coin is known as a "loonie", after the bird on one face; no one's come up with a suitable name for the newer $2 coin – "twoonie" has been tried but hasn't really caught on. Paper currency comes in $5, $10, $50, $100, $500 and $1000 denominations. Although US dollars are widely accepted, it's often on a one-for-one basis, and as the US dollar is usually worth more than its Canadian counterpart, it makes sense to exchange US currency.

At the time of writing, the **rate of exchange** is Can$2.30 to the pound sterling, Can$1.50 to the US dollar, and Can$0.93 to the Australian dollar. For the most up-to-date rates, check the currency converter website ⓦwww.oanda.com.

Traveller's cheques

The main advantage of buying **traveller's cheques** is that they are a safe way of carrying funds. All well-known brands of traveller's cheque in all major currencies are widely accepted in Toronto, with US dollar and Canadian dollar cheques being the most common. The usual fee for their purchase is one to two percent of face value, though this fee is often waived if you buy the cheques through a bank where you have an account. You'll find it useful to purchase a selection of denominations. When you **cash your cheques**, almost all banks make a percentage charge per transaction on top of a basic minimum charge.

In the event that your cheques are **lost or stolen**, the issuing company will expect you to report it immediately. Make sure you keep the purchase agreement, a record of cheque serial numbers, and details of the company's emergency contact numbers or the addresses of their local offices, **safe and separate from the cheques themselves**. Most companies claim to replace lost or stolen cheques within 24 hours.

ATMs, debit and credit cards

Toronto is rife with **ATMs**, with a particular concentration in the city centre. Most ATMs accept a host of **debit cards**, including all those carrying the Cirrus coding. If in doubt, check with your bank to find out whether the card you wish to use will be accepted – and if you need a new (international) PIN. You'll rarely be charged a transaction fee, as the banks make their profits from applying different exchange rates. **Credit cards** can be used in ATMs too, but in this case transactions are treated as loans, with interest accruing daily from the date of withdrawal. All major credit cards, including American Express, Visa and Mastercard, are widely accepted in Toronto.

Visa TravelMoney (ⓦwww.visa.com) combines the security of traveller's cheques with the convenience of plastic. It's a disposable debit card, charged up before you leave home with whatever amount you like, separate from your normal banking or credit accounts. You can then access these dedicated travel funds from any ATM that accepts Visa worldwide, with a PIN that you select yourself. When your money runs out, you just throw the card away. Since you can buy up to nine cards to access the same funds – useful for families travelling together – it's recommended that you buy at least one extra card as a back-up in case your first is lost or stolen. Travelex/Interpayment outlets sell the card worldwide (see ⓦwww.travelex.com for locations).

Banks and exchange

If you need to change money, Toronto's **banks** usually offer the best deals. Banks are legion and although opening hours vary, all are open Mon–Fri 10am–3pm at the very least. Outside these times, you might consider a **bureau de change**. Two of the more reliable are Thomas Cook, 10 King St E (Mon–Fri 9am–5pm; ☎416/863-1611), and Cafforex (formerly Currencies International), whose main branch is at 170 Bloor St W (daily 8.30am–7pm; ☎416/921-4872).

American Express checks can be cashed at their downtown office, 50 Bloor St W (Mon–Wed & Sat 10am–6pm, Thurs & Fri 10am–7pm, closed Sun; ☎416/967-3411).

Wiring money

Having **money wired** from home using one of the companies listed below is never convenient or cheap, and should only be considered as a last resort. It can actually be slightly cheaper to have your own bank send the money through. For that, you need to nominate a receiving bank in Toronto and confirm the arrangement with them before you set the wheels in motion back home – any large branch will do. The sending bank's fees are geared to the amount being transferred and the urgency of the service you require – the fastest transfers, taking two or three days, start at around £25/US$40 for the first £300–400/US$450–600.

Money-wiring companies

Thomas Cook Canada ☎1-888/823-4732; Ireland ☎01/677 1721; UK ☎01733/318 922; US ☎1-800/287-7362; ⓦwww.us.thomascook.com.
Travelers Express Moneygram Canada ☎1-800/933-3278; US ☎1-800/926-3947; ⓦwww.moneygram.com.
Western Union Australia ☎1800/501 500; Ireland ☎1800/395 395; New Zealand ☎09/270 0050; UK ☎0800/833 833; US and Canada ☎1-800/325-6000; ⓦwww.westernunion.com.

Post, phones and email

Canada in general and Toronto in particular has an efficient postal system and a first-rate telephone network. Furthermore, after a tardy start, mobile coverage across the city and the rest of southern Ontario is fairly comprehensive. Telephone booths and mail boxes are liberally distributed across the city and charges for both types of service are reasonable. Internet cafés are increasingly common, too.

Post

Canada Post operates branches in scores of locations, mostly as one part of a larger retail outlet, mainly pharmacies and stationery stores. Usual opening hours are Mon–Fri 9am–6pm and Sat 9am–noon. Specific **post offices** are thinner on the ground, but there are a number dotted across the city centre. These include post offices at 31 Adelaide St East (℡416/214-2352); 595 Bay St (℡416/506-0911); and Commerce Court at 25 King St West (℡416/925-7452). If you're posting letters to a Canadian address, always include the postcode or your mail may never get there. Apart from Canada Post branches or offices, **stamps** can be purchased from automatic vending machines, the lobbies of larger hotels, airports, train stations, bus terminals and many retail outlets and newsstands. Current **postal charges** are 48¢ for letters and postcards up to 30g within Canada, 65¢ for the same weight to the US, and Can$1.25 for international mail (also up to 30g).

Phones

Domestic and international **telephone calls** can be made with equal ease from public and private phones. **Public telephones** are commonplace, though the irresistible rise of the mobile means that their numbers will not increase and may well diminish. All are equipped for the hearing-impaired and take coins. Most also accept pre-paid calling cards, as well as credit cards. Local calls cost 25¢ from a public phone, but are free on private phones (though not usually hotel phones). All **phone books** contain maps of the downtown core and display Toronto Transit Commission (TTC) routes; the *Yellow*

Pages, a compendium of all business phone numbers, grouped by service, are especially informative.

When **dialling** any Canadian number, either local or long-distance, you must include the area code – ℡416 or ℡647 in Toronto. Long-distance calls – to numbers beyond the area code of the telephone from which you are making the call – must be prefixed with "1". On public telephones, this "1" puts you through to the operator, who will tell you how much money you need to get connected. Thereafter, you'll be asked to shovel money in at regular intervals – so unless you're making a reverse-charge/collect call you'll need a stack of quarters (25¢ pieces) handy, if your call will be of any length.

To confuse matters, some connections within a single telephone code area are charged at the long-distance rate, and thus need the "1" prefix; a recorded message will tell you this is necessary as soon as you dial the number. To save the hassle of carrying all this change, you could consider either buying a telephone card back home (see below) or here. In Toronto, there are several to choose from, but one of the more widely available is Bell's **Hello Phone Pass**, sold in denominations of Can$10 and Can$20. For further details of Bell's other phone cards, contact their customer service department on ℡1-800/803 0077. As for **tariffs**, the cheap-rate period for calls is between 6pm and 8am during the week and all the weekend. Detailed rates are listed at the front of the telephone directory. Note also that many businesses, especially hotels, have **toll-free numbers** (prefixed by ℡1-800 or ℡1-888). Some of these can only be dialled from phones in the same province, others from anywhere within Canada, and a few from anywhere in North America; as a rough guideline, the larger the organization, the wider its toll-free net. Finally, remember that although most hotel rooms have phones, there is almost always an exorbitant surcharge for their use.

Useful phone numbers

Directory enquiries local (from private and public phones) ☎411; long-distance within North America from private phones ☎411, from public phones ☎1+ area code + 555-1212; international, call the operator ☎0.

Emergencies Police, fire and ambulance ☎911.

Operator (Domestic and international) ☎0.

Phoning abroad from Toronto To Australia: ☎011 + 61 + area code minus zero + number; to the Republic of Ireland: ☎011 + 353 + area code minus zero + number; to New Zealand: ☎011 + 64 + area code minus zero + number; to the UK: ☎011 + 44 + area code minus zero + number; to the US: ☎1 + area code + number.

Phoning Toronto from abroad Dial your country's international access code, then the area code, followed by the number.

Calling home from abroad with a telephone charge card

One of the most convenient ways of phoning home from abroad is via a **telephone charge card** from your phone company back home. Using a PIN number, you can make calls from most hotels, public and private phones that will be charged to your home account – and not locally. Since most major charge cards are free to obtain, it's certainly worth getting one at least for emergencies; bear in mind, however, that rates aren't necessarily cheaper than calling from a Toronto public phone – it's just more convenient, not having to carry quarters around.

In the US, AT&T, MCI, Sprint, Canada Direct and other North American long-distance companies all enable their customers to make credit-card calls while overseas, billed to your home number. Call your company's customer service line for details of the toll-free access code in Toronto. **In the UK and Ireland**, British Telecom (☎0800/345 144, ⓦwww.chargecard.bt.com) will issue free to all BT customers the BT Charge

Card, which can be used in Canada, along with a host of other countries. Alternatively, AT&T (☎0800/890 011, then 888/641-6123 when you hear the AT&T prompt) offers the Global Calling Card.

To call **Australia and New Zealand** from overseas, telephone charge cards such as Telstra Telecard or Optus Calling Card in Australia, and Telecom NZ's Calling Card can be used to make calls abroad, which are charged back to a domestic account or credit card. Apply to Telstra (☎1800/038 000), Optus (☎1300/300 937), or Telecom NZ (☎04/801 9000).

Mobile phones

If you want to use your **mobile phone** in Toronto, you'll need to check cellular access and call charges with your phone provider before you set out. Note in particular that you are likely to be charged extra for incoming calls when abroad, as the people calling you will be paying the usual rate. The same sometimes applies to text messages, though in many cases these can now be received easily and at ordinary rates. The mobile network now covers almost all of the city and, working on GSM 1900 – which means that mobiles bought in **Europe** need to be **triband** to gain cellular access.

Email

Toronto is well geared-up for Internet and email access with a healthy supply of **Internet cafés** – see below for a selection. In addition, note that many of the better hotels provide email and Internet access for their guests free or at a minimal charge.

One of the best ways to keep in touch while travelling is to sign up for a **free Internet email address** that can be accessed from anywhere in the world, for example Yahoo!Mail or Hotmail – accessible through ⓦwww.yahoo.com and ⓦwww.hotmail.com, respectively. Once you've set up an account, you can use these sites to pick up and send mail from any computer with access to the Internet. In addition, ⓦwww.kropla.com is a useful website giving details of how to plug your laptop in when abroad; the site also lists international phone codes and provides information about electrical systems in different countries.

Selected Internet cafés

Cyber Orbits 1 Gloucester ☎416/920-5912.
Open 24 hrs.
Internet Café 370 Yonge St ☎416/408-0400.
Open 6am–1am.

Net Space 275 Queen St W ☎416/597-2005.
Open 8am–1am.
Net Space 2 2305 Yonge St ☎416/486-9071.
Open 8am–1am.
SX Gaming 752 Yonge St ☎416/963-5000. Open
24 hrs.

The media

Toronto does well for radio stations, newspapers and magazines, some of which
are free. The TV channels on offer, both broadcast and cable, are largely uninspiring until after 11pm, at which point any number of truly strange and exotic
programmes spring up. Many shows that are deemed too risqué for general
North American audiences find their previews on Toronto TV channels during the
wee hours.

Newspapers

Toronto has two first-rate daily **newspapers**,
the *Globe and Mail*, and the *Toronto Star*.
Both provide an insight into every facet of
the city, but the *Globe and Mail* is better for
international and Canada-wide coverage.
The *Globe* is also Canada's main nationwide
newspaper, its only rival being the troubled
National Post. Initially a right-wing ranter, the
Post was aquired by a media mogul with
very strong Liberal connections, with an
ensuing editorial bloodletting.

Magazines

The **magazine** Torontonians rush to is
Toronto Life, which has a wonderful oblivi-
ousness about the rest of the world that's
very particular to Toronto. In addition, it does
an excellent line of small, red-covered special listings publications; the "Where to Get
Good Stuff Cheap" is a particular favourite
and tends to sell out quickly.

   A few **literary publications** deserve special note: *Brick* continues on towards its third
decade as Canada's national poetry magazine. *Blood & Aphorisms*, despite its gothic
title, publishes new writers of speculative fiction and has somehow managed to stay
afloat for over a decade. If one is serious
about local 'zines and comics, **The
Beguiling**, 601 Markham (☎416/533-9168)

is a must-visit, as it stocks most of the indie
publications.

TV and radio

Canadian TV is dominated by US sludge,
though the publicly-subsidized **Canadian
Broadcasting Corporation** (CBC) does
fight a rearguard action for quality programmes, from drama through to documen-
tary. The main local TV station is the chatty
and really rather inconsequential **City TV**.
Cable television is commonplace, both in
private homes and in the vast majority of
hotel and motel rooms.

   As regards **radio**, CBC Radio One (99.1
FM) is Toronto's frequency for the Canadian
Broadcasting Corporation, an excellent
source for public affairs, news and arts programming. For just news, try CFTR (680 AM)
or CFRB (1010 AM). For easy rock, tune in
to CHUM (104.5 FM) or MIX (99.9 FM).
Harder rock is found on Q 107 (107.1 FM),
and alternative sounds are on CFNY (102.1
FM). CISS (92.5 FM) does country, and for
classical try CFMX (96 FM) or CBC Two
(94.5 FM). There are also two excellent student stations that feature alternative and
world artists, as well as news and events:
CJRT (91.1 FM) from Ryerson Polytechnic,
and CIUT (89 FM) from the University of
Toronto.

Opening hours and public holidays

Shopping is a major Toronto pastime and opening hours are consequently generous. Still, many places are closed on public holidays – though not the city's bars, restaurants and hotels. Public transport keeps moving on holidays, too, operating a scaled-back restricted service. For a list of select celebrations the city puts on, see Chapter 16, "Festivals and events".

Opening hours

Shopping hours are fairly uniform, with most places open seven days a week, 10am–7pm Monday to Wednesday, 10am–9pm Thursday and Friday, 10am–6pm on Saturday and noon–6pm on Sunday. In addition, convenience stores, like 7-11, are routinely open much longer, often round the clock. **Office hours** are more restricted, characteristically Monday to Friday 9/9.30am–4.30/5pm. Most major **museums** are open daily from around 10am to 5pm or 5.30pm, with one late-night a week, usually Thursday until 8pm. As for **restaurants**, these are usually open daily from 11am to 11pm, with or without an afternoon break, from around 2.30/3pm to 5/6pm. **Bars** are open daily from 11am to 2am.

Public holidays

New Year's Day Jan 1
Good Friday varies; March/April
Easter Sunday varies; March/April
Easter Monday varies; March/April
Victoria Day third Monday in May
Canada Day July 1
Simcoe Day first Monday in Aug
Labour Day first Monday in Sept
Thanksgiving second Monday in Oct
Remembrance Day Nov 11
Christmas Day Dec 25
Boxing Day Dec 26

Crime and personal safety

There's little reason why you should ever come into contact with either the Toronto Police Service or the Ontario Provincial Police, who safeguard the rest of the province: Toronto is one of the safest cities in North America and although there are a few crime hotspots, these are mostly on the city's peripheries.

Few citizens carry arms, muggings are uncommon, and street crime less commonplace than in many other major cities – though the usual cautions about poorly lit urban streets and so forth stand. Note also that the police are diligent in enforcing traffic laws.

Petty crime

Almost all the problems tourists encounter in Toronto are to do with **petty crime** – pick-pocketing and bag-snatching – rather than more serious physical confrontations. As such, it's good to be on your guard and know where your possessions are at all times. Thieves often work in pairs and, although **theft** is far from commonplace, you should be aware of certain ploys, such as: the "helpful" person pointing out "birdshit" (actually shaving cream or similar) on your coat, while someone else relieves you of your money; being invited to read a card or paper on the street to distract your attention; or someone in a café moving for your drink with one hand while the other goes for your bag. If you're in a crowd of tourists, watch out for people moving in unusually close.

Sensible **precautions** against petty theft include: carrying bags slung across your neck and not over your shoulder; not carrying anything in pockets that are easy to dip into; and having photocopies of your passport, airline ticket and driving licence, while leaving the originals in your hotel. When you're looking for a hotel room, never leave your bags unattended, and, similarly, if you have a car, don't leave anything in view when you park: vehicle theft is still fairly uncommon, but luggage and valuables do make a tempting target.

If you are robbed, you'll need to go to the **police** to report it, not least because your insurance company will require a police report. Remember to make a note of the report number – or, better still, ask for a copy of the statement itself. Don't expect a great deal of concern if your loss is relatively small, and don't be surprised if the process of completing forms and formalities takes ages.

Personal safety

Although generally you can walk around the city without fear of **harassment or assault**, certain parts of Toronto are decidedly shady and neither is the overall downtown atmosphere improved by the large number of (sometimes aggressive) beggars. There are no clearly defined "no-go" areas as such – though Sherbourne Street to the south of

Queen Street East comes close – but on the other hand, pockets of seedy roughness are dotted here and there seemingly at random. Consequently, and especially until you are familiar with the city's layout, it's always best to err on the side of caution, particularly at night. Using **public transport**, even late at night, isn't usually a problem – but if in doubt take a taxi.

In the unlikely event that you are **mugged**, or otherwise threatened, never resist, and try to reduce your contact with the robber to a minimum; either just hand over what's wanted, or throw money in one direction and take off in the other. Afterwards go straight to the police, who will be much more sympathetic and helpful on these occasions than if you're merely pickpocketed, say.

The **Toronto Police service** is divided into two commands: Central Field, 75 Eglington Avenue West, which covers central Toronto, and Area Field, 30 Ellerslie Avenue, which covers outer Toronto. For **emergencies** (police, fire, or ambulance), call ☎911. To reach the police in a **non-emergency situation**, call ☎416/808 2222, or TDD 416/467-0493.

Being arrested

If you're **detained** by the police, the arresting officer(s) must identify him/herself. At the police station, detainees have the right to free but reasonable use of a telephone and legal counsel. For certain sorts of suspected offence – primarily gun- and drug-related – the police are likely to strip-search detainees, though these searches, and the frequency of them, remain controversial.

Travellers with disabilities

Toronto is one of the best places in the world to visit if you have mobility problems or other physical disabilities. All public buildings are required to be wheelchair-accessible and provide suitable toilet facilities, almost all street corners have dropped kerbs, and public telephones are specially equipped for hearing-aid users.

Operated by the TTC, the city's public transport system (see p.22) is disability-friendly, its bespoke Wheel-Trans service providing a door-to-door accessible transit service seven days a week (Mon–Fri 6am–1am, Sat & Sun 7am–1am). Further Wheel-Trans information is available on ☏416/393-4111 (Mon–Fri 8am–4pm); make reservations on ☏416/393-4222.

Contacts for travellers with disabilities

In the US and Canada

Access-Able ⊛www.access-able.com. Online resource for travellers with disabilities.
Directions Unlimited 123 Green Lane, Bedford Hills, NY 10507 ☏1-800/533-5343 or 914/241-1700. Travel agency specializing in bookings for people with disabilities.
Mobility International USA 451 Broadway, Eugene, OR 97401 ☏541/343-1284, ⊛www.miusa.org. Information and referral services, access guides, tours and exchange programmes.
Society for the Advancement of Travelers with Handicaps (SATH) 347 5th Ave, New York, NY 10016 ☏212/447-7284, ⊛www.sath.org. Non-profit educational organization that has actively represented travelers with disabilities since 1976.
Wheels Up! ☏1-888/38-WHEELS, ⊛www.wheelsup.com. Provides discounted airfare, tour and cruise prices for disabled travellers, also publishes a free monthly newsletter and has a comprehensive website.

In the UK and Ireland

Access Travel 6 The Hillock, Astley, Lancashire M29 7GW ☏01942/888 844, ⊛www.access-travel.co.uk. Small, personal-service tour operator that can arrange flights, transfer and accommodation.
Holiday Care 2nd floor, Imperial Building, Victoria Rd, Horley, Surrey RH6 7PZ ☏0845/124 9971, minicom ☏0845/124 9976, ⊛www.holidaycare.org.uk. Provides free lists of accessible accommodation across North America.
Irish Wheelchair Association Blackheath Drive, Clontarf, Dublin 3 ☏01/818 6400, ⊛www.iwa.ie. Useful information provided about travelling abroad with a wheelchair.
Tripscope Alexandra House, Albany Rd, Brentford, Middlesex TW8 0NE ☏0845/7585 641, ⊛www.tripscope.org.uk. Registered charity providing free advice on international transport.

In Australia and New Zealand

ACROD (Australian Council for Rehabilitation of the Disabled) PO Box 60, Curtin ACT 2605; Suite 103, 1st floor, 1–5 Commercial Rd, Kings Grove 2208 ☏02/6282 4333, TTY ☏02/6282 4333, ⊛www.acrod.org.au. Provides lists of travel agencies and tour operators for people with disabilities.
Disabled Persons Assembly 4/173–175 Victoria St, Wellington, New Zealand ☏04/801 9100 (also TTY), ⊛www.dpa.org.nz. Resource centre with lists of travel agencies and tour operators for people with disabilities.

The City

The City

Downtown Toronto

The skyscrapers etched across **Downtown Toronto's** skyline witness the clout of a city that has shed its dowdy provincialism to become the economic and cultural focus of English-speaking Canada. There's no false modesty here, beginning with Toronto's mascot, the **CN Tower**, and continuing with **SkyDome** and the herd of tower blocks that dominate the nearby **Banking District**. Modern behemoths like the **Toronto Dominion Centre** and the gold-coated towers of the **Royal Bank Plaza** are beacons of modern-day prosperity, but the downtown area is also dotted with older skyrises – the **Dominion Bank** and the **Canada Permanent Trust building** for example – whose sumptuous designs (circa 1920) once trumpeted the aspirations of previous generations. Toronto's business elite also funded downtown's two most enjoyable art galleries, the **Toronto Dominion Gallery of Inuit Art** and the superb **Hudson's Bay Company Gallery**, which boasts a connoisseur's collection of Canadian paintings.

At Queen Street, the Banking District gives way to the main **shopping** area, which revolves around the sprawling **Eaton Centre**. Immediately to the west is **City Hall**, another striking example of modern design, and the **Art Gallery of Ontario**, which houses the province's finest collection of paintings, as well as an entire gallery of sculptures by Henry Moore. Finally, on the western periphery of downtown is **Fort York**, a pleasing reconstruction of the British fort established here in 1793.

Downtown is best explored on **foot**, though the tower blocks can be a bit claustrophobic and local complaints that the city centre lacks a human dimension are legion. To be fair, this sentiment has been taken into account, and although it's a bit late in the day, efforts have been made to make the downtown core more people-friendly, with plazas, pavement cafés and street sculptures.

The CN Tower and around

Much to the dismay of many Torontonians, the **CN Tower**, 301 Front St West (daily: Jan–April 10am–10pm, May–Dec 8am–11pm; observation deck $18, Sky Pod $8 extra; ☎416/868-6937, @www.cntower.ca; Union Station subway), has become the city's symbol. It's touted on much of the city's promotional literature, features on thousands of postcards and holiday snaps, and has become the obligatory start to most tourist itineraries. From anywhere in the city, it's impossible to miss its slender form poking high above the skyline, reminding some of French novelist Guy de Maupassant's quip about another

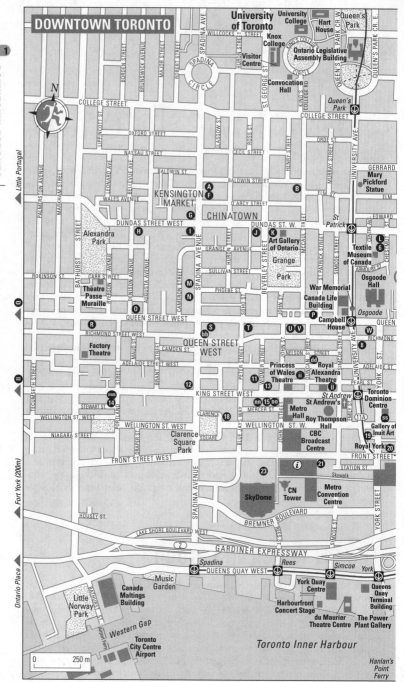

DOWNTOWN TORONTO

Little Portugal ◄

Fort York (200m) ◄

Ontario Place ◄

University of Toronto

University College

Hart House

Queen's Park

Knox College

Visitor Centre

Ontario Legislative Assembly Building

Convocation Hall

Queen's Park

COLLEGE STREET

WILLCOCKS STREET

SPADINA CIRCLE

COLLEGE STREET

OXFORD STREET

NASSAU STREET

BALDWIN ST

WALES AVENUE

KENSINGTON MARKET

Ⓐ Ⓕ

Ⓑ

CHINATOWN

Ⓖ

DUNDAS STREET WEST

Ⓗ Ⓘ

Ⓙ Ⓚ

Art Gallery of Ontario

Grange Park

Alexandra Park

Theatre Passe Muraille

ROBINSON ST.

CARR STREET

Ⓠ

Ⓜ Ⓝ

Ⓞ

QUEEN STREET WEST

PHOEBE ST.

War Memorial

Canada Life Building

Ⓟ **Campbell House**

GERRARD

Mary Pickford Statue

ELM

St Patrick

Ⓛ Ⓖ

Textile Museum of Canada

Osgoode Hall

Osgoode

Ⓡ

ⓑⓑ Ⓢ

QUEEN STREET WEST

Ⓣ

ⓊⓋ

Ⓦ

RICHMOND STREET WEST

Factory Theatre

ADELAIDE STREET

Ⓠ ⓑⓑ

Ⓣ

Princess of Wales Theatre

ⓕⓕ

Royal Alexandra Theatre

ⓓⓓ

ⓙⓙ

Toronto Dominion Centre

Ⓗ

ⓜⓜ

⑭

⑫

⑪ ⑬

KING STREET WEST

ⓝⓝ ⑮ ⓞⓞ

St Andrew's

St Andrew

WELLINGTON ST. WEST

⑱

Clarence Square Park

Metro Hall

Roy Thompson Hall

CBC Broadcast Centre

ⓢⓢ

⑲ **Gallery of Inuit Art**

Royal York ⑳

FRONT STREET

STATION ST.

Skywalk

FRONT STREET WEST

ⓘ ㉑

㉓

SkyDome

CN Tower

Metro Convention Centre

BREMNER BOULEVARD

LAKE SHORE BOULEVARD WEST

② **GARDINER EXPRESSWAY**

Spadina

Rees

Simcoe

York

QUEENS QUAY WEST

Music Garden

Canada Maltings Building

York Quay Centre

Queens Quay Terminal Building

Harbourfront Concert Stage

du Maurier Theatre Centre

The Power Plant Gallery

Little Norway Park

Western Gap

Toronto City Centre Airport

Toronto Inner Harbour

Hanlan's Point Ferry

0 — 250 m

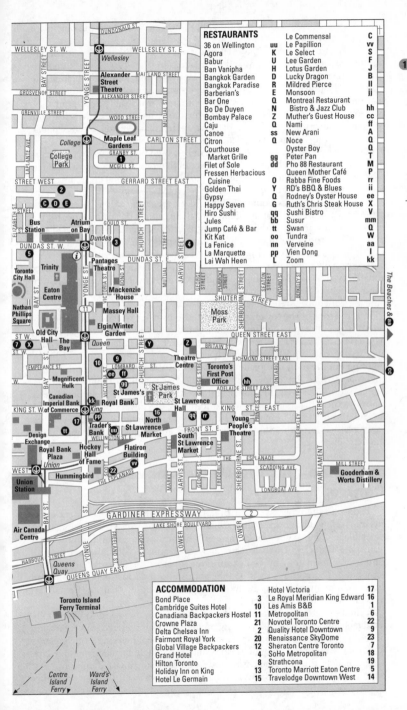

famous tower: "I like to lunch at the Eiffel Tower because that's the only place in Paris I can't see it."

Unlikely as it may seem, the celebrity status of the CN Tower was entirely unforeseen, its origins plain and utilitarian. In the 1960s, the Canadian Broadcasting Company (CBC) teamed up with the railway conglomerate Canadian National (CN) to propose the construction of a bigger and better transmission antenna. CBC eventually withdrew from the project, but CN, who owned the land and saw a chance for profit, forged ahead. Much to the company's surprise, they found that the undertaking stirred intense public interest – so much so that long before the tower was completed, in April 1975, it was clear that its potential as a tourist sight would be huge: today, broadcasting only accounts for about twenty percent of the tower's income, with the rest provided by the two million tourists who throng here annually. Come early (especially on school holidays) to avoid the crowds.

Only die-hard critics could deny the sleek elegance of the tower, which tapers to a minaret-thin point 553m (or 1815ft) above the city centre. It's the tallest structure in the world, and details of its construction are provided in a series of **photographs** and **touch-screen displays** on the main access ramp and on the mezzanine level beyond. The background information is interesting – especially tidbits revealing that the tower is hit by lightning between sixty and eighty times a year – but the "Daredevil Thrills" film simulations (for an extra charge) of bungee jumping, tightrope walking and the like, in the neighbouring concourse, are eminently missable.

From the foot of the tower, **glass-fronted elevators** whisk you up the outside of the building to the indoor and outdoor **Look Out level** galleries at 346m. These circular galleries provide views over the whole of the city, which appears flattened and without much perspective – though markers help by pointing out the most conspicuous sights. This is also where you'll find *360 The Restaurant* (which slowly revolves around the tower, taking 72 minutes to make one revolution), as well as experience the vertigo shock of the reinforced **glass floor** – a thrill that goes some way to justifying the tower's pricey admittance fee. You're still 100m from the top of the tower, though; a separate set of lifts carry visitors up to the **Sky Pod**, a confined little gallery that doesn't justify the extra expense.

SkyDome and the Metro Convention Centre

Next door to the CN Tower, at 1 Blue Jays Way, is **SkyDome** (frequent guided tours depending on event schedules; call ☎416/341-2770 for latest timetable; $12.50; ⓦwww.skydome.com), home to two major Toronto sports teams: the Blue Jays baseball team, and the Argonauts, of Canadian football fame (for information on both teams, see Chapter 14, "Sports and outdoor activities"). The stadium seats 53,000, and is also used for special events and concerts, sometimes within the **SkyTent**, which encloses a part of the stadium to create a more intimate arena.

Opened in 1989, SkyDome was the first stadium in the world to have a fully retractable roof – it only takes twenty minutes to cover the stadium's eight acres of turf and terrace. It was an extraordinary feat of engineering (four gigantic roof panels mounted on rail tracks), and was much heralded by the city. Unfortunately, the end result was pretty ugly, and remains so despite the best efforts of artist **Michael Snow**, who added a pair of giant cartoon sculptures to the exterior – *The Audience Part 1* and *Part 2* – in an effort to enhance its aesthetic appeal. The sculptures are endearing (check out the Eaton Centre, p.52, for more of Snow's work), but when the roof is closed SkyDome still looks like a giant armadillo. Hour-long **guided tours**, which are worth it only if you're sticking around for a sporting event, begin with a fifteen-minute film about the stadium's construction; the walking tour that follows the film takes in the media centre, a dressing room and a stroll on the field.

On the other side of the CN Tower, the **Metro Convention Centre** straddles the rail lines into Union Station (see p.40), with the dreary North Building on one side, and the smart, chic South Building, with its acres of glass and steel, on the other. The former faces onto Front Street West, and the latter onto Bremner Boulevard. The South Building has the main entrance, where the foyer displays a delightful mosaic of frogs, frogspawn and turtles – *The Turtle Pond*. Here also, just outside the building, is an engaging sculpture of two giant woodpeckers pecking away at a steel tree.

West of the CN: Fort York

Modern-day Toronto traces its origins to **Fort York**, an appealing reconstruction of a colonial stockade located a twenty-minute stroll west of the CBC Broadcasting Centre, on Garrison Rd, off Fleet St (mid-May to Aug daily 10am–5pm; Sept to late May Mon–Fri 10am–4pm, Sat & Sun 10am–5pm; $5; ☎416/392-6907). To get there from CBC, follow Front St West to its end, turn left along Bathurst St and, after crossing the railway bridge, take the signposted footpath on the right; this leads to the fort's rear entrance. To reach the front entrance, take either the Bathurst streetcar (#511) or streetcar #509 from Union Station, and get off on Fleet St at the foot of Garrison Rd; from here the fort is a ten-minute walk.

Built in 1793 on the shores of Lake Ontario to bolster British control of the Great Lakes, Fort York was initially a half-hearted, poorly fortified affair, partly because of a lack of funds, but mainly because it was too remote to command much attention – never mind that the township of York was the capital of Upper Canada. However, in 1811, the deterioration in Anglo-American relations put it on active duty. There was a sudden flurry of activity as the fort's ramparts and gun emplacements were strengthened – but it was still too weak to hold off the American army that marched on York in 1813. Hurriedly, the British decided to evacuate the fort and blow up the gunpowder magazine to stop its contents falling into enemy hands. Unfortunately, they completely underestimated the force of the explosion, and killed or wounded ten of their own men as well as 260 of the advancing enemy, the fatalities including the splendidly named American general Zebulon Montgomery Pike. After the war, Fort York was rebuilt and its garrison made a considerable contribution to the development of Toronto, as York was renamed in 1834. The British army moved out in 1870 and their Canadian replacements stayed for another sixty years, by which time landfill had pushed the lakeshore to the south; nowadays the fort is marooned in the shadow of the Gardiner Expressway.

Opened as a **museum** in 1934, Fort York is staffed by guides who provide informative, free forty-minute **tours**; or you can wander around on your own, but be sure to pick up a plan at reception. The carefully restored earthen **ramparts** are low-lying, thick and constructed in a zigzag pattern, both to mitigate against enemy artillery and to provide complementary lines of fire. They enclose a haphazard sequence of log, stone and brick buildings, notably a couple of well-preserved **blockhouses**, complete with heavy timbers and snipers'

The Fenian raids

During the American Civil War, the British continued to trade with the Confederacy, much to the chagrin of the Union army. After the war, tensions between the two countries abated, though many northerners still hankered for retribution – no group more so than the **Fenian Brotherhood**, formed by Irish exiles in New York in 1859. Many of these Irishmen had a deep and abiding hatred for the British, whose cruel administration of their homeland had caused the Catholic population endless suffering. To the Brotherhood, Britain's continued control of Canada was unbearable, and they hoped to capitalize on the residue of ill-feeling left from the Civil War to push the US into military action against its northern neighbour. Their tactics were simple: they organized a series of cross-border raids, hoping that if they provoked a military retaliation from the British, the US government would feel obliged to come to their aid and invade Canada. The most serious Fenian raid crossed the border in 1866 with 1000 men. The British drove the Fenians out without too much difficulty, and although there were significant casualties, Congress didn't take the military bait.

loopholes. In one of them – **Building No.5** on the plan – an introductory video outlines the history of the fort and an exhibit explores the various military crises that afflicted Canada from 1792 to 1967, including the War of 1812 and the curious affair of the Fenian Raids (see box above). Here also is a small but particularly good display on late eighteenth- and early nineteenth-century **artillery**. The prize pieces are a 1793 British rampart gun, a cross between a rifle and an artillery piece, and a hot-shot furnace for heating cannon balls. A certain **Lieutenant Colonel Shrapnel**, who saw military service in Canada, wasn't at all impressed by cannon balls and invented his own much more lethal shell, which fragmented on impact. To prove his invention, Shrapnel arranged a test firing at the arsenal in Woolwich, back in London, and a card copy of the results is displayed here; needless to say, the top brass were suitably persuaded.

Moving on, **Building No.6** started out as a magazine but ended up as a storehouse. Its ground floor now holds a modest display on the role of black soldiers and settlers in the early history of Ontario. Interestingly, the Upper Canada legislature banned the importation of slaves in 1793, forty years before it was abolished right across the British Empire. Up above, an archeological section displays the various bits and pieces unearthed at the fort – buckles, brooches, plates, clay pipes, tunic buttons and so forth. The most interesting piece is a "Sacred to Love" stick-pin, an example of the mourning jewellery that was popular amongst Victorians. Across the fort, **Building No.4**, the Blue Barracks, is a 1930s reconstruction of the junior officers' quarters, whilst **Building No.3** is the former Officers' Quarters and Mess. The latter boasts several period rooms and two original money vaults, hidden away in the cellar. Opposite, the stone and brick powder magazine – **Building No.8** – has two-metre-thick walls and spark-proof copper and brass fixtures.

Union Station and the Air Canada Centre

The **Skywalk** is a sheltered walkway that leads from the Metro Convention Centre to **Union Station**, at Front St W and Bay St, a distinguished Beaux Arts structure designed in 1907 and finally completed in 1927. The exterior is imposing, with its long serenade of Neoclassical columns, but its interior is the real highlight, the vast **main hall** boasting a coffered, tiled ceiling of graceful design. Like other North American railway stations of the period, Union Station has the flavour of a medieval cathedral, with muffled sounds echoing through its stone cloisters, and daylight filtering through its high arched windows. The station's grandiose quality was quite deliberate. In the days when the steam train was the most popular form of transport, architects were keen to glorify the train station, and, in this case, to conjure up images of Canada's vastness – a frieze bearing the names of all the Canadian cities reachable by rail at the time of construction runs around the hall.

A short walk south from Union Station, the **Air Canada Centre**, 40 Bay St (℡416/815-5982, ₩www.theaircanadacentre.com), is home to hockey's Maple Leafs and basketball's Raptors; see Chapter 14, "Sports and outdoor activities," for information on these two teams. **Tours** of the Air Canada Centre ($12) are available, and include a visit to a dressing room and the baseball practice area.

The Royal York Hotel

Directly opposite the west end of the railway station, the **Royal York Hotel**, 100 Front St W, was the largest and tallest building in the British Empire when it opened in 1929. It, too, was designed in the Beaux Arts style, by Montreal architects Ross and Macdonald. However, instead of the formal symmetries of Union Station, the *Royal York* has a cascading, irregular facade with stylistic flourishes reminiscent of a French chateau. It was built to impress. Originally, the hotel had its own concert hall, mini-hospital and 12,000-book library; each of the hotel's one thousand rooms also had a radio, private shower and bath. The hotel soon became a byword for luxury, where every well-heeled visitor to the city stayed, and although its pre-eminent position has been usurped by other, newer hotels in the last decade or two, a recent refurbishment has restored it as a favourite with visiting big wigs. For full contact details, as well as what it costs to stay here, see p.118.

The Banking District

Union Station and the *Royal York Hotel* mark the southern boundary of the **Banking District**, home to many of the city's most impressive buildings, from flamboyant 1920s high-rises to dynamic, modern skyscrapers, sheathed in glass and steel. It's also a district of bizarre juxtapositions: old, low buildings are packed tight alongside their mighty, newer neighbours.

Royal Bank Plaza and the Toronto Dominion Centre

Opposite the east end of Union Station, the two massive towers of the **Royal Bank Plaza**, 200 Bay St, were designed by local architect Boris Zerafa during the architectural boom of the mid-1970s. Each tower is completely coated with a thin layer of gold, and despite Zerafa's assertion that the gold simply added texture to his creation, it's hard not to believe that the Royal Bank wanted to show off a bit, too.

In between the *Royal York Hotel* and the Royal Bank, a gated **stone stairway** climbs up from Front Street West to a tiny plaza overseen by a phalanx of skyscrapers. It's a delightful spot, in a heart-of-the-city sort of way, and Catherine Widgery's *City People* (1989), a folksy set of life-size metal figures attached to the stairway's walls, add a touch of decorative elan. The walkway continues down to Wellington Street West, just a few metres from the southern tower of the **Toronto Dominion Centre**, whose four reflective black blocks straddle Wellington Street between Bay and York. Arguably the most appealing of the city's modern skyscrapers, the four towers are without decoration, but as an ensemble they achieve an austere beauty that can't help but impress. Begun in 1964, they were designed by **Ludwig Mies van der Rohe** (1886–1969), one of the twentieth century's most influential architects. Born to a family of German stone carvers, the magpie-like Rohe was influenced by a wide range of architectural styles, including Prussian Classicism and Russian Constructivism; he also served as the director of Bauhaus. In his last decades, he refined his architectural vision, seeking to establish contemplative, neutral spaces guided by his maxim-cum-motto "Less is more"; the Toronto Dominion Centre is a case in point.

The Toronto Dominion Gallery of Inuit Art

The **Toronto Dominion Gallery of Inuit Art**, in the South Tower of the Toronto Dominion Centre (Mon–Fri 8am–6pm, Sat & Sun 10am–4pm; free), boasts an outstanding collection of over a hundred pieces of Inuit sculpture. Spread over two levels, the collection is owned by the Dominion Bank, who commissioned a panel of experts to celebrate Canada's Centennial in 1965 by collecting the best of postwar Inuit art. The gallery contains examples of all the favourite themes of Inuit sculpture, primarily animal and human studies supplemented by a smattering of metamorphic figures, in which an Inuit adopts the form of an animal, either in full or in part. Other sculptures depict deities, particularly Nuliayuk the sea goddess (also known as Sedna). Inuit religious belief was short on theology, but its encyclopedic animism populated the Arctic with spirits and gods, the subject of all manner of Inuit folk tales. Christianity destroyed this traditional faith, but the legends survived and continue to feature prominently in Inuit art. Most of the sculptures are in soapstone, a greyish-blue stone that is easy to carve, though there are bone, ivory and caribou-antler creations, too.

In the **foyer**, beside the revolving doors, the gallery begins with **Johnny Inukpuk**'s raw, elemental *Mother Feeding Child* (1962), an exquisite piece in which a woman holds her child in an all-encompassing embrace. Hailing from Port Harrison, on the eastern shores of Hudson Bay, Inukpuk was one of the first Inuit sculptors to establish a reputation in the south, and his work has been collected since the late 1950s. There's another of his soapstone sculptures in the foyer: *Tattooed Woman*, a fine, almost fierce, portrayal of a woman in traditional attire, whose eyes stare out into the distance.

Upstairs, distributed among a dozen glass cabinets, is a superb selection of soapstone sculptures. In the first cabinet are two striking representations of Sedna, one by **Saggiak**, the other by **Kenojuak Ashevak**, both carved in Cape Dorset in 1965. Half-woman, half-seal, Sedna, the goddess of the sea and sometimes of life itself, is one of the key figures of Inuit mythology. Her story is a sad one. She was deceived by a young man who posed as a hunter, but was in fact a powerful shaman. Sedna married him and he promptly spirited her away from her family. Sedna's father gave chase and rescued his daughter, but on the return journey they were assailed by a violent storm conjured by the shaman. Terrified, the father threw his daughter overboard, and when she repeatedly attempted to get back into the boat, he chopped off her fingers and then her hands. These bits and pieces (according to legend) became whales, seals, walruses and fish – but Sedna herself sank to the depths of the ocean, where she remains.

Other striking works to look out for include – in an adjacent cabinet – **Joe Talirunili**'s *Migration*, a dynamic stone and antler carving depicting a traditional *umiak* (boat) crowded with migrating Inuit, and, further on, the magnificent *Bear*, by Cape Dorset's **Pauta Saila**. The bear is crudely carved, but the jaws are all that's needed to convey the animal's ferocity, and the blurring of the trunk and the legs gives the appearance of great strength. For more top-quality Inuit art, you should visit the Art Gallery of Ontario; see p.58 for the account.

St Andrew's Presbyterian Church

Crossing over Wellington Street, and walking between the other three towers of the Toronto Dominion Centre, you soon pass Joe Fafard's herd of grazing cows – seven extraordinarily realistic bronze **statues**. From here, it's a short detour west along King Street to **St Andrew's Presbyterian Church**, 75 Simcoe St (daily: 9am–4pm; free; St Andrew subway). Marooned among the city's skyscrapers, this handsome sandstone church is a reminder of an older Toronto, and its Romanesque Revival towers and gables have a distinctly Norman appearance. Built in 1876 for a predominantly Scottish congregation, the church has a delightful interior. Its cherrywood pews and balcony slope down towards the chancel, and dappled light streams through the stained-glass windows. Most importantly, though, St Andrew's has an admirable history of social action. Since the earliest days of the city's settlement, this and many other Toronto churches have played a leading role in the campaign against poverty and homelessness. It is perhaps a bit surprising, then, that the church basement has been turned into the **48th Highlanders' Museum** (Wed & Thurs 10am–3pm; donation), honouring the regiment that has attracted Scottish Canadians to its colours since its formation in 1891. The museum displays uniforms and weaponry alongside an intriguing collection of old photographs, tracking the regiment through its involvement in the Boer and both world wars.

Roy Thompson Hall, Metro Hall and the CBC Centre

Across Simcoe Street from St Andrew's, **Roy Thompson Hall** is the home of the Toronto Symphony Orchestra (for more on the orchestra, see p.158). It was completed in 1982 to a design by Canada's Arthur Erickson, and although it looks like an upturned soup bowl by day, at night its glass-panelled walls transform its appearance with a skein of filtered light.

Next door, **Metro Hall**'s trio of glass-and-steel office blocks is set around an attractive plaza of water fountains and lawns. Built in the early 1990s, the complex represents a break from the brash architectural harshness of previous decades and a move toward more fluid, people-friendly designs.

To the south, Metro Hall abuts the **CBC Broadcasting Centre**, 250 Front St West, a ten-storey edifice whose painted gridiron beams make the building aesthetically bearable, but not much more. CBC – the Canadian Broadcasting Company – offers one-hour **guided tours** ($7) of the building; these take in visits to TV and radio studios, sets and newsrooms. For times, call ☏416/205-8605. Here also is a **CBC museum** (Mon–Fri 9am–4pm, Sat noon–4pm; free; ⓦwww.cbc.ca/museum), where several thousand artefacts illustrate the history of CBC since its foundation in 1936. Highlights include a CBC Hall of Fame, the opportunity to listen to old CBC radio programmes, and a theatre which screens vintage CBC TV shows.

The Toronto Stock Exchange

Doubling back from the CBC Centre along King Street West, it's a short walk to the old **Toronto Stock Exchange**, 234 Bay St at King, which has been corrupted by its incorporation within a skyrise that imitates – but doesn't match – the sober blocks of the adjacent Toronto Dominion Centre. Nevertheless, the facade has survived, and its stone lintel is decorated with muscular Art Deco carvings of men at work. This glorification of labour pleased the stockbrokers to no end, but an unknown stonemason was not so impressed: look closely at the frieze and you'll see that the top-hatted figure – the capitalist – is dipping his hand into a worker's pocket, a subversive subtext that seems to have gone unnoticed by the original owners. Inside, the ground floor is routinely modern, but the trading floor upstairs has been preserved in all its Art Deco pomp, the geometric panelling decorated with a series of delightful ribbon murals celebrating industry. On the ground floor, the Stock Exchange now accommodates the temporary exhibitions of the **Design Exchange** (Tues–Fri 9am–6pm, Sat & Sun noon–5pm; admission charged for some exhibitions), or "DX", whose purpose is to foster innovative design. Recent displays have covered everything from local furniture design to prototype plans for making the city more environmentally conscious.

The CIBC buildings

Across the street from the Exchange, the formidable (and formidably named) **Canadian Imperial Bank of Commerce**, 243 Bay St, is a stainless-steel behemoth erected in the 1970s to a design by renowned architect **I.M. Pei** (born 1917). Born in China, Pei moved to the USA in the 1930s, where he eventually established a worldwide reputation for his sleek modern designs, such as Boston's John Hancock Tower and the glass pyramids at the Louvre museum in Paris. Pei's CIBC tower is typical of his work, its sheer, overween-ing size emphasized by its severe angles and sleek trajectory. The tower stands in sharp contrast to the former **CIBC building**, next door to the north at 25 King St West. This older structure, erected just after the stock market crash of 1929, has a restrained stone exterior, where the cathedral-like doors, draped with carved reliefs, are the only hint of the magnificent chandeliers, gilt-cof-fered ceilings, and sinuous marble tracery inside.

The Bay-Adelaide development

Walking north up Bay Street from King Street West, turn right on Temperance Street for a glimpse of the **Bay-Adelaide development**, the city's biggest real-estate fiasco. The big wheels of the business community decided to plonk a mammoth office complex right here in the mid-1980s, when property spec-ulation was at a fever pitch. Millions of dollars were invested, but in 1988 the bottom fell out of the office rental market just as construction had begun. In a near panic, the developers cancelled further work on the project, leaving a scat-tering of foundations and a rough, concrete block six storeys high that was intended to be the core of the main skyscraper. Many Torontonians were delighted by the collapse of the project, and a *Toronto Star* columnist promptly christened the concrete stump the "**Magnificent Hulk**" – and the name stuck. What will happen to the site now is anybody's guess, but further devel-opment seems unlikely.

The Royal and Trader's banks

At the east end of Temperance Street, turn right down Yonge Street and you'll soon reach the **Royal Bank**, 2 King St East, which was designed by Ross and Macdonald, also the creators of Union Station and the *Royal York Hotel*. Clumsily modernized, the ground floor is less than inspired, but the austere symmetries of the building as a whole still impress, as do the classical motifs that were gracefully worked into the main frieze.

A quick step to the south, **Trader's Bank**, 67 Yonge St at King (no public access), was Toronto's first skyscraper, a fifteen-storey structure completed in 1906. The owners were apprehensive that the size of the building might prompt accusations of vanity, so they insisted on overhanging eaves and stumpy classical columns in an effort to make it look shorter. They need not have both-ered: as soon as it was finished visitors thronged the bank and the top floor was turned into an observation deck. Newer skyscrapers now dwarf Trader's, though, and the once unhindered view is long gone.

The Hockey Hall of Fame

From Trader's Bank, it's a short haul south to the **Hockey Hall of Fame**, 30 Yonge St at Front St West (Sept to late June Mon–Fri 10am–5pm, Sat 9.30am–6pm, Sun 10.30am–5pm; late June to Aug Mon–Sat 9.30am–6pm, Sun 10am–6pm; $12, children 4–13 years old $8; ☎416/360-7735, ⓦwww.hhof.com), a highly commercialized, ultra-modern tribute to Canada's national sport – though you wouldn't think so from the outside. The only part of the complex visible from the street is the old **Bank of Montréal building**, a Neoclassical edifice dating back to 1885. The bank is actually one of Toronto's finer structures – its intricately carved stonework is adorned by a dainty sequence of pediments and pilasters – but its incorporation into the Hockey

Hall of Fame is awkward. The bank's entrance has been blocked off and the interior bowdlerized to house a collection of hockey trophies.

The **entrance** to the Hockey Hall of Fame is below ground in the adjacent **BCE Place**, a glitzy retail complex on the west side of Yonge St between Front and Wellington streets. Inside the museum are a series of exhibition areas, with particularly enjoyable sections on the evolution of the goalie's mask and a replica of the Montréal Canadiens' locker room. Other areas, including endless biographical displays on the sport's great names and details of the various National Hockey League (NHL) teams, are geared to the most rabid of fans, but there's plenty to keep the less-obsessed entertained as well. Highlights include the mini ice-rink where visitors can blast away at hockey pucks and a small theatre showing films of hockey's most celebrated games. The film of the 1972 "World Summit Series" between the USSR and Canada is filled with Cold War resonance and is gripping stuff even for the non-enthusiast. Finally, the **trophy room**, located inside the old bank, contains the very first **Stanley Cup**. The trophy was originally donated by Lord Stanley, the Governor General of Canada, in 1893. An English aristocrat, Stanley was convinced that sports raised the mettle of the men of the British Empire. Concerned that Canadian ice hockey lacked a trophy of any stature, he inaugurated the Stanley Cup, which has become the defining emblem of the sport. For more on ice hockey, see "Sports and outdoor activities", p.179.

The St Lawrence District

The **St Lawrence District**, lying just to the east of Yonge St, between Adelaide St East, Frederick St and The Esplanade, is one of the city's oldest, enjoying its first period of rapid growth after the War of 1812. In Victorian times, St Lawrence became one of the most fashionable parts of the city, and although it hit the skids thereafter, it has recently been revamped and (partly) gentrified.

The district is best approached by heading east from Yonge Street along Front Street East. From this direction, you'll soon spot the distinctive trompe l'oeil **mural** on the back of the **Flatiron building**, a sturdy office block of 1892, which fills in the narrow triangle of land between Wellington and Front streets – hence its name. From here, it's a short hop to the **South St Lawrence Market**, at Front and Jarvis (Tues–Thurs 8am–6pm, Fri 8am–7pm & Sat 5am–5pm), a capacious Neoclassical red-brick building of 1844 that holds the city's best food and drink market (see p.175 for a review). Spread out across the main and lower levels, there are stalls selling everything from fish and freshly baked bread to international foodstuffs, all sorts of organic edibles and Ontario specialities: cheese, jellies, jams and fiddlehead ferns to name but four. The market is at its busiest on Saturday. Up above, the old city council chamber – the building served as the town hall from 1845 to 1899 – accommodates the **Market Gallery** (Wed–Fri 10am–4pm, Sat 9am–4pm & Sun noon–4pm; free), which displays regularly rotated exhibitions, often of sketches and photographs drawn from the city's archives. Visiting on Saturdays also means that you can drop by **North St Lawrence Market**, a farmers' market (Sat 5am–5pm) housed in a plain brick building just opposite the main market, on the north side of Front Street.

△ The Henry Moore sculpture collection at the Art Gallery of Ontario

St Lawrence Hall

Strolling north along Jarvis Street, it only takes a couple of minutes to reach **St Lawrence Hall**, at Jarvis and King, one of the city's most attractive Victorian buildings, a palatial edifice whose columns, pilasters and pediments are surmounted by a dinky little cupola. Dating from 1850, the hall was built as the city's main meeting-place, with oodles of space for balls, public lectures and concerts. Some performances were eminently genteel, others decidedly mawkish – it was here that the "Swedish songbird" **Jenny Lind** (1820–1887) made one of her Canadian appearances – and yet others more urgent, like the anti-slavery rallies of the 1850s. The bad taste award goes to the American showman and circus proprietor **P.T. Barnum** (1810–1891), one-time mayor of his hometown of Bridgeport, Connecticut, and author of the bizarre *The Humbugs of the World*. It was Barnum who saw the potential of his fellow Bridgeportonian, the diminutive Charles Sherwood Stratton, aka **Tom Thumb** (1838–1883), exhibiting him as a curiosity here in St Lawrence Hall as well as anywhere else that would pay. Poor old Stratton was just 60cm (2ft) tall when he first went on tour.

St James Cathedral

On the other side of King Street, a couple of hundred metres from St Lawrence Hall, rises the graceful bulk of **St James Anglican Cathedral**, whose yellowish stone is fetchingly off-set by copper-green roofs and a slender spire. An excellent example of the neo-Gothic style once popular in every corner of the British Empire, the cathedral boasts scores of pointed-arch windows and acres of sturdy buttressing. Inside, the nave is supported by chunky high-arched pillars and flanked by an ambitious set of **stained-glass windows** that attempts to trace the path by which Christianity reached Canada from Palestine via England. It's all a little confusing, but broadly speaking, the less original windows depict Biblical scenes, whereas those that focus on English history are noticeably inventive. These stained-glass windows were inserted at the end of the nineteenth century, but those of **St George's Chapel**, in the southeast corner of the church, were added in 1935 to celebrate the Silver Jubilee of King George V. They exhibit an enthusiastic loyalty to the British Empire that is echoed in many of the cathedral's funerary plaques: take, for example, that of a certain **Captain John Henry Gamble**, who was born in Toronto in 1844, but died on active service at the Khyber Pass in 1879.

Toronto's First Post Office

Located about five minutes' walk northeast of St James Cathedral, in a tatty part of town, **Toronto's First Post Office**, 260 Adelaide St East (Mon–Fri 9am–4pm, Sat & Sun 10am–4pm; free), occupies an old brick building that dates back to 1833. Returned to something approaching its original appearance, and staffed by costumed volunteers, the museum gives the flavour of the times and features displays on postal history. It also doubles up as a working post office, where visitors can write a letter with a quill pen, seal it with wax and tie it up with a ribbon ($1).

From the post office, it takes about twenty minutes to walk west to Nathan Philips Square (see below) or, heading southeast, around fifteen minutes to reach the Distillery District.

The Distillery District

The **Distillery District**, just fifteen minutes' walk southeast from the First Post Office, is home to Toronto's newest arts and entertainment complex, sited in the former **Gooderham and Worts distillery**, an extremely appealing industrial "village" at 55 Mill St, just east of the foot of Parliament St (Mon–Wed 11am–7pm, Thurs–Sat 11am–9pm, Sun 11am–7pm; ☎416/866-8687, ⓦwww.distillerytours.ca). In use as a distillery until 1990, this rambling network of over forty old brick buildings once comprised the largest distillery in the British Empire, and now lays claim to be the best-preserved Victorian industrial complex in the whole of North America. The distillery was founded in 1832, when ships could sail into its own jetty (though landfill subsequently marooned it in the lee of the railway lines and the tail-end of the Gardiner Expressway). Otherwise unruffled for decades, much of the distillery's machinery has survived, as have its walkways and bottle runways, features that have been carefully integrated into the revamp. One of the architectural highlights is the **Pure Spirits building**, which features French doors and a fancy wrought-iron balcony. When the complex is complete, it will hold, amongst much else, over twenty art galleries, a visitor centre (offering guided tours), furniture designers, bakeries, shops, a microbrewery, and no less than three performance venues. The redevelopment of the distillery has been led by a small group of entrepreneurs, who decided (with refreshing integrity) to exclude all multinational chains. Try not to miss it.

Nathan Phillips Square and City Hall

Back in the city centre, **Nathan Phillips Square**, one of Toronto's most distinctive landmarks, lies on Queen St, just north of the Banking District and close to Queen subway. Designed by the Finnish architect Viljo Revell (1910–1964), the square is framed by an elevated walkway and focuses on a reflecting pool, which becomes a skating rink in winter. The square is overlooked by Revell's **City Hall**, whose curved glass and concrete towers stand behind and to either side of a mushroom-shaped entrance. In front of this is *The Archer*, a **Henry Moore** sculpture resembling nothing so much as a giant propeller. Surprising as it seems today, when such architectural designs are fairly commonplace, Revell won all sorts of awards for this project, which was considered the last word in 1960s dynamism – though today its rain-stained blocks look rather dejected. In its creation, however, the square became a catalyst for change. Named after its sponsor, Nathan Phillips, Toronto's first Jewish mayor, the space suddenly provided the kind of public gathering-place the city so sorely lacked, kick-starting the process by which the private Toronto of the 1950s became the extrovert metropolis of today.

Had Revell's grand scheme been carried out fully, the city would have bulldozed the **Old City Hall** – it wasn't, though, and so the flamboyant pseudo-Romanesque building on the east side of the square still stands. Completed in 1899, it was designed by **Edward J. Lennox**, who developed a fractious relationship with his paymasters on the city council. They had a point: the original cost of the building had been estimated at $1.77 million, but Lennox spent an extra $750,000 and took all of eight years to finish the project. Nevertheless, Lennox had the last laugh, carving gargoyle-like representations of the city's fathers on the arches at the top of the front steps and placing his name on each side of the building – something the city council had expressly forbidden him to do. Lennox was also responsible for the construction of Casa Loma; see p.72.

Lastly, standing in the southwest corner of Nathan Phillips Square, a statue of **Winston Churchill** (1874–1965) recalls Toronto's British connection. Inscribed upon the statue are five famous quotations, one of which is drawn from the speech Churchill delivered to the Canadian House of Commons on December 30, 1941: "[The losing French] generals advised France's divided cabinet 'In three weeks, the English will have their necks wrung like a chicken'. Some chicken! Some neck!"

The Hudson's Bay Company Gallery

Across the street from the Old City Hall, the **Hudson's Bay Company Gallery** (Tues–Sat 11am–5pm; $4; Queen subway) is located on the ninth floor of The Bay department store at Queen St and Yonge (for more on the department store, see p.173). The gallery offers an outstanding introduction to many of Canada's finest artists, especially the Group of Seven (see box p.57); its paintings are on loan from the newspaper tycoon Ken Thomson. One of the gallery's strengths is its modest size, providing an intimate setting for what is very much a connoisseur's collection – but unfortunately there are plans afoot to close the place down and move into the AGO (see p.55), probably in 2005.

For now, well-organized and -labelled, gallery highlights include an impressive selection of paintings by **Lawren Harris** (1885–1970), one of the Group of Seven's most distinctive artists. His surreal *Lake Superior* (1923) is a representative piece; it's one of several inspired by the wild, cold landscapes of the lake's north shore. Harris was also partial to city street scenes and there are three here – including two of Toronto – each painted in a careful pointillist style very different from his wilderness works. **J.E.H. MacDonald** (1873–1932), another member of the Group of Seven, also features prominently; amongst a fine sample of his canvases, look out for the superb *Rowan Berries*, painted in 1922, and the startling sweep of *October Shower Gleam*. Their colleague **Tom Thomson** (1877–1917) is well-represented by over thirty preparatory sketches of lakes and canyons, waterfalls and forests, each small panel displaying the vibrant, blotchy colours that characterize his work. Larger Thomson paintings include the sticky dabs of colour of *Maple Springs*, as well as his *Autumn's Garland*, an oil on panel finished the year before he died. The talents of **A.J. Casson** are perhaps best recalled by the jumble of snow-covered roofs of his *House Tops in the Ward*, though his work is slight when compared with the vital canvases of **A.Y. Jackson** (1882–1974), the sweeping colours and forms of his *Yellowknife Country* being a case in point. Yet another member of the Group of Seven, **Arthur Lismer** (1885–1969) spent every summer at his cottage in Georgian Bay (for more on which, see p.107), where he concentrated on painting shoreline and island vistas; there are several examples on display here. A contemporary of the Group – but not a member – the gifted **Emily Carr** (1871–1945) focused on the Canadian west coast in general, and its dense forests and native villages in particular, as in her dark and haunting *Thunderbird* of 1930.

In a separate section, the gallery's assortment of paintings by early and mid-nineteenth century Canadians is less distinguished than the Group of Seven, but there are still some fascinating works. One noteworthy canvas is a curiously unflattering *Portrait of Joseph Brant* by **William Berczy** (1748–1813). A Mohawk chief,

Joseph Brant (1742–1807), was consistently loyal to the British interest, his followers fighting alongside them during the American War of Independence. Brant's reward was a large chunk of Ontario land and a string of official portraits; this was one of them. Brant is shown in a mix of European and native gear – he carries an axe and has a Mohawk hairdo, but wears a dress coat with a sash – an apt reflection of his twin loyalties. Brant spoke English fluently, even translating parts of the Bible into Mohawk, and was a Freemason and Anglican as well, feted by high society during a visit to England in 1776. At the same time, under his Mohawk name, Thayendanega (Two Bets), Brant was a powerful figure in the Iroquois Confederacy, leading one of its four main clans in both war and peace.

Near to Brant's portrait, there are also a number of winter scenes by **Cornelius Krieghoff** (see box below). In particular, look out for his *The Portage Aux Titres*, whose autumnal colours surround a tiny figure struggling with a canoe, and the light-hearted humour of his (larger) *Toll Gate*.

Equally interesting is the work of **Paul Kane** (1810–1871). Born in Ireland, Kane first emigrated to Toronto in the early 1820s. In 1840, he returned to Europe, where, curiously enough, he was so impressed by a touring exhibition of paintings on the American Indian that he promptly decided to move back to Canada. In 1846, he wrangled a spot on a westward-bound fur-trading expedition, beginning an epic journey: he travelled from Thunder Bay to Edmonton by canoe, crossed the Rockies by horse, and finally returned to Toronto two years later. During his trip, Kane made some seven hundred sketches, which he then painted onto canvas, paper and cardboard. Interestingly, and like many early Canadian artists, Kane's paintings often displayed a conflict in subject and style – that is, the subject was North American but the style European; indeed, it wasn't until the Group of Seven that a true Canadian aesthetic emerged. Perfect examples of this conflict are Kane's *Landscape in the Foothills with Buffalo Resting* and *At Buffalo Pound*, where bison are pictured in what looks more like a placid German valley than a North American prairie. Finally, there's *The Passing Storm* by **Homer Watson** (1855–1936), whose glossy Ontario landscapes, with their vigorous paintwork and dynamic compositions, made him a popular artist; Queen Victoria even purchased one of his paintings, and Oscar Wilde dubbed him "the Canadian Constable".

Cornelius Krieghoff

A prolific artist, **Cornelius Krieghoff** (1815–1872) led a roller-coaster life. Born in Amsterdam, he trained as an artist in Düsseldorf before emigrating to New York, where, at the age of 21, he joined the US army, serving in the Second Seminole War in Florida. Discharged in 1840, Krieghoff immediately re-enlisted, claimed three months' advance pay and deserted, hot-footing it to Montréal with the French-Canadian woman he had met and married in New York. In Montréal, he picked up his brushes again, but without any commercial success – quite simply no one wanted to buy his paintings. That might have been the end of the matter, except for the fact that Krieghoff moved to Québec City in 1852, where he found a ready market for his paintings among the well-heeled officers of the British garrison, who liked his folksy renditions of Québec rural life. This was the start of Krieghoff's most productive period. Over the next eight years he churned out dozens of souvenir pictures – finely detailed, anecdotal scenes that are his best work. In the early 1860s, however – and for reasons that remain obscure – he temporarily packed in painting, returning to Europe for five years before another stint in Québec City, though this time, with the officer corps gone, he failed to sell his work. In 1871, he went to live with his daughter in Chicago and died there the following year, a defeated man.

The Eaton Centre

A second-floor walkway crosses Queen Street to connect The Bay with the **Eaton Centre** (Mon–Fri 10am–9pm, Sat 9.30am–7pm, Sun noon–6pm; Queen or Dundas subways), a three-storey assortment of shops and restaurants spread out underneath a glass-and-steel arched roof. By shopping mall standards, the design is appealing, and the flock of fibreglass Canada geese suspended from the ceiling adds a touch of flair. Maps of the shopping mall are displayed on every floor, but the general rule is the higher the floor, the more expensive the shop.

The centre takes its name from **Timothy Eaton**, an immigrant from Ulster who opened his first store here in 1869. His cash-only, fixed-price, money-back-guarantee trading revolutionized the Canadian market and made him a fortune. Soon a Canadian institution, Eaton kept a grip on the pioneer settlements in the west through his mail-order catalogue, known as the "homesteader's bible" – or the "wish book" among native peoples – whilst Eaton department stores sprang up in all of Canada's big cities. In recent years, however, the company has struggled to maintain its profitability; this branch, in fact, has now been taken over by Sears.

About two-thirds of the way along the Eaton Centre from Queen Street – just before Sears – a side exit leads straight from Level 3 to the **Church of the Holy Trinity**, an appealing nineteenth-century structure whose yellow brickwork is surmounted by a pair of sturdy turrets and matching chimneys. Much to its credit, the church campaigns hard on issues of poverty; beside the entrance there's the **Toronto Homeless Memorial**, which lists those who have died as a result of their homelessness. The church also figures in Canadian movie history. It was here, with the church set against the skyscrapers that crowd in on it, that Canadian director **David Cronenberg** filmed the last scene of *Dead Ringers*. The dubious moral content of the film – the unscrupulous exploits of twin rogue gynaecologists, both played by Jeremy Irons – prompted Cronenberg to defend his subject matter thusly: "I don't have a moral plan. I'm a Canadian."

The Eaton Centre ends at the corner of Dundas and Yonge streets, once the city's main intersection and now, after years of decay, partly revamped with the construction of a public piazza – **Dundas Square** – at its southeast corner. Further redevelopment is planned.

Glenn Gould

In the 1970s, anyone passing the Eaton Centre's department store around 9pm on any day of the year might have seen the door unlocked for a distracted-looking figure swaddled in overcoat, scarves, gloves and hat. This character, making his way to a recording studio set up for his exclusive use inside the shop, was perhaps the most famous citizen of Toronto and the most charismatic pianist in the world – **Glenn Gould**.

In 1964, aged just 32, Gould retired from the concert platform, partly out of a distaste for the accidental qualities of any live performance, partly out of hatred for the cult of the virtuoso. Yet no pianist ever provided more material for the mythologizers. He possessed a memory so prodigious that none of his acquaintances was ever able to find a piece of music he could not instantly play perfectly. He loathed much of the standard piano repertoire, dismissing romantic composers such as Chopin, Liszt and Rachmaninoff as little more than showmen, but was nonetheless an ardent fan of Barbra Streisand – an esteem that was fully reciprocated – and once wrote an essay titled "In Search of Petula Clark". He travelled everywhere with bags full of medicines and would never allow anyone to shake his hand, and even in a heatwave he was always dressed as if a blizzard were imminent. To many of his colleagues, Gould's eccentricities were maddening, but what mattered was that nobody could play like Glenn Gould. As one exasperated conductor put it, "the nut's a genius".

Gould's first recording, Bach's *Goldberg Variations*, was released in 1956 and became the best-selling classical record of that year. Soon after, he became the first Western musician to play in the Soviet Union, where his reputation spread so quickly that for his final recital more than a thousand people were allowed to stand in the aisles of the Leningrad hall. On his debut in Berlin, the leading German critic described him as "a young man in a strange sort of trance", whose "technical ability borders on the fabulous". The technique always dazzled, but Gould's fiercely wayward intelligence made his interpretations controversial, as can be gauged from the fact that Leonard Bernstein, conducting Gould on one occasion, felt obliged to inform the audience that what they were about to hear was the pianist's responsibility, not his. Most notoriously of all, Gould had a very low opinion of Mozart's abilities, going so far as to record the Mozart sonatas in order to demonstrate that Wolfgang Amadeus died too late rather than too soon. Gould himself died suddenly in 1982 at the age of 50 – the age at which he had said he would give up playing the piano entirely.

The Elgin Theatre and Winter Garden and Mackenzie House

Across from the Eaton Centre, the **Elgin Theatre and Winter Garden**, 189 Yonge St, just north of Queen (guided tours only, Thurs 5pm & Sat 11am; 90min; $7; ☎416/597-0965; Queen subway), is one of the city's most unusual attractions. The first part of the guided tour covers the Elgin, an old vaudeville theatre whose ornate furnishings and fittings, including a set of splendid gilt mirrors, have been restored after years of neglect. The Elgin was turned into a cinema in the 1930s and, remarkably enough, its accompaniment, the top-floor **Winter Garden**, also a vaudeville theatre, was sealed off. Such double-decker theatres were introduced in the late nineteenth century in New York, and soon became popular along the east coast, but only a handful have survived. Even better, when this one was unsealed, its original decor was found to be intact, the ceiling hung with thousands of preserved painted beech leaves, illuminated by coloured lanterns. Still, much of the decor had to be replaced, but the restoration work was painstakingly thorough and the end result is delightful. Lastly, being an informal business, with customers coming and going and performances following each other non-stop, every vaudeville theatre had a ready supply of **backcloths**, and several were discovered here when the Winter Garden was unsealed; they are now a feature of the tour.

It's hardly an essential visit, but the **Mackenzie House** (Jan–April Sat & Sun noon–5pm, May–Aug Tues–Sun noon–5pm, Sept–Dec Tues–Fri noon–4pm, Sat & Sun noon–5pm; $3.50; Dundas subway), a five-minute walk east of Eaton Centre along Dundas, at 82 Bond St, is of some interest as the home of **William Lyon Mackenzie** (1795–1861). Born in Scotland, Mackenzie moved to Toronto where he scraped together a living publishing *The Colonial Advocate*, a radical anti-Tory newspaper. Frustrated with the politics of the colony's early leaders, Mackenzie was one of the instigators of the Rebellion of 1837 (see p.202), after which he was exiled to the US for twelve years before being pardoned. Mackenzie lived in this house between 1859 and 1861, and it has been restored to an approximation of its appearance at the time, complete with a print shop (circa 1845) whose workings are demonstrated by costumed guides.

Osgoode Hall, Campbell House and Queen Street West

Immediately to the west of Nathan Phillips Square, along Queen Street, stands **Osgoode Hall** (no public access), a Neoclassical pile built in the nineteenth century for the Law Society of Upper Canada. Looking like a cross between a Greek temple and an English country house, it's protected by a sturdy wrought-iron fence with fancy gates that was designed to keep cows and horses off the lawn. Metres away, in the middle of University Avenue, stands a **War Memorial** honouring those Canadians who fought (for the British imperial interest) in the South African – or Boer – War at the turn of the twentieth century. The memorial features two Canadian soldiers of heroic disposition, and the column is engraved with the names of the battles where Canadian regiments fought.

The elegant Georgian mansion on the west side of University Avenue is **Campbell House** (daily: Mon–Fri 9.30am–4.30pm, late May to Sept also Sat & Sun noon–4.30pm; $4.50; Osgoode subway), originally built on Adelaide Street for Sir William Campbell, Chief Justice and Speaker of the Legislative Assembly. The house was transported to its current location in 1972. There are regular **guided tours** of the period interior, which is distinguished by the immaculately carved woodwork and sweeping circular stairway. The tours also provide a well-researched overview of early nineteenth-century Toronto, in which Campbell was a surprisingly progressive figure: he eschewed the death penalty whenever possible, and even awarded the radical William Mackenzie (see above) damages when his printing press was wrecked by a mob of Tories in 1826.

Beyond the Campbell House, **Queen Street West** between University and Spadina is one of the grooviest parts of the city, its assorted cafés and bars attracting the sharpest of dressers. Meanwhile, the alternative crew of students and punks who once hung around here have moved further west, out to what is known as **Queen West West**, between Spadina and Bathurst. In the daytime, this whole section of Queen Street is a great place to be – but at night it's even better.

The Canada Life Building and the Textile Museum of Canada

Behind the Campbell House rises the **Canada Life building**, whose monumental Art Deco lines are capped by a chunky tower-cum-weather beacon – the cube on top signifies white for snow, red for rain and green for sun. The Canada Life building is but one of the long sequence of bristling tower blocks which flank **University Avenue** as it slices across the city, running north from Front Street to the Ontario Legislative Assembly Building (see p.60). Strolling north up University from Queen Street West, it only takes a couple of minutes to reach **Armoury Street**, the site of the old city armoury and the place where the province's soldiers mustered before embarking overseas for the battlefields of both world wars. Just off Armoury Street, the **Textile Museum of Canada**, housed in part of an office block at 55 Centre Ave (Tues, Thurs & Fri 11am–5pm, Wed 11am–8pm, Sat & Sun noon–5pm; $8, students & seniors $6; ☎416/599-5321, ⓦwww.textilemuseum.ca), offers a rolling programme of temporary exhibitions. International in outlook, the museum has featured everything from contemporary domestic textile pieces to traditional work such as Oriental rugs and the hooked mats that were once handmade in Newfoundland and Labrador. The displays are often very good and are supplemented by practical demonstrations of different textile techniques.

Just north of the Textile Museum, back on the east side of University Avenue, just beyond Elm Street, watch out for the bust of **Mary Pickford** (1893–1979). Pickford was born in Toronto, but left on a theatrical tour at the tender age of eight. She dropped her original name – Gladys Mary Smith – when she began working as a motion-picture extra in Hollywood in 1909. Renowned as "America's sweetheart", she earned the cinematic sobriquet with her cute face and fluffy mop of hair, which enabled her to play little-girl roles well into her thirties.

The Art Gallery of Ontario

Just west of University Avenue along Dundas Street West, the **Art Gallery of Ontario** (Tues, Thurs & Fri 11am–6pm, Wed 11am–8.30pm, Sat & Sun 10am–5.30pm; $12, or free after 6pm on Wed; St Patrick subway; ☎416/979-6648, ⓦwww.ago.net) is celebrated both for its wide-ranging collection of foreign and domestic art and its excellent temporary exhibitions. They also run a first-rate programme of free guided tours. The gallery is, however, housed in an oddly discordant and rather confusing building, the result of several different phases of construction. Neither is there enough room to exhibit all of the permanent collection at any one time, which means that the exhibits are rotated, though this problem will be at least partly resolved with the opening of a new extension in 2005 or 2006. The exterior of the AGO (as it's commonly known) is a stern, modern facade decorated by a scaffold-like tower and a matching pair of **Henry Moore** sculptures, large and chunky bronzes uninspiringly called *Two Forms*. Inside, the AGO's **Street Level** boasts European works as well as an art shop and café, whilst the **Upper Level** is devoted to contemporary art, a superb clutch of Canadian paintings and an extensive collection of Henry Moore sculptures. Museum **maps** are issued free at reception.

Street Level: Walker Court and the European collection

Just beyond the main entrance, turn right and stroll down the corridor (S2), where a long series of cabinets display a marvellous sample of European applied art, including ivory and alabaster pieces, exquisite cameos and fine porcelain. All are on permanent loan from Ken Thomson's private collection – the same tycoon who equips the Hudson's Bay Company Gallery (see p.50). The corridor leads to the first part of S10, a rectangular room given over to selected items from the permanent collection, noteworthy sculptures by the likes of Moore and Hepworth and paintings by such luminaries as Picasso, Van Gogh, Monet and Francis Bacon, among others. Just to the left, **Walker Court** is surrounded on three sides by the main **European art galleries** (S3–S9), which cover the Italian Renaissance through to French Impressionism. Early works include some rather pedestrian Italian altarpieces, though Pieter Brueghel the Younger weighs in with the incident-packed *Peasant Wedding*; there's a strong showing for Dutch painters of the Golden Age – Rembrandt, Van Dyck, Frans Hals and Goyen to name but four. Look out also for Carel Fabritius's exquisite *Portrait of a Lady with a Handkerchief*, one of only a few of the artist's works to have survived the powder-magazine explosion that killed him in Delft in 1654 – though the authorship of the painting has been disputed. **French** painters are much in evidence, too, with distinguished works including *St Anne with the Christ Child* by Georges de la Tour, and Poussin's *Venus Presenting Arms to Aeneas*. Amongst the **Impressionists,** there's Degas's archetypal *Woman in the Bath*, Renoir's screaming-pink *Concert*, and Monet's wonderful *Vétheuil in Summer*, with its hundreds of tiny jabs of colour.

Upper Level: the Canadian collection

The Upper Level of the AGO holds the outstanding **Canadian Art to 1960** section (U8–U20), whose strongest suite is the work of the **Group of Seven** (see box on p.57) and their contemporaries, bundled together in rooms U11–U12. To provide some artistic context, it's best to start with the earliest Canadian works – in U17 – and work backwards to U16 and so forth. U17 kicks off with a light scattering of early to mid-nineteenth-century paintings, including the cheery *Passenger Pigeon Hunt* by **Antoine Plamondon** (1802–1895). Trained in Paris, Plamondon worked in the Neoclassical tradition, but here he allows some freedom of movement amongst the young hunters, with the St Lawrence River as the backdrop. Here also is **Paul Kane's** (see p.51) *Indian encampment on Lake Huron*, a softly hued oil on canvas dating to 1845. The adjacent U16 features several paintings by **Cornelius Krieghoff** (see p.51), characteristic winter scenes – like his *Settler's Log House* – intermingled with portraits. In this room too is **John O'Brien**'s (1832–1891) *The Ocean Bride leaving Halifax Harbour*. Self-taught, O'Brien specialized in maritime scenes, turning out dozens of brightly coloured pictures of sailing ships and coastal settings.

Moving on, U14 and U13 concentrate on the folksy and/or romanticised country scenes and landscapes that were in vogue from the 1850s through to the early twentieth century. By and large this is pretty dull stuff, but **Homer Watson**'s (see p.51) *The Old Mill* is an especially handsome and well-composed canvas, whilst his *Death of Elaine* – inspired by a Tennyson poem – stands out as a bizarrely unsuccessful venture into ancient legend. U13 also holds a couple of important paintings by the Newfoundlander **Maurice Cullen** (1866–1934), beginning with the precise angles and dappled brushwork of *Moret in Winter*, which is generally regarded as the beginning of Canadian Impressionism. Cullen was trained in Paris, where he was greatly influenced by the work of Monet, producing this French riverscape just before he returned to Canada, where he applied a similar approach to the landscapes of the St Lawrence River, as in his *The Last Loads*, also present.

One of the most distinctive artists of the Group of Seven, whose works are displayed in U11–U12, was **Lawren Harris** (1885–1970), whose 1922 *Above Lake Superior* is a pivotal work – its clarity of conception, with bare birch stumps framing a dark mountain beneath Art Deco clouds, is quite exceptional. The adjacent *West Wind* by **Tom Thomson** (1877–1917) is another seminal work, an iconic rendering of the northern wilderness that is perhaps the most famous of all Canadian paintings. Thomson was the first to approach wilderness landscapes with the determination of an explorer and the sense that they could encapsulate a specifically Canadian identity. Several of his less familiar (but no less powerful) works are here as well, including the moody *A Northern Lake* and the Cubist-influenced preparatory painting, *Autumn Foliage 1915*.

The Group of Seven

In the autumn of 1912, a commercial artist by the name of **Tom Thomson** returned from an extended trip to the Mississauga country, north of Georgian Bay, with a bag full of sketches that were to add a new momentum to Canadian art. His friends, many of them fellow employees of the art firm of Grip Ltd in Toronto, saw Thomson's naturalistic approach to indigenous subject matter as a pointer away from the influence of Europe, declaring the "northland" as the true Canadian "painter's country". World War I and the death of Thomson – who drowned in 1917 – delayed these artists' ambitions, but in 1920 they formed the **Group of Seven**. Initially, the group was comprised of Franklin H. Carmichael, Lawren Harris, A.Y. Jackson, Arthur Lismer, J.E.H. MacDonald, F.H. Varley and Frank Johnston; later, they were joined by A.J. Casson, L.L. Fitzgerald and Edwin Holgate. Working under the unofficial leadership of **Lawren Harris**, they explored the wilds of Algoma in Northern Ontario in the late 1910s, travelling around in a converted freight car, and later foraged even further afield, from Newfoundland and Baffin Island to British Columbia.

They were immediately successful, staging forty shows in eleven years, a triumph due in large part to Harris's many influential contacts. However, there was also a genuine popular response to the intrepid frontiersman element of their aesthetic. Art was a matter of "taking to the road" and "risking all for the glory of a great adventure", as they wrote in 1922, whilst "nature was the measure of a man's stature", according to Lismer. Symbolic of struggle against the elements, the Group's favourite symbol was the lone pine set against the sky, an image whose authenticity was confirmed by reference to the "manly" poetry of Walt Whitman.

J.E.H. MacDonald (1873–1932) was fond of dynamic, sweeping effects, and his panoramic *Falls, Montreal River* sets turbulent rapids beside hot-coloured hillsides. His friend **F.H. Varley** (1881–1969) dabbled in portraiture and chose soft images and subtle colours for his landscapes, as exemplified by the sticky-looking brushstrokes he used for *Moonlight after Rain*. A sample of **A.Y. Jackson**'s (1882–1974) work includes the characteristically carpet-like surface of *Algoma Rocks, Autumn*, painted in 1923, while **A.J. Casson**'s (1898–1992) bright, rather formal *Old Store at Salem* offers a break from the scenic preoccupations of the rest of the Seven. **Emily Carr** (1871–1945), represented by several works here, was a great admirer of the Seven, but she was never accepted as a member despite her obvious abilities – the deep green foliage of her *Indian Church* and *Western Forest*, both painted in 1929, are good examples of her talent.

Close by, in U8, there are two small galleries of **Inuit art**, mostly sculpture, beside and above the spiral staircase. Highlights here include **Pauta Saila**'s (born 1916) *Dancing Bear* and **Joe Talirunili**'s (1906–1976) *Migration*, in which a traditional Inuit boat – an *umiak* – is crowded with Inuit seemingly bent on escaping danger. Talirunili carved a large number of migration boat scenes throughout his long career (see p.43 for another), the inspiration derived from a dramatic incident in his childhood when the break-up of the pack ice caught his family unawares, forcing them to hurriedly evacuate their encampment. Look out also for the work of **John Tiktak** (1916–1981), generally regarded as one of the most talented Inuit sculptors of his generation. The death of Tiktak's mother in 1962 had a profound effect on him, and his *Mother and Child* forcefully expresses this close connection, with the figure of the child carved into the larger figure of the mother. Tiktak's *Owl Man* is another fine piece, an excellent example of the metamorphic figures popular amongst the Inuit, as is **Thomas Sivuraq**'s (born 1941) *Shaman Transformation*.

Contemporary art and the Henry Moore Sculpture Gallery

Most of the rest of the Upper Level (U3–U7) is given over to the AGO's collection of **contemporary art**, showcasing works by European, British and American artists. Pieces are regularly rotated, but watch out for Warhol's *Elvis I and II*, Mark Rothko's strident *No.1 White and Red* and Claes Oldenburg's quirky if somewhat frayed *Giant Hamburger*. The contemporary art section culminates in the **Henry Moore Sculpture Gallery** (U1), the world's largest collection of pieces by Moore (1898–1986), with the emphasis firmly on his plaster casts, alongside a selection of his bronzes. Given a whole gallery, the sheer size and volume of Moore's output is impressive, but actually it was something of an accident that his work ended up here at all. In the 1960s, Moore had reason to believe that London's Tate Gallery was going to build a special wing for him. When the Tate declined, Moore chose the AGO instead, persuaded to do so by the gallery's British representative, Anthony Blunt, the art expert who was famously uncovered as a Soviet spy in 1979.

The Grange

Attached to the back of the AGO is **The Grange**, an early nineteenth-century brick mansion with Neoclassical trimmings built by the Boultons, one of the city's most powerful and reactionary families. The last of the line, William Henry – "a privileged, petted man...without principle", according to a local journalist – died in 1874, and his property passed to his widow, Harriette, who promptly married an English expatriate professor named Goldwin Smith. Goldwin enjoyed Toronto immensely, holding court and boasting of his English connections, and when he died in 1910 (after Harriette) he bequeathed the house to the fledgling Art Museum of Toronto, the predecessor of the AGO. The Grange remains part of the AGO and it has been restored to its mid–nineteenth-century appearance. Guides dressed in period costume show you around, enthusiastically explaining the ins and outs of life in nineteenth-century Toronto. Several of Harriette's paintings have survived, and while the antique furnishings and fittings are appealing, it's the beautiful wooden staircase that really catches the eye.

Chinatown and Kensington Market

The Art Gallery of Ontario is hemmed in by **Chinatown**, a bustling, immensely appealing neighbourhood cluttered with shops, restaurants (for recommendations, see p.133) and street stalls selling any and every type of Asian delicacy. The boundaries of Chinatown are somewhat blurred, but its focus, ever since the 1960s, when the original Chinatown was demolished to make way for the new City Hall, has been Dundas Street West between Bay Street and Spadina Avenue. The first Chinese to migrate to Canada arrived in the mid–nineteenth century to work in British Columbia's gold fields. Subsequently, a portion of this population migrated east, and a sizeable Chinese community sprang up in Toronto in the early twentieth century. Several more waves of migration – the last influx following the handing over of Hong Kong to mainland China by the British in 1997 – have greatly increased the number of Toronto's Chinese, bringing the population to approximately 250,000 (about eight percent of the city's total).

Next door to Chinatown, just north of Dundas Street West, between Spadina and Augusta avenues, lies Toronto's most ethnically diverse neighbourhood, pocket-sized **Kensington Market**. It was here, at the turn of the twentieth century, that Eastern European immigrants squeezed into a patchwork of modest little brick and timber houses that survive to this day. On Kensington Avenue they established the **open-air street market**, the main feature of the neighbourhood ever since, a lively, entertaining bazaar whose stall owners stem from many different ethnic backgrounds. The lower half of the market, just off Dundas Street, concentrates on secondhand clothing, while the upper half is crowded with fresh food stalls. Even if you don't want to actually buy anything, Kensington Market is one of the city's funkiest neighbourhoods, a great place to hang out.

Uptown Toronto

eginning north of Gerrard Street, **uptown Toronto** is something of an architectural hodgepodge. To start with, there are the bristling, monochromatic office blocks of University Avenue, which lead straight to the contrasting **Ontario Legislative Assembly Building**, one of the city's finest Victorian structures. The Assembly Building also marks the start of a small museum district, made up of the delightful **Gardiner Museum of Ceramic Art** and the large but somewhat incoherent **Royal Ontario Museum**, which possesses one of the country's most extensive collections of applied art. The Assembly Building is also located close to the prettiest part of the sprawling **University of Toronto** campus, on and around King's College Circle. Moving north, office blocks and shops choke Bloor Street West, though it's here you'll find the fanciful **Bata Shoe Museum**, as well as the ritzy little neighbourhood of **Yorkville**. From here, it's a short subway ride – or a thirty-minute walk – to the city's two finest historic homes, the neo-baronial **Casa Loma** and the debonair **Spadina House** next door.

Bloor Street is uptown's principal east-west corridor, intersecting with **Yonge Street**, the main north–south drag, which cuts a lively, if somewhat seedy, route north from Gerrard Street, lined along the way with bars, cafés and shops. At Wellesley Street, Yonge cuts through the edge of the **Gay Village**, but the only sights hereabouts are further east in **Cabbagetown**, a pleasant old neighbourhood of leafy streets and terrace houses.

The Ontario Legislative Assembly Building

Peering down University Avenue, from just north of College Street, the pink sandstone mass of the **Ontario Legislative Assembly Building** dates to the 1890s (late May to late Sept daily 10am–4pm, late Sept to late May Mon–Fri 10am–4pm; free, with frequent 30min guided tours; ☎416/325-7500, Ⓦwww.ontla.on.ca; Queen's Park subway). Elegant it certainly isn't, but although the building is heavy and solid, its ponderous symmetries do have a certain appeal, with block upon block of roughly dressed stone assembled in the full flourish of the Romanesque Revival style. Seen from close up, the design is even more engaging, its intricacies a pleasant surprise: above the chunky columns of the main entrance is a sinuous filigree of carved stone, with mythological creatures and gargoyle-like faces poking out from every nook and cranny. The main facade also sports a Neoclassical frieze in which the Great Seal of Ontario is flanked by allegorical figures representing art, music, agriculture and so forth.

Inside, the foyer leads to the wide, thickly carpeted Grand Staircase, whose massive timbers are supported by gilded iron pillars. Beyond, among the long corridors and arcaded galleries, is the **Legislative Chamber**, where the formal mahogany and sycamore panels are offset by a series of whimsical little carvings: look for the owl overlooking the doings of the government and the eagle overseeing the opposition benches. Under the Speaker's gallery, righteous inscriptions have been carved into the pillars – which is a bit of a hoot considering the behaviour of the building's architect, Richard Waite. Waite was chairman of the committee responsible for selecting an architect; and, as chairman, he selected himself.

A fire burned down the building's **west wing** in 1909, and to avoid a repeat performance, parliament had its replacement built in marble the following year. No expense was spared in the reconstruction, so there was a substantial fuss when one of the MPPs (Members of the Provincial Parliament) noticed what appeared to be blemishes in the stone on several of the pillars. The blotches turned out to be dinosaur fossils, and nowadays they are pointed out on the guided tour. The provincial assembly typically sits from late September to late June, with breaks at Christmas and Easter, and although guided tours avoid the chamber when the body is in session, the **visitors' gallery** is open to the public during its deliberations Monday through Thursdays; call for further details and times.

Back outside, in front of the main entrance, are a pair of Russian **cannons** that were captured during the Crimean War. Queen Victoria gave them to the city in 1859 in honour of those Canadian regiments who had fought alongside the British during the siege of Sevastopol. The cannons are flanked by a series of **statues** of politicians and imperial bigwigs that spread across the manicured lawns of **Queen's Park**. Two of the more interesting are just a few metres to the east of the assembly's main entrance, beginning with Queen Victoria, who sits on her throne with a rather paltry crown on her head. Strangely, Victoria looks very male and, as if to compensate, her bust appears much too large for her slender frame. The adjacent statue of John Graves Simcoe (1752–1806; see p.201) is a much happier affair, with the one-time lieutenant-governor of Upper Canada cutting a dashing figure with a tricorn hat in one hand and a cane, held at a jaunty angle, in the other. On the west side of the building stands a **bust** of anti-Tory radical William Lyon Mackenzie (see p.54 & p.202) and immediately behind it is an over-blown **memorial** to "The struggle for responsible government" – that is, the campaign for representative government as opposed to rule by British appointees. Mackenzie was the first figure of any note to champion this cause. Behind the memorial is a **plaque** honouring the **Mac-Paps**. Named after the joint leaders of the Rebellion of 1837 – Mackenzie and Louis Joseph Papineau – the Mac-Paps were a 1500-strong Canadian battalion of the International Brigades, who fought Franco in the Spanish Civil War. The plaque is attached to a hunk of rock from the Spanish town of Gandesa, scene of some of the war's bloodiest fighting.

There's more **statuary** behind the Legislative Building on the other section of Queen's Park. Here, right in the middle of the greenery, lording it over the pigeons and the squirrels, is a heavyweight equestrian statue of King Edward VII in full-dress uniform. Originally plonked down in Delhi, this imperial left-over looks a bit forlorn – and you can't help but feel the Indians must have been pleased to off-load it.

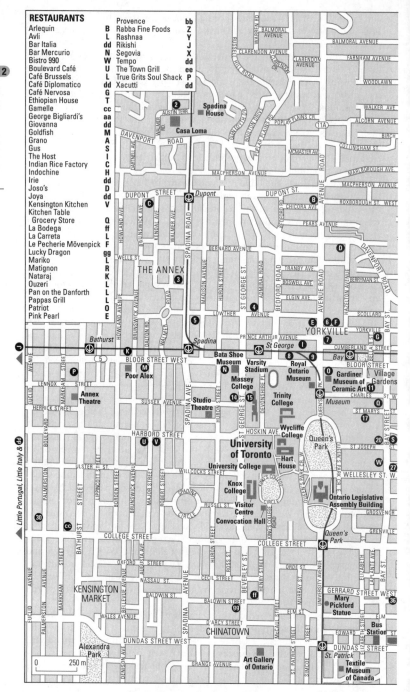

RESTAURANTS

Arlequin	**B**	Provence	**bb**
Avli	**L**	Rabba Fine Foods	**Z**
Bar Italia	**dd**	Rashnaa	**Y**
Bar Mercurio	**N**	Rikishi	**J**
Bistro 990	**W**	Segovia	**X**
Boulevard Café	**U**	Tempo	**dd**
Café Brussels	**L**	The Town Grill	**ee**
Café Diplomatico	**dd**	True Grits Soul Shack	**P**
Café Nervosa	**G**	Xacutti	**dd**
Ethiopian House	**T**		
Gamelle	**cc**		
George Bigliardi's	**aa**		
Giovanna	**dd**		
Goldfish	**M**		
Grano	**A**		
Gus	**S**		
The Host	**I**		
Indian Rice Factory	**C**		
Indochine	**H**		
Irie	**dd**		
Joso's	**D**		
Joya	**dd**		
Kensington Kitchen	**V**		
Kitchen Table			
Grocery Store	**Q**		
La Bodega	**ff**		
La Carreta	**F**		
Le Pecherie Mövenpick	**gg**		
Lucky Dragon	**L**		
Mariko	**R**		
Matignon	**K**		
Nataraj	**L**		
Ouzeri	**L**		
Pan on the Danforth	**L**		
Pappas Grill	**O**		
Patriot	**E**		
Pink Pearl			

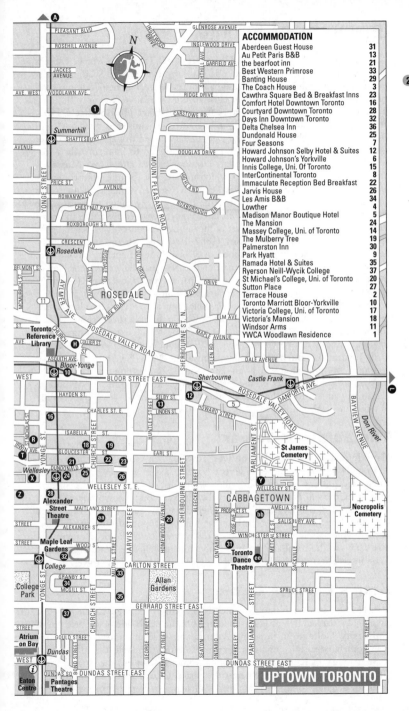

ACCOMMODATION

Aberdeen Guest House	31
Au Petit Paris B&B	13
the bearfoot inn	21
Best Western Primrose	33
Banting House	29
The Coach House	3
Cawthra Square Bed & Breakfast Inns	23
Comfort Hotel Downtown Toronto	16
Courtyard Downtown Toronto	28
Days Inn Downtown Toronto	32
Delta Chelsea Inn	36
Dundonald House	25
Four Seasons	7
Howard Johnson Selby Hotel & Suites	12
Howard Johnson's Yorkville	6
Innis College, Uni. Of Toronto	15
InterContinental Toronto	8
Immaculate Reception Bed Breakfast	22
Jarvis House	26
Les Amis B&B	34
Lowther	4
Madison Manor Boutique Hotel	5
The Mansion	24
Massey College, Uni. of Toronto	14
The Mulberry Tree	19
Palmerston Inn	30
Park Hyatt	9
Ramada Hotel & Suites	35
Ryerson Neill-Wycik College	37
St Michael's College, Uni. of Toronto	20
Sutton Place	27
Terrace House	2
Toronto Marriott Bloor-Yorkville	10
Victoria College, Uni. of Toronto	17
Victoria's Mansion	18
Windsor Arms	11
YWCA Woodlawn Residence	1

UPTOWN TORONTO

University of Toronto

The sprawling campus of the **University of Toronto**, which extends south–north from College to Bloor and east–west from Bay to Spadina, is dotted with stately college buildings and halls of residence. The best-looking – and most interesting – are to be found close to the Legislative Assembly Building at the west end of Wellesley Street, beginning on **Hart House Circle**. Here, the ivy-covered walls, neo-Gothic architecture and cloistered quadrangles of **Hart House**, which dates from the early twentieth century, are reminiscent of Oxford and Cambridge – just as they were designed to be. Primarily a students' social and cultural facility, Hart House is named after **Hart Massey**, a member of the eponymous family, which made a vast fortune from the manufacture of farm machinery. It was Daniel Massey, an Ontario farmer, who started the business in the 1840s, but the money really rolled in towards the end of the nineteenth century, when the Masseys began to specialize in grain-harvesting machines. One of the last of the family to be directly associated with the company was **Vincent Massey** (1887–1967), an extraordinarily influential man, sometimes (gently) ribbed as Canada's representative in heaven. Vincent was the one-time Chairman of the National Gallery, Chancellor of the University of Toronto, and the first native-born Governor-General of Canada from 1952 to 1959. Hart House was built at Vincent's instigation and he also helped equip it with a sizeable collection of modern Canadian paintings, in which the Group of Seven (see box p.57) makes a strong showing. The collection is too large to display at any one time, so the exhibits are regularly rotated, and they can be viewed both in the public rooms of Hart House and in its **Justina M. Barnicke Gallery** (July–Aug Mon–Fri 11am–6pm & Sat 1–4pm; Sept–June Mon–Fri 11am–7pm, Sat & Sun 1–4pm; free; ☏416/978-8398). This gallery focuses on the earlier, less well-known paintings of modern Canadian painters from the 1920s onwards, and also runs a lively programme of temporary exhibitions.

The Soldiers' Tower

Hart House is attached to the **Soldiers' Tower**, a neo-Gothic memorial erected in 1924 to honour those students who had died in World War I. It adjoins an arcaded **gallery**, which is inscribed with a list of the dead and Canadian **John McCrae**'s *In Flanders Fields*, arguably the war's best-known poem: "...We are the Dead. Short days ago/We lived, felt dawn, saw sunset glow,/Loved and were loved, and now we lie,/In Flanders fields...". Optimistically, the builders of the memorial didn't leave any space to commemorate the dead of any further war – so the names of the university students killed in World War II had to be inscribed on the walls under the arches at the foot of the tower.

King's College Circle

Hart House Circle leads into the much larger **King's College Circle**, where a large field is flanked by university buildings. On the north side of the field stands **University College**, an imposing Romanesque-style structure with a whopping, somewhat surly central tower. Further around the circle, the rough sandstone masonry of **Knox College**, dating from 1874, repeats the studied stone Gothicism of its neighbours, whereas the adjacent **Convocation Hall** makes a break for a lighter tone, its elegant rotunda having been erected in the 1920s.

Toronto's first Anglican bishop was the redoubtable **John Strachan**, a one-time schoolmaster who made a name for himself in the War of 1812. The Americans may have occupied Toronto easily enough, but Strachan led a spirited civil resistance, bombarding the occupiers with a veritable deluge of requests and demands about everything from inadequate supplies to any lack of respect the Americans showed to private property. Perhaps surprisingly, the Americans treated Strachan's complaints very seriously, though they did get mightily irritated. After the war, Strachan turned his formidable energies to education. All of moneyed Toronto believed in the value of university education, but the problem was agreeing who should provide it, as Canada's various religious denominations all wanted a piece of the educational action.

In 1827, Strachan obtained a royal charter for the foundation of Toronto's first college of higher education, but his plans for an Anglican-controlled institution were resisted so forcibly that **King's College**, as Strachan's college was called, didn't open its doors until 1843. Even then, Strachan's triumph was short-lived: Anglican control lasted just six years before the provincial government secularized the institution and renamed it the **University of Toronto**.

Over the ensuing decades the university was brow-beaten by theological colleges that considered a secular university to be immoral. But by the turn of the twentieth century, the University of Toronto had made a name for itself, ultimately becoming one of North America's most prestigious educational institutions. It was here that **insulin** was discovered in 1921, and here that **Marshall McLuhan**, who taught at the university, wrote the seminal *The Medium is the Massage*.

Philosopher's Walk

Backtracking to Hart House Circle, walk through the arch of the Soldiers' Tower, turn right along Hoskin Avenue and – just before you reach the traffic island – watch for the footpath on the left. This is **Philosopher's Walk**, an easy, leafy stroll which leads north, slipping around the back of the Royal Ontario Museum (see below) on the way to Bloor Street West.

The Royal Ontario Museum

From the Legislative Assembly Building, it's a brief walk north along the boulevard to the **Royal Ontario Museum**, at 100 Queen's Park (Mon–Thurs 10am–6pm, Fri 10am–9.30pm, Sat 10am–6pm & Sun 11am–6pm; $10, children 5–14 years old $6, free after 4.30pm on Fri; ☎416/586-8000, ⓦwww.rom.on.ca; Museum subway). Usually known as the ROM, this is Canada's largest and most diverse museum, with ambitious collections of fine and applied art from all over the world, as well as a varied programme of temporary exhibitions. Opened in 1914, the museum occupies a handsome five-storey building whose precise neo-Gothic symmetries were subsequently embellished with Art Deco flourishes. The main doors are imposingly large and above them a complement of muses, astrological symbols and mythological beasts stands guard. Beyond lies an enormous collection of over six million objects and artefacts, though the museum is currently in the middle of a major redevelopment and, until the new wing opens in late 2005, visitors have to take potluck as to which galleries are open. Amongst the ROM's many sections, two particular highlights are the internationally acclaimed Chinese collection and the Dinosaurs Gallery. Museum **plans** are available for free at the entrance.

The ROM makes a cheerful start with a domed and vaulted **entrance hall** whose ceiling is decorated with a brilliant mosaic of imported Venetian glass. Just beyond, bolted into the stairwells, are four colossal and stunningly beautiful Native Canadian **crest poles** (commonly but erroneously referred to as totem poles). Dating from the 1880s, and the work of craftsmen from the Haida and Nisga'a peoples of the west coast, these poles (the tallest is 24.5 metres high) are decorated with stylized carvings representing the supernatural animals and birds that were associated with particular clans. Currently, the crest poles are the most significant Canadian artefacts on display – the rest are in storage until the construction work makes further progress. The ROM's **Canadian collection** is strong on prehistoric archeology and late eighteenth- and early nineteenth-century trade silver, comprising an intriguing assortment of silver ornaments – brooches, earrings, crucifixes, medals and the like – which European traders swapped with natives for furs. It also includes the iconic *Death of Wolfe* by **Benjamin West**. The British general James Wolfe inflicted a crushing defeat on the French outside Quebec City in 1759, but was killed during the battle. West's painting transformed this grubby colonial conflict into a romantic extravagance, with the dying general in a Christ-like pose, a pale figure held tenderly by his subordinates. West presented the first version of his painting to the Royal Academy of Arts in 1771 and it proved so popular that he spent much of the next decade painting copies.

Chinese art

Beyond the crest poles, straight back from the main entrance on **Level 1** is the **Bishop White Gallery of Chinese Temple Art**, one of the ROM's most significant sections. The gallery features three Daoist and Buddhist wall paintings dating from around 1300 AD, including a matching pair of Yuan Dynasty murals depicting the lords of the Northern and Southern Dipper, each of whom leads an astrological procession of star spirits. The murals are complemented by an exquisite sample of Buddhist sculpture, temple figures dating from the twelfth to the fourteenth centuries.

Close by, the **South Asian Gallery** contains artefacts spanning six millennia, from 4500 BC to 1900 AD. Among the most important pieces is a remarkable collection of toy-sized tomb figurines – a couple of hundred ceramic pieces representing funerary processions of soldiers, musicians, carts and attendants. Dating from the early sixth to the late seventh century, they re-create the habits of early China – how people dressed, how horses were groomed and shod, changes in armoury and so forth. There is also a fabulous collection of **snuff bottles**, some carved from glass and rock crystal, others from more exotic materials – amber, ivory, bamboo and even tangerine skin. Europeans introduced tobacco to China in the late sixteenth century, and although smoking did not become popular in China until recent times, snuff went down a storm and anyone who was anybody at court was snorting the stuff by the middle of the seventeenth century. Perhaps the most popular component of the Chinese galleries, however, is the **Ming Tomb**. The aristocracy of the Ming Dynasty (1368–1644 AD) evolved an elaborate style of monumental funerary sculpture and architecture, and this is the only example outside of China – though it is actually a composite tomb drawn from several sources rather than an intact, original whole. Central to the Ming burial conception was a Spirit Way, a central avenue with large-scale carved figures of guards, attendants and animals placed on either side. At the end of the alley was the tumulus, or burial mound – in this case the tomb-house of a seventeenth-century Chinese general by the name of Zu Dashou.

Life Sciences

Upstairs, the focal point of **Level 2**'s Life Sciences exhibits is the **Dinosaurs Gallery**. Dioramas and simulations have made this one of the most informative parts of the museum and also one of the most popular. Among the assorted fossil-skeletons, the pick are those retrieved from the Alberta Badlands, near Calgary. These Badlands are the richest source of dinosaur fossils in the world, having yielded over 300 complete skeletons and 35 dinosaur species – ten percent of all those known today. Millions of years ago, the Badlands were lush lowlands attractive to hundreds of dinosaurs; their remains accumulated in the region's sediments, which were then, over hundreds of thousands of years, turned to stone. The first fossilised skeleton, that of the aptly named Albertosaurus, was stumbled upon by the palaeontologist Joseph Tyrrell in 1884. Many of the Alberta dinosaur fossils have been dispatched to museums across the world, though the ROM still has a superb collection, including several **Albertosaurus**. However, it's the rampant herd of **Allosaurus** – a Jurassic-period carnivore of large proportions and ferocious appearance – that commands the most attention.

Other popular sections on Level 2 are the replica **bat cave** and a large display on Canada's **insects** – and a fearsome-looking bunch they are too, including the No-see-um, which drives caribou to distraction by burrowing into their nostrils. There's also the **Discovery Gallery**, one of the best education facilities in Toronto, giving children the opportunity to handle and study museum artefacts. Over a dozen workstations are set up with slides and microscopes, or identification drawers containing butterflies, insects, minerals and prehistoric pottery. Kids can try on virtual reality headsets or seventeenth-century helmets, handle the leg bone of a Stegosaurus dinosaur, and learn how to write in hieroglyphics. Expect queues when the gallery is at its busiest, Monday through Friday 10am to noon during school terms. Children under ten must be accompanied by an adult, while ten- to twelve-year-olds must have an adult supervisor on the premises.

Europe and the Mediterranean World

Level 3 holds the **Samuel European Galleries**, which kick off with a beginner's exposition on the History of Style, exploring changing fashions and tastes, and continue with a string of period rooms, mostly English, from the sixteenth to the eighteenth century. There are also discrete collections of Arms and Armour, Art Nouveau and Art Deco, metalwork, glass and ceramics. Amongst the latter is a superb collection of Delftware and Italian majolica (see below, under the Gardiner Museum, for more on majolica).

Level 3 also has a substantial section devoted to the **Mediterranean World**, including galleries devoted to Imperial Rome, Mesopotamia, Nubia, the Greeks and the Etruscans. The particular highlight here is the **Ancient Egypt Gallery**, where there are several finely preserved mummies, including the richly decorated sarcophagus of a certain Djedmaatesankh, a court musician who died around 850 BC. Even more unusual is the assortment of mummified animals, including a crocodile, a hawk and a weird-looking cat. The same gallery also has the **Punt Wall**, a 1905 plaster cast of the original in Queen Hatshepsut's temple in Deir el-Bahri, Egypt. The events depicted on the wall occurred in the year 1482 BC, and represent a military expedition to Punt, which lay south of Egypt near present-day Somalia.

The George R. Gardiner Museum of Ceramic Art

Named after its wealthy patron, the **George R. Gardiner Museum of Ceramic Art** (Mon, Wed & Fri 10am–6pm, Tues & Thurs 10am–8pm, Sat 10am–5pm, Sun 11am–5pm; $5, but free the first Tues of every month; ☎416/586-8080, ⓦwww.gardinermuseum.on.ca; Museum subway), just across the street from the ROM at 111 Queen's Park, holds a superb connoisseur's collection of ceramics. Spread over two small floors, the museum's exhibits are beautifully presented, and key pieces are well-labelled and explained. There is, however, insufficient room to display all the permanent collection at any one time, so some of the exhibits are regularly rotated – which means the description below should be taken with a grain of salt. An audioguide is also available.

Downstairs, the **pre-Columbian** section is especially fine, composed of over three hundred pieces from regions stretching from Mexico to Peru. One of the most comprehensive collections of its kind in North America, it provides an intriguing insight into the lifestyles and beliefs of the Mayan, Incan, and Aztec peoples. The sculptures are all the more remarkable for the fact that the potter's wheel was unknown in pre-Columbian America, and thus everything on display was necessarily hand-modelled. While some of the pieces feature everyday activities, it is the **religious sculptures** that mostly catch the eye, from wonderfully intricate Mexican incense burners and lurid Mayan plates and cylindrical vases to the fantastical zoomorphic gods of the Zapotecs. Also downstairs is an exquisite sample of fifteenth- and sixteenth-century tin-glazed **Italian majolica**, mostly dishes, plates and jars depicting classical and Biblical themes designed by Renaissance artists. The early pieces are comparatively plain, limited to green and purple, but the later examples are brightly coloured, for in the second half of the fifteenth century Italian potters learnt how to glaze blue and yellow – and ochre was added later. The most splendid pieces are perhaps those from the city – and pottery centre – of Urbino, including two wonderful plates portraying the fall of Jericho and the exploits of Hannibal.

The upstairs level is devoted to eighteenth-century **European porcelain**, with fine examples of hard-paste wares (fired at very high temperatures) from Meissen, Germany, as well as an interesting sample of Chinese-style blue and white porcelain, long the mainstay of the European ceramic industry. Here also is an unusual collection of English ware, which features both well-known manufacturers – notably the ornate products of Royal Worcester – as well as less familiar pieces, including the demure and modest crockery produced in the village of Pinxton, on the edge of Sherwood Forest, in the eighteenth century. On this floor also is a charming collection of Italian *commedia dell'arte* figurines, doll-sized representations of theatrical characters popular across Europe from the middle of the sixteenth to the late eighteenth century. The predecessor of pantomime, the *commedia dell'arte* featured stock characters in improvised settings, but with a consistent theme of seduction, age and beauty: the centrepiece was always an elderly, rich merchant and his beautiful young wife. Lastly, the museum **gift shop** also merits special mention, as it specialises in contemporary Canadian ceramics.

△ Chinese guardian sculptures front the Royal Ontario Museum

Yorkville

From the Gardiner Museum, it's a couple of minutes' walk north to Bloor Street West, and another short hop to the chic and well-heeled **Yorkville** neighbourhood, whose centre of gravity is Cumberland Street and Yorkville Avenue between Bay and Avenue Road. Jam-packed with chi-chi cafés, restaurants and shops, Yorkville makes for a pleasant stroll (especially if you've got some spare cash), one of its most agreeable features being the old timber-terrace houses that are still much in evidence. These same houses have actually seen much grimmer days: in the late 1950s, Yorkville was run-down and druggy, but then the hippies arrived and soon turned the area into a counter-cultural enclave, a diminutive version of Haight-Ashbury with Joni Mitchell and Gordon Lightfoot in attendance. Things are much less inventive today – big cars and big jewellery – but the **Village Gardens**, at the corner of Cumberland and Bellair streets, is a particularly appealing and cleverly designed little park. The centrepiece is a hunk of granite brought from northern Ontario and around it are arranged a variety of neat little gardens, displaying every native habitat from upland conifers to wetlands.

The Toronto Reference Library

At the east end of Cumberland Street, at 789 Yonge, the **Toronto Reference Library** (Mon–Fri 10am–8pm, Sat 10am–5pm & Sept to late June Sun 1.30–5pm; ☎416/395-5577, ⓦwww.tpl.toronto.on.ca) occupies a striking modern building designed by Canada's own **Raymond Moriyama** (see below). The exterior is actually a good deal less becoming than the interior, which is arranged around a large and airy atrium with a pool and waterfall in the foyer. An enormous stock of books and a wide range of audiobooks and music recordings are readily accessible to the general public; there's also the **Special Collections, Genealogy and Maps Centre** on the fourth floor. This comprises the library's rare and specialized research collections, which are divided into four main sections: contemporary and historical maps; genealogy and local history; Canadian history primary sources; and the art room, where pride of place goes to the exquisitely drawn John James Audubon *Birds of America*. The library puts on regular exhibitions illustrating various aspects of the special collections, but it's the fifth section, the **Arthur Conan Doyle Room** (Tues, Thurs & Sat 1–4pm; free), which steals the show, possessing the world's largest collection of books, manuscripts, letters and so forth written by Conan Doyle, including of course the illustrious Sherlock Holmes.

Bata Shoe Museum

Within easy walking distance of both the ROM and Yorkville, the **Bata Shoe Museum**, 327 Bloor St West at St George St (Tues, Wed, Fri, Sat 10am–5pm, Thurs 10am–8pm, Sun noon–5pm, closed Mon; $6; ☎416/979-7799, ⓦwww.batashoemuseum.ca; St George subway), was designed by **Raymond Moriyama**, the much-lauded Vancouver-born architect whose other creations include the Ontario Science Centre and the Scarborough Civic Centre (see p.88). Opened in 1995, the museum was designed to resemble a shoe box – the roof supposedly suggests a lid resting on an open box – and was built for **Sonja Bata**, of the Bata shoe manufacturing family, to house the extraordinary assortment of footwear she has spent a lifetime collecting.

A leaflet issued at reception steers visitors around the museum, starting with an introductory section entitled "All About Shoes" on **Level B1**, which presents an overview on the evolution of footwear, beginning with a plaster cast of the oldest human footprint ever discovered, roughly 3,700,000 years old. Among the more interesting exhibits in this section are pointed shoes from medieval Europe, where different social classes were allowed different lengths of toe, and tiny Chinese silk shoes used by women whose feet had been bound. Banned by the Chinese Communists when they came to power in 1949, foot binding was common practice for over a thousand years, and the "ideal" length of a woman's foot was a hobbling three inches. Begun in early childhood, the process effectively crippled women and, in its contraction and bending of the foot, created a U-shaped orifice that was commonly used for sexual penetration by the master of the house. A small adjoining section is devoted to specialist footwear, including French chestnut-crushing clogs from the nineteenth century, inlaid Ottoman platforms designed to keep aristocratic feet well away from the mud, and a pair of US army boots from the Vietnam War with the sole shaped to imitate the sandal prints of the Vietcong.

The stairs leading up from Level B1 are flanked by a small but unusual collection of stirrups – the iron ones look spectacularly uncomfortable – and at the top, on **Level G**, a large glass cabinet showcases all sorts of celebrity footwear. The exhibits are rotated regularly, but look out for Buddy Holly's loafers, Marilyn Monroe's stilettos, Princess Diana's red court shoes, Shaquille O'Neal's colossal Reebok trainers and Elton John's ridiculous platforms. **Level 2** and **Level 3** are used for temporary exhibitions – some of which are very good indeed – and there's also a small section explaining the museum's role in restoring and repairing old footwear.

Cabbagetown

The precise boundaries of **Cabbagetown** continue to be a matter of dispute between local historians and real estate agents – the former try to narrow the area and the latter try to expand it – but, roughly speaking, this Victorian neighbourhood is bounded by Dundas Street to the south, Parliament to the west, Wellesley to the north, and the Don River to the east. Cabbagetown got its name from nineteenth-century Irish immigrants who grew cabbages in their yards instead of flowers. Contemporary Cabbagetowners have embraced the vegetable and even have their own flag with a large, leafy cabbage prominently displayed at the centre. In the early twentieth century, the area was pocked by substandard homes and dire living conditions, prompting novelist Hugh Garner to anoint it "the largest Anglo-Saxon slum in North America". Today, most of the houses have been renovated by new, better-off owners, and the neighbourhood has become a haven for the city's hip and moderately well-to-do.

Specific sights in Cabbagetown are thin on the ground, but **Metcalfe Street**, running one block east of Parliament, does possess a particularly appealing ensemble of Victorian houses, as does adjoining **Winchester Street**. Common architectural features include high-pitched gables, stained-glass windows, stone lintels and inviting timber verandas. At the east end of Winchester Street, the entrance to one of the city's oldest cemeteries is marked by a handsome Gothic Revival **chapel** and matching **pavilion**, whose coloured tiles and soft yellow brickwork date to the middle of the nineteenth century. Inside the **cemetery**, the gravestones are almost universally modest and unassuming, but their straightforward accounts of the lives of the dead give witness to the extraordinary British diaspora that populated much of Victorian Canada. Cabbagetown is also home to the oldest neighbourhood festival in Toronto; for details, see p.192 in Chapter 16, "Festivals and events".

Casa Loma

From Dupont subway station, it's a brief walk north up the slope of Spadina Road to the corner of Davenport Road, where a flight of steps leads to **Casa Loma**, 1 Austin Terrace (daily 9.30am–5pm, last admission 4pm; $10, parking $2.30; ☎416/923-1171, ⊛www.casaloma.org). The house, Toronto's most bizarre attraction, is an enormous towered and turreted mansion built to the instructions of Sir Henry Pellatt and his architect Edward J. Lennox between 1911 and 1914. A free diagram of the layout of the house is available at the reception, as are audioguides.

The clearly numbered route around the house goes up one side and down the other. It begins on the ground floor in the **Great Hall**, a pseudo-Gothic extravaganza with an eighteen-metre-high cross-beamed ceiling, a Wurlitzer organ and enough floor space to accommodate several hundred guests. Hung with flags, heavy-duty chandeliers and suits of armour, it's a remarkably cheerless place, but in a touch worthy of Errol Flynn, the hall is overlooked by a balcony at the end of Pellatt's second-floor bedroom: presumably Sir Henry could, like some medieval baron, welcome his guests from on high. Pushing on, the **Library** and then the walnut-panelled **Dining Room** lead to the **Conservatory**, an elegant and spacious room with a marble floor and side-panels set beneath a handsome Tiffany domed glass ceiling. Well-lit, this is perhaps the mansion's most appealing room, its flowerbeds kept warm even in winter by the original network of steam pipes. The nearby **Study** was Sir Henry's favourite room, a serious affair engulfed by mahogany panelling and equipped with two secret passageways, one leading to the wine cellar, the other to his wife's rooms. Also of note is the ground-floor **Oak Room**, which comes complete with an elaborate stucco ceiling and acres of finely carved oak panelling.

On the second floor, **Sir Henry's Suite** has oodles of walnut and mahogany panelling, which stands in odd contrast to the 1910s white-marble, high-tech bathroom, featuring an elaborate multi-nozzle shower. **Lady Pellatt's Suite** wasn't left behind in the ablutions department, either – her bathroom had a bidet, a real novelty in George V's Canada – and she had a lighter decorative touch, too, eschewing wood panelling for walls painted in her favourite colour, Wedgwood Blue, with pastel furniture to match. This suite also contains a small display on Lady Pellatt's involvement with the Girl Guides, a uniformed organization encouraging good imperial habits – self-reliance, honesty, self-discipline and so forth. In the photos, Lady Pellatt looks serious and concerned,

Sir Henry Pellatt

Sir Henry Pellatt (1859–1939) made a fortune by pioneering the use of hydro-electricity, harnessing the power of Niagara Falls to light Ontario's expanding cities. Determined to become a man of social standing, Pellatt threw his money around with gusto. He levered his wife into a key position as a leader of the Girl Guides and managed to become a major general of the Queen's Own Rifles, bolstering his appointment by taking 640 soldiers to a military training camp in Aldershot, in England, at his own expense. Pellatt's enthusiasm for the British interest went down well, and he even secured a knighthood, though he was much too nouveau to be fully accepted into the old elite – for one thing, he was fond of dressing up in a costume that combined a British colonel's uniform with the attire of a Mohawk chief.

In 1911, Pellatt started work on **Casa Loma**, gathering furnishings from all over the world and even importing Scottish stonemasons to build a wall around his six-acre property, the end result being an eccentric mixture of medieval fantasy and early twentieth-century technology. Pellatt spent more than $3 million fulfilling his dream, but his penchant for reckless business dealings finally caught up with him, forcing him to move out and declare himself bankrupt in 1923. He died penniless sixteen years later, his dramatic fall from grace earning him the nickname "Pellatt the Plunger".

the girls suitably keen and dutiful. At the other end of the main second-floor corridor are the **Round Room**, with its curved doors and walls, and the smartly decorated **Windsor Room**, named after – and built for – the Royal Family, in the rather forlorn hope that they would come and stay here. Of course they never did; Pellatt was much too parvenu for their tastes. Up above, the third floor holds a mildly diverting display on Pellatt's one-time regiment, the **Queen's Own Rifles**, tracing their involvement in various campaigns from the suppression of the Métis rebellion in western Canada in 1885 through to World War I and beyond. The old photographs are the most interesting feature, along with biographies of some of the soldiers who were awarded medals for gallantry. From the third floor, wooden staircases clamber up to two of the house's **towers**, from where there are pleasing views over the house and gardens.

Back on the ground floor, stairs lead down to the Lower Level, which was where Pellatt's money ran out and his plans ground to a halt. Work never started on the bowling alleys and shooting range he had designed, and the swimming pool only got as far as the rough concrete basin that survives today – never mind that Pellatt conceived a marble pool overlooked by golden swans. Pellatt did, however, manage to complete the 250-metre-long **tunnel** that runs from the house and pool to the **carriage room** and **stables**, where his thoroughbred horses were allegedly better-treated than his servants, chomping away at their oats and hay in splendid iron and mahogany stalls.

The stables are a dead-end, so you'll have to double back along the tunnel to reach the house and the exit. Before you leave, spare time for the **terraced gardens** (May–Oct daily 9.30am–5pm; no extra charge), which tumble down the ridge at the back of the house. They are parcelled up into several different sections and easily explored along a network of footpaths, beginning on the terrace behind the Great Hall. Highlights include the Rhododendron Dell, the lily pond and waterfall of the Water Garden and the Cedar Grove, a meadow garden flanked by cool, green cedars.

Spadina Historic House and Gardens

What the occupants of **Spadina House** (guided tours only, May–Aug Tues–Sun noon–5pm; Sept–Dec Tues–Fri noon–4pm, Sat & Sun noon–5pm; $5; ☎416/392-6910; Dupont subway) must have thought when Casa Loma went up next door can only be imagined, but there must have been an awful lot of curtain-twitching. The two houses are a study in contrasts: Casa Loma a grandiose pile, and Spadina an elegant Victorian property of genteel appearance dating from 1866. Spadina was built by James Austin, an Irish immigrant from County Armagh who was a printer's apprentice before becoming a successful businessman and a co-founder of the Toronto Dominion Bank. After his death, Spadina House passed to Albert Austin, who enlarged and modernized his father's home, adding a billiard and laundry room, a garage and a refrigerator room to replace the old ice house. Albert's property eventually passed to his three daughters, who lived in the house until the last of the sisters, Anna Kathleen, moved out in 1983, the year before she died. Anna bequeathed Spadina House to the City of Toronto, which now manages and maintains the place. The Austins' uninterrupted occupation of Spadina House means that the house's furnishings are nearly all genuine family artefacts, and they provide an intriguing insight into the family's changing tastes and interests.

Narrated by enthusiastic volunteers, the **guided tour** is a delight. Particular highlights include the conservatory trap door that allowed the gardeners to come and go unseen by their employers, an assortment of period chairs designed to accommodate the largest of bustles, the original gas chandeliers and a couple of canvases by **Cornelius Krieghoff** (for more on whom, see p.51). Pride of place, however, is the Billiard Room, where an inventive Art Nouveau decorative frieze dating from 1898 is complemented by several fine pieces of furniture, including a sturdy oak desk, bentwood chairs and a swivel armchair that imitated the designs of Englishman William Morris. Also of interest are the unusual arcaded arches at the top of the first flight of stairs, installed in the 1890s as part of a scheme to improve the circulation of air. Curiously, this was inspired by Florence Nightingale (1820–1910), a Victorian philanthropist who became famous in every corner of the British Empire when she took over the military hospital at Scutari during the Crimean War of the 1850s. Appalled by the unsanitary conditions at the hospital, she took matters into her own hands, applying basic standards of hygiene and thereby substantially reducing the mortality rate amongst the British wounded. After the war, she effectively founded nursing as a profession for women and her treatises were widely disseminated, including her theories linking health and the good circulation of air.

The waterfront and the Toronto Islands

espite its industrial blotches, and the heavy concrete brow of the Gardiner Expressway, there is much to enjoy on the shore of **Lake Ontario**. Footpaths and cycling trails now nudge along a fair slice of the waterfront, and the **Harbourfront Centre** offers a year-round schedule of activities – music festivals, theatre, dance and the like. Here also is the adventurous **Power Plant Contemporary Art Gallery**, as well as **Ontario Place**, a leisure complex spread over three man-made islands, that provides all sorts of kids' stuff throughout the summer.

Even better are the **Toronto Islands**, whose breezy tranquillity attracts droves of city-dwellers during Toronto's humid summers. It only takes fifteen minutes to reach them by municipal ferry, but the contrast between the city and the islands could hardly be more marked, not least because the islands are almost entirely **vehicle-free**: many locals use wheelbarrows to move their tackle, while others walk or cycle.

The waterfront and around

Toronto's grimy docks once disfigured the shoreline nearest the city centre, a swathe of warehouses and factories that was unattractive and smelly in equal measure. Today it's another story: the port and its facilities have been concentrated further east, beyond the foot of Parliament Street and the Distillery District (see p.49), while the **waterfront** west of Yonge Street has been redeveloped in grand style, sprouting luxury condominium blocks, jogging and cycling trails, offices, shops and marinas. The focus of all this activity is the **Harbourfront Centre**, whose various facilities include an open-air performance area and the **Power Plant Contemporary Art Gallery**. To reach the Harbourfront Centre by public transport, take streetcar #509 or #510 from Union Station and get off at the Queens Quay Terminal.

The Harbourfront Centre

The centrepiece of Toronto's downtown waterfront is the ten-acre **Harbourfront Centre**, an expanse of lakefront property stretching from the foot of York Street in the east to the conspicuous outdoor Harbourfront

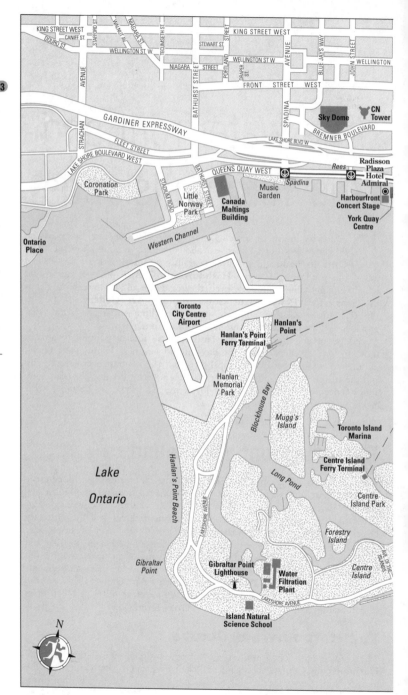

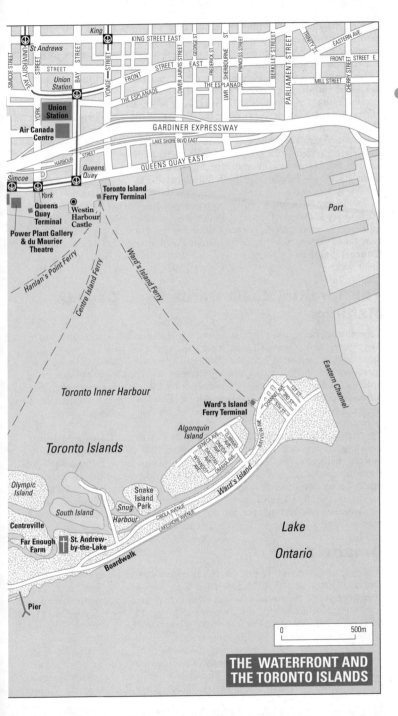

King

KING STREET EAST

St Andrews

STREET

STREET

Union
Station

KING

STREET

EAST

SIMCOE STREET

UNIVERSITY AVE

STREET

BAY

YONGE STREET

FRONT

LOWER JARVIS STREET

GEORGES ST

FREDERICK ST

PRINCESS STREET

ST

SHERBOURNE STREET

BERKELEY STREET

PARLIAMENT STREET

TRINITY ST

FRONT STREET E.

EASTERN AVE

MILL STREET

CHERRY STREET

THE ESPLANADE

THE ESPLANADE

LWR

Union
Station

Air Canada
Centre

YORK

GARDINER EXPRESSWAY

LAKE SHORE BLVD EAST

STREET

HARBOUR

Queens
Quay

QUEENS QUAY EAST

Simcoe

York

Queens
Quay
Terminal

Westin
Harbour
Castle

Toronto Island
Ferry Terminal

Port

Power Plant Gallery
& du Maurier
Theatre

Hanlan's Point Ferry

Centre Island Ferry

Ward's Island Ferry

Toronto Inner Harbour

Ward's Island
Ferry Terminal

Eastern Channel

Toronto Islands

Algonquin
Island

SENECA AVE

OMAHA AVE

DURBAN AVE

ONEIDA AVE

DACOTAH AVE

AVOCA

WYANDOT
AVE

BAYVIEW AVE

CHIPPEWA AVE

3RD ST

4TH ST

5TH ST

1ST ST

Olympic
Island

Snake
Island
Park

Ward's Island

Centreville

South Island

Snug
Harbour

CIBOLA AVENUE

LAKESHORE AVENUE

Lake

Far Enough
Farm

St. Andrew-
by-the-Lake

Ontario

Boardwalk

Pier

0   500m

Concert Stage, about five minutes' walk to the west from York. This is one of Toronto's most creative quarters, and many of the city's artistic and cultural events are held here, either outside or indoors at one of several venues, principally the du Maurier Theatre Centre (see p.159).

The east end of the Harbourfront Centre is marked by the **Queens Quay Terminal building**, a handsome, glassy structure built as a combined warehouse and shipping depot in 1927. Attractively refurbished, it now holds cafés, offices and smart shops. Next door, the **Power Plant Contemporary Art Gallery** (Tues & Thurs–Sun noon–6pm, Wed noon–8pm; $4, but free on Wed after 5pm; ☎416/973-4949, ⓦwww.thepowerplant.org) is housed in an imaginatively converted 1920s power station. Every year, the gallery presents about a dozen exhibitions of contemporary art, often featuring emerging Canadian artists. It's mostly cutting-edge stuff, indecipherable to some, exciting to others. The gallery shares the power station with the du Maurier Theatre Centre.

Close by, just to the west, another former warehouse has been turned into the **York Quay Centre**, which holds performance areas, meeting spaces and craft galleries. The south entrance of the Centre lets out to a shallow pond that converts into a skating rink during the winter. Further west is the **Harbourfront Concert Stage**, which boasts a graceful fan-like roof designed to suggest a ship's deck.

The Toronto Music Garden and Canada Maltings

Cross the footbridge on the west side of the Harbourfront Centre and you're a few metres from **Queens Quay West**, once a busy boulevard but now much more subdued, separated from the Gardiner Expressway by a raft of brand-new apartment blocks. Walking west along the road, it's about 500m to the foot of Spadina Avenue, and a slice of old industrial land that has been reclaimed and turned into the landscaped **Toronto Music Garden** – essentially a series of rockeries with vague musical allusions which meanders west along the lakeshore.

Just beyond the Music Garden lurk the giant silos of the **Canada Maltings building**, an imposing concrete hulk erected in 1928 for the storage of barley brought here from the Prairies by the ships which once thronged the St Lawrence Seaway. Closed in 1987, the building is derelict today, but architecturally – as a prime example of industrial Modernism – it's much too fine a structure to be demolished, and Torontonians have been debating its future for years. On its far side is Bathurst Street, and the dinky little ferry that shuttles across the narrow Western Channel to the Toronto City Centre Airport (see p.21).

Ontario Place

A couple of kilometres west of the Harbourfront Centre along the lakeshore, **Ontario Place**, at 955 Lakeshore Blvd West (late May & Sept Sat & Sun 10am–6pm; June–Aug mostly, though times can vary, daily 10am–8pm; day pass covering most rides $28 for visitors aged 6–64 years, $14 for 4–5 years and $16 for those 65 and older; ☎416/314-9900, ⓦwww.ontarioplace.com), rises out of the lake like a postmodern Atlantis. Architect Eberhard Zeidler was given a mandate to create "leisure space in an urban context", and he came up with these three man-made islands, or "pods", covering ninety-five acres with landscaped parks, lagoons and canals. The attractions here are almost entirely themed around water, and rides like the Rush River Raft Ride, the Purple

Pipeline and the Pink Twister provide exciting ways to get dizzy and wet. Visitors looking for less frenetic activities can rent **pedal boats** (available at all of the park's various lagoons) or two-seater aquatic bicycles, which are used to thrash through the canals that separate the pods.

Both an amusement park and an entertainment complex, Ontario Place was the template for facilities like Florida's EPCOT Center, and it teems with young families and teenagers during the day. The atmosphere at night tends to be a bit more mature, particularly at the **Molson Amphitheatre**, which puts on a series of summer concerts, dominated by headliner rock groups. In addition, every June and July a spectacular international fireworks competition called **Symphony of Fire** overwhelms Ontario Place. Pyrotechnic teams from around the world congregate at the water's edge and try to beat out their rivals with creative routines and sheer firepower.

Also at Ontario Place is the **Cinesphere**, whose distinctive geodesic dome, containing a 750-seat theatre with a curved, six-storey screen, was the world's first IMAX theatre, opened in 1971. IMAX technology was first developed by the Toronto-based IMAX Corporation in 1967. Distinguishing IMAX from normal cinema, the frames of an IMAX film are physically larger than in any other processing format; the film runs through a behemoth projector at twenty-four frames per second; and the screens average 20m (65 feet) in height. The cumulative sensation is one of being immersed in the film, and it has certainly proved a popular formula – there are now IMAX theatres all over the world. To see an IMAX film here, it is a good idea to book ahead, either in person at the Ontario Place Box Office or by calling ☎416/870-8000; tickets cost $8–10.

To get to Ontario Place by **public transport**, either take the Bathurst streetcar, #511, which drops passengers a short walk away, or catch the free shuttle bus which leaves Union Station every 30 minutes.

The Toronto Islands

Originally a sandbar peninsula, the **Toronto Islands**, arching around the city's harbour, were cut adrift from the mainland by a violent storm in 1858. First used as a summer retreat by the Mississauga Indians, the islands went through various incarnations during the twentieth century: they once hosted a baseball stadium, where slugger Babe Ruth hit his first professional home run, and they even served as a World War II training base for the Norwegian Air Force. Today, this archipelago, roughly 6km long and totalling around 800 acres, seems worlds away from the bustle of downtown, a haven for rest and relaxation – and a place where visitors' motor cars are **banned**.

The city side of the archipelago is broken into a dozen tiny islets dotted with cottages, leisure facilities, neat gardens and clumps of wild woodland. By comparison, the other side of the archipelago is a tad wilder and more windswept, consisting of one long sliver of land, which is somewhat arbitrarily divided into three "islands". From the east, these are **Ward's Island**, a quiet residential area with parkland and wilderness; **Centre Island**, the busiest and most developed of the three, itself divided in twain by a narrow waterway; and **Hanlan's Point**, edging Toronto's pint-sized City Centre Airport. Hanlan's Point also holds the city's best **sandy beach** – though, as Lake Ontario is generally regarded as being too polluted for swimming, most visitors stick to sunbathing.

Mrs Simcoe and the Toronto Islands

Mrs Elizabeth Simcoe (1766–1850), the energetic wife of the lieutenant-governor of Upper Canada, John Graves Simcoe, arrived in York, today's Toronto, in 1793 and returned to England three years later. An avid diarist, Mrs Simcoe recorded the day-to-day happenings of colonial life in her diary, a lively, attractively illustrated text dotted with shrewd observations and descriptions of Canada's flora. Mrs Simcoe took a shine to the Toronto Islands – as it was then – and rode there frequently. Her first jaunt is recorded thusly: "We met with some good natural meadows and several ponds. The trees are mostly of the poplar kind, covered with wild vines, …[and] on the ground were everlasting peas creeping in abundance, of a purple colour. I am told they are good to eat when boiled…The diversity of scenes I met with this morning made the ride extremely pleasant. I was very near riding into what appeared a quicksand…[which was]…the only unpleasant incident that occurred this day." If this extract whets your appetite, *The Diary of Mrs John Graves Simcoe* is available at the World's Biggest Bookstore (see p.169), even though it's currently out of print.

Practicalities

Three separate **ferries** depart for the Toronto Islands from the mainland **ferry terminal**, which is located behind the conspicuous *Westin Harbour Castle Hotel*, between the foot of Yonge and Bay streets. To get to the ferry terminal from Union Station, take the #509 or #510 streetcar and get off at the first stop – Queen's Quay (Ferry Docks). The Ward's Island and Hanlan's Point ferries run year-round, while the ferry shuttling visitors over to Centre Island only operates from spring to early fall. During peak season (May to early Sept), all the ferry lines depart every twenty minutes; at other times of the year they operate at regular intervals, either every half-hour, every forty-five minutes, or on the hour. Ferries begin running between 6.30am and 9am and end service between 9pm and 11.30pm, depending on the service and the season. For schedule details, telephone ☏416/392-8193. Regardless of the time of year, a return **fare** for adults is $6, or $3.50 for seniors and students.

Cars are not allowed on the Toronto Islands without a special permit, which is only available to island residents. Aside from walking, cycling or rowing, the other means of conveyance is a free but irregular trackless **train** that runs between the ferry docks at Hanlan's Point and Ward's Island; you can board the train at any of the three ferry docks. Several hours are needed to cover the islands' trails by **bicycle**, and a full day can easily be spent exploring on foot. Rollerblades are allowed on the islands, but must be removed while on board the ferries. Bicycles are allowed on the ferries, though restrictions may apply on busy weekends.

Ward's Island

Named after the Ward family, who settled on the then-peninsula in 1830, **Ward's Island** possesses a sloping, sandy beach and a pleasant boardwalk, which scoots along the Lake Ontario side of the island, and is lined with cottages, some of which double as artists' studios. The island is home to approximately 700 full-time residents, but remains one of the least-developed of the chain – the landscape is still dominated by primeval-looking scrub, reed and birches mixed with wild apple trees and grape vines. A network of footpaths explores this terrain, and a trio of small footbridges connects the island with its tiny neighbours – Algonquin, Snake Island and Snug Harbour, just to the north.

Centre Island

Centre Island is where most of the action takes place during the summer season, when ferries arrive at its harbour carrying boatloads of day-trippers. The first building you'll see as the ferry docks is the *Paradise Restaurant*, a favourite watering hole for the thirsty sailors of the adjacent **Toronto Island Marina**. From the dock, it's a five-minute walk east to **Centreville** (mid-May to Aug daily, plus early May & Sept weekends, from 10.30am–5pm, 6pm, 7pm or 8pm; ☏416/203-0405, ⓦwww.centreisland.ca), a children's amusement park with charmingly old-fashioned rides. There are around thirty rides altogether, from paddle boats shaped as swans to a carousel, a Ferris Wheel and the Lake Monster roller-coaster. Each ride costs a specified number of tickets, from two to board the carousel up to a maximum of six to experience the Lake Monster. Individual tickets are 70¢, or you can splash out on an all-day pass costing \$23 for adults (and anyone over four feet tall), or \$16.50 for kids under four feet. At the east end of Centreville is the **Far Enough Farm**, a small farm and petting zoo popular with very young children.

Just to the south of Centreville, a footbridge spans the narrow waterway that separates the two parts of Centre Island to reach the **Avenue of the Islands**, a wide walkway surrounded by trim gardens. At its southern end, this walkway extends into a forked **pier** that pokes out beyond the stone breakwater into the lake. At the foot of the pier is one of the island's two **Toronto Island Bicycle Rental** outlets (☏416/203-0009), which stocks conventional bicycles, tandems, and even quadracycles; reservations are strongly advised. **Boat rental** is available near the Avenue of the Islands, too, and from here you can paddle through the lagoons and explore tiny islands like **Forestry Island**, which is otherwise inaccessible. One other attraction, just east of the Avenue of the Islands, across the water from Far Enough Farm, is the Anglican **St Andrew-by-the-Lake**, a dinky clapboard church dating from 1884 and featuring attractive stained-glass windows.

Hanlan's Point

Hanlan's Point is named after another old island family, who first settled here at Gibraltar Point, on the island's southwestern tip, in 1862. The most famous member of the family was **Edward "Ned" Hanlan**, who earned Canada's first Olympic gold medal as a champion rower, a skill he honed rowing back and forth to the mainland. The Hanlans built a hotel-resort on the island and others followed, though none has survived and neither has the old amusement park, which was demolished in the 1930s to make way for what is now the Toronto City Centre Airport.

Ferries arrive on the northeast side of the island close to the airport. The ferry dock is the location of the other **Toronto Island Bicycle Rental** outlet (see above), as well as washrooms, showers and a snack bar. From here, footpaths and bicycle trails run south, passing behind – and just east – of **Hanlan's Point Beach**, a stretch of tawny sand which is perhaps more valued as an environmentalist's haven than a sunbathers' retreat. Indeed, generations of budding biologists have been nurtured at the nearby **Toronto Islands Natural Science School**, which teaches city children about the flora and fauna of both the islands and Lake Ontario. The school is on the south side of the island, and nearby are both a water filtration plant and the **Gibraltar Point Lighthouse**, a sturdy limestone structure with a bright-red iron top. Erected at the beginning of the nineteenth century, the original lighthouse was sixteen metres high, and equipped with a lamp that burned sperm oil. This set-up was updated in the 1830s, when the lighthouse was heightened by about four metres and its lamp replaced by one fuelled by coal oil; an electric lamp was installed in 1916. In its early days, when Toronto harbour was crowded with sailing ships, the Gibraltar was a vitally important beacon. It also achieved notoriety when its first keeper, a certain Radan Muller, disappeared in 1815. The York Gazette was quick to pronounce Muller of "inoffensive and benevolent character", and was pleased to report that two suspects in his disappearance had been picked up by the police. In the event, the suspects – two soldiers from Fort York (see p.39) – were never charged, but nevertheless popular legend continued to assert their guilt. The story went that they dropped in on Radan for a drinking session, but a quarrel ensued in which the lighthouse keeper was accidentally killed. More murkily, it's possible that Radan was a whisky smuggler, and the fight started over the profits of some contraband booze. Whatever the truth, the remains of Radan's body were finally discovered in 1893, buried just to the west of the lighthouse, by a later keeper.

The suburbs

oronto's **suburbs** surround the city in a mixture of parkland, residential neighbourhoods and monotonous stretches of malls, car parks and high-rises. The discerning eye, however, will see beyond the monochromatic urban sprawl to notice that the ethnic diversity so prevalent downtown extends to the suburbs as well, keeping the city's environs from sinking into the yawning blandness characteristic of many North American city outskirts.

In 1998, Ontario's provincial government decided that the City of Toronto and its suburban municipalities would amalgamate into one huge city. This "Mega City", as it's colloquially known, has a population of over four million people and covers an area of 632 square kilometres. While the consolidation was a major social and political controversy for residents, to outsiders it is of little consequence, and the only potential for confusion might be the continued use of the different suburbs' names by the local population.

Venturing outside the city centre is certainly worth your while, particularly since a fair amount of major attractions – like the **Toronto Zoo**, the **Ontario Science Centre** and **Black Creek Pioneer Village** – are found in the suburbs, especially the **Scarborough** and **North York** neighbourhoods. Toronto's extensive **transit system** takes passengers to the perimeters of Toronto's suburbs for the adult flat fare of $2.25 – the same price as a subway ride in the downtown core. It's advisable to rely on public transport rather than a rental car, as the arterial roadways can be a scary prospect during rush hour traffic when you are unfamiliar with the routes. On weekends, suburban bus and train routes run less frequently. Contact the Toronto Transit Commission (TTC) for route information: ☎416/393-4636 or ⍟www.city.toronto.on.ca /ttc.

The Beaches

A century ago, **The Beaches**, located to the east of downtown Toronto, was what the Toronto Islands are today: a summer vacation area used for frolicking about the shores of Lake Ontario. Today, The Beaches is more a residential than a holiday spot, but its overall atmosphere has retained the look and feel of a turn-of-the-century seaside resort. It has a three-kilometre boardwalk, ample Queen Anne-style houses with generous front porches, and a charming bandshell in Kew Park, which serves as the main stage for the neighbourhood's many festivals; see Chapter 16, "Festivals and events," for some of these. The fact that

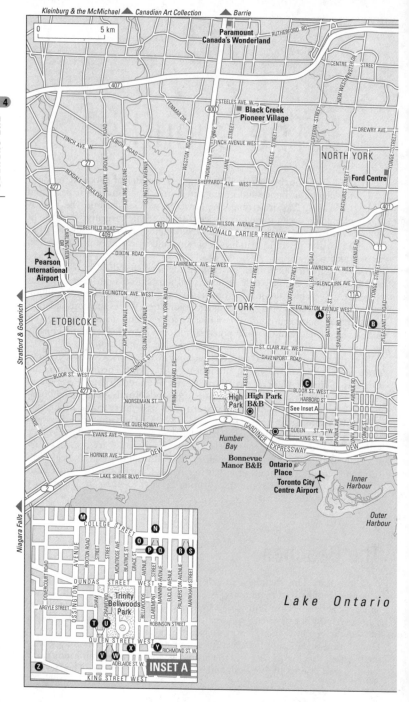

Kleinburg & the McMichael ▲ Canadian Art Collection   ▲ Barrie

0   5 km

**Paramount
Canada's Wonderland**

RUTHERFORD RD.

CENTRE STREET

NEW WESTMINSTER DR.

STEELES AVE. W.

**Black Creek
Pioneer Village**

FINCH AVENUE WEST

DREWRY AVE.

NORTH YORK

SHEPPARD AVE. WEST

Ford Centre

WILSON AVENUE

MACDONALD CARTIER FREEWAY

LAWRENCE AVE. WEST

GLENCAIRN AVE.

YORK

EGLINTON AVENUE WEST   **A**

B

**Pearson
International
Airport**

ETOBICOKE

ST. CLAIR AVE. WEST

DAVENPORT ROAD

C   BLOOR ST. WEST

HARBORD ST.

5

High Park

**High Park
B&B**

See Inset A

QUEEN ST. W.

KING ST. W.

*Humber
Bay*

GARDINER EXPRESSWAY

**Bonnevue
Manor B&B**

Ontario Place

**Toronto City
Centre Airport**

*Inner
Harbour*

*Outer
Harbour*

Lake Ontario

INSET A

M   COLLEGE STREET

N

O   **P** **Q**   **R** **S**

DUNDAS STREET WEST

**Trinity
Bellwoods
Park**

ROBINSON STREET

T **U**

QUEEN STREET WEST

V **W**   **X**   **Y**   RICHMOND ST. W.

ADELAIDE ST. W.

Z

KING STREET WEST

Stratford & Goderich ◄

Niagara Falls ◄

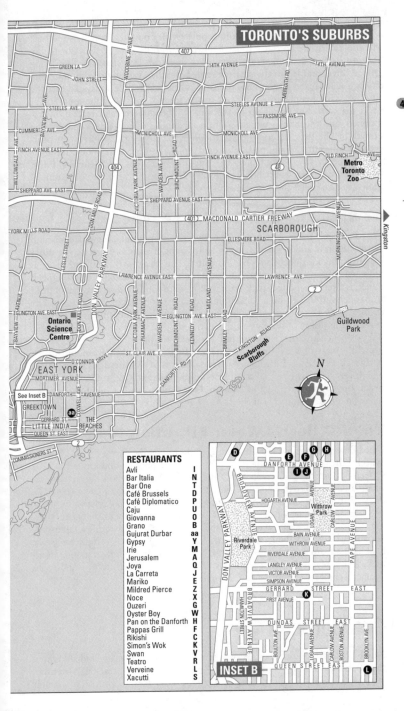

TORONTO'S SUBURBS

Metro Toronto Zoo

SCARBOROUGH

Kingston

Guildwood Park

Ontario Science Centre

Scarborough Bluffs

EAST YORK

See Inset B

GREEKTOWN

LITTLE INDIA

THE BEACHES

N

RESTAURANTS

Avli	I
Bar Italia	N
Bar One	T
Café Brussels	D
Café Diplomatico	P
Caju	U
Giovanna	O
Grano	B
Gujurat Durbar	aa
Gypsy	Y
Irie	M
Jerusalem	A
Joya	Q
La Carreta	J
Mariko	E
Mildred Pierce	Z
Noce	X
Ouzeri	G
Oyster Boy	W
Pan on the Danforth	H
Pappas Grill	F
Rikishi	C
Simon's Wok	K
Swan	V
Teatro	R
Verveine	L
Xacutti	S

INSET B

DANFORTH AVENUE

Withrow Park

Riverdale Park

DON VALLEY PARKWAY

BROADVIEW AVENUE

HOGARTH AVENUE

BAIN AVENUE

WITHROW AVENUE

RIVERDALE AVENUE

LANGLEY AVENUE

VICTOR AVENUE

SIMPSON AVENUE

GERRARD STREET EAST

FIRST AVENUE

DUNDAS STREET EAST

HAMILTON STREET

BOULTON AVE

LOGAN AVENUE

CARLOW AVENUE

BOSTON AVENUE

BROOKLYN AVE

PAPE AVENUE

QUEEN STREET EAST

The Beaches has been so successfully preserved is remarkable, especially considering that Toronto's downtown core is only twenty minutes away by streetcar.

In the 1880s, the Toronto Street Railway Company (the predecessor to the Toronto Transit Commission) installed a streetcar line that ran east along Queen Street and led to the sparsely settled Beaches. Initially, the churchgoing city was scandalized by the TSR's idea to run its trams on Sundays, so that the city's working people could get out in the fresh air and visit the amusement parks that were springing up in the area. But commerce and recreation triumphed, and the line – which continues running to this day – spurred the growth of The Beaches community. In 1903, the city began a thirty-year project to acquire the private parks clustered along the waterfront. The consolidation of the private parks led to the opening of the public **Beaches Park**, whose tennis courts, parklands, boardwalks and unspoiled beaches offer unparalleled rest and relaxation to the city's masses.

Kew, Balmy and Cherry beaches

There are two main sections to The Beaches community, **Kew Beach** and **Balmy Beach**, and neither wants to be thought of as subordinate to the other – hence the insistence on pluralization ("The Beaches"). Kew, however, is probably the most popular. Here, **Kew Beach Park**, situated just below Queen Street, is a picture-perfect park with rolling, grassy hills and a sandy beachfront that is delightful even on a packed Sunday afternoon. Balmy Beach is separated from Kew Beach by a tiny inlet at the foot of Silverbirch Avenue, but there is very little distinction between the two – despite what some locals may say, Balmy's beach and parklands are just as nice as Kew's.

Slightly west of Kew Beach is **Cherry Beach,** a favourite among hikers, birdwatchers and cyclists. Cherry Beach begins at **Ashbridges Bay Park**, which is at the corner of Lakeshore Boulevard East and Coxwell Avenue. Signs inside the park point out the **Martin Goodman Trail**, a hiking route that spans the entire Toronto waterfront.

The RC Harris Water Filtration Plant

One of the strangest and most intriguing sights in The Beaches is the **RC Harris Water Filtration Plant**, built during the Great Depression and located at 2701 Queen St East (☎416/392-3566). Commissioner Harris, whose career achievements are referred to in Michael Ondaatje's novel *In the Skin of a Lion* (see p.212), decided that a project as grand as turning the water of Lake Ontario into safe, clean drinking water for the people of Toronto demanded a magnificent building. A palatial, Byzantine-style edifice, the plant looks like something a multi-millionaire would have built for himself. Instead, it's Toronto's temple to public health. There are free tours (Sat 10am, 11.30am and 1pm) of the filtration complex, which reveal the inner workings of the mammoth architecture and monstrous machines – a must for fans of architectural exotica.

Scarborough

Scarborough, unjustly best-known for its dreary strip malls and doughnut shops, has been stuck with the unfortunate nickname "Scarberia" by other Torontonians. In actuality, though, the area does have a couple of notable attractions and boasts proudly of native son Mike Myers, whose parody of growing up in this suburb was repackaged as the American midwest and released as the motion picture *Wayne's World*.

Toronto Zoo

Set on the hilly edge of the Rouge Valley, the **Toronto Zoo** (daily: Mar–Sept 9am–7.30pm, Oct–Feb 9.30am–5.30pm; $18, children age 4–12 $10; ☎416/392-5900, ⓦwww.torontozoo.com) encompasses a 710-acre site that does its best to place animals in their own environments. To this end, seven **pavilions** representing different geographic regions are filled with indigenous plants and more than five thousand animals. Hardy species live outside in large paddocks, and an open train, the **Zoomobile** ($5), zips around the vast site for those opposed to hiking between enclosures. In addition to grizzly bears, musk oxen, Siberian tigers and camels, a variety of wildlife – racoons, chipmunks and foxes – drop in from the woodland surrounding the zoo for frequent visits.

Some of the most popular attractions include the **Underwater Exhibits**, featuring South African fur seals, beavers and the ever-popular otters; and **Edge of Night**, an extension of the Australasian Pavilion, which simulates nighttime in the Australian outback. The zoo also has an extensive breeding, recovery and reintroduction programme, which has helped a variety of threatened species back into their indigenous environment. The Puerto Rican crested toad, the wood bison and the black-footed ferret are three such species. Conservation programmes apply as much to the local flora and fauna as to the exotic inhabitants of the zoo. On the flashier front, media relations go on overdrive when zoo babies are born, such as with the naming contest that greets every new arrival.

Arriving by **car**, take Hwy-401 to Scarborough (exit 389) and drive north on Meadowvale Road, following the signs for the zoo. Via **public transport** – which takes about fifty minutes from downtown – catch the Sheppard East #85B bus from the Sheppard subway station. **Eating** at the zoo is dominated by McDonald's, which has a monopoly on the hot food concessions. There are, however, pleasant picnic areas if you wish to bring your own lunch.

Scarborough Bluffs

When Elizabeth Simcoe, the wife of Upper Canada's first lieutenant-governor, sailed past these bluffs, she remarked how they reminded her of the Scarborough cliffs in England – and hence the most easterly part of Toronto got its name. The **Scarborough Bluffs** are indeed a beautiful and significant geological feature, and they have been preserved from rampant development by the Metropolitan Toronto and Region Conservation Authority, which has created three parks: **Bluffer's Park**, which features a public marina, **Scarborough Heights**, the smallest and least spectacular of the three, and **Cathedral Bluffs Park**, which has dramatic spires of eroded sandstone cliffs rising more than 90m above Lake Ontario. All are within a short walk of the Kingston Road (#12) bus stop on Kingston Road. For more information about these or any of Toronto's parks call ☎416/392-8186 or visit ⓦwww.city.toronto.on.ca/parks.

Guildwood Park

Another scenic stop along the bluffs is **Guildwood Park**, accessible either by turning south onto Guildwood Parkway from Kingston Road, or by taking the Morningside #116 bus, which departs from the Kennedy subway station and heads east into the park. The current park is on the grounds of a former estate. Although a succession of people have owned the property since the eighteenth century, its name and reputation were established in 1932, when Spencer and Rosa Clark decided to turn their 36-acre estate into a "Guild of all arts", and established a rent-free colony for artists and craftspeople. Guildwood became an infirmary for victims of battle fatigue during World War II and the artists' residence programme was permanently suspended – though the Ontario Crafts Council's Guild Shop on Cumberland Avenue in Yorkville (see p.70) continues as a legacy of the Clarks' vision. Another example of Rosa and Spencer's foresight was their collection of over seventy architectural ornaments from several of the historic Toronto buildings that were torn down to make way for the skyscrapers that dominate the skyline today. Huge keystones and fanciful patios, arches and doorways (minus their buildings) dot the Guildwood Park grounds. At the centre of the park, the Clarks' pseudo-Georgian house was, until recently, an inn and restaurant; today it awaits a new set of owners. Guildwood Park's stunning view of Lake Ontario amid the ecclectic, even surrealistic collection of architectural fragments makes it a popular spot for film shoots and photographers of all kinds. The gardens are laid out country-estate style, containing some interesting varieties, while the woods that surround Guildwood have a good cross-section of local flora.

Finally, tucked in behind the Guild Inn estate is an early nineteenth-century **log cabin**, similar in style to the late eighteenth-century homes built by Upper Canada's earliest settlers. The cabin and its site, which are part of an ongoing archeological excavation, are open to the public free of charge during the summer months.

North York

The suburb of **North York** finds itself on many itineraries because of the **Toronto Centre for the Arts** (see "Performing arts and film", p.158), which has hosted some of the city's biggest musicals and theatrical productions. The most popular attraction in North York, however, is the **Ontario Science Centre**, a sprawling testament to the notion that science and technology can be fun. To reach North York from downtown, take the Yonge subway line north to the North York Centre stop.

The Ontario Science Centre

The over eight hundred exhibits on science and technology at the **Ontario Science Centre**, 770 Don Mills Rd (daily 10am–5pm; $13, children ages 5–12 $7, students & seniors $9; ☎416/696-1000, ⊛ www.ontariosciencecentre.ca), are so captivating that visitors can forget they're in the midst of an educational experience. Although children are the primary audience, adults shouldn't deprive themselves of the pleasure of exploring interactive displays on subjects like genetics and electromagnetics. One of the most popular exhibits is **The Human Body**, where visitors can discern the inner workings of human biology through life-sized three-dimensional displays and various quizzes and games. There's also information on complex medical advances like bioengineering, DNA fingerprinting and immunology, all presented in an easily accessible format.

One of the biggest draws at the Science Centre is the **OMNIMAX Theatre** (call ☎416/696-1000 for show schedules). The 320-seat theatre features a 24-metre-high wraparound screen with digital sound that creates an enveloping cinematic experience. Admissions to the Omnimax shows are either separate from the general admission ($10 for adults) or can be combined with general admission, which costs $18 for adults, $10 for children ages 5–12, and $12 for students and seniors.

To reach the Science Centre by **car** from downtown Toronto, take the Don Valley Parkway and follow the signs from the Don Mills Road North exit. By **public transport**, take the Yonge Street subway line north to Eglington station and transfer to the Eglington East bus; get off at Don Mills Road. The trip should take about thirty minutes from the vicinity of downtown's Union Station.

Black Creek Pioneer Village

A distant second in popularity to the Ontario Science Centre, North York's **Black Creek Pioneer Village**, 100 Murry Ross Parkway (May–June Mon–Fri 9.30am–4pm, Sat & Sun 10am–5pm, July–Sept daily 10am–5pm, Oct–Dec Mon–Fri 9.30am–4pm, Sat & Sun 10am–4.30pm; $10, children ages 5–14 $6, students and seniors $9; ☎416/736-1733, ⓦwww.trca.on.ca/ parks_and_recreation), is nonetheless worth a visit. Like the Fort York "living history" site in Toronto proper (see p.39), Pioneer Village is staffed by guides dressed in period attire. Here visitors are immersed in a country village dating from the 1860s, and learn about the everyday activities of the early settlers. The site has over 35 authentically restored buildings, heritage gardens and a host of working pioneers: gunsmiths make muskets, smiths work the forge, and women perform various domestic chores like churning butter, carding and spinning wool, and weaving cloth. On the whole, the Village presents a pleasing but somewhat sentimentalized view of the past and pioneer self-sufficiency. In that sense, it has more to do with nostalgia than it does with history. The details are all there, but it lacks an authentic spirit.

Arriving by **car**, travel north on Hwy-400 and exit on Steels Avenue East. From here, turn west on Murray Ross Parkway, which is one block east of Jane Street, to find the Village's parking lot. Via **public transport** (about forty minutes from downtown), take the Yonge subway line to Finch station and board the Steels bus (#60 B, D or E).

Paramount Canada's Wonderland

Paramount Canada's Wonderland, Hwy-400, Rutherford exit (May–Oct, opening hours vary; one-day pass covering all rides $52, children ages 3–6 $26; ☎905/832-7000, ⓦwww.canadas-wonderland.com) is Toronto's de facto Disney World. A theme park featuring over fifty different rides, it is spread over a large chunk of land about 30km north of downtown in the suburb of **Vaughan**. Visiting the park is an all-day proposal: among the many attractions here are roller-coasters, a twenty-acre water park with sixteen water slides, souped-up go-karts, mini-golf and roaming cartoon and TV characters – everything from Fred Flintstone to *Star Trek*'s "Klingons". The roller-coaster rides are enough to make the strongest stomachs churn, if the kitsch of the place doesn't do it first. During the peak summer season, the "extreme" special events, such as stunt shows put together by Hollywood crews, are scheduled. By public transport, you can get here by catching the Wonderland Express GO bus from the Yorkdale or York Mills subway stations; buses leave every hour and take forty minutes.

McMichael Canadian Art Collection

Situated in the village of Kleinburg, the **McMichael Canadian Art Collection**, 10365 Islington Ave (daily May–Oct 10am–5pm, Nov–Apr Tues–Sat 10am–4pm, Sun 10am–5pm; $15; ℡905/893-1121 or 1-888/213-1121, ⊛www.mcmichael.com), is housed in a series of handsome log and stone buildings in the wooded Humber River valley. The collection was put together by Robert and Signe McMichael, devoted followers of the Group of Seven (see p.57), and given to the province in 1965.

On the collection's **Lower Level**, a series of small galleries focuses on various aspects of the Group of Seven's work. Gallery Two, for example, begins with the artistic friends and contemporaries who influenced the Group's early style, while Gallery Three zeroes in on the Group's spiritual founder, Tom Thomson, who died in a canoeing accident three years before the Group showed as a collective. The galleries boast fine paintings here by J.E.H. MacDonald, Lawren Harris, Edwin Holgate, F.H. Varley and L.L. Fitzgerald, as well as works by their talented contemporary Emily Carr. Other artists who later bcame associated with the Group of Seven, notably A.J. Casson, are also strongly represented.

The museum's **Upper Level** is devoted primarily to modern First Nations Art and Inuit soapstone carvings and lithographs. Rotating temporary exhibitions appear on the Upper Level as well. The variety of exhibits on this level have posed a thorny question for the Collection: namely, is the gallery's function to advance Canadian art, or is it to collect, present and conserve the works of the Group of Seven and their contemporaries? The latest round in this curatorial struggle goes to the Group, and it must be said that recent shows reinterpreting the works of their members and associates have been extraordinarily successful.

When you've finished with the paintings, allow a little time to stroll the footpaths that lattice the **woods** surrounding the McMichael. Maps are provided free at reception, and as you wander around you'll bump into various pieces of sculpture, as well as Tom Thomson's old wooden shack, moved here from Rosedale in 1962. For true Group of Seven devotees, the McMichael grounds also contain the graves of five Group members.

To get here by **driving** from downtown, take Hwy-401 to Hwy-400 north to Major Mackenzie Drive. Turn left (west) on Major Mackenzie Drive to Islington Avenue. Turn right (north) on Islington Avenue to the village of Kleinburg. **Public transport** requires a few transfers: from the Islington subways take the TTC Bus #37 north to Steels and Islington, then transfer to York Region bus #13, continuing up Islington to the McMichael Collection entrance. Alternatively, a taxi ride from Islington subway station is about $24.

High Park district

There have been Poles in Toronto since the middle of the nineteenth century, but the first major influx came in the 1890s when their homeland was wracked by famine. These early immigrants were reinforced on several subsequent occasions, most notably during and immediately after World War II, when the Germans and then the Russians occupied Poland, driving thousands into exile. In the 1950s, the Poles, along with other Slavic speakers from Eastern Europe, gravitated to the **High Park district** of Toronto, about 5km west of Yonge Street. It's not a particularly attractive neighbourhood, consisting for the most part of a low tangle of undistinguished brick buildings, but the long main street – **Roncesvalles Avenue** – is lined with Eastern European eateries and shops.

High Park

On Roncesvalles' western edge is the hilly expanse of **High Park**, a rectangle of greenery running north from the Gardiner Expressway to Bloor Street West. The park traces its origins to John George Howard, an Englishman who bought the land hereabouts shortly after his arrival in Toronto in 1832. The Howard family later bequeathed their estate to the city, but the old family home, **Colborne Lodge** (guided tours only; Tues–Fri noon–4pm, Sat–Sun noon–5pm; $3.50), has survived, tucked away among the wooded ravines on the southern edge of the park. The lodge looks pretty dreary from the outside, but the interior has been delightfully restored to its appearance in the middle of the nineteenth century. John Howard was a keen watercolourist, painting dozens of early Toronto scenes. A regularly rotated selection of his work is displayed at the lodge, and although he was hardly an outstanding artist, his watercolours are enjoyable, especially in the eccentric way he manages to squeeze a jubilant animal (or two) into each and every one of his paintings. John and his wife, Jemima Francis, were buried a short stroll north of the lodge beneath the large **stone cairn**.

The flatter, northern half of the park is prime picnic territory, with primly mown lawns and a scattering of sports facilities. The park's southwest corner boasts the charming **Hillside Gardens**, a manicured stretch that borders the wooded slopes above **Grenadier Pond**. The pond was supposedly named after the British grenadiers who paraded here on the winter ice, though there are more lurid theories: the most widely believed has a young skater spotting a grinning grenadier frozen under the ice. Unfortunately, the pond – really a mini-lake – is currently in a bit of a mess, its ecosystem unbalanced by a surfeit of saline stormwater from the drain runoffs of the surrounding neighbourhoods. Efforts to rectify matters by integrating water treatment facilities into the natural environment, and introducing controls to improve the quality of runoff, have had a noticable effect on the Pond's bass and pike population. Flora repopulation is taking a bit longer but appears to be progressing.

The north side of the park is a short walk from the High Park subway station; the south and east sections are readily reached on bus #80, which leaves Keele subway station and travels down the eastern edge of the park along Parkside Drive.

Day-trips

Without a doubt, the most popular day-trip destination from Toronto is **Niagara Falls**, a vast arc of water crashing over a 52-metre cliff and the most conspicuous feature of the Niagara River, which links lakes Ontario and Erie. One of the most celebrated sights in North America, the Falls are just 130km south of Toronto, along and around the heavily industrialized Lake Ontario shoreline. They adjoin the uninspiring **town of Niagara Falls**, which bills itself as the "Honeymoon Capital of the World" – and its hotels and motels have the heart-shaped double beds to prove it. Much more enticing, especially as a place to stay overnight, is the beguiling little town of **Niagara-on-the-Lake**, whose colonial villas abut Lake Ontario 26km downstream from the Falls. You should note that vacant rooms get very thin on the ground here in the high season, when you'd be well-advised to book in advance.

Less familiar to visitors is the **Lake Huron shoreline**, 210km west of Toronto across a thick band of fertile farmland. The lakeshore is dotted with pretty little country towns, especially **Goderich** and **Bayfield**. The first has a charming small-town air and one key sight, the intriguing **Huron Historic Gaol**, while the second possesses leafy streets flanked by elegant clapboard villas, a far cry from the fast-food joints and neon billboards that disfigure many Canadian towns.

A couple of hours north of Toronto by car, there's **Severn Sound**, the southeastern inlet of **Georgian Bay**, whose bare, glacier-shaved rocks, myriad lakes and spindly pines were immortalized by the Group of Seven painters. This is one of the most beautiful parts of southern Ontario, and although the region is dotted with country cottages, its pristine landscapes have been conserved in the **Georgian Bay Islands National Park**, accessible by water taxi from the tiny resort of **Honey Harbour**. Also on Severn Sound are the region's two outstanding historical reconstructions: the seventeenth-century Jesuit complex of **Sainte-Marie among the Hurons** and the British naval base at **Discovery Harbour**, founded outside Penetanguishene in 1817.

East from Toronto, it's a fast 260km along the Lake Ontario shoreline to **Kingston**, a handsome old town with a clutch of attractive colonial buildings and a genial lakeshore setting. Theatre enthusiasts might also be keen to visit the town of **Stratford**, which puts on North America's largest classical theatre festival every year, from May to November. For more details, see "Performing arts and film", p.156.

Buses and trains link Toronto with Niagara Falls and Kingston, but otherwise you'll be struggling to reach any of the other destinations mentioned above by **public transportation**; car rental is, however, reasonably priced – see p.195 for contact info.

Niagara Falls

In 1860, thousands watched as Charles Blondin walked a tightrope across
Niagara Falls. Midway, he paused to cook an omelette on a portable grill, and
then had a marksman shoot a hole through his hat from the *Maid of the Mist*
boat, fifty metres below. As attested by Blondin's antics, and by the millions of
waterlogged tourists who jam the tour boats and observation points, Niagara
Falls is a dramatic attraction. Still, the stupendous first impression doesn't last
long, and to prevent each year's crop of visitors from getting bored, the
Niagarans have created an infinite number of vantage points: you can ogle the
52-metre drop from boats, viewing towers, helicopters, cable cars and even
tunnels in the rock face behind the cascade. Of these options, the tunnels and
boats best capture the extraordinary force of the waterfall, a perpetual white-
crested thundering pile-up that had Austrian composer Gustav Mahler bawl-
ing "At last, fortissimo!" over the din.

Arrival, information and getting around

From Toronto's main bus terminal (see p.21), there are regular **Coach Canada
buses** (7 daily; 1hr 45min to 2hrs; ☎1-800/461-7661) to Niagara Falls; there
is also a less frequent **VIA train** service (2 daily; 2hrs; ☎1-888/842-7245)
from Toronto's Union Station (see p.21). The train trip is the more pleasant
journey of the two, though delays on the return leg – the train linking Niagara
with Toronto originates in New York City – can be a real pain. If you're travelling by **car**, a day is more than enough time to see the Falls and squeeze in
a visit to the delightful town of Niagara-on-the-Lake, just 26km downstream;
allow an hour and a half for the drive from Toronto to the Falls.

Trains to Niagara pull in at the **VIA train station**, on Bridge Street, in the
commercial heart of the town, about 3km north of the Falls. The **bus station**
is across the street, at 420 Bridge St at Erie Ave. Next door to the bus station,
Niagara Transit (☎905/356-1179) operates the **Falls Shuttle bus service**
(daily: May–Oct every 30min, Oct–April hourly; single ticket $3, all-day pass
$6), which runs across town, stopping – amongst many other places – at the
foot of Clifton Hill and beside the Skylon Tower. The Shuttle links with the
Niagara Parks' **People Mover** system (mid-May to Aug Mon–Fri 11am–8pm,
Sat & Sun 10am–9pm; Sept to mid-Oct daily 11am–6pm), whose buses travel
30km along the riverbank between Queenston Heights Park, north of the
Falls, and the Rapids' View car park to the south, pausing at all the major
attractions in between. People Movers appear at twenty-minute intervals and
an all-day pass costs $5.50. Car drivers should be aware that **parking** anywhere
near the Falls can be a major hassle in the summer; try to arrive before 10am,
when the tourists begin to arrive in force.

For **visitor information**, steer clear of the gaggle of privately run tourist
centres that dot the area, and head instead for the main **Niagara Parks information centre** (☎905/371-0254 or 1-877/NIA-PARK, ⓦwww.niagara-
parks.com) at the Table Rock complex beside the Falls. Here, from mid-May
to mid-October, you can purchase the **Niagara Falls Great Gorge
Adventure Pass**, a combined ticket covering four of the main attractions –
the Journey Behind the Falls, Maid of the Mist, White Water Boardwalk and
the Butterfly Conservatory; see below for info on these – plus all-day transportation on the People Mover system; it costs $32 for adults, or $19 for children ages 6–12.

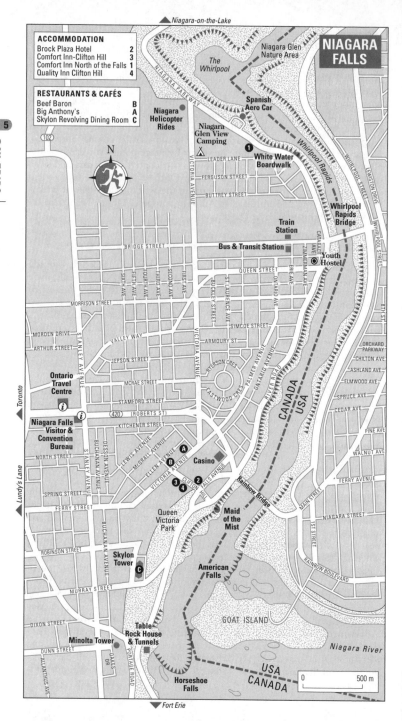

▲ Niagara-on-the-Lake

NIAGARA FALLS

ACCOMMODATION
Brock Plaza Hotel	2
Comfort Inn-Clifton Hill	3
Comfort Inn North of the Falls	1
Quality Inn Clifton Hill	4

RESTAURANTS & CAFÉS
Beef Baron	B
Big Anthony's	A
Skylon Revolving Dining Room	C

Niagara Glen
Nature Area

The Whirlpool

Spanish
Aero Car

Niagara
Helicopter
Rides

Niagara
Glen View
Camping

White Water
Boardwalk

NIAGARA PARKWAY

Whirlpool Rapids

LEADER LANE

VICTORIA AVENUE

FERGUSON STREET

BUTTREY STREET

N

Whirlpool
Rapids
Bridge

Train
Station

Bus & Transit Station

Youth
Hostel

QUEEN STREET

BRIDGE STREET

SIXTH AVE.
FIFTH AVE.
FOURTH AVE.
THIRD AVE.
SECOND AVE.
FIRST AVE.

BUCKLEY STREET
ST LAURENCE AVE.
ERIE AVE.
ONTARIO AVE.
ZIMMERMAN AVE.
CATARACT AVE.

MORRISON STREET

SIMCOE STREET

8TH ST.

MORDEN DRIVE

ARMOURY ST.

ORCHARD
PARKWAY

ARTHUR STREET

VALLEY WAY

JEPSON STREET

MCRAE STREET

STAMFORD STREET

CHILTON AVE.
ASHLAND AVE.
ELMWOOD AVE.
SPRUCE AVE.
CEDAR AVE.

RYERSON CRES.
EASTWOOD CRES.
PALMER AVENUE
RIVER ROAD
ONTARIO AVE.

Toronto ◀

Ontario
Travel
Centre
ⓘ

Niagara Falls
Visitor &
Convention
Bureau
ⓘ

STANLEY AVENUE

(420) (ROBERTS ST.)

KITCHENER STREET

PINE AVE.

WALNUT AVE.

NORTH STREET

LEWIS AVENUE
MCRAL AVENUE
VICTORIA AVENUE
CLIFTON HILL

BUCHANAN AVENUE
DESSON AVENUE

CASINO

Ⓐ
Ⓑ
Ⓒasino
❸ ❷
❹

Casino

FERRY AVENUE

NIAGARA STREET

Lundy's Lane ◀

SPRING STREET

FERRY STREET

CLIFTON HILL
FALLS AVENUE

Rainbow Bridge

MAIN STREET
1ST STREET

ROBINSON STREET

Queen
Victoria
Park

Maid
of the
Mist

RAINBOW BOULEVARD

Skylon
Tower
Ⓒ

American
Falls

MURRAY STREET

DIXON STREET

BUCHANAN AVENUE

GOAT ISLAND

Niagara River

Minolta Tower

Table
Rock House
& Tunnels

DUNN STREET

ALLANTHUS AVE.

OAKES DR.
PORTAGE ROAD

Horseshoe
Falls

USA
CANADA

CANADA
USA

0   500 m

CANADA
USA

94

▼ Fort Erie

Other places to pick up visitor information include the municipal **Niagara Falls Visitor and Convention Bureau**, just off Hwy-420 as you head into town from the QEW, at 5515 Stanley Ave (May–Aug daily 8am–8pm, Sept–April Mon–Fri 8am–6pm, Sat 10am–6pm & Sun 10am–4pm; ☎905/356-6061 or 1-800/563-2557, ⓦwww.niagarafallstourism.com), and the **Ontario Welcome Centre** (daily: generally at least 8.30am–5pm; ☎905/358-3221), which is well-stocked with literature on the whole of the province. The Welcome Centre is located beside Hwy-420 at the Stanley Avenue intersection.

5

Accommodation

For details on accommodation price codes – ❺, etc – see p.117.

Brock Plaza Hotel 5685 Falls Ave ☎905/374-4444 or 1-800/263-7135, ⓦwww.niagarafallshotels .com. Just metres from the foot of Clifton Hill, this is one of Niagara's older hotels, a tidy tower block whose upper storeys have splendid views over the American Falls. Marilyn Monroe stayed here in Room #801 while filming *Niagara*. ❺
Comfort Inn – Clifton Hill 4960 Clifton Hill ☎905/358-3293 or 1-800/801-8557, ⓦwww.comfortniagara.com. Nothing extraordinary perhaps, but this chain motel has entirely adequate rooms decorated in a brisk, modern style, and is handily located near the falls. ❺

Comfort Inn North of the Falls 4009 River Rd ☎905/357-3366 or 1-800/503-3666, ⓦwww .niagarafallscomfortinn.com. Similar to the *Comfort Inn* listed above, but with a more attractive location, flanked by parkland near the Spanish Aero Car (see p.96). ❻
Quality Inn – Clifton Hill 4946 Clifton Hill ☎905/358-3601 or 1-800/801-8557, ⓦwww.qualityniagara.com. Comfortable, pleasantly furnished motel-style rooms in a 300-room inn on its own grounds (or rather car park) on Clifton Hill. ❺

The falls

Though you can hear the growl of the **falls** miles away, nothing quite prepares you for your first glimpse of the fearsome white arc shrouded in clouds of dense spray, with riverboats struggling far below. There are actually two cataracts, as tiny Goat Island – which must be one of the wettest and bleakest places on earth – divides the accelerating water into two channels: on the American side, the river slips over the precipice of the **American Falls**, 320m wide but still only half the width of **Horseshoe Falls**, on the Canadian side. The spectacle is even more amazing in winter, when snow-covered trees edge a jagged armoury of freezing mist and heaped ice blocks. It may look like a scene of untrammelled nature, but it isn't. Since the early twentieth century, hydroelectric schemes have greatly reduced the water flow, and all sorts of tinkering has spread what's left of the Niagara River more evenly across the Fall's crest line. As a result, the process of erosion – which has moved the Falls some 11km upstream in twelve thousand years – has slowed from one metre a year to just 30cm. This obviously has advantages for the tourist industry, but the environmental consequences of harnessing the river in such a way are still unclear.

Beside Horseshoe Falls, **Table Rock House** has a small, free observation platform and elevators that travel to the base of the cliff, where **tunnels** (open daily from 9am to dusk; $7), grandly named the "**Journey Behind the Falls**", lead to points directly behind the waterfall. For a more panoramic view, a small **Incline Railway** ($1) takes visitors up the hill behind Table Rock House to the **Minolta Tower**, 6732 Oakes Drive (daily: June–Sept 9am to midnight, Oct–May 9am–11pm; $8), which has observation decks – though the views are better from the Skylon Tower (see below).

From Table Rock House, a wide and crowded path leads north along the cliffs, with the manicured lawns of Queen Victoria Park to the left and views of American Falls to the right. After a few minutes' march, turn left up Murray Street to the **Skylon Tower** (daily 8am to midnight; $5), whose observation deck is high above the Falls, or continue along the path to the foot of Clifton Hill, the main drag linking the riverside with the town of Niagara Falls. From the jetty below Clifton Hill, **Maid of the Mist boats** edge out into the river and push up towards the Falls, an exhilarating and extremely damp trip that no one should miss (daily: April to mid-June 9.45am–5.45pm, late June to July 9am–7.45pm, Aug 9am–7pm, Sept–Oct 9.45am–5pm; boats leave every 15mins in high season, otherwise every 30mins; $13, or $8 for children ages 6–12, including waterproofs).

Clifton Hill itself is a tawdry collection of fast-food joints and bizarre attractions like the eminently missable "Believe It or Not Museum", where, amongst other wonders, you can see a dog with human teeth and a Chinese chap with two pupils in each eye. If you stick to the river's edge, though, you can avoid both this unattractive side of Niagara and the area's second-biggest crowd-puller – the 24hr, bristlingly modern **casino**, near the Rainbow Bridge that connects to the United States.

Downstream from the falls

The **Niagara River Recreation Trail** is a combined bicycle and walking track that travels the entire length of the Niagara River from Lake Ontario to Lake Erie, running parallel to the main road, the **Niagara Parkway**. Downstream from the falls, the trail cuts across the foot of Clifton Hill (see above) before continuing north for a further 3km to the **White Water Boardwalk** (May–Oct daily dawn–dusk; $6.15). This comprises an elevator and then a tunnel leading to a boardwalk that overlooks the Whirlpool Rapids, where the river seethes and fizzes as it makes an abrupt turn to the east. From here, it's a further 1km to the brightly painted **Spanish Aero Car** (daily mid-June to Aug, 9 or 10am to dusk; $6; rest of year call ☏905/371-0254 for times), a cable-car ride across the gorge that's as close as you'll come to emulating Blondin's tightrope trick. Another 1.5km brings you to **Niagara Helicopter Rides**, 3731 Victoria Ave (☏905/357-5672, ⊛www.niagarahelicopters.com), which offers a twelve-minute excursion over the Falls for $100 per person, though costs can be reduced considerably if you are in a group. You don't need to book ahead, as the helicopters whiz in and out with unnerving frequency from 9am to sunset, weather permitting.

Pushing on, the trail soon reaches the **Niagara Glen Nature Area** (daily dawn to dusk; free), where paths lead down from the clifftop to the bottom of the gorge. It's a hot and sticky trek in the height of the summer, and strenuous at any time of the year, but rewarding for all that – here at least you get a sense of what the gorge was like before all the tourist hullabaloo. Nearby, about 800m further downstream, lie the spick-and-span **Niagara Parks Botanical Gardens** (daily dawn to dusk; free), whose splendid **Butterfly Conservatory** (daily: May–Sept 9am–9pm, Oct–April 9am–6pm; $8.50) attracts visitors in droves.

About 3km further on, **Queenston Heights Park** marks the original location of the Falls, before the force of the water – as it adjusts to the hundred-metre differential between the water levels of lakes Erie and Ontario – eroded the riverbed to its present point, 11km upstream. Soaring above the park, there's a grandiloquent **monument** to Sir Isaac Brock, the Guernsey-born general who was killed here in the War of 1812, leading a head-on charge against the Americans. From beside the park, the Niagara Parkway begins a curving descent down to the little village of **QUEENSTON**, whose importance as a transit centre disappeared when the Falls were bypassed by the Welland Canal, running west of the river between lakes Erie and Ontario and completed in 1829. In the village, on Partition Street, the **Laura Secord Homestead** (May–Aug daily 10am–5pm; $2.50) is a reconstruction of the simple timber-frame house of Massachusetts-born Laura Ingersoll Secord (1775–1868). Secord's dedication to the imperial interest was such that she ran 30km through the woods to warn the British army of a surprise attack planned by the Americans in the War of 1812.

Eating and drinking

Beef Baron 5019 Centre St. A ribs and steak joint that's always popular, despite being opposite a disturbing waxworks museum. Inexpensive.

Big Anthony's 5677 Victoria Ave ☎905/354-9844. Tasty, reasonably priced Italian food at this small, family-run place; it's owned by a well-known ex-professional wrestler, pictures of whom decorate the windows. Close to Clifton Hill.

Skylon Tower's Revolving Dining Room 5200 Robinson St ☎905/356-2651. This smart and fairly formal restaurant, 236m up the Skylon Tower, offers panoramic views over the falls and well-prepared traditional dishes – salmon, rack of lamb and so forth. It takes an hour to complete one revolution – a gentle, almost imperceptible ride.

Niagara-on-the-Lake

One of the prettiest places in Ontario, **NIAGARA-ON-THE-LAKE**, 26km downstream from the falls, boasts elegant clapboard houses and well-kept gardens, all spread along tree-lined streets. The town, much of which dates from the early nineteenth century, was originally known as Newark, and became the first capital of Upper Canada in 1792. Four years later it lost this distinction to York (Toronto) because it was deemed too close to the American frontier, and therefore vulnerable to attack. The US army did, in fact, cross the river in 1813, destroying the town, but it was quickly rebuilt and renamed. Even better, it has managed to avoid all but the most sympathetic of modifications ever since. The town attracts a few too many day-trippers for its own good, but the crowds are rarely oppressive, except on weekends in July and August. Niagara-on-the-Lake is also popular as the location of one of Canada's most acclaimed theatre festivals, the Shaw Festival, which celebrates the works of George Bernard Shaw with performances from April to late October; see p.157 for further details.

Arrival, information and getting around

At time of writing, there are no **public transport** links between Niagara Falls and Niagara-on-the-Lake – the shuttle bus that linked the two has been discontinued. It's possible that someone will pick up the service – Niagara Parks (ⓦwww.niagaraparks.com) for one – but in the meantime the best bet is **5-0 Taxis** (☎905/358-3232), who charge $10 for the one-way fare, or $15 return.

The Niagara-on-the-Lake **tourist office** is on the main drag at 26 Queen St, in the lower level of the Court House (daily: May to mid-Oct 10am–7.30pm; mid-Oct to April 10am–5pm; ☎905/468-1950, ⓦwww.niagaraonthelake.com).

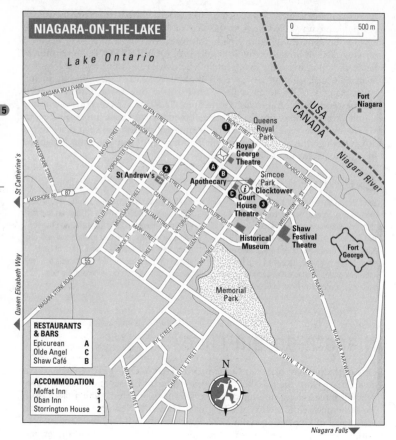

NIAGARA-ON-THE-LAKE

0   500 m

Lake Ontario

NIAGARA BOULEVARD

QUEEN STREET

JOHNSON STREET

NASSAU STREET

DORCHESTER STREET

SHAKESPEARE STREET

LAKESHORE RD   87

GAGE STREET

BUTLER STREET

MISSISSAGA STREET

CENTRE STREET

WILLIAM STREET

SIMCOE ST

MARY STREET

GATE STREET

REGENT STREET

VICTORIA STREET

KING STREET

CASTLEREAGH ST

55

NIAGARA STONE ROAD

PRIDEAUX ST

FRONT STREET

RICARDO STREET

PICTON ST

BYRON ST

DAVY ST

WELLINGTON ST

QUEENS PARADE

NIAGARA PARKWAY

JOHN STREET

RYE STREET

CHARLOTTE STREET

NIAGARA STREET

① Queens
Royal
Park

**Royal
George
Theatre**

② St Andrew's

Ⓐ Ⓑ
Ⓒ Apothecary

Simcoe
Park

ⓘ Clocktower

**Court
House ③**
Theatre

**Historical
Museum**

**Shaw
Festival
Theatre**

Fort
Niagara ■

USA
CANADA

Niagara River

Fort
George

Memorial
Park

N

**RESTAURANTS
& BARS**

Epicurean   **A**
Olde Angel   **C**
Shaw Café   **B**

ACCOMMODATION

Moffat Inn   **3**
Oban Inn   **1**
Storrington House   **2**

Niagara Falls ▼

They issue town maps and operate a free **room reservation service**, which can be a great help in the summer when the town's hotels and B&Bs – of which there are dozens – get very busy. Bed-and-breakfast rates range from $60 to $120.

It only takes a few minutes to stroll from one end of town to the other, but to venture further afield – especially to the falls – you might consider renting a **bicycle** from Zoom, 275 Mary St (☎905/468-2366).

Accommodation

For details on accommodation price codes – ❺, etc – see p.117.

Adam Lockhart's Storrington House 289 Simcoe St ☎905/468-8254, ⓦwww .storringtonhouse.com. Niagara-on-the-Lake boasts dozens of charming B&Bs, but this is one of the best, with each of the guest bedrooms of this 1817 house decked out in impeccable style. Breakfasts are a treat, too, and it's an easy stroll from here to the town centre. ❻

Moffat Inn 60 Picton St ☎905/468-4116, ⓦwww.moffatinn.com. This modest hotel is located in a modernized building close to the centre of town. The rooms are pleasant but undistinguished – which means that its prices are lower than most of its rivals and there is sometimes space here when everyone else is full. ❹

Oban Inn 160 Front St ☎ 905/468-2165 or 1-888/669 5566, ⊛ www.vintageinns.com. A delightful and luxurious hotel across from the lake and within easy walking distance of the town centre.

The original *Oban* burnt to the ground in 1992, but its replacement was built in true colonial style, with an elegant wooden veranda. The gardens are beautiful and the breakfasts are first-rate. ❼

The Town

It's the general flavour of Niagara-on-the-Lake that appeals rather than any specific sight, but **Queen Street**, the main drag, does hold the **Apothecary** (mid-May to Sept daily noon–6pm; free), which is worth a look for its beautifully carved walnut and butternut cabinets and porcelain jars. There is also the **Niagara Historical Museum**, at 43 Castlereagh St and Davy (daily: May–Oct 10am–5.30pm, Nov–April 1–5pm; $5), whose accumulated tackle tracks through the early history of the town and includes mementoes of the Laura Secord family (see p.97).

More diverting still is the British military post of **Fort George** (May–Oct daily 10am–5pm; $8), 700m southeast of town via Picton Street. In the early nineteenth century, so many of its soldiers were hightailing it off to the States that the British had to garrison the fort with the Royal Canadian Rifle Regiment, a troop of primarily married men approaching retirement who

Ontario wines

Until the 1980s **Canadian wine** was something of a joke. The industry's most popular product was a sticky, fizzy concoction called "Baby Duck," and other varieties were commonly called "block-and-tackle" wines, after a widely reported witticism of a member of the Ontario legislature: "If you drink a bottle and walk a block, you can tackle anyone." This state of affairs was, however, transformed by the **Vintners Quality Alliance** (VQA), who have, since 1989, come to exercise tight control over wine production in Ontario, which produces around eighty percent of Canadian wine. The VQA's appellation system distinguishes between – and supervises the quality control of – two broad types of wine. Those bottles carrying the Provincial Designation on their labels (ie Ontario) must be made from 100 percent Ontario-grown wines from an approved list of European varieties of grape and selected hybrids; those bearing the Geographic Designation (ie Niagara Peninsula, Pelee Island or Lake Erie North Shore), by comparison, can only use *Vitis vinifera*, the classic European grape varieties, such as Riesling, Chardonnay and Cabernet Sauvignon. As you might expect from a developing wine area, the results are rather inconsistent, but the **Rieslings** have a refreshingly crisp, almost tart flavour with a mellow, warming aftertaste – and are perhaps the best of the present range, white or red.

More than twenty **wineries** are clustered in the vicinity of Niagara-on-the-Lake, and most are very willing to show visitors around. Local tourist offices carry a full list with opening times, but one of the most interesting is **Inniskillin**, Line 3 (Service Road 66), just off the Niagara Parkway, about 5km south of Niagara-on-the-Lake (daily: May–Oct 10am–6pm, Nov–April 10am–5pm; ☎ 905/468-3554, ⊛ www.inniskillin.com). Here you can follow a twenty-step self-guided tour or take a free guided tour, sip away at the tasting bar and buy at the wine boutique. Inniskillin has produced a clutch of award-winning vintages and has played a leading role in the improvement of the industry. They are also one of the few Canadian wineries to produce **ice wine**, an outstanding sweet dessert wine made from grapes that are left on the vine till December or January, when they are hand-picked at night when frozen. The picking and the crushing of the frozen grapes is a time-consuming business and this is reflected in the price – about $50 per 375ml bottle.

were unlikely to forfeit their pensions by deserting. If they did try and were caught, they were branded on the chest with the letter "D" (for "Deserter"), and were either lashed or transported to a penal colony – except in wartime, when they were shot.

The fort was destroyed during the War of 1812, but today's site is a splendid reconstruction. The palisaded **compound** holds ten buildings, among them three pine blockhouses and the powder magazine, its inside finished in wood and copper to reduce the chances of an accidental explosion; as an added precaution, the soldiers working in here wore shoes with no metal fastenings. There are also lantern-light **ghost tours** of the fort – good fun with or without an apparition (May–June Sun at 8.30pm; July–Aug Mon, Wed, Thurs & Sun at 8.30pm; $10). Tours leave from the car park in front of the fort; tickets can be purchased either in advance at the fort's gift shop, or from the guide at the beginning of the tour.

Eating and drinking

By sheer weight of numbers, the day-trippers set the gastronomic tone here in Niagara-on-the-Lake, but one or two good **cafés** and **restaurants** have survived the deluge to offer tasty meals and snacks.

Epicurean 84 Queen St. Inexpensive but very competent café, featuring Mediterranean dishes. Vegetarian options offered most days. Inexpensive.

Olde Angel Inn 224 Regent St. With its low-beamed ceilings and flagstone floors, this is the town's most atmospheric pub, serving a first-rate range of draught beers. Also offers first-class and very affordable bar food – Guinness steak-and-kidney pies and so forth – and has a smart a la carte restaurant at the back. Just off Queen St.

Shaw Café and Wine Bar 92 Queen St at Victoria. This café-restaurant caters to theatre-goers rather than day-trippers. The decor is a tad overdone, but the pastas and salads are tasty and well prepared. Closes at 8pm.

Goderich and Bayfield

A popular summer resort area, the southern section of the **Lake Huron shoreline** is trimmed by sandy beaches and a steep bluff that's interrupted by the occasional river valley. The water here is much less polluted than Lake Ontario, the sunsets are beautiful, and in **Goderich** and neighbouring **Bayfield**, the lakeshore possesses two of the most appealing places in the whole of the province. It's about 210km – a good three hours by car – from Toronto, which makes a day-trip just about feasible, though it's better to stay the night – Bayfield has the choicer accommodation. There's no public transport to either destination.

Goderich

Perched on the edge of Lake Huron, **GODERICH** is a delightful country town of eight thousand inhabitants. It began life in 1825 when, amid rumours of bribery and corruption, the British-owned Canada Company bought two and a half million acres of fertile southern Ontario – the so-called Huron Tract – from the government for logging and then sold it off for settlement at the ridiculously low rate of twelve cents an acre. Today, the wide tree-lined avenues of Goderich radiate from a grand **octagonal circus**, which is dominated by a white stone courthouse. From here, the four main streets follow the points of the

△ Thrilling Niagara Falls, which straddles the Canadian / American border

compass, with North Street leading to the compendious **Huron County Museum** (May–Aug Mon–Sat 10am–4.30pm & Sun 1–4.30pm; Sept–April Mon–Fri 10am–4.30pm; $5, $7.50 with jail, see below), which concentrates on the exploits of the district's pioneers. Highlights include a fantastic array of farm implements, from simple hand tools to gigantic, clumsy machines like a steam-driven thresher. There's also a beautifully restored Canadian Pacific steam engine, as well as exhibition areas featuring furniture and military memorabilia.

From the County Museum, it's a ten-minute walk to the high stone walls of the **Huron County Gaol**, at 181 Victoria St (mid-May to early Sept daily 10am–4.30pm; $5): to get there, walk up to the far end of North Street, turn right along Gloucester Terrace and it's at the end of the street on the right. This joint courthouse and jail was constructed between 1839 and 1842, but the design was most unpopular with local judges, who felt threatened by the proximity of those they were sentencing. The other problem was the smell: several judges refused to conduct proceedings because of the terrible odour coming from the privies in the exercise yard below. In 1856, the administration gave in and built a new courthouse in the town centre. On a visit, don't miss the original **jailer's apartment** and a string of well-preserved **prison cells**, which reflect various changes in design between 1841 and 1972, when the prison was finally closed. The worst is the leg-iron cell for "troublesome" prisoners, where unfortunates were chained to the wall with neither bed nor blanket.

Back in the centre, West Street leads the 1km through a cutting in the bluffs to the harbour and salt workings on the Lake Huron shoreline. From here, a footpath trails north round the harbourside silos to the **Menesetung Bridge**, a former railway bridge that is now a pedestrian walkway spanning the Maitland River. On the north side of the river, you can pick up the **Maitland Trail**, which wanders down the north bank of the river as far as the marina. In the opposite direction, the shoreline has been tidied up to create a picnic area, and although the sunsets are spectacular the beach is a tad scrawny.

Accommodation and information

The Goderich **tourist office** (mid-May to Aug daily 9am–7pm, Sept–April Mon–Fri 9am–4.30pm; ☎519/524–6600, ⓦ www.town.goderich.on.ca) is at Nelson and Hamilton streets, beside Hwy-21, a couple of minutes' walk northeast of the central circus. They have details of the town's **bed-and-breakfasts**, which average about $65 for a double.

For details on accommodation price codes – ❺, etc – see p.117.

Bedford Hotel 92 The Square ☎519/524–7337, ⓦ www.hotelbedford.on.ca. Right on the central circus, this hotel is certainly distinctive. Built in 1896, the *Bedford* has a grandiose wooden staircase just like a saloon in a John Ford movie – though the unimaginatively modernized rooms at the top are something of a disappointment. Friendly and family-run. ❹

Colborne Bed & Breakfast 72 Colborne St ☎519/524–7400 or 1-800/390–4612, ⓦ www.colbornebandb.com. In a plain brick building dating from the early twentieth century, this bed-and-breakfast is a short walk from the central circus. There are four air-conditioned rooms with en-suite facilities available, and gourmet breakfasts are provided. ❹

Eating and drinking

Big Daddy's Pizza & Grill 42 West St ☎519/524–7777. Big pizzas and steaks served up in an inexpensive diner-cum-café.
Park House 168 West St. The liveliest bar in town, with views of the lake and filling pub food. Inexpensive.

Robindale's 80 Hamilton St ☎519/524–4171. Situated in a lavishly restored Victorian house across from the tourist office, this restaurant has an imaginative menu featuring tasty seafood. Moderate prices. Closed Mon.

Bayfield

Just 20km south of Goderich, pocket-sized **BAYFIELD** is a wealthy town with handsome timber villas, nestled beneath a canopy of ancient trees. The towns-folk have kept modern development at arm's length – there's barely a neon sign in sight, never mind a concrete apartment block – and almost every house has been beautifully maintained. Historical plaques give the low-down on the older buildings that line Bayfield's short **Main Street**, and pint-sized **Pioneer Park**, on the bluff overlooking the lake, is a fine spot to take in the sunset. Bayfield is mainly a place to relax and unwind, but you can also venture down to the harbour on the north side of the village, where, in season, you can pick wild mushrooms and fiddleheads along the banks of the Bayfield River.

Accommodation and information

The Bayfield **tourist office** (May–Sept daily 10am–6pm; ☏519/565-2499, ⓦ www.bayfieldchamberofcommerce.on.ca), in the village hall beside the green at the end of Main Street, will help you find **accommodation** – though their assistance is only necessary in July and August when vacancies are thin on the ground.

For details on accommodation price codes – ❻, etc – see p.117.

Albion Main St ☏519/565-2641, ⓦ www.albion-hotel.com. Bang in the middle of Bayfield, this old, pleasant inn has four en-suite bedrooms, the better of which overlook Main Street. ❻
Clair on the Square 12 The Square ☏519/565-2135, ⓦ www.claironthesquare.ca. Occupying a charming Victorian villa, this first-rate bed-and-breakfast is right in the town centre. It offers attractive, comfortable double rooms, all en suite. ❻

Little Inn of Bayfield 26 Main St ☏519/565-2611 or 1-800/565-1832, ⓦ www.littleinn.com. The best hotel for miles around, the *Little Inn* inhabits a tastefully modernized nineteenth-century timber-and-brick building with a lovely second-floor veranda and delightfully furnished rooms, most with whirlpool baths. A wonderful spot. ❼

Eating and drinking

Albion Hotel Main St ☏519/565-2641. A casual dining room offering tasty bar food and a good range of beers at reasonable prices. Attractive old premises, too.
Little Inn of Bayfield Main St ☏519/565-2611. A superb restaurant whose speciality is fresh fish from Lake Huron – perch, pickerel and steelhead.

Smart but informal, though expensive. The attached bar is similarly appealing.
Red Pump Main St ☏519/565-2576. Popular and polished restaurant in the heart of Bayfield. The seafood is especially good here. Closed Jan–March.

Severn Sound

Some 150km north of Toronto along Hwy-400, **Severn Sound** is one of the most beguiling parts of Ontario, its sheltered southern shore lined with tiny ports and its deep-blue waters studded by thousands of rocky little islands. There's enough here for several day-trips, beginning with two of the province's finest historical reconstructions, **Discovery Harbour**, a British naval base, and **Sainte-Marie among the Hurons**, a Jesuit mission. Be sure, also, to spare some time for the wonderful scenery of the **Georgian Bay Islands National Park**, whose glacier-smoothed rocks and wispy pines were so marvellously celebrated by the Group of Seven painters (see p.57).

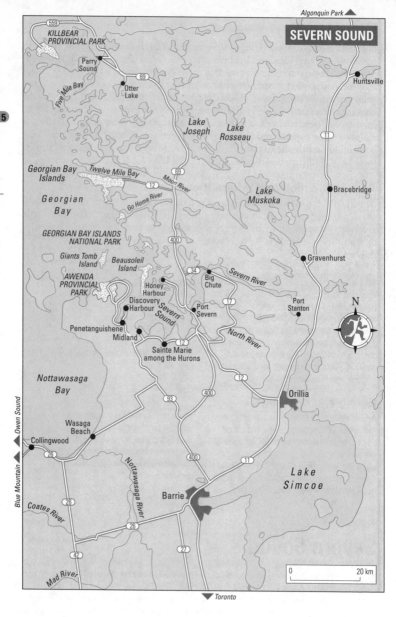

PMCL (☎1-800/461-1767, ©pmcl@greyhound.caa) runs three **buses** daily from Toronto to the regional towns of **Penetanguishene** and **Midland**. Beyond that, however, local bus services are very patchy, and your best bet is to rent a car in Toronto.

Penetanguishene

The westernmost town on Severn Sound is homely **Penetanguishene** ("place of the rolling white sands"), the site of one of Ontario's first European settlements, a Jesuit mission founded in 1639 then abandoned a decade later. Thereafter, in the eighteenth century, Europeans established a trading station here, but the settlement remained insignificant until the British built a naval dockyard following the War of 1812. This attracted both French- and English-speaking shopkeepers and suppliers, and even today Penetanguishene is one of the few places in southern Ontario to maintain a bilingual tradition.

The town's primary thoroughfare, **Main Street**, is a pleasant place for a stroll, its shops and cafés installed behind sturdy red-brick facades, which slope down towards the waterfront. Take a peek also at the **Centennial Museum**, 13 Burke St (May–Sept Mon–Sat 9am–4.30pm & Sun 12–4.30pm, Oct–April usually Mon–Fri 9am–4.30pm; $4.50), a couple of minutes' walk east of Main Street along the waterfront's Beck Boulevard. The museum occupies the old general store and offices of the Beck lumber company, whose yards once stretched right along the town's lakeshore. The company was founded in 1865 by Charles Beck, a German immigrant who made himself immensely unpopular by paying his men half their wages in tokens that were only redeemable at his stores. The museum has examples of these "Beck dollars" as well as a fascinating selection of old photographs featuring locals at work and play in the town and its forested surroundings.

From the jetty at the north end of Main Street, the MS *Georgian Queen* provides enjoyable, three-hour **cruises** of the **Thirty Thousand Islands**, the collective name for the myriad islands that confetti the southern reaches of Georgian Bay (mid-June to Aug 1–2 cruises daily; late May to early June plus Sept & early Oct occasional sailings; $20; ☎705/549-7795 or 1-800/363-7447, ⓦwww.georgianbaycruises.com). Advance reservations are advised at least a day ahead of time.

Arrival, information and getting around

Penetanguishene's tiny **bus depot** is at Main Street and Robert, a five- to ten-minute walk from the harbour, where the **tourist office** (Mon–Fri 9am–5pm, plus May–Sept Sat & Sun 9am–5pm; ☎705/549-2232) has details of local hotels and bed-and-breakfasts. **Union Taxi** (☎705/549-7666), next door to the bus station, will whisk you off to Discovery Harbour (see overleaf) and Sainte-Marie among the Hurons (see overleaf for both) if required.

Accommodation

For details on accommodation price codes – ❺, etc – see p.117.

Hillside Inn B&B 27 Church St ☎705/549-3508, ⓦwww.hillsideinn.ca. This good-looking old house with a wraparound veranda has four well-appointed guest rooms, decorated in fluffy, cosy style and with shared facilities. The house stands on a wooded ridge with views out across the bay, near the centre of Penetanguishene. ❸

No. 1 Jury Drive 1 Jury Drive ☎705/549-6851, ⓦwww.jurydrbb.huronia.com. This delightful bed-and-breakfast, in a leafy suburban setting at the entrance to Discovery Harbour (see below), occupies an immaculate modern house built in the style of a Victorian clapboard. Has five extremely comfortable, en-suite rooms and provides a fantastic breakfast – ask for the carrot muffins. Highly recommended. ❹

Eating and drinking

Arthur's 3 Beck Blvd. Not exactly haute cuisine, but this harbourside bar-cum-restaurant offers reasonably priced seafood dishes. Very popular with the locals.

Blue Sky Family Restaurant 48 Main St.
Agreeable small-town diner offering good-quality

snacks and meals at very affordable prices. Great
place for a gossip, too.

Discovery Harbour

Discovery Harbour (late May to June Mon–Fri 10am–5pm; July to early Sept daily 10am–5pm; $5.50; ☎705/549-8064, ⓦwww.discoveryharbour.on.ca), located about 5km north along the bay from Penetanguishene's town centre on Jury Drive, is an ambitious reconstruction of the British naval base that was established here in 1817. The purpose of the base was primarily to keep an eye on American movements on the Great Lakes, and between 1820 and 1834 up to twenty Royal Navy vessels were stationed here. **Lieutenant Henry Bayfield**, who undertook the monumental task of surveying and charting the Great Lakes, used the base as his winter quarters, informing his superiors of his determination "to render this work so correct that it shall not be easy to render it more so". He lived up to his word, and his charts remained in use for decades. The naval station, unfortunately, was more short-lived. By 1834, relations with the US were sufficiently cordial for the navy to withdraw, and the base was turned over to the army, who maintained a small garrison here until 1856.

Staffed by enthusiastic costumed guides, the sprawling site spreads along a hillside above a tranquil inlet, its green slopes scattered with accurate reconstructions of everything from a sailors' barracks to several period houses, the prettiest of which is the **Keating House**, named after the base's longest-serving adjutant, Frank Keating. Only one of the original buildings survives, the dour limestone **Officers' Quarters**, which dates from the 1840s, but the complex's pride and joy is the working harbour-cum-dockyard. Here, a brace of fully rigged **sailing ships**, the HMS *Bee* and HMS *Tecumseth*, have been rebuilt to their original nineteenth-century specifications. Both schooners take on volunteers as members of their crews and make occasional outings; for sailing times and prices, call ahead.

Sainte-Marie among the Hurons

One of Ontario's most arresting historical attractions is the reconstructed Jesuit mission of **Sainte-Marie among the Hurons** (late May to mid-Oct daily 10am–5pm; $9.75; ☎705/526-7838), which marks the site of a crucial episode in Canadian history. The mission is located 8km southeast of Penetanguishene off Hwy-12; there are no buses, but Penetanguishene's Union Taxi (☎705/549-7666) charges about $12 each way to make the trip.

In 1608, the French explorer **Samuel de Champlain** returned to Canada convinced that the only way to make the fur trade profitable was by developing partnerships with native hunters. Three years later, he formed an alliance with the **Huron** of southwest Ontario, cementing the agreement with a formal exchange of presents. However, his decision to champion one tribe against another – and particularly his gift of firearms to his new allies – disrupted the balance of power among the native societies of the St Lawrence and Great Lakes areas. Armed with Champlain's rifles, the Huron attacked their ancient enemies, the **Iroquois**, with gusto, inflicting heavy casualties; the Iroquois licked their wounds, determined to get even whenever they could. Meanwhile, in 1639, the **Jesuits** had established their centre of operations here at Sainte-Marie. They converted a substantial minority of the native people to Christianity, thereby undermining the social cohesion of the Huron – but much more importantly they had unwittingly infected and enfeebled the Huron with three European sicknesses: measles, smallpox and influenza.

In 1648 the Dutch, copying Champlain, began to sell the Iroquois firearms, and in March of the following year the Iroquois launched a full-scale invasion of Huron territory, or **Huronia**, slaughtering their enemies as they moved in on Sainte-Marie. Fearing for their lives, the Jesuits of Sainte-Marie burned their settlement and fled. Eight thousand Hurons went with them; most starved to death on Georgian Bay, but a few made it to Québec. During the campaign, two Jesuit priests, fathers **Brébeuf and Lalemant**, were captured at the outpost of Saint-Louis (near present-day Victoria Harbour), where they were bound to the stake and tortured – as per standard Iroquois practice. Despite the suffering brought upon the Hurons, it was the image of Catholic bravery and Iroquois cruelty that long lingered in the minds of French Canadians.

The Mission

A visit to Sainte-Marie starts in the impressive **reception centre**. An audio-visual show provides some background information, ending with the screen lifting dramatically away to reveal the painstakingly restored **Mission**. The twenty-odd wooden buildings are divided into two sections: the Jesuit area with its watchtowers, chapel, forge and farm buildings; and the native area, including a hospital and a pair of bark-covered long houses – one for Christian converts, the other for heathens. Relatively spick-and-span today, it takes some imagination to see the long houses as they appeared to Father Lalemant, who saw "a miniature picture of hell... on every side naked bodies, black and half-roasted, mingled pell-mell with the dogs... you will not reach the end of the cabin before you are completely befouled with soot, filth and dirt".

Costumed guides act out the parts of Hurons and Europeans with vim, answering questions and demonstrating crafts and skills, though they show a reluctance to eat the staple food of the region: *sagamite*, a porridge of cornmeal seasoned with rotten fish. The cemetery contains the remains of several Hurons who died here, and in the adjacent wooden church of St Joseph is the **grave** where the remains of Brébeuf and Lalemant were interred. At the end of the tour, a path leads from the site to the excellent **museum**, which traces the story of early Canada with maps and displays on such subjects as fishing and the fur trade.

Martyrs' Shrine

Overlooking Sainte-Marie from across Hwy-12, the twin-spired church of the **Martyrs' Shrine** (late May to mid-Oct daily 9am–9pm; $3) was built in 1926 to commemorate the eight Jesuits who were killed in Huronia between 1642 and 1649. Blessed by Pope John Paul II in 1984 – when he bafflingly remarked that it was "a symbol of unity of faith in a diversity of cultures" – the church is massively popular with pilgrims, who have left a stack of discarded crutches in the transept, in sight of the assorted reliquaries that claim to contain the body parts of the murdered priests. The most conspicuous reliquary is the alleged skull of Brébeuf, which is displayed in the glass cabinet near the transept door.

Georgian Bay Islands National Park

Georgian Bay Islands National Park consists of a scattering of about sixty islands spread between Severn Sound and Twelve Mile Bay, about 50km to the north. The park's two distinct landscapes – the glacier-scraped rock of the Canadian Shield and the hardwood forests and thicker soils of the south – meet at the northern end of the largest and most scenic island, **Beausoleil**. This beautiful island is a forty-minute boat ride west of **Honey Harbour**, the park's nearest port, which contains little more than a jetty, a couple of shops and a few self-contained hotel resorts.

Beausoleil has eleven short **hiking trails**, including two that start at the Cedar Spring landing stage on the southeastern shore: Treasure Trail (3.8km), which heads north behind the marshes along the edge of the island, and the Christian Trail (1.5km), which cuts through beech and maple stands to balsam and hemlock groves overlooking the rocky beaches of the western shoreline. At the northern end of Beausoleil, the Cambrian (2km) and Fairy trails (2.5km) are two delightful routes through harsher glacier-scraped scenery, while, just to the west, the Dossyonshing Trail (2.5km) tracks through a mixed area of wetland, forest and bare granite that covers the transitional zone between the two main landscapes.

Practicalities

Honey Harbour is around 170km north of Toronto – take Hwy-400 and watch for the turn-off onto Route 5 (Exit 156), just beyond Port Severn. There's no public transport, so having your own car is essential. The **national park office** in Honey Harbour (late June to early Sept Mon–Fri 8am–4.30pm, Sat 8am–4pm & Sun 8am to noon; ☎705/756-2415) provides a full range of information on walking trails and flora and fauna. Three Honey Harbour operators run **water taxis to Beausoleil**, with a one-way trip costing $35–40 in summer, a few dollars less in spring and fall. Of the three, Honey Harbour Boat Club (☎705/756-2411), about 700m beyond the park office, is probably your best bet. There are no set times, but in summer boats leave for Beausoleil quite frequently. Fares to several of the park's other islands are negotiable. In all cases, advance reservations are required, and you should be sure to agree on a pick-up time before you set out. With less time to spare, the national park's **Georgian Bay Islands Day Tripper boat** leaves from Honey Harbour three times daily from July to early September bound for Beausoleil, where passengers get four hours' hiking time. The round-trip fare is $15; further details can be had and reservations can be made at the national park office (☎705/756-2415). Prospective hikers and campers bound for the Georgian Bay Islands National Park need to come properly equipped – this is very much a wilderness environment. And whatever you do, don't forget the insect repellent.

If you decide to stay overnight, Beausoleil has eleven small **campsites**. The charge is $13 a night and all operate on a self-registration, first-come, first-served basis, with the exception of Cedar Spring ($17), where the Cedar Spring visitor centre near the main boat dock (☎705/756-5909) takes reservations for an additional $10. The campsites can get packed to the gills, so check availability before departure. Less arduously, Honey Harbour has one good **hotel**, the seasonal, lakeshore *Delawana Inn Resort* (☎705/756-2424 or 1-888/335-2926, ⓦwww.delawana.com; ❼), which has spacious chalet-cabins dotted round its extensive, pine-forested grounds (though note that the resort is geared up for family holidays rather than overnight travellers). Guests have use of the resort's canoes, kayaks and windsurfing equipment. A more economical option – and one where overnight stays are more usual – is *Rawley Lodge* (☎705/538-2272 or 1-800/263-7538, ⓦwww.rawleylodge.on.ca; ❹), a pleasantly old-fashioned, 1920s timber hotel located on the water's edge in the hamlet of **Port Severn**, some fifteen kilometres from Honey Harbour, just off Hwy-400 (Exit 153 or 156). **Restaurants** hereabouts are few and far between – the pick is *The Inn at Christie's Mill* (☎705/538-2354), at Port Severn, where the brisk modern and reasonably priced restaurant offers tasty steaks and seafood; reservations are advised.

Kingston

Birthplace of Bryan Adams but prouder of its handsome limestone buildings, the town of **KINGSTON**, a fairly quick 260km east of Toronto along Hwy-401, is the largest and most enticing of the communities along the northern shore of Lake Ontario. It occupies an attractive and strategically important position where the lake narrows into the St Lawrence River, its potential first recognized by the French who built a fortified fur-trading post here in 1673. It was not a success. The commander, the Comte de Frontenac, managed to argue with just about everybody, and his deputy, Denonville, pursued a risky side-line in kidnapping, inviting local Iroquois to the fort and then forcibly shipping them to France as curiosities.

The British succeeded the French in the middle of the eighteenth century, and shortly afterwards there was an influx of **United Empire Loyalists** – that is, those Americans who had no truck with their compatriots' struggle for independence against Britain. These Loyalists promptly developed Kingston into a major shipbuilding centre and naval base. In 1841, Kingston became the capital of Upper Canada, and although it lost this distinction just three years later it remained the region's most important town into the 1880s. In recent years, Kingston has had as many economic downs as ups, but it does benefit from the presence of **Queen's University**, one of Canada's most prestigious academic institutions, and of the **Royal Military College**, the country's answer to Sandhurst and West Point.

Kingston's attractions include a cluster of especially fine nineteenth-century limestone buildings – most notably **City Hall** and the **Cathedral of St George** – as well as the first-rate **Agnes Etherington Art Centre** gallery and **Bellevue House**, once the home of Prime Minister Sir John A. Macdonald. Add to this several delicious **B&Bs**, a cluster of good **restaurants** and scenic **boat trips** round the **Thousand Islands** just offshore, and you have a town that is well worth a visit.

Arrival and information

Trains from Toronto (4–6 daily; 2hrs 40mins) terminate at the **VIA Rail station** on Hwy-2, an inconvenient 7km northwest of the city at the junction of Princess and Counter streets; Kingston Transit bus #4 (Mon–Sat only; every 30mins) connects with downtown Kingston. The terminus for long-distance **Coach Canada buses** is on the corner of Division and Counter streets, about 6km to the north of the city centre; Kingston Transit bus #2 (Mon–Sat only; hourly) runs downtown from here. Kingston Transit's **local bus** information line is ☎613/546-0000.

Kingston's helpful **tourist office** is in the city centre, across from the waterfront at 209 Ontario St (☎613/548-4415 or 1-888/855-4555, ⊛www .kingstoncanada.com). They have a wide range of local and regional

---

Freshwater diving

In the 1950s, the creation of the St Lawrence Seaway regulated the depth of Lake Ontario and flooded its various rapids. Before then, the waters off Kingston had been extremely treacherous, and the bottom of the lake is still dotted with **shipwrecks**. The tourist office (see above) publishes an excellent booklet explaining what is where and several companies rent out **diving** gear and organize diving trips. One of them is Kingsdive Limited, 119 Princess St (☎613/542-2892).

information and operate a free room reservation service. Indeed, Kingston has an excellent range of accommodation, from hotels through to hostels, but it is mainly noted for its **B&Bs**, the pick of which occupy grand Victorian mansions; advance reservations are advised in the high season.

Accommodation

For details on accommodation price codes – ❺, etc – see p.117.

Alexander Henry Bed and Breakfast 55 Ontario St ☎613/542-2261, ⓦwww.marmuseum.ca. Kingston's most unusual lodgings are provided here in this former coastguard ice-breaker, moored downtown next to the Marine Museum. Berths vary from a bunk in a tiny cabin ($35 per person) to more comfortable quarters ($80–100 for a two-person cabin). The ship itself dates from the 1960s and is a sturdy affair with narrow stairways and corridors and the salty taste of the sea. Open mid-May to late Sept. ❸

Hochelaga Inn 24 Sydenham St ☎613/549-5534 or 1-800/267-0525, ⓦwww.someplacesdifferent .com. This twenty-room inn occupies a good-looking

Victorian mansion with a playful central tower, bay windows and wraparound veranda. There are 23 guestrooms, all en suite, and although the furnishings and fittings are rather pedestrian, each is very comfortable. In a residential area within easy walking distance of the centre. ❼

Rosemount B&B Inn 46 Sydenham St ☎613/531-8844 or 1-888/871-8844, ⓦwww.rosemountinn.com. An eminently appealing B&B in a strikingly handsome, distinctively Italianate old limestone villa – arguably Kingston's finest. The *Rosemount* has nine guestrooms, all en suite, decorated in period style. The breakfasts are delicious. ❻

The City

The obvious place to start a visit is **City Hall** (free guided tours late May to Oct Mon–Fri 10am–4pm, plus Sat & Sun in July & Aug 11am–3pm; 30mins), a copper-domed, stone extravagance which, with its imposing Neoclassical columns and portico, dominates the waterfront as was intended, a suitably grand structure for what was scheduled to be the Canadian Parliament. By the time the building was completed in 1844, however, Kingston had lost its capital status and – faced with colossal bills – the city council had to make some quick adjustments, filling the empty corridors with shops and stalls and even a saloon. Things are more sedate today, with municipal offices occupying most of the space, but the tour provides a fascinating insight into the development of the city and includes a trip up the **clock tower** via a magnificent circular stairway.

Back outside, the **Market Square**, at the back of City Hall, is home to an excellent open-air **farmers' market** on Tuesdays, Thursdays and Saturdays, while on Sundays the square is given over to craft and antiques stalls. Opposite, the site of the original French outpost is marked by the waterfront **Confederation Park**, whose manicured lawns run behind the harbour with its marina and squat, nineteenth-century Martello tower (see Murney Tower below). From the dock at the foot of Brock Street, there are regular **cruises of the Thousand Islands**, which litter the St Lawrence River as it leaves Lake Ontario and range from tiny hunks of rock to much larger islands with thick forest and lavish second homes. It's a pretty cruise at any time of the year, but especially so in autumn when the leaves turn. Several companies offer cruises, but the benchmark is set by **Kingston 1000 Islands Cruises** (☎613/549-5544, ⓦwww.1000islandscruises.ca), whose bread-and-butter, three-hour cruises in a replica steamboat, the *Island Queen*, are as good as any (mid-May to mid-Oct 1–2 daily; $22.50).

The Cathedral of St George

Back on dry land, it's a couple of minutes' walk from Confederation Park to Kingston's finest limestone building, the **Anglican Cathedral of St George**,

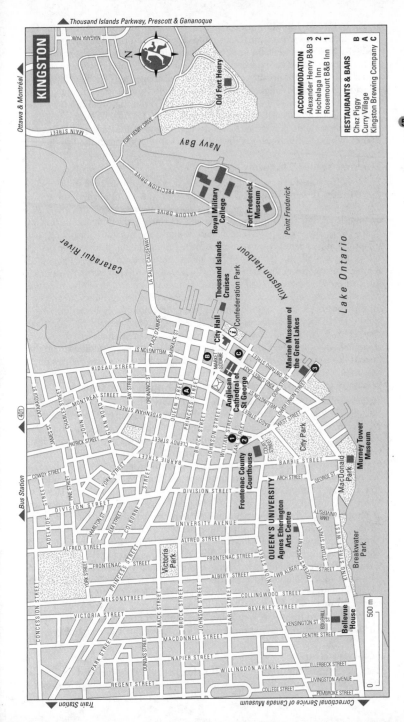

Thousand Islands Parkway, Prescott & Gananoque

KINGSTON

Ottawa & Montréal

MAIN STREET

NIAGARA PARK

Old Fort Henry

N

FORT HENRY DRIVE

Navy Bay

PRECISION DRIVE

Royal Military College

VALDOUR DRIVE

Fort Frederick Museum

Point Frederick

Cataraqui River

LA SALLE CAUSEWAY

Thousand Islands Cruises

City Hall

Confederation Park

Kingston Harbour

Marine Museum of the Great Lakes

Lake Ontario

PLACE D'ARMES

WELLINGTON ST

BARRACK ST

RIDEAU STREET

BAY STREET

ORDNANCE ST

Market Square

Anglican Cathedral of St George

B

C

KING STREET EAST

ONTARIO STREET

WELLINGTON ST

GORE ST

LOWER UNION STREET

WEST STREET

3

CATARAQUI STREET

MONTREAL STREET

CHARLES STREET

JOHN STREET

RAGLAN ROAD

SYDENHAM STREET

QUEEN STREET

PRINCESS STREET

BROCK STREET

JOHNSON STREET

WILLIAM STREET

CLERGY STREET

EARL STREET

BAGOT STREET

A

1

2

Frontenac County Courthouse

COURT STREET

City Park

JAMES STREET

PATRICK STREET

BARRIE STREET

CLERGY STREET

BARRIE STREET

ARCH STREET

GEORGE ST

MacDonald Park

Murney Tower Museum

401

COWDY STREET

PINE STREET

YORK STREET

DIVISION STREET

DIVISION STREET

UNIVERSITY AVENUE

ALFRED STREET

QUEEN'S UNIVERSITY

Agnes Etherington Arts Centre

LWR UNIVERSITY

STUART STREET

Breakwater Park

Bus Station

ADELAIDE STREET

HAMILTON ST

ELM STREET

COLBORNE STREET

ALFRED STREET

FRONTENAC STREET

ALBERT STREET

LWR ALBERT ST

COLLINGWOOD STREET

BEVERLEY STREET

KING STREET WEST

QUEEN'S CRESCENT

UNION STREET

KING STREET WEST

CONCESSION STREET

PRINCESS STREET

MACK STREET

BROCK STREET

JOHNSON STREET

EARL STREET

VICTORIA STREET

NELSON STREET

Victoria Park

VICTORIA STREET

MACDONNELL STREET

NAPIER STREET

WILLINGDON AVENUE

KENSINGTON ST

EDGEHILL ST

CENTRE STREET

Bellevue House

PARK STREET

DUNDAS STREET

REGENT STREET

ELLERBECK STREET

LIVINGSTON AVENUE

COLLEGE STREET

PEMBROKE STREET

Train Station

Correctional Service of Canada Museum

0   500 m

111

at King St and Johnson (mid-April to Sept Mon–Thurs 10am–4pm, Fri 10am–7pm & Sat 10am–1pm; Oct to mid-April Mon–Fri 1–4pm; free). Dating from the 1820s, the graceful lines of the cathedral, with its Neoclassical portico and dainty domes, are deceptively uniform, for the church was remodelled on several occasions, notably after severe fire damage in 1899. The capacious interior holds some delightful Tiffany stained-glass windows and, attached to the wall of the nave, a plain **memorial** to Molly Brant (1736–1797), a Mohawk leader and sister of Joseph Brant (see p.51).

From the cathedral, it's a brief stroll to the main commercial drag, **Princess Street**, whose assorted shops, offices and cafés stretch up from the lakeshore.

Murney Tower Museum

From the corner of Princess and King streets, it's a good ten-minute stroll west to the **Murney Tower Museum**, on Barrie St (mid-May to Aug daily 10am–5pm; $2). The most impressive of four such towers built in Kingston to defend the dockyards against an anticipated US attack, during the Oregon Crisis of 1846–1847, this one holds incidental military memorabilia including old weapons, uniforms and re-created nineteenth-century living quarters. The design of the tower, built as a combined barracks, battery and storehouse, was copied from a Corsican tower (at Martello Point) which had proved particularly troublesome to the British navy. A self-contained, semi-self-sufficient defensive structure with thick walls and a protected entrance, the Martello design proved so successful that towers like this were built throughout the empire, only becoming obsolete in the 1870s with advances in artillery technology. Incidentally, on Christmas Day 1885, members of the Royal Canadian Rifles regiment left the tower equipped with their **field hockey sticks** and a lacrosse ball, skidding round the frozen lake and thereby inventing the sport that has become a national passion.

West of the Centre: the Agnes Etherington Art Centre

Striking inland up Barrie Street, with City Park on the right, it's a ten-minute walk to the top of the park, where the **Frontenac County Courthouse** of 1858 is another grand limestone pile whose whopping Neoclassical portico is fronted by a fanciful water fountain and surmounted by a copper dome. Head west from here, along Union Street, and you'll soon be in the midst of the **Queen's University** campus, whose various sturdy stone college buildings fan out in all directions. The place to aim for is the first-rate **Agnes Etherington Art Centre**, on the corner of University Ave and Queen's Crescent (Tues–Fri 10am–4.30pm, Sat & Sun 1–5pm; $4). The gallery has an excellent reputation for its temporary exhibitions, so paintings are regularly rotated, but the first room (Room 1) usually kicks off in dramatic style with a vivid selection of Canadian Abstract paintings (1940–1960), with French-speaking artists on one side and English-speaking artists on the other. Beyond, there is a strong showing for the **Group of Seven**, including a striking *Evening Solitude* by **Lawren Harris** and the carpet-like, rolling fields of **Lismer**'s *Quebec Village*, while **Tom Thomson** weighs in with his studied *Autumn, Algonquin Park*. Other exhibits to look out for are the **Inuit** prints of Kenojuak and Pitseolak – two of the best-known Inuit artists of modern times – as well as heritage **quilts** from eastern Ontario, which date back to 1820, and an excellent collection of West African sculpture.

Bellevue House

Born in Glasgow, **Sir John A. Macdonald** (1815–1891) emigrated to Canada in his youth, settling in Kingston, where he became a successful corporate

Algonquin Park

Algonquin Provincial Park (⊛ www.algonquinpark.on.ca) is a giant slab of untamed wilderness boasting dense hardwood and pine forests, canyons, rapids, scores of lakes and, amongst a rich wildlife, loons, beavers, moose, timber wolves and black bears. The nearest entrance is a slowish 260km north of Toronto, too far for a day-trip, but worth considering for a longer excursion. To get there, make your way to Huntsville on Hwy-11 and then continue 45km along Hwy-60 to the park's west gate, where there is a visitor centre (☎705/633-5572). Canoeing and hiking are the big deals here, and several Toronto companies offer all-inclusive wilderness packages, including meals, permits, guides, equipment and transport to and from Toronto. The pick of the bunch is **Call of the Wild**, 23 Edward St, Markham, Ontario (☎905/471-9453 or 1-800/776-9453, ⊛ www.callofthewild.ca), which runs a varied programme that includes three-day ($345) and five-day ($545) canoeing trips deep into the park.

lawyer, an MP – representing the town for well-nigh forty years – and ultimately prime minister (1867–1873 and 1887–1891). A shrewd and forceful man, Macdonald played a leading role in Canada's Confederation, with a little arm-twisting here and a little charming there, to ensure the grand plan went through.

In the 1840s, Macdonald rented **Bellevue House** (daily: April–May & Sept 10am–5pm; June–Aug 9am–6pm; $3.50), a bizarrely asymmetrical, pagoda-shaped building located about 2km to the west of the city centre, beyond the university campus, at 35 Centre Street. The idea was that the country air would improve the health of Macdonald's wife, Isabella, whose tuberculosis was made worse by the treatment – laudanum. Isabella never returned to good health and died after years as an invalid, leaving Macdonald alone (with the bottle). Both the house and gardens have been restored to the period of the late 1840s, when the Macdonalds lived here.

Eating and drinking

Chez Piggy 68 Princess St at King St E ☎613/549-7673. Kingston's best-known restaurant is housed in restored stables dating from 1810. The patio is packed in summer and the attractive interior has handcrafted pine and limestone walls. The wide-ranging menu features all manner of main courses, from Thai and Vietnamese through to South American and standard North American dishes. Probably the best

place in town; main courses average around $19.
Curry Village 169A Princess St ☎613/542-5010. Popular, reasonably priced Indian restaurant above a shoe shop. Just north of Bagot St. Reservations recommended.
Kingston Brewing Company 34 Clarence St. The best pub in town, serving natural ales and lagers brewed on the premises, as well as tasty bar food. Outside patio area, too.

Listings

Listings

Accommodation

A s Toronto's popularity as a travel destination has increased, the availability of hotel **accommodation**, especially in the mid-price range, has shrunk. During peak season (late June–Aug), and especially around popular summer events like Gay Pride (see p.190), it is essential to book well in advance. Prices tend to fluctuate depending on when and for how long you stay, but in general, a clean, centrally located hotel room starts at $80–100; the best places are pretty much all in Downtown. **Bed-and-breakfast** accommodations tend to be slightly cheaper – even with breakfast thrown in. Although many B&Bs are not as central as the city's hotels, they take you off the beaten path and into some of Toronto's quaint, leafy neighbourhoods. Budget-conscious travellers might want to consider Toronto's **hostels**, but the best deal in town is the **summer residences** at local universities. You'll get bare essentials here, but the rooms are much cheerier than the hostels, and prices start at about $40.

Maps, with all the accommodations below keyed to them, can be found in the main part of the Guide: see p.36 for Downtown, p.62 for Uptown, p.76 for the waterfront, and p.84 for the suburbs.

Hotels

Downtown is the epicentre of Toronto's **hotel** scene – outside the downtown core the range is almost entirely dictated by bland chains. Any downtown hotel will be sufficiently close to all the main attractions and easily accessible by public transport. The bread and butter of most Toronto hotels is a constant stream of business travellers, but some (like the *Delta Chelsea* in particular; see below) offer special features and packages geared toward families.

Accommodation price codes

The price codes given in the reviews below reflect the price of the least expensive double room throughout most of the year, excluding room taxes. There is a seven percent federal Goods and Service Tax (GST) and a Provincial Sales Tax (PST) of five percent on all accommodations.

❶ Under $40	❹ $80–100	❼ $175–240
❷ $40–60	❺ $100–125	❽ Over $240
❸ $60–80	❻ $125–175	

Bond Place 65 Dundas St W ☎416/362-6061 or 1-800/268-9390, ⓦwww.bondplacehoteltoronto .com. Subway: Dundas. A favourite of the tourist-bus crowds, this establishment is just steps away from the Eaton Centre (see p.52) and Dundas Square, with all modern conveniences and reasonable rates. ❹

Cambridge Suites Hotel 15 Richmond St E ☎416/368-1990 or 1-800/463-1990, ⓦwww.cambridgesuiteshotel.com. Subway: Queen. A good option if you want to stay in the heart of downtown Toronto in comfort and style, with plenty of privacy. Caters mainly to a business clientele (and the odd movie star), the hotel is close to theatres, shops and excellent restaurants. ❻

Crowne Plaza Toronto 225 Front St W ☎416/422-7969, ⓦwww.torontocentre .crowneplaza.com. Subway: Union Station. A short walk from the Metro Toronto Convention Centre as well as the CN Tower, SkyDome and the Financial District, this relatively glitzy hotel is an obvious choice for business travellers as well as families. The well-equipped air-conditioned rooms include mini bars, dataports, coffeemakers and hairdryers. Close to the King West theatres and restaurants. ❼

Delta Chelsea Inn 33 Gerrard St W ☎416/595-1975, ⓦwww.deltachelsea.com. Subway: Dundas. A huge establishment replete with bars, restaurants and facilities like day care and play centres for families with young children. The rooms are comfortable and well appointed, and the location very central. ❻

Fairmont Royal York 100 Front St W ☎416/368-2511 or 1-800/441-1414, ⓦwww .fairmont.com. Subway: Union Station. As huge, overstuffed and comfortable as your grandfather's favourite armchair, the *Royal York* offers luxury-level services for less than you'd expect. The lobby is a sight in itself, with its mosaic floors, coffered ceilings and massive chandeliers. Dependable quality, unflappable staff and a central location have kept this a favourite for generations. ❻

Grand Hotel & Suites Toronto 225 Jarvis St, ☎416/863-9000, ⓦwww.grandhoteltoronto.com. Streetcar: Dundas (#505). The neighbourhood, in the beginning stages of gentrification, is a tad funky but the *Grand* is a beautiful, full-service surprise, complete with a rooftop Jacuzzi and cathedral-windowed suites on the third floor. All rooms have kitchenettes and sofa beds. ❼

Hilton Toronto 145 Richmond St W ☎416/ 869-3456, ⓦwww.hilton.com. Streetcar: Queen (#501). A massive refurbishment spruced up this full-service, downtown property, giving it the stylistic cachet one would expect of a hotel on the edge of the Queen Street West neighbourhood. ❼

Holiday Inn on King 370 King St W ☎416/599-4000 or 1-800/263-6364, ⓦwww.hiok.com. Streetcar: King St (#504). Especially popular with business travellers, this large hotel is close to theatres, the SkyDome, Roy Thompson Hall and many fine restaurants and nightclubs. ❼

Hotel Le Germain 30 Mercer St ☎416/ 345-9500 or 1-866/7345-9501, ⓦwww.hotelgermain .com. Streetcar: King St (#504). Spanking new from the ground up, this stylish boutique hotel offers well-appointed rooms done in minimal modernist style, and the attractive staff strives to be helpful. ❻

Hotel Victoria 56 Yonge St ☎416/363-1666 or 1-800/363-8228, ⓦwww.hotelvictoria-toronto .com. Subway: King. A charming boutique hotel, located in the heart of downtown, with 48 recently refurbished rooms. Complimentary continental breakfast is served daily, and service is excellent. ❻

Le Royal Meridian King Edward 37 King St E ☎416/863-3131 or 1-800/543-4300, ⓦwww .lemeridien-kingedward.com. Subway: King. This dowager of a hotel was designed by E.J. Lennox (see p.49) in 1903 and its famous guests have included everyone from Mark Twain to John and Yoko. A recent facelift has restored the Beaux Arts opulence of its exterior and main floor while an ongoing room renovation gives guests the choice of chic minimalist and Edwardian-inspired decors. ❼

Metropolitan 108 Chestnut St ☎416/599-0555 or 1-800/668-6600, ⓦwww.metropolitan.com. Subway: St Patrick. This small, handsomely decorated hotel is located right behind the new City Hall, and is perfectly located for a visit to the nearby Art Gallery of Ontario (see pp.55–58). ❼

Novotel Toronto Centre 45 The Esplanade ☎416/367-8900 or 1-800/668-6835, ⓦwww .novotel.com. Subway: Union Station. Part of a Swiss chain, this hotel offers excellent service at moderate prices. Its affordability may be linked to its noisy location: the hotel abuts the busiest stretch of railway in

Canada. Otherwise, the location on the Esplanade is excellent, close to a number of shopping districts, theatres, restaurants and bars, as well as the Harbourfront (see p.75) and the stunning Distillery District (see p.49). ❺

Quality Hotel Downtown 111 Lombard St ☎416/367-5555, ⓦwww.toronto.com /qualityhoteldowntown. Streetcar: King St (#504). Clean and affordable, this place is located on a quiet street in an older part of town, and is a ten-minute walk from downtown. Book early; this is a favourite among travellers looking for good value. ❻

Renaissance (SkyDome) Hotel 1 Blue Jays Way ☎416/341-7100 or 1-800/228-9290, ⓦwww.renaissancehotels.com. Subway: Union Station. This hotel's claim to fame is its location – overlooking the SkyDome field. The CN Tower is also right next door, and the Harbourfront and the King West theatre district are close by. ❼

Sheraton Centre Toronto 123 Queen St W ☎416/361-1000 or 1-800/325-3535, ⓦwww .sheratontoronto.com. Subway: Queen. Behind the bland exterior, the snazzy insides of this hotel feature a waterfall and islands of soft leather couches scattered throughout the lobby. The *Sheraton* is connected to the Underground City (see p.173), and is a short walk from the clubs, restaurants and shops on the Queen West strip, as well as the Eaton Centre and Dundas Square. ❻

SoHo Metropolitan 318 Wellington St W. ☎416/977-5000 or 1-800/668-6600, ⓦwww .metropolitan.com/soho. Streetcar: King St (#504). A chic, high-end boutique hotel, located close to the hive of restaurants, bars, clubs and theatres between Queen West and King West. The hotel occupies three floors, while the rest are taken up by condominiums. ❽

Strathcona 60 York St ☎416/363-3321 or 1-800/268-8304, ⓦwww.toronto.com /strathconahotel. Subway: Union Station. A good bet for the business traveller, with all the standard amenities. Except for the location – about half a block from Union Station, and five minutes from the SkyDome and the CN Tower – it's nothing to write home about, though. ❺

Toronto Marriott Eaton Centre 525 Bay St ☎416/597-9200 or 1-800/228-9290, ⓦwww .marriott.com. Subway: Dundas. If staying in Eighties-style glitz next door to one of the largest malls in North America (Eaton

Centre; see p.52) is your idea of heaven, search no further. Part of the Marriott chain, the hotel's best feature is the attentive staff. ❻

Travelodge Toronto Downtown West 621 King St W ☎416/504-7441 or 1-800/578-7878, ⓦwww.TravelodgeTorontoDowntown.com. Streetcar: King St (#504). Once a quirky alternative to Downtown's mainstay hotels, the refurbished *Executive* became a *Travelodge* and all the retro-hip cachet went out the window. On the plus side the neighbourhood has perked up considerably and is filled with good bars and clubs. ❹

Uptown

Best Western Primrose 111 Carlton St ☎416/977-8000 or 1-800/268-8082, ⓦwww .torontoprimrosehotel.com. Subway: College. A ten-minute walk from Downtown, this place has all the basic amenities you'd expect from a large chain hotel, including an outdoor pool. ❺

Comfort Hotel Downtown Toronto 15 Charles St E ☎416/924-1222 or 1-800/221-2222, ⓔcomfort@nhgi.com. Subway: Wellesley. One of the better budget hotel chains, the *Comfort Hotel* is centrally located on a leafy side street, close to the bustling intersection of Yonge Street and Bloor West. ❹

Courtyard Downtown Toronto 475 Yonge St ☎416/924-0611 or 1-800/847-5075. Subway: Carlton. Clean, affordable and comfortable option without lots of frills but all the necessary conveniences. Close to the Gay Village restaurants, shops, cinemas and all-night action of the Yonge Street strip. ❻

Days Inn Toronto Downtown 30 Carlton St ☎416/977-6655 or 1-800/DAYS-INN, ⓦwww .daysinn.com. Subway: College. Located just up the block from Maple Leaf Gardens, the former home of the Toronto Maple Leafs hockey team (see "Sports and outdoor activities", p.178), and a good bet if you want to be near the Gay Village (see "Gay Toronto", p.163). This chain offers all the basic amenities and a convenient location, with all-night eateries and a multiplex cinema just steps away. ❺

Four Seasons 21 Avenue Rd ☎416/964-0411 or 1-800/332-3442, ⓦwww.fourseasons.com. Subway: Bay. This well-appointed establishment, situated in the heart of the costly Yorkville neighbourhood, has a reputation for hosting the city's most famous guests. The hotel's restaurants and wine cellar are as stellar as the impeccable service, and while the prices here are off the charts, this is a fine place to be if you want to splurge. **❻**

Howard Johnson Selby Hotel and Suites 592 Sherbourne St ☎ 416/921-3142 or 1-800/387-4788, 🌐 www.toronto.com/selby. Subway: **Sherbourne.** A friendly, budget chain hotel located inside what was once a Victorian mansion, its beautiful exterior now sensitively restored. Close to the Danforth strip and Greektown, and major shopping areas. **❻**

Howard Johnson Yorkville 89 Avenue Rd ☎ 416/964-1220 or 1-877/967-5845, 🌐 www .hojo.com. Subway: **Bay.** This small, budget-friendly hotel is tucked away in a busy section of Avenue Road, just blocks from the luxury *Four Seasons Hotel* and Yorkville and Annex neighbourhoods. The helpful staff is attentive, and the large rooms are tidy, comfortable and equipped for the business traveller. **❹**

InterContinental Toronto 220 Bloor St W ☎ 416/960-5200 or 1-800/327-0200, 🌐 www .intercontinental.com. Subway: **Museum or St George.** This place offers its guests all the extras, including fireplaces in a few of the suites. The decor is sleek and classic, and there are frequent celebrity sightings in the lobby. **❼**

Madison Manor Boutique Hotel 20 Madison Ave ☎ 416/922-5579 or 877-561-7048, 🌐 www .madisonavenuepub.com. Subway: **St George.** Located in the heart of the Annex, this neighbourhood inn has 22 comfortable, non-smoking rooms, some with fireplaces and all with en-suite bathrooms as well as the amenities (hairdryers, Internet access) that you would expect in luxury hotels. A great find. **❹**

Park Hyatt 4 Avenue Rd ☎ 416/924-5471 or 1-800/977-4197, 🌐 www.hyatt.com. Subway: **Museum or Bay.** Centrally located at the edge of the posh Yorkville neighbourhood, this luxury hotel also boasts a rooftop cocktail bar with spectacular views of the city. The recently refurbished rooms offer the ultimate in comfort, albeit at a premium price. **❼**

Ramada Hotel & Suites 300 Jarvis St ☎ 416/977-4830 or 1-800/567-2233, 🌐 www .ramadahotelandsuites.com. Streetcar: **Carlton (#506).** A comfortable, small hotel on busy Jarvis street. The facilities are on par with the larger chain hotels, and Yonge Street is just a five-minute walk away. **❻**

Sutton Place 955 Bay St ☎ 416/924-9221 or 1-800/268-3790, 🌐 www.suttonplace.com. Subway: **Wellesley.** Long associated with the Toronto International Film Festival (see p.161), this classy hotel is a favourite with visiting celebrities, and the service and amenities are predictably excellent. Nicely situated for all the downtown sights, and only a five-minute walk from the Gay Village (see "Gay Toronto", p.189). **❼**

Toronto Marriott Bloor-Yorkville 90 Bloor St E ☎ 416/961-8000 or 1-800/264-6116, 🌐 .marriott.com. Subway: **Yonge-Bloor.** The bunker-like exterior is a bit of a turn-off, but this establishment has one of the best prices for its very central location. The service is professional, and there's plenty of shopping, restaurants and cinemas nearby. **❻**

Windsor Arms 18 St Thomas St ☎ 416/971-9666, 🌐 www.windsorarmshotel.com. Subway: **Bay.** A jewel among boutique hotels, the *Windsor Arms* is a faithful reconstruction of the 1911 original, which was razed in the early 1990s. What's new are the condominiums on top, the opulent spa, the designer guest rooms with their 300 thread-count sheets and abundant electronic gadgets. What hasn't changed, however, are the beautiful street on which it's located, the superb downstairs restaurant and the top-notch service. **❽**

The waterfront

Radisson Plaza Hotel Admiral 249 Queens Quay W ☎ 416/203-3333 or 1-800/333-3333, 🌐 www.radisson.com/torontoca_admiral. Subway: **York Quay.** Located right on the waterfront, this full-service chain hotel divides its attention between families and conventioneers. While not as central as other comparable hotels, it's still just 5min from Downtown by taxi or 10min by public transport. **❼**

Westin Harbour Castle 1 Harbour Square ☎ 416/869-1600 or 1-800/937-8461, 🌐 www .westin.com. York Quay stop on the LRT from Union Station. This massive hotel right on Lake Ontario's edge, is a terrific base for forays to the Toronto Islands – ferries dock at the plaza out in front. The *Westin Harbour* makes up for its lack of intimate charm by catering to its guests' every whim and offering many nicely furnished rooms with splendid views of Lake Ontario or Downtown's skyscrapers. **❻**

Bed-and-breakfasts

Often cheaper than the city's hotels – and certainly more intimate – are **bed-and-breakfasts**, which can be the best bet for a quality, good-value stay. While you might not get access to a swimming pool or room service, you will certainly get a better sense of what it's like to live in Toronto. Many B&Bs require a tram or subway ride to reach Downtown, but Toronto's transit system (see pp.22–23) is efficient, and none of the addresses listed below is more than twenty minutes from the city centre; the odd one (or two) are in Downtown. If there is a particular area you wish to stay in, or if you have special needs as a traveller, contact the Federation of Ontario Bed and Breakfast Accommodation (☎613/515-1293, ℱ475-5267, ⓦ www.fobba.com) or Bed and Breakfast Homes of Toronto (☎416/363-6362, ⓦ www.bbht.ca).

Aberdeen Guest House 52 Aberdeen Ave, Uptown ☎416/922-8697, ⓦ www .aberdeenguesthouse.com. Streetcar: College (#506). This Cabbagetown house has four rooms (two with private baths), laundry facilities and some parking. Close to parks, restaurants, shops and a dance theatre as well in one of Toronto's most interesting neighbourhoods. ❺

Au Petit Paris B&B 3 Selby St, Uptown ☎ 416/928-1348, ⓦ www.bbtoronto.com /aupetitparis. Subway: Sherbourne. Attractive B&B in a meticulously renovated Victorian house. Each of the guest rooms is decorated in modern style, with hardwood floors and pastel-painted walls, and comes complete with a queen-size bed and en-suite facilities. Vegetarian breakfasts are the house speciality. ❺

Bonnevue Manor 33 Beaty Ave, Downtown ☎ 416/536-1455, ⓦ www.toronto.com /bonnevuemanor. Streetcar: King (#504). This large Victorian home has six rooms (three with private bathrooms) and a self-contained family suite. Close to Ontario Place and the quirky shops, cinemas and restaurants of its surrounding neighbourhood, which has a distinctive Eastern European feel. ❹

The Coach House 117 Walmer Rd, Uptown ☎416/899-0306, ⓦ www.thecoachhouse.ca. Subway: Spadina. This Annex guest house differs from the average B&B in that it offers weekly instead of daily rates for its two, self-contained rooms. Monthly rates are negotiable. Each suite has its own kitchenette, so guests put together their own breakfasts. ❹

Dundonald House 35 Dundonald St, Uptown ☎416/961-9888 or 1-800/260-7227, ⓦ www.dundonaldhouse.com. Subway: Wellesley. This establishment offers handy

extras like bicycles and a workout room. Five rooms are available, all with shared baths. Close to the Gay Village and the theatres and restaurants on Yonge Street. ❸

High Park B&B 4 High Park Blvd, High Park ☎416/531-7963, ℱ416 531-0060. Subway: Dundas West. This spacious home has three rooms, two of which share a bath. The largest room has its own balcony, which overlooks the leafy confines of the surrounding Victorian neighbourhood. The breakfasts here are scrumptious, and the service is friendly. ❷

Jarvis House 344 Jarvis St, Uptown ☎416/975-3838, ⓦ www.jarvishouse.com. Subway: College. Once upon a time, Jarvis Street was where all the fashionable millionaires lived, and this house is a relic of bygone days. All twelve rooms have private baths, and the location is close to popular sights like Maple Leaf Gardens and Cabbagetown (see p.71). ❹

Les Amis B&B 31 Granby St, Downtown ☎416/591-0635, ⓦ www.bbtoronto.com. Subway: College. Downtown B&B, a short stroll from the Eaton Centre, holding a handful of pleasantly furnished rooms with shared facilities. Vegetarian breakfasts are a speciality – the crepes go down a treat. Air conditioned. ❹

Lowtherhouse 72 Lowther Ave, Uptown ☎416/323-1589 or 1-800/265-4158, ⓦ www .lowtherhouse.ca. Subway: St George. This Annex guest house offers six rooms with private or share bathrooms, full breakfasts, air-conditioning, cable TV and other conveniences within steps of Yorkville, the Royal Ontario Museum (see p.65), the Bata Shoe Museum (see p.70) and the University of Toronto's downtown campus. ❹

The Mansion 49 Dundonald Ave, Uptown ℡ 416/963-8385, ⊛ www.themansion.com. Subway: Wellesley. Located on a pleasant tree-lined street between the Yonge Street strip and the Gay Village on Church Street. The B&B has three rooms, some parking, amenities like fridges, cable TV, air-conditioning and, as a special service, your hosts will arrange day-trips to Niagara Falls. ❸

The Mulberry Tree 122 Isabella St, Uptown ℡ 416/960-5249, ⊛ www.bbtoronto.com. Subway: Wellesley. This delightful B&B, one of Toronto's most agreeable, occupies a tastefully decorated heritage home close to the city centre. Each of the guest rooms is comfortable and relaxing - indeed the whole atmosphere of the place is just right, combining efficiency and friendliness. Breakfasts are first-rate too, home cooking at its best and eaten at one large table where guests can chat away with each other. A short walk from Wellesley or Bloor-Yonge subway stations. Highly recommended. ❺

Palmerston Inn 322 Palmerston Blvd, Uptown ℡ 416/920-7842, ⊛ www.toronto.com /palmerstoninn. Streetcar: College (#506). This oak-panelled mansion, situated on the edge of the trendy College Street strip, has eight rooms of varying degrees of comfort, with features such as fireplaces, fresh flowers and bathrobes. Extras include afternoon sherry and a daily maid service. ❸

Terrace House 52 Austin Terrace, Uptown ℡ 416/535-1493, ⊛ www.terracehouse.com. Subway: St Clair West. This pre-World War I, mock-Tudor house is perched high on a hill overlooking the city. The neighbourhood includes noteworthy piles like Casa Loma and Spadina House (see p.72–74), and is close to some of the most exclusive residential districts in the city. There are three rooms (two with fireplaces, one with a private bath), all decked out with antiques and North African rugs. It's only a five-minute walk from the Dupont subway station, but it's all uphill. ❹

University residences and hostels

Two large **universities** are set in the city centre: the University of Toronto and Ryerson Polytechnic University. From the second week in May to the end of August there is an abundance of student residences available to budget-wise tourists of all ages on a daily, weekly or monthly basis. Quite often this is the best bargain for clean, affordable and relatively private accommodation. Most residences require a night's or week's deposit, depending on the length of your stay. Students with valid IDs can often get a discount of around ten percent; enquire at reception.

Toronto's range of **hostels** has improved in recent years, with several of the more recently opened ones being agreeable options. Most have private or family rooms as well as dormitories, and we've included two hostels below. Although the YMCA no longer accepts overnight guests, the **YWCA** Woodlawn Residence is a good budget option for women travellers.

Canadiana Backpackers Hostel 42 Widmer St, Downtown ℡ 416/598-9090 or 1-877/215-1225, ⊛ www.canadianalodging.com. Streetcar: King St (#504). This hip, clean hostel is right in the midst of Toronto's clubs, steps away from Queen Street W and within easy walking distance of all Downtown. Dorm bed $25; 10 percent off with HI or student card.

Global Village Backpackers 460 King St W, Downtown ℡ 416/703-8540 or 1-888/844-7875. Streetcar: King (#504). This former hotel (once famed for a free-wheeling Art Deco tap room) has four private/family rooms; everything else

is dormitory-style with shared bathrooms. The above-standard facilities include laundry facilities, a kitchen and a games room. Close to the Richmond Street/Queen Street West action as well as the up-and-coming King West strip. Dorm bed $25; 10 percent off with HI or student card.

Ryerson Neill-Wycik College 96 Gerrard St E, Downtown ℡ 416/977-2320, ⊛ www.neill-wycik .com. Subway: Dundas. All available accommodations (singles, doubles and quads) are apartment suites with shared kitchens. There are telephones in all rooms, laundry facilities and limited on-site parking. The campus itself is scenic and quiet, but the youth-magnet intersection of Yonge and Dundas is only a short walk away – which could be good or bad depending on how you like your Saturday nights. Daily, weekly and monthly rates available on all units. Private room $42, or $33 with HI or student card.

University of Toronto, Innis College 111 St George St, Uptown ☏416/978-2553, ⓦwww .utoronto.ca/innis/residence/summer. Subway: St George. This recently built residence, with air-conditioning and a daily maid service, offers daily and weekly rentals for single rooms, while doubles are only available for long-term stays. Single room $30.

University of Toronto, Massey College 4 Devonshire Place, Uptown ☏416/978-2549, ⓦwww.utoronto.ca/massey. Subway: St George. Apart from being the one-time stomping grounds of author Robertson Davies, this beautiful college reportedly boasts the presence of at least one ghost. Singles and doubles are available with breakfast included on weekdays May–July; rates are lower in August, when breakfast is no longer served. $50/single room May–July; $40/single room in August.

University of Toronto, St Michael's College 81 St Mary's St, Uptown ☏416/926-7296, ⒻEnv416/926-7139. Subway: Museum. This is the college where Marshall McLuhan taught for much of his professional life. Singles and doubles are available at weekly rates and include maid service. This is a popular campus, so call ahead to see about availability. Season ends on August 16th. Single room $209/week, double room $187/week.

University of Toronto, Victoria College 140 Charles St W, Uptown ☏416/585-4524, ⓦvicu .utoronto.ca/conference.htm. Subway: Museum. This huge campus site includes accommodation in Annesley Hall, Burwash Hall, Law House and Margaret Addison Hall. The daily rates for doubles and singles include a full cafeteria breakfast. Single room $47.

YWCA Woodlawn Residence 80 Woodlawn Ave, Uptown ☏416/923-8454, ⓦwww.ywcator.org. Subway: Summerhill. Tucked away in a cul-de-sac in the pretty Summerhill neighbourhood, this women-only residence offers dormitory, single and double rooms at daily and monthly rates, and includes a continental breakfast. There are laundry facilities and vending machines on site, and a good cafés, restaurants and speciality shops close by. Dorm bed $22.

Cafés and light meals

Toronto's thriving **cafés** are the seam in the city's social fabric – roughly analogous to pubs in London. Locals head there for a morning latte, a quick meal, an evening drink, or just to meet up with friends for some social activity. The scene gets especially busy during the summertime, when many cafés roll out onto terraces and sidewalks, providing excellent vantage points for people-watching or just hanging about. We've grouped spots into two broad categories: places that are best for beverages and socializing – though you'll find even these places typically serve some sort of snacks – and places that can be considered for **light meals**, or even full meals.

Coffee- and teahouses

As in many other cities, the ubiquitous Seattle coffee chain, Starbucks, is making its presence felt in Toronto's **coffee bar scene**. Canadian versions of the chain are Timothy's and The Second Cup. While these franchises are giving independent establishments a run for your money, they simply don't offer the character and sense of place that many of the independent shops do.

As for tea, you'll find many different varieties on offer in the city, including **high tea**, which is served by some hotels, chai and, most recently, the latest Taiwanese fad to catch on in Hong Kong, Vancouver, Los Angeles and Toronto: bubble tea, recognizable by the large globules of tapioca sitting at the bottom of this sweet, Technicolor drink.

Downtown

Balzac's 55 Mill St ☏416/207-1709. Streetcar: King (#504). Bus: Parliament St (#65A from Castle Frank Station). In the midst of the Distillery District, *Balzac's* has the look and feel of an airy Parisian café, and churns out nicely presented espresso-type coffees and some sweets to go with them.

Café Bernate 1024 Queen St W ☏416/535-2835. Streetcar: Queen (#501). The steam machine is in full swing at this neighbourhood spot where the walls are hung with local artists' work. The menu offers a wide variety of plump sandwiches for all tastes, and the regular coffee comes with free refills.

Java House 537 Queen St W ☏416/504-3025. Streetcar: Queen (#501). The exterior of this popular local hangout is painted to look like a hut from some fabulist South Pacific village, while inside it is all café, steamy and busy serving up light meals and gallons of caffeinated beverages of all descriptions.

Moon Bean Coffee 30 St Andrew's St ☏416/595-0327. Streetcar: Spadina (#501). One of a dwindling number of cafés that care enough to roast its own beans, *Moon Bean* is a Kensington Market tradition. Its patio is a perfect spot to watch the daily parade go by.

Sugar Café 942 Queen St W ☎ 416/532-5088. **Streetcar: Queen (#501).** This little café on the West Queen West strip has all the usual elements – espresso coffees, sweets and light fare – but presented in a charming, light-hearted way.

Tequila Bookworm 490 Queen St W ☎ 416/504-7335. **Streetcar: Queen (#501).** The exposed brick walls in the front of the café are lined with magazines for sale, while the back section is filled with floor-to-ceiling bookshelves stuffed with old text books, yesterday's star biographies, romance novels and the odd Penguin classic. Garage-sale armchairs and coffee tables await patrons willing to make a serious time commitment. Espresso drinks and simple desserts are served without fussy embell-ishments.

Vienna Home Bakery 626 Queen St W ☎ 416/703-7278. **Streetcar: Queen (#501).** Part of the original, pre-cool Queen West land-scape, the *Vienna Bakery* has been pro-viding starving-artist types with caffeine and sugar rushes for decades. This earnest slice of central Europe is a wonderful anti-dote to ludicrously named coffee drinks and low-cal snacks.

Uptown

Avenue Coffee Shop 222 Davenport Rd ☎ 416/744-1617. **Subway: Bay.** One of the city's coffee shops that has hardly changed, this Art Deco sliver on the northern edge of Yorkville keeps its food simple and its coffee straightforward.

Café Doria 1094 Yonge St ☎ 416/944-0101. **Subway: Rosedale.** A recent change in owner-ship and name hasn't altered the neigh-bourhood character of this place one bit. This charming little coffee bar still serves up fortifying espresso drinks for patrons worn out from shopping at the many beautiful antique stores lining this strip near the upscale Rosedale neighbourhood.

Café Elise 673 Spadina Ave ☎ 416/598-5522. **Subway: Spadina.** Generations of students from the nearby University of Toronto have pondered existentialism over the beverages and light meals served at the venerable *Café Elise*.

The Coffee Mill 99 Yorkville Ave ☎ 416/967-3837. **Subway: Bay.** This Hungarian establish-ment dates back to Yorkville's coffee house days when the likes of Joni Mitchell and Neil Young were getting their start in that very neighbourhood. It serves a variety of coffees, its influences more Viennese than Italian.

Insomnia Internet Bar Café Inc 502 Bloor St W ☎ 416/588-3907. **Subway: Bathurst.** This fully licensed Internet café has six computer ter-minals and a kitchen that stays open until 2am, plus a large screen TV and couches on which to snuggle. Booths are available, too.

Jaka's Coffee and Bubble Tea 1033 Bay St ☎ 416/925-6607. **Subway: Wellesley.** Located on the edge of the University of Toronto's St Michael's campus, this spacious and airy upmarket café is a favourite with students as well as office workers looking for some-thing other than the usual coffees.

Jet Fuel Coffee Shop 519 Parliament St ☎ 416/968-9982. **Streetcar: Carlton/College (#506).** This is one of the oldest independent coffee establishments in town and the unof-ficial club house of bicycle couriers. It only serves beverages that can be made with an espresso machine (tea included), and imports a few baked goods for dunking. An excellent choice for relaxing with a huge, inexpensive latte and a newspaper.

Lettieri Espresso Bar Café 94 Cumberland St ☎ 416/515-8764. **Subway: Bay.** Amidst the surge of espresso-bar chains that have blighted Toronto as of late, this one is actu-ally deserving of praise. The paninis (Italian sandwiches made from flatbread) are deli-cious, and make for the cheapest meal in Yorkville. The atmosphere is nothing to write home about, but the coffee drinks are good, as is the selection of pastas and salads (and the full wine list).

Tea Shop 168 419 College St ☎ 416/633-9168. **Streetcar: College (#506).** Trust the trendy College Street strip to be one of the early downtown outlets for this popular bubble tea chain. A wide variety of the refreshing drinks in just about every tropical fruit flavour is paired with sweet Chinese pas-tries.

The suburbs

Athens Pastries 509 Danforth Ave, Greektown ☎ 416/463-5144. **Subway: Chester.** True to its name this café-cum-bakery sells sweet and savoury Greek pastries with coffee, and

If you find yourself awake and hungry between 3am and 6am, the following establishments will be open to serve you seven days a week.

7 Charles Street West	p.129	Iliada Café	p.126
Athens Pastries	p.125	Mars Restaurant	p.127
Bonjour Brioche	p.129	Soda Market Café	p.130
Fran's	p.127	Tango Palace Coffee Co	p.126
Golden Griddle	p.127	Tournayre Patisserie	p.126
Hello Toast	p.127		

7

CAFÉS AND LIGHT MEALS | Light meals

nothing else. Huge trays of *baklava*, *spanakopita* and a delectable custard and filo confection empty out in rapid succession as sit-down or takeaway customers file in for their filo pastry fix.

Iliada Café 550 Danforth Ave, Greektown ☎416/462-0334. Subway: Chester. The Greek coffee served here, which comes in a tiny cup three-quarters full of fine coffee grounds, makes espresso seem as tame as baby formula. Regular coffee and espresso-type beverages are also available.

Tango Palace Coffee Co. 1156 Queen St E, Leslieville ☎416/465-8085. Streetcar: Queen (#501). Ensconced in an Edwardian storefront amongst a row of antique stores, *Tango* serves up huge cups and bowls of café au lait, cappuccinos and just plain coffee with a bewildering variety of sweets, all to the strains of jitterbug and doowop tunes. Some savoury snacks are available but desserts are the strong suit here.

Tournayre Patisserie 1856 Queen St E, The Beaches ☎416/693-7997. Streetcar: Queen (#501). Most business is conducted in French at this gem of a patisserie. The customers don't bat an eye and reply in kind for they tend to be serious Francophiles hungering for a divinely flaky croissant, golden-crusted baguettes or a zingy lemon tarte. Imported French bonbons are stacked by the cash register as a final, ultra-Gallic enticement.

Light meals

Somewhere in-between Toronto's more casual cafés and its full-blown restaurants are smaller, bistro-type dining spots that serve light and generally inexpensive **meals**. These are often the best places to sample the diverse cuisines that the city has to offer, at very affordable prices. The listings below are **price-coded** into three categories: budget (under $15), inexpensive ($15–20), and moderate ($20–35).

American and Canadian

52 Inc. 394 College St, Uptown ☎416/960-0334. Streetcar: College (#506). Blink and you'll miss this tiny but worthwhile neighbourhood bar. The owners sell domestic art magazines and hang works by up-and-coming artists on the walls. The light menu includes a range of sandwiches named after Sixties art flicks (eg the L'Aventura, with roasted red peppers, asiago and watercress). The extensive cocktail list also vies for patrons' attention. Inexpensive to moderate.

Brownstone Café & Wine Bar 603 Yonge St, Downtown ☎416/920-6288. Subway: Wellesley. The *Brownstone* is proof positive that neighbourhood cafés are in every nook and corner of the city, even on busy Yonge Street. Its glass storefront provides a prime view for people-watching. Light meals with plenty of vegetarian options are available throughout the day and when the sun slips down coffee drinks give way to a thoughtful and reasonably priced wine list. Moderate.

Dooney's Café 511 Bloor St W, Uptown ☎416/536-3292. Subway: Spadina. This is the David to *Starbuck's* Goliath. When the latter tried to usurp *Dooney's* lease, the café's regular patrons rebelled and kept the *Dooney* dream alive. The interior is cosy with exposed brick throughout, and the full menu boasts items like fat slices of French toast smothered in maple syrup and fresh fruit, pizzas, sandwiches and pastas. Inexpensive to moderate.

Fran's 20 College St, Uptown ☎416/923-9867. Streetcar: College (#506). The last remaining branch of a Toronto institution. Glenn Gould was keen on their grilled cheese sandwiches and the King of Denmark (who resided in Toronto with his family during World War II) was fond of *Fran's* famed apple pie with cinnamon sauce. Both items are still on the menu alongside inexpensive grill offerings, breakfasts, pastas and the odd blue plate special. Inexpensive.

Golden Griddle 45 Carlton St, Uptown ☎416/9775044, Subway: Carlton; also 11 Jarvis St, Downtown, ☎416/865-1263, Subway: Union Station. A road-house type atmosphere where the late-night, early-morning types that roll in are an attraction all to themselves. This 24-hour joint serves mainly an array of pancakes, but a full menu is also available. Inexpensive.

Hello Toast 993 Queen St E, Leslieville ☎416/778-7299. Streetcar: Queen (#501). The flea market chic furnishings are your first clue that *Hello Toast* positions itself on the lighter side of serious. It is famous for its Sunday brunch, which features the house specialties, French toast and Belgium waffles. The espresso drinks are just right and the cappuccinos pack a wallop. Inexpensive.

Maggies 400 College St, Uptown ☎416/323-3248. Streetcar: College (#506). Although you can get very nice lunches here, the real draw is the inexpensive, all-day breakfasts, including items like eggs Benedict, omelettes, and French toast served with mounds of fresh fruit, and free refills on regular coffees and tea. Inexpensive.

Mars Restaurant 432 College St, Uptown ☎416/921-6332. Streetcar: College (#506). A full-service diner frequented for its all-day breakfast special: two eggs prepared any way you like, sausage and bacon, and thick slices of toast with jam. Cheap and filling. Budget.

Upmarket Café 533 Parliament St, Cabbagetown ☎416/922-9998. Streetcar: Carlton/College (#506). A recent addition to Parliament Street, this tiny, charming café offers Cabbagetowners a good selection of substantial salads, pastas, frittatas, sandwiches and sweets to complement its espresso coffees and wide range of teas. Inexpensive.

Asian fusion

Colony Kitchen 153 Bloor St W, Uptown ☎416/591-9997. Subway: Museum or Bay. If you can find the door (it's under the *Club Monaco*, across from the Royal Ontario Museum) you're in for a treat. Light but satisfying Asian fusion dishes are served in a stylishly understated metal and dark glass decor, with knowledgeable staff offering just the right amount of help. The tandoori salmon is one delicious example of local ingredients being given an Asian flair. This reasonably priced option in a haughtily expensive neighbourhood also has one of the best summer patios in town. Moderate.

Red Tea Box 696 Queen St W, Downtown ☎416/203-8882. Streetcar: Queen (#501). Little tables covered in decorative cloth and an assortment of antimacassared chairs make up the front tearoom of this pretty lunch spot. Bento boxes of dainty Asian fusion dishes are the house speciality along with a bewildering array of teas served in china teapots. There is also a larger tearoom out back beside a garden patio, and a little gift shop. Moderate.

Silk Road Café 341 Danforth Ave, Uptown ☎416/63-8660. Subway: Chester. Owner Tom Wong's trip across China along the ancient silk and spice trade route was the inspiration for this neighbourhood favourite and pictures of his odyssey grace the walls. Hot, spicy beef dishes from Turfan share menu space with a highly recommended vegetarian appetizer. Family recipes make it onto the list as well, notably Grandma Wong's hot pot, a spicy stew of tofu, vegetables and meat. Inexpensive to moderate.

Spring Rolls 58 Front St E, Downtown. ☎416/365-7655. Subway: Union. Also at 693 Yonge St ☎416/972-7655. A broad range of Asian cuisines and influences (Japanese, Chinese, Thai) make up the menu at both attractive locations. Stir-fries, soups, noodles, satay and salads are the mainstays, and nothing should take longer than 10 minutes to reach your table. Inexpensive to moderate.

CAFÉS AND LIGHT MEALS | Light meals

Caribbean

Ali's West Indian Roti Shop 1446 Queen St W, Parkdale ☏ 416/532-7701. Streetcar: Queen (#501). *Ali's* is one of the city's best roti shops, featuring succulent *dhalpoori*, and *paratha roti* stuffed with your choice of meat, seafood or vegetarian options. Stews and full dinners are also available. Island juices and a home-made soursop ice cream are on hand to cool spice-excited palates. Budget.

Bacchus 1376 Queen St W, Parkdale ☏ 416/532-8191. Streetcar: Queen (#501). This tiny restaurant offers a Guyanese version of roti, filled with a selection of stuffings such as curried goat, squash, spinach or conch, to name but a few. Feather-light dumplings and fritters, peanut butter cakes and fried plantains can be accompanied by a wide selection of tropical fruit drinks and ginger beers. Budget.

Flava Restaurant 606 Yonge St, Uptown ☏ 416/967-0700. Subway: Wellesley. Besides having a devoted lunchtime following the restaurant opens at night on Thursday and Friday as a cabaret. Roti, saltfish/ackee combos and rib-sticking stews of chicken, goat or beef are served up in an island of calm on busy Yonge Street. Inexpensive.

Irie Food Joint 745 Queen St W, Downtown ☏ 416/366-4743. Streetcar: Queen (#501). A recent addition to the Queen Street strip west of Bathurst Street, *Irie* serves Caribbean-style cuisine in a trendy, upscale setting. Entrees of jerk chicken, beef or pork and a wide array of roti arrive with sides of island slaw and peas and rice. Surprisingly affordable for such an attractive space. Inexpensive.

The Real Jerk 709 Queen St E, Riverdale ☏ 416/463-6055. Streetcar: Queen (#501). *The Jerk* dishes up platters of hot, spicy chicken and beef with mounds of rice and peas to take away the heat, as well as bottles of Red Stripe beer. Seafood and a few vegetarian entrees round out the offerings but this is really a place for heat-loving carnivores. Inexpensive.

Ritz Caribbean Foods 10 Roy Square, Uptown ☏ 416/972-7480. Subway: Yonge/Bloor. A good Caribbean lunch spot catering to uptown office workers, the *Ritz* has all the high points (roti, *callaloo*, jerk and ackee and saltfish), plus Chinese Caribbean food – an Island take on low mein. Service is excellent, and the generously portioned lunch specials can cost as little as $4. Eat at tables or take away. Budget.

Chinese

Bright Pearl Seafood 346-348 Spadina Ave (upstairs), Uptown ☏ 416/979-3988. Streetcar: Spadina (#510) or College (#506). You can't miss this seafood and dim sum palace: huge lion statues, paws aloft, seemingly wave to passing streetcars from the entrance. A big draw is the 100 item dim sum lunch, as popular with locals as it is with the tourists. Servers who zip around the huge, pink banquet hall with carts of dim sum are happy to explain the contents of the little bamboo baskets, dishes and trays. You can also order from the menu. Inexpensive.

Champion House 480 Dundas St W, Downtown ☏ 416/977-8282. Streetcar: Dundas (#505). This Chinatown favourite is known equally for its Peking Duck and its well-rounded list of vegetarian entrees, the latter featuring tofu as a stand-in for gluten. Even though a few courses have been trimmed, the Peking Duck experience still takes a bit of time and involves some pleasant theatricality in the service. Moderate.

Indian

Debu Saha's Biryani House 25 Wellesley St E, Uptown ☏ 416/ 927-9340. Subway: Wellesley. Recently relocated to this much larger, second-storey location, *Debu Saha's* serves some of Toronto's best north Indian food. The bigger space has meant a bigger kitchen and thus more menu choices, and the best way to sample the expanded menu is to attend the weekday buffet. Inexpensive to moderate.

Kama 214 King St W (downstairs), Downtown ☏ 416/599-5262. Streetcar: King (#504). Handily located across the street from Roy Thompson Hall, *Kama* offers a lighter, modern interpretation of Indian classics. Nothing on the menu is too hot nor too buttery, nor too exotic, making *Kama* a good introduction for those not ready for full-blown Indian cuisine. Moderate.

Udupi Palace 1460 Gerrard St E ☏ 416/405-8138. Streetcar: Carlton (#506). This mall space in Little India doesn't win any beauty prizes but no one pays attention to their surroundings when they bite into the delicious Southern Indian–style food, which pairs green chillis with coconut chutney in countless ways. For an authentic taste of India, be sure to sample the chilli *pakora* with a *raita* (a thick, home-made yogurt dish) or a *lassi* (a yogurt drink) to extinguish any fire you can't ride out. Budget.

Italian

7 Charles Street West 7 Charles St, Uptown W ☎ 416/928-9041. This old Victorian house has been renovated into a three-floor café. The first floor is a traditional bistro-type dining area, the second is an espresso bar/cafe, and the third is like a friend's attic, complete with a tiny pool table and murals. The simple food, available on the first two floors, is relatively inexpensive and has an Italian twist. The desserts are lovely and there is a bargain-basement brunch on Sunday. Inexpensive.

Café Diplomatico 594 College St, Uptown ☎ 416/534-4637. Streetcar: College (#506). This vestige of an earlier time has managed to hold its own among newer, chichi neighbours. Substantial, no-nonsense pizzas with a selection of market-fresh toppings, as well as pastas, are served inside or on the packed patio. Inexpensive.

John's Italian Café 27 Baldwin, Downtown ☎ 416//5596-8848. Streetcar: College (#506). A pleasant, unpretentious little café specializing in pizzas and pastas with Italian sweets to round out the meal, although regulars also treasure it as a place to chat with friends over bowls of coffee or glasses of wine. Inexpensive.

Terroni 720 Queen St W, Downtown ☎ 416/504-0320. Streetcar: Queen (#501). Also at 106 Victoria St ☎ 416/955-0258. Subway: Queen. The menu is structured around salads and pizza, the latter being a huge draw because of their thin, crispy crusts. Also available are stuffed pastas, daily specials and a small menu of desserts (mainly ice cream), along with espresso coffees, beer and wine. The spaces at both locations are crammed tight with tables and chairs, but the service is unfailingly polite. Moderate.

International

By the Way Café 400 Bloor St W, Uptown ☎ 416/967-4295. Subway: Spadina. An eclectic mixture of Middle East standards including Jewish delicacies, along with substantial soups, salads and daily specials, keep this spot packed on summer evenings and weekends. This is a prime spot for people watching and conversation in the Annex neighbourhood. Plenty of vegetarian options are available. Moderate.

Bonjour Brioche 812 Queen St E ☎ 416/406-1250. Streetcar: Queen (#501). This patisserie/café draws hordes from all over the city with its jewel-like fruit tarts, buttery croissants, puffy brioche and delectable *pissaladiere*, a variation on pizza from Provence. The sit-down menu is a blackboard full of soups, sandwiches, omelettes and quiche. There's always a line for Sunday brunch, and almost everything is eaten by 2pm, so come early. Moderate.

Café la Gaffe 24 Baldwin St, Uptown ☎ 416/596-2397 Streetcar: Carlton/College (#506). Cosy, exposed brick walls, a well-stocked Art Deco bar and an open kitchen create a convivial atmosphere in this lively neighbourhood bistro. The menu is heavily Italian (pastas, pizzas, salads), with a selection of fusion finger food. Moderate.

Epicure Café 512 Queen St W, Downtown ☎ 416/504-8942. Streetcar: Queen (#501). Unpretentious, funky and comfortable, the *Epicure* serves up a selection of tasty fare. Polenta makes a nice change from pasta and their regulars swear by the burger menu. Apart from coffee there's a good selection of local microbrews and regional wines. Moderate.

Kalendar Koffee House 546 College St, Uptown ☎ 416/923-4138. Streetcar: Carlton/College (#506). Perhaps the loveliest café in town, with dark wood panelling and intimate booths providing an old-world atmosphere. A popular place to start an evening's bar and restaurant crawl along the College Street Strip or end one with a coffee and dessert. Innovative light meals are served by excellent staff, and a well-stocked bar complements a full range of espresso drinks. Moderate.

Kensington Café 73 Kensington Ave, Downtown ☎ 416/971-5632. Streetcar: Spadina (#510). The international soup-and-sandwich menu gives a nod to the Middle East. A small, cosy place to slip into if the hectic pace of Kensington Market gets to be too much. Moderate.

CAFÉS AND LIGHT MEALS | Light meals

Living Well 692 Yonge St, Uptown ☎ 416/922-6770. **Subway: Yonge.** The two terraces fill up fast in summer, and the casual clientele selects from a full menu of inexpensive, well-prepared snacks and entrees, particularly custom-made sandwiches and pastas. The burger list is solid and makes a rib-sticking meal for carnivores and vegetarians alike. Inexpensive to moderate.

Loftus Lloyd 401 Richmond St, Downtown ☎ 416/596-7100. **Streetcar: Queen (#501).** Loftus Lloyd was the owner of the tin box factory that now houses the architecturally stunning studio and gallery space known as 401 Richmond, and this attractive, on-site café is named for him. Apart from the fact that a coffee or snack gets you inside this facility, the global fusion menu is a distinct attraction. Moderate.

The Peartree Restaurant 507 Parliament St, Uptown ☎ 416/962-8190. **Streetcar: Carlton/College (#506).** A neighbourhood café with a leafy, open-air patio for summer lingering. The international menu features stir fries, pastas and plenty of Tex Mex–style entrees. The Sunday brunch is hugely popular with locals, so come early. Recommended. Moderate.

Soda Market Café 425 Danforth Ave, Uptown ☎ 416/466-5227. **Subway: Chester.** This attractive lunch spot offers a menu of substantial but inexpensive items such as large, fluffy omelettes with a variety of fillings and a choice of home-fried potatoes or salad, pizzas, or a platter of Greek dips and grilled pita, in addition to lattes, espressos, cappuccinos and juices. Inexpensive to moderate.

Thai

Green Mango 707 and 730 Yonge St, Uptown ☎ 416/928-0021. **Subway: Yonge/Bloor.** This popular establishment has both a sit-down dining spot and a cafeteria-style outlet, right across the road from one another. Both are perfect for inexpensive, quick lunches. Spicy noodles are dressed up with tofu, chicken or vegetables, and fresh (ie unfried)

spring rolls and sticky rice desserts are on the menu as well. Inexpensive to moderate.

Salad King 335 Yonge St, Downtown ☎ 416/971-7041. **Subway: Dundas.** The door to this popular Thai hole-in-the-wall is around the corner from Yonge Street; to find it simply follow the line that snakes along the sidewalk. Most people choose to take out, patrons can sit down if they don't mind the frenetic activity. Regulars come for the punchy spicing (beware the Evil Jungle Prince, a fiery vegetable stir-fry), and there are plenty of vegetarian options amid the varieties of chicken dishes, and imported Thai beer, too. Inexpensive.

Vegetarian

Fresh 894 Queen St W, Downtown ☎ 416/9132720. **Streetcar: Queen (#501).** A welcome change from the usually uninspired vegetarian food served in unappealing surroundings. *Fresh* lives up to its name with a sleek modernist interior and a varied and health-conscious menu. Rice bowls with names such as "Tantric" and "Warrior" are the speciality and feature delicious combinations of tempeh, tofu, greens and gravies over brown basmati rice. Burgers, wraps and burritos are other tempting options, and apart from *Fresh's* signature shakes, smoothies and juices, there's a decent selection of wines and microbeers too. Moderate.

King's Café 192 August Ave, Uptown ☎ 416/591-1340. **Streetcar: College (#506).** This attractive café, with a Chinese vegetarian bent is located in the midst of bustling Kensington Market. Eat in the soft green interior, with its blonde wood and brushed aluminium accents, or on the spacious patio out front. Cheap breakfast specials go for less than $3, while the rest of the menu features pages of "mock meat" dishes (gluten styled vaguely to resemble meat). Committed carnivores will find the rich desserts and espresso coffees more than enough reason to stop by. Budget to inexpensive.

Restaurants

D ining out in Toronto is one of the city's most pleasurable experiences. The passion with which residents embrace gastronomy is readily evident – so don't be surprised if, during your stay, you overhear someone holding forth on where they found a particularly good olive oil, or which hot new restaurant enticed which chef, or how so-and-so's pate foie gras is a near-religious experience. And, contrary to what you might expect, such interest in fine food is not snobbish: with more than 5000 restaurants in the city, everyone is sure to find someplace where they can educate their palates and discover new and unfamiliar cuisines. Competition between restaurants is fierce, so the **service** and the quality of the food is usually excellent, as well.

As for pricing, restaurants in Toronto are often on the **expensive** side – though one needn't break the bank for a superior dining experience. A good trick for sampling the food at pricier establishments is to take advantage of lunch menus, offered from 11.30am–3pm at roughly 25 percent less than the cost of dinner menus. As well, we've listed plenty of places where you can eat light or full meals in a **more casual setting**, usually quite inexpensively, in Chapter 7, "Cafés and light meals".

For an up-to-the minute scoop on who the chefs are and where to dine, consult ⓦ www.martiniboys.com or the glossy *Toronto Life* magazine, which has a much-coveted annual restaurant review guide.

The listings below are **price-coded** into four categories: inexpensive ($15–20), moderate ($20–35), expensive ($35–50) and very expensive ($50 and over). This assumes a three-course meal for one person, not including drinks,

---

Celebrity chefs

As an apocryphal local legend goes, there was a very famous rock star standing in a hotel lobby and trying hard not to be recognized, when he heard an excited squeal from a group of fans. As he readied himself to sign autographs, the group walked directly past him, having spotted a well-known local chef hanging about in the same hotel lobby.

In Toronto, chefs really are celebrities. Often, these culinary superstars are followed by their fans – who read avidly about them in gossip columns devoted to foodie chit-chat, and save up for special occasions at their restaurants – from kitchen to kitchen. Five-star Toronto chefs, and their respective restaurants, are as follows:

Susur Lee	*Susur* (see p.132)
Chris McDonald	*Avalon*, 270 Adelaide St W ☎416/979-9918
Mark McEwan	*Bymark*, 66 Wellington St W ☎416/7771144
Marc Thuet	*The Fifth*, 225 Richmond St W ☎416/979-3005
Anne Yarymowich	*Agora* (see p.134)

tax or tip. Restaurant **opening hours** and times of peak flow vary, so it's probably a good idea to call ahead to the place you have in mind.

Maps, with all the restaurants in this chapter keyed to them, can be found in
the main part of the Guide: see p.36 for the Downtown map, p.62 for the
Uptown map, and p.84 for the suburbs map.

Downtown

Asian fusion

Monsoon 100 Simcoe St ☎416/979-7172.
Subway: St Andrew. The award-winning interior here reflects the Asian influence on the
menu. Make time to stop for a martini in the
glamorous bar before going on to the
dining room. Starters are served on delicate
rakku dishes, and the light, assured
cooking boasts imaginative combinations
(seared tofu in green tea marinade, maple-
ginger grouper). An excellent place to mark
a special occasion. Expensive.

Queen Mother Café 208 Queen St W
☎416/598-4719. **Streetcar: Queen (#501).**
Neither the name nor the cosy, wood-panelled interior gives a hint about the menu:
Asian specialities like pad Thai, crispy
spring rolls, and lots of chicken-and-shrimp
entrees. Vegetarians take heart: the house
veggie burger is a local tradition. Moderate
to expensive.

Susur 601 King St W ☎416/603-2205.
Streetcar: King (#504). Susur Lee is consistently ranked as one of the ten best chefs
in the world, and people come to Toronto
expressly for the purpose of eating at his
restaurant. If you ever wondered why
someone would spend serious money for a
meal, make a reservation (well in advance):
it will be a quantum leap in your taste
experience. The best thing to do is to
place yourself in the chef's hands and
order a tasting menu (approximately $65
per person for three dishes, $90 for five
and $110 for seven). The extraordinary
waitstaff will bring you bowls of this and
little dishes of that and explain each one of
them. The underlying sensibility is more-or-
less Chinese, and aspects of the technique
are classically French – but the absolute
purity and clarity of taste defies adjectives
or labels. Vegetarian and other special
diets can be easily accommodated if you
explain your needs at the outset. Very
expensive.

Canadian and American

Canoe in the Toronto Dominion Tower, 66
Wellington St W ☎416/364-0054. **Subway: King
or St Andrew.** Way up on the 54th floor of an
office tower, this elegant restaurant serves
up highly imaginative Canadian cuisine
(Yukon caribou, feral greens, wild berries)
alongside one of the best wine lists in the
city. Very expensive.

Le Papillion 16 Church St ☎416/363-0838.
Subway: Union Station. Large Breton crepes
served sweet or savoury with a Québecois
flair are the house specialities. The menu
also includes tortier (a Québec meat pie),
and bistro standards like onion soup and
steak frites. Convivial, solicitous service in a
casually trendy environment. Moderate.

Montreal Restaurant Bistro and Jazz Club
65 Sherbourne St ☎416/363-0179. **Streetcar:
King (#504).** Like Montreal itself, the menu is
a mishmash of Quebecois, French, Italian
and American influences, meaning that you
can have split pea soup with your burgers
and fries. The real draw, though, are the top
jazz acts it books, which attract enthusiastic crowds out for a night sur la ville.
Cover charges usually apply and it's a good
idea to call ahead. Moderate to expensive.

Oyster Boy 872 Queen St W ☎416/534-3432.
Streetcar: Queen (#501). For maritimers home-
sick for a taste of Down East, and those
who want to eat like Bluenosers, visit
Oyster Boy for twelve varieties of the tasty
bivalve. Although oysters are king here,
other items such as clam fritters, fish and
chips in beer batter and lobster are also
served. Moderate.

RD's BBQ and Blues 14 Duncan St. ☎416/
598-5209. **Streetcar: King (#504).** Everything
has to grow up, even the Red Devil. The
frat boy elements are gone (no more baseball cap selection), but the core elements of
barbecued back ribs, chicken and steak are
still on the menu. Garlicky mashed potatoes, Memphis coleslaw and Southern

baked beans are the after-thought additions to the slow-cooked, piquantly-sauced meat mains. Moderate to expensive.

Tundra 145 Richmond St W ☎416/869-3456. **Streetcar: Queen (#501).** As the name suggests, this sleekly turned-out dining room – its rich woods, granite embellishments, glass-topped bar and canvas-wrapped pillars all suggest geographic elements – is intended to be as Canadian as the Great White North. In this case, "Canadian" means the ingredients (Arctic char, venison tenderloin, Malpeque oysters) more than any particular cuisine. Moderate to expensive.

Chinese

Happy Seven 358 Spadina Ave ☎416/971-9820. **Streetcar: Dundas (#505).** Predominantly Cantonese-style cooking with a few spicy Szechuan dishes, tanks of soon-to-be seafood, and large, attractively presented servings. Bright and spotless, this establishment is always filled with satisfied customers. Open until 5am. Inexpensive.

Lai Wah Heen Metropolitan Hotel, 108 Chestnut St ☎416/977-9899. **Streetcar: Dundas (#505).** The name means "elegant meeting place", which it most certainly is. The high-end dining room atmosphere is matched by the complex menu, best described as Hong Kong moderne, with dishes like Lustrous Peacock (a salad of barbecued duck, chicken and jellyfish on slivered melons garnished with eggs). Very popular on Sundays for dim sum. Expensive.

Lee Garden 331 Spadina Ave ☎416/593-9524. **Streetcar: Dundas (#505).** Expect long lines at this beloved restaurant. Locals esteem *Lee's* for the boneless chicken with black bean sauce and the large selection of fresh fish dishes. The cuisine is mostly Cantonese with plenty of daily specials that may demand your waiter's translation. Inexpensive to moderate.

Lucky Dragon 418 Spadina Ave ☎416/598-7823. **Streetcar: Spadina (#510).** The extensive pan-China menu features over 500 items, making the *Lucky Dragon* a prime spot for anyone seeking a crash course in all the Middle Kingdom's cuisines. The noodle dishes contain some delicate surprises, like a fine noodle dressed simply in green onion and ginger. There are a wide variety of soups, hearty hot pots, lots of pork and seafood dishes, and plenty of vegetarian

options available to those who ask. Delicious and authentic. Inexpensive.

French

Jules 147 Spadina Ave ☎416/348-8886. **Streetcar: Queen (#501).** Tucked between coffeeshops and the Fashion District wholesalers, this small French bistro is a real find. Huge bowls of steamed mussels in a garlicky white wine sauce complement rosemary rubbed chicken, a daily selection of savoury crepes or toothsome quiche. The wine list is thoughtful if somewhat limited, and the desserts are *comme Mama fait* ("like Mum makes"). Moderate.

La Maquette 111 King St E ☎416/366-8191. **Streetcar: King (#504).** If for nothing else, *La Maquette* would be worth visiting for the views alone: the summer patio runs alongside the Toronto Sculpture Garden, and, in winter, cosy upstairs rooms overlook the steeple of St James Cathedral. As for the menu, it's French with pronounced Italian tendencies, meaning that meaty mains like seared pate foie gras and beef tenderloin share space alongside veggie-friendly options like a respectable range of pastas. The service here is warm and friendly, the setting is opulently pretty, and the ambience is leisurely and contemplative. Moderate to expensive.

Le Select 328 Queen St W ☎416/596-6406. **Streetcar: Queen (#506).** Rib-sticking Gallic favourites are served in a bistro atmosphere, with embellishments like a genuine Parisian zinc bar and little baskets of bread raised and lowered at each table by a Rube Goldberg-esque pulley system. Use Sunday brunch as an excuse to sample an ultra-fluffy omelette served with the best *frites* in town. If your main intent is to lounge on the enclosed patio and people-watch, the beer and wine list is sterling, and the service is consistently excellent. Moderate to expensive.

Indian

Babur 237 Queen St W ☎416/599-7720. **Streetcar: Queen (#501).** Rich, buttery sauces, delicately spiced stews and fluffy naan and pori breads, all delivered to your linen-cloth table by a helpful waitstaff. Moderate.

Bombay Palace 71 Jarvis St ☎416/368-8048. **Streetcar: King (#504).** Mostly northern-style cooking with a nod towards Delhi. Crispy pakoras and samosas are good bets for starters. Main courses of mulligatawny soup and a full range of fish, meat and vegetable dishes are served with flourish in a serene, attractive dining room. Moderate.

New Arani 402 Spadina Ave ℡416/979-8105. **Streetcar: Spadina (#510) or Dundas (#501).** Located in the middle of Chinatown, this is one of Toronto's best-loved Indian restaurants. Specializing in southern Indian fare, in which more subtle spice combinations with occasional fire predominate, the small, narrow dining room here fills up quickly. Inexpensive to moderate.

International

Agora 317 Dundas St W ℡416/979-6612. **Streetcar: Dundas (#505)** The cuisine theme of this beautiful atrium restaurant, in the Art Gallery of Ontario (see p.55), depends on the gallery's current major exhibit. For a Gauguin and Van Gogh show, the tastes and colours of Provence dominated the menu, while during a Tom Thomson exhibit, prosaic Canadian favourites such as the humble grilled-cheese sandwich or lake trout were reinterpreted with gourmet flair. The wine list also reflects these theme variations, though the cellar consistently stocks some of the best Ontario vintages, such as a Henry of Pelham baco noir 1999 or the hard-to-find Cave Springs Chardonnay 2001. Service is solicitous and waitstaff know their stuff. Moderate to expensive.

Citron 813 Queen St W ℡416/504-2647. **Streetcar: Queen (#501).** A pleasant neighbourhood surprise on the bustling West Queen West strip. The kitchen casually veers between laid-back pastas and Middle Eastern starters to sophisticated entrees like duck confit. A solid vegetarian selection demonstrates an understanding of the neighbourhood, and everything is market-fresh. The interior is old-style diner, and the back patio is extremely pleasant, with old trees shading benches and banquettes at their base. Service is good if unrushed. Moderate.

Courthouse Market Grille 57 Adelaide St E ℡416/214-9379. **Streetcar: King (#504).** This building – once Toronto's courthouse, where ringleaders of the 1837 Upper Canada Rebellion were sentenced to death, and, just around the corner, hanged – commemorates its stirring history in a downstairs bar where the jail used to be.

Upstairs is a series of beautiful rooms, each giving way onto one another with the promise of fine dining. In actuality, the mainly steak and seafood entrees do not fulfil the promise of the setting – but if you want to stop off for a drink and snacks before moving on to some of the neighbourhood's better kitchens, you can't do better for a backdrop to end or begin an evening. Expensive.

Gypsy 817 Queen St W ℡416/703-5069. There are so many reasons to come to *Gypsy*: it's a genuine Toronto experience, the environment is like a big, comfy chair and the meals are wonderful. The varied menu offers stylish spins on comfort food – though in Toronto, comfort food belongs to many different cultures, so expect to see a variety of cuisines represented, according to market freshness. Moderate to expensive.

Jump Café and Bar 18 Wellington St W, **Commerce Court East** ℡416/363-340. **Subway: King.** Wheelers and dealers love this fine Financial District eatery, and lunchtime often sees a who's who of Canadian money and politics sitting down to sophisticated treatments of meat and potatoes. An impressive range of meal-sized salads, as well as the weekly specials, carry a light touch, featuring chicken and freshwater fish – so patrons won't have to worry about nodding off during those post-prandial briefings. The wine list is very good, with a nice emphasis on New World vintages. Expensive.

Mildred Pierce 99 Sudbury Ave ℡416/ 588-5695, ⊛www.mildredpierce.com. **Streetcar: King (#504).** The name alone should be enough to intrigue you. However, nothing about this fine restaurant suggests the Joan Crawford tearjerker: its interior is reminiscent of an Italian Renaissance palazzo, and the menu wafts through the Mediterranean via Italy, with a nod to Thailand and even the odd Canadian reference. Moderate to expensive.

Peter Pan 373 Queen St W ℡416/593-0917. **Streetcar: Queen (#501).** This long, thin Queen West icon is where many Torontonians had their first foodie epiphanies back in the early 1980s, though it wears its age and reputation well. Perhaps less interested in staying on top of trends than in doing a solid bistro-type menu well, the only caveat may be that vegetarian options are limited; otherwise, bon appetit! Moderate to expensive.

TAKE OUT
SERVICE

...LY LICENSED

△ At Lawrence Market, there's creative food and advertising

Swan Restaurant 892 Queen St W ☎416/532-0452. **Streetcar: Queen (#501).** Once an ugly-duckling lunch counter, this little eatery was the first sign that the neighbourhood was in the midst of a big transition. Today, the warm, wood-panelled interior maintains the vestiges of its past – booths, swivel stools at the counter and 1940s light fixtures – while meal-sized salads, creamy risottos and numerous oyster dishes, like Angels on Horseback (oysters wrapped in bacon), are served by a youthful, friendly staff. Moderate.

Verveine 1097 Queen St E ☎416/ 405-9906. **Streetcar: Queen (#501).** When well-decorated restaurants serving contemporary takes on bistro classics – steamed mussels bathed in mango butter, fat sandwiches served with crispy pommes frites – pop up in formerly proletarian sections of town, locals cluck their tongues at the gentrification of yet another neighbourhood... and then line up to sample the menu. All of the above is true of *Verveine*, which, despite its name and lovely green interior, has few herbaceous items on its menu. It's a very popular Sunday brunch spot, so you'd do well to make reservations if that's when you plan to visit. Moderate to expensive.

Zoom 18 King St E ☎416/861-9872. **Expensive. Subway: King.** A midtown eatery popular with lunching corporate types and CEOs. The dramatic steel-and-glass interior seems designed to give diners clear sight lines of all the other tables, and the quality food – a confident mix of Asian, North American and Latin cuisines – is given excellent presentation. Expensive.

Italian

Bar One 924 Queen St W ☎416/535-1655. **Streetcar: Queen (#501).** The first thing you'll notice about *Bar One* is that the place is long, narrow and looks fabulous. On one side of the space are intimate blonde wood booths, and on the other is the best long bar in town. Stretching the full length of the interior, this two-sided seating arrangement promotes lots of chat with fellow diners; if you want intimacy, stick to the booths. Essential menu elements are pizzas and pastas, with an emphasis on fresh, quality ingredients. Also has a good wine list and a great staff. Moderate.

Kit Kat 297 King St W ☎416/977-4461. **Streetcar: King (#504).** Pastas, steaks and seafood dominate the uncomplicated menu at *Kit Kat*. Even though it's typically busy, the atmosphere here is friendly and the service is attentive. First-timers are invited to pat the tree growing in the middle of the kitchen for good luck. Moderate.

La Fenice 319 King St W ☎416/585-2377. **Streetcar: King (#504).** The high standards of this long-time favourite are one reason its clientele keep coming back. Another is the deliberate unfashionability of the antipasti, pastas, risottos and fish dishes. Tradition reigns in the kitchen – venison, veal and lamb are featured as the weighty mains – as well as in the dining room. Waitstaff take their jobs seriously and are knowledgeable. Expensive.

Noce 875 Queen St W ☎416/504-3463. **Streetcar: Queen (#501)** On the corner of Queen West and Walnut (hence the nut name), this little house has become an exceptional Italian restaurant. The pasta is rolled by hand, the beef carpaccio virtually melts on the tongue, and the meat from the roasted capon breast falls right off the bone. Service is personable, as befits such a small place, and although the wine list is short, it is well considered. A wonderful choice for a special occasion. Moderate to expensive.

Japanese

Hiro Sushi 171 King St E ☎416/304-0550. **Streetcar: King (#504).** Hiro-san raised the bar for Toronto's sushi establishments when he opened this sliver of a restaurant. It offers unparalleled subtlety in all respects: decor, presentation and, of course, the food itself. Considered by many to be the best sushi spot in town. Expensive.

Nami 55 Adelaide St E ☎416/362-7373. **Streetcar: King (#504).** A very fine Japanese restaurant with a dark, elegant interior lined with discrete private booths. The sushi bar is the standard fare, but the robata counter (grilled seafood prepared in front of you) is the main draw. Expensive.

Sushi Bistro 204 Queen St W ☎416/971-5315. **Streetcar: Queen (#501).** At the moment, there are any number of sushi chains churning out stuff that tastes like the plastic food models *Sushi Bistro* has in its window. Not here, though: this venerable Queen West hangout has freshly made sushi selections and bento boxes as varied as its clientele. Entrees come with soup, salad, tea and rice, and there is an impressive sake selection. Moderate.

Latin

Caju 922 Queen St W ☎416/532-2550. **Streetcar: Queen (#501)** This Brazilian newcomer to the West Queen West strip is making friends quickly. Its svelte interior is warmly minimal and the menu is similarly compact, with just seven appetizers and six main course offerings, plus vegetarian options. Distinctive features are the varied uses of cassava root (as flour, rosti, in stews, as chips), the zingy treatment seafood gets, and the hearty soups of the day. Desserts are attractive and so is the cocktail list. Moderate to expensive.

Seafood

Filet of Sole 11 Duncan St ☎416/598-3256. **Streetcar: Queen (#501).** Serving an extensive range of fairly straightforward, extra-fresh seafood (lobsters, scallops, trout and salmon), in lively warehouse-style surroundings. Downstairs, *The Whistling Oyster* oyster bar is especially popular with the after-office set, and features a dim sum list, as well. Moderate to expensive.

Rodney's Oyster House 209 Adelaide St E ☎416/363-8105. **Streetcar: King (#504).** Toronto's favourite oyster bar serves up tons of the slippery delicacies, along with scallops, mussels and shrimp. The only regular fish available is the smoked salmon. The wine and dessert menus are short, but the selection of beer and scotch is impressive. Expensive.

Steakhouses

36 On Wellington 36 Wellington Ave E ☎416/306-0221. **Subway: Union Station or Streetcar: King (#504).** A really good-looking restaurant, like a brasserie in a Degas painting. There are intimate booths and a dark carved-wood, seemingly antique bar in the front, beside a generous nineteenth-century picture window perfect for those who want to be seen. Bistro-style viands and grilled steak are the mains. Cornish game hens are about the lightest food on the menu. Substantive wine list, solicitous service. Expensive.

Barberian's 7 Elm St ☎416/597-0335. **Subway: Dundas.** *Barberian's* hasn't changed much since it opened its doors in 1959, catering to Richard Burton and Elizabeth Taylor during the opening days of *Camelot*. It continues to offer no-nonsense dining geared towards carnivores in a comfy, clubby environment. The wine list is excellent. Expensive.

Ruth's Chris Steak House 145 Richmond St W ☎416/955-1455. **Subway: Osgoode.** For those who know their beef, the corn-fed distinction of the cattle here at this outpost of the Ruth's Chris chain is an important one, as is the fact that the steaks are hand-cut and arrive at your table in varying appetizing shades of pink, sizzling away. Moderate to expensive.

Thai

Ban Vanipha 638 Dundas St W ☎416/340-0491. **Streetcar: Dundas (#505).** A recent move from its old Augusta Avenue location has led to a less distinguished atmosphere, though the menu has actually expanded, and continues to offer subtle, sophisticated versions of dishes that may be familiar by name (fresh spring rolls, shrimp soup, glass noodles) but which tend to receive a heavy hand in other kitchens. Here, peppers, ginger, and coconut are used with care, not abandon. Vegetarians will be pleased with the number of options. Moderate.

Bangkok Garden 18 Elm St ☎416/977-6748. **Subway: Dundas.** Set in one of Elm Street's beautiful old brownstones, *Bangkok Garden* features a fine dining room with Southeast Asian embellishments, soft lighting and plenty of nooks. The heat on the curries is turned down a notch to accommodate all tastes. Specialities include a Thai take on fresh lake fish, and a standard selection of salads, noodles and curries. Moderate to expensive.

Bangkok Paradise 506 Queen St W ☎416/504-3210. **Streetcar: Queen (#501).** This is funky Thai for the Queen West crowd. Informal and usually packed, *Bangkok Paradise* has a goofy thatched hut motif that has an off-centre appeal. The menu has all the satay, noodle and curry classics you'd expect, with a wide range of vegetarian options. Moderate.

Golden Thai 105 Church St ☎416/868-6668. **Streetcar: King (#504).** It's almost worth visiting *Golden Thai* for the space alone: huge, Neoclassical fan windows, high ceilings and a cavernous interior make this space an island of calm. And, with over eighty dishes of Royal Thai cuisine to choose from, the menu lives up to the decor's promise, with an emphasis on freshness, enabling the taste of the ingredients to shine through, firey spices and all. The lemon shrimp soup is recommended, and vegetarians have a good range of choice. Moderate.

Vegetarian

Bo De Duyen 254 Spadina Ave (upstairs) ☎416/703-1247. Streetcar: Spadina (#510). This popular walk-up greets guests with puffs of incense and an ancestral shrine halfway up the stairs. It offers Chinese-Vietnamese cooking for vegetarians. The utter absence of any animal by-products means that even the strictest vegan can eat here with a clear conscience. Pages and pages of selections, including "mock" meat and seafood items. Moderate.

Fressen Herbacious Cuisine 478 Queen St W ☎416/504-5127. Streetcar: Queen (#501). This restaurant is too cool to bill itself as being vegetarian per se; the tag line here is "herbacious cuisine" – but, veggie it is, replete with vegan options. Regulars pass over the pastas and pizzas for the entrees. A full meal can also be made of the excellent appetizers, and the juice/smoothie list is extensive. Moderate.

Gujurat Durbar 1386 Gerrard St E ☎416/406-1085. Streetcar: Carlton (#506). This vegetarian restaurant, in the midst of the East End's Little India, serves up aromatic dishes from India's northwest Gujrati region. Your best bet is the generously proportioned thali, which features a variety of daily curries, dhal, pickles and rice. Inexpensive.

Le Commensal 655 Bay St (entrance off Elm Street) ☎416/596-9364. Subway: Dundas. The cafeteria-style set-up of this large, airy restaurant is its only drawback. Otherwise, the variety of offerings is excellent: soups, great salads, hearty pot-pies, stews, casseroles and baked goods are clearly marked for vegans or lacto-ovo vegetarians. A large dessert counter tempts with delectables like maple sugar pie, fruit cobblers and sweet pastries. Licensed for beer and wine. Takeout is also available. Moderate.

Lotus Garden 393 Dundas St W ☎416/598-1883. Streetcar: Dundas (#505). A huge fibreglass moose, decked out in vaguely Taoist colours and symbols, stands in front of this little Vietnamese eatery, which is the only vegetarian Vietnamese restaurant in Toronto. Ignore the "mock" beef, pork, seafood dishes and go straight for the soups, noodle dishes, or stuffed vegetables. The Vietnamese crepes are particularly tasty, and the iced coffee is habit-forming in the extreme. Suitable for vegan diets. Inexpensive.

Simon's Wok 797 Gerrard St ☎416/ 778-9836. Streetcar: Carlton (#506) This wonderful

24-7 grocery stores and delis

Rabba Fine Foods 256 Jarvis St ☎416/595-9679, Downtown, Streetcar: King (#504); 4 Wellesley St W ☎416/922-4451, Subway: Wellesley; 9 Isabella, Uptown ☎416/928-2300, Subway: Wellesley; plus four other locations.
This handy, well-run deli/grocery store chain has large deli counters that stock prepared foods for takeaway meals, picnics and snacks at bargain prices, including salads, Mediterranean dips, pastas, sliced meats and cheeses and sweet and savoury pastries. As befits Toronto, there's a cosmopolitan array of foodstuffs on offer, ranging from Greek dolimadas to Indian samosas to Japanese sushi. You can also purchase toiletries, gadgets like can-openers and corkscrews, and fresh-cut flowers for those last-minute gifts. Rabba also has ATMs.

Kitchen Table Grocery Store 595 Bay St, Uptown ☎416/977-2225, Subway: Bay. Just in case you wake up at 3.30am and decide you have to have fresh fusili pasta with marinara sauce and a shrimp cocktail chaser, this is the place to head. However, you should expect to pay premium prices for the 24-7 convenience. Kitchen Table also has a range of prepared deli-type foods for more simple late-night snacks. There's an ATM on the premises.

Chinese restaurant sits at the east end of Chinatown East, and has a menu with wide enough appeal to draw in all types, from hippie-esque Riverdalers and elderly Asian ladies, to young university types resplendent in tattoos and multiple piercings. Many items on the menu contain gluten, a chewy wheat-based staple that can be crafted to resemble fish, chicken or meat – which it doesn't taste like at all – and there are long lists of delicious casseroles, soups, noodle and rice dishes. The subtlety of the flavours is explained by the absence of MSG, garlic or even onion. Suitable for vegan diets. Inexpensive.

Vietnamese

Pho 88 Restaurant 270 Spadina Ave ☎416/971-8899. **Streetcar: Spadina (#510).** The speciality here is pho, a spicy noodle soup with beef and vegetables that can have numerous variations, according to the customer's choice. Inexpensive.
Vien Dong 359 Spadina Ave ☎416/593-6265. **Streetcar: Spadina (#510).** Primarily a Vietnamese restaurant, with lots of Cantonese influence and a few Gallic touches (frog legs, for example). Also serves a variety of fresh tropical fruit shakes. Inexpensive.

Uptown

African

Ethiopian House 4 Irwin Ave ☎416/923-5438. **Subway: Wellesley.** A two-storey restaurant with cosy, muralled rooms, the food here is graced with aromatic, complex spicing. Moist towelettes and huge discs of sourdough bread called injera replace cutlery, while large platters covered with yurt-like raffia caps replace ho-hum dishes. And, for a nominal fee, a full-blown coffee ceremony replaces a plain cup o' joe at the end of the delicious meal. Inexpensive to moderate.

Asian fusion

Indochine 4 Collier St ☎416/922-5840. **Subway: Yonge/Bloor.** A sexy new renovation draws the Yorkville crowd, though the menu (and the prices) have remained the same. The French accent in the Vietnamese dishes is fairly pronounced, especially with the shellfish, while gentle touches of fragrant lemongrass, coriander and curry prevail in the soups and noodle dishes. The pho soup is the best bargain, and the crab curry is much recommended, with an agreeable amount of spice. The yellow chicken curry is really hot, and not for the uninitiated. Thai favourites like pad Thai and purple basil beef also find their way onto the menu. Desserts are more a suggestion than an actual course, but the sweet iced coffee will take care of any post-prandial sugar cravings. Inexpensive to moderate.

Tempo 596 College St ☎416/531-2822. **Streetcar: College (# 506).** This slim, minimalist restaurant continues to host the construction of some of the city's most desirable sashimi, while non-vegetarian thermaphobes can't get enough of the hamachi tartare. Although the top notes at *Tempo* are Japanese, the menu reflects what Toronto food critics have started to describe as "multi-culti": sea bass is given a maple glaze, red snapper gets the sushi treatment, and Italian touches like balsamic vinegar and olive oil work as accents on an Asian background, while simultaneously referring back to the neighbourhood's Little Italy origins. Moderate to expensive.
Xacutti 503 College St ☎416/323-3957. **Streetcar: College (#506).** Pronounced sha-KOO-tee, this deeply hip space makes an immediate impression with a pair of decorative chandeliers made from small handwritten notes in many languages and alphabets. After seeing these, slip to the lounge at the back and order a drink from the innovative cocktail list, or sit down at the long, communal table that slices through the middle of the restaurant. The food is pan-Asian via India (Thai noodles, curries, pakora), made mostly with indigenous ingredients. A good introduction to the chef's vision is to order lots of small dishes or appetizers. Moderate to expensive.

Canadian and American

Patriot Restaurant and Brasserie 131 Bloor St W, 2nd floor ☎416/922-0025. Subway: Bay/Museum. Owner Scott Willows has nurtured *Patriot* in a manner befitting a personal passion. His establishment reinterprets Canadian regional dishes (ie tortier from Québec, Mennonite sausages from Ontario, and variations on every crustaceous Maritime dish) and sources the best in craft fromageries, ultra-fresh, often organic fruits and vegetables, and somewhat exotic game birds and animals. The service is excellent, and the calm celadon-and-wood interior opens onto a dynamic view of Bloor Street's Golden Row. *Patriot* also serves the best Sunday brunch on this pricey strip. Moderate to expensive.

True Grits Soul Shack 603 Markham St ☎416/536-8383. Subway: Bathurst. Creole and Southern US specialities like grits, chicken-fried steak, and candied yams are dished up with laid-back elan in this comfy Victorian renovation. The walls are packed with funky naif paintings by artist Robin Grindley and the furniture is a flea market mishmash. Make time to eat slowly and enjoy the party that surrounds you. Moderate to expensive.

Caribbean

Irie 808 College St ☎416/531-4743. Streetcar: College (#506). Island standards like jerk chicken, pork or shrimp, rice and peas and rotis of every description are given a chef's touch at this modest restaurant at the end of the thriving College strip. The extreme heat of some preparations is toned down for a greater subtlety of flavours, the interplay between herbs and spices being one of the joys of Caribbean cooking. There are plenty of veggie options, a rich dessert menu, and a slight – but well-chosen – wine list. Moderate.

Chinese

Pink Pearl 120 Avenue Rd ☎416/966-3631. Subway: Bay. You won't find many Chinese restaurants in the Yorkville area, but *Pink Pearl* is the happy exception. Serves mostly dependable Cantonese-style dishes. The desserts (fried banana, for one) leave something to be desired, but the ambience makes up for this slight digression in taste. Moderate to expensive.

French and Belgian

Arlequin 134 Avenue Rd ☎416/928-9521. Subway: Bay. Commedia dell'arte motifs decorate this tried-and-true outpost of traditional French fare, featuring bistro standards like duck leg confit, a slightly spicy rabbit dish, and *le bifteque* with pommes frites (of course). There are also a number of tasty salads with a Moroccan twist, available from the lunch counter right by the door. Luncheon diners can avail themselves of a prix-fixe menu. Expensive.

Bistro 990 990 Bay St ☎416/921-9990. Subway: Wellesley. This cosy favourite of corporate types (and the odd movie star) offers robust bistro fare, with a strong emphasis on meaty dishes (rabbit, lamb). The caramelized onion tart with a melt-in-the-mouth flake pastry crust is a real showstopper. Prix-fixe menus take the sting out of what can be a pricey outing. Expensive.

Café Brussels 124 Danforth Ave ☎416/465-7363. Subway: Broadview. The popularity of this huge space is entirely due to the fact that it does one or two simple things well: moules et frites with garlic mayonnaise, savoury or sweet crepes and huge fluffy waffles, for Sunday brunch. Service is friendly but not over-solicitous, and, like all good Belgian establishments, the beer list is as serious as the wine. The Art Deco promise of the chrome lettering outside carries through to the interior, right down to the last angular wall sconce. Moderate.

Gamelle 468 College St ☎416/923-6254. Streetcar: College (#506). Every neighbourhood should be so lucky as to have a little French bistro like *Gamelle* tucked in its midst. Touches of Québec and Morocco find their way onto the menu in the form of salads or roasted meats. Brunch is both popular and charming, and space is limited, so be sure to make reservations. Moderate.

La Bodega 30 Baldwin St ☎416/977-1287. Streetcar: College (#506) The eclectic Baldwin Street stretch of restaurants is perhaps an odd place to look for traditional French dining – but *La Bodega* manages to meet the standards of the most critical Francophile, with its respectful approach to sweetbreads, pates, beef and – for those who have room – desserts. Moderate to expensive.

Matignon 51 St Nicholas St ☎416/921-9226. Subway: Wellesley. Less than a block from gritty Yonge Street, St Nicholas Street seems

a world away, with its cobblestone paving, Victorian cottages and wonderful gems like *Matignon*. The approach to traditional French mains here is very light, with some Moroccan (or perhaps Lebanese?) refinements, which are especially noticeable in the lunchtime menu's salads. Four prix-fixe selections make this one of the more affordable French restaurants in town. Moderate to expensive.
Provence 12 Amelia St ☎416/924-9901. **Streetcar: Carlton (#506).** This renovated Cabbagetown cottage serves a small but highly competent menu, with pronounced nouvelle cuisine leanings: there's plenty of attention to vegetables, meats served au jus rather than in heavy sauces and there's lots of fresh-fruit desserts. Vegetarian options are a recent, good addition to the menu. A particularly charming place for brunch. Expensive.

Greek

Avli 401 Danforth Ave ☎416/461-9577. **Subway: Chester.** An authentic Greek restaurant with a strong emphasis on fancy starters, a combination of which could easily make a full meal. Classic seafood dishes, a variety of pot-pies and sublime *baklava* round out the meal, all served with Hellenic elan. The most theatrical dish in the house is saganaki, a slab of a mozzarella-like cheese doused in brandy and set aflame. The wine list is good, but ask about the owner's cellar for something really special. Moderate to expensive.
Ouzeri 500 A Danforth Ave ☎416/466-8158. **Subway: Chester.** The later the hour, the more festive the atmosphere at this raucous joint. A long list of classic mezze (Greek tapas) starters like skardalia, humous, stuffed vine leaves and home-made pita vie with entrees such as moussakas, pastas, racks of lamb and a solid wine list for guests' attention and capacity. Loud music, clattering glasses, pans and dishes and animated conversation make each visit a party. Moderate to expensive.
Pan on the Danforth 516 Danforth Ave ☎416/466-8158. **Subway: Chester.** This long, thin eatery is where Greek classics meet Athenian nouvelle cuisine. Check out the upmarket interpretations of seafood classics like kakavia, a type of Greek bouillabaisse. Attentive service on even the busiest nights. Moderate to expensive.
Pappas Grill 440 Danforth Ave ☎416/469-9595. **Subway: Chester.** This is very much a family

establishment, with two-and-a-half levels and plenty of space for large tables. All the standard items are featured: souvlaki, mezze appetizers, grilled seafood and lamb served with rice and potatoes. Everything comes with baskets of pita and lashings of olive oil. Moderate.

Indian and Sri Lankan

The Host 14 Prince Arthur Ave ☎416/962-4678. **Subway: Bay or St George.** An unusually delicate approach to Northern style Indian cuisine frees spices from heavy sauces and lets the interplay of flavors and ingredients work their magic in a fine dining room. Carnivores may want to stray over onto the vegetarian side of the menu, which has many options and features a light touch.
Indian Rice Factory 414 Dupont St ☎416/961-3472. **Subway: Dupont.** This venerable Annex favourite has recently had a face-lift and now sports a look that dips into *Wallpaper* territory. Nevertheless, the fare remains dependable and the family atmosphere lurks just below the new, sleek decor. The spicing of the main dishes is on the mild side, but the samosas and pakoras are perfectly crisp, the entree sauces are voluptuously rich to the taste, and the dessert offerings are very sweet. Moderate.
Nataraj 394 Bloor St W ☎416/928-2925. **Subway: Spadina.** Delhi-specific dishes with a tandoori twist. The air is perfumed with delectable naan baking on the sides of the tandoori oven, which is on view to diners through a window to the kitchen. Try the spicy stews, near-addictive shrimp pakoras, and sugar-rush desserts. Moderate.
Rashnaa 307 Wellesley St E ☎416/929-2099. **Streetcar: Carlton (#506).** This tiny restaurant, crammed into a small Cabbagetown cottage, offers intriguing Southern Indian and Sri Lankan dishes, including a red lentil linguine served with coconut chutney and a variety of dhosas, a habit-forming Sri Lankan crepe that comes with a variety of fillings. One of the city's best dining bargains. Inexpensive.

International

Goldfish Restaurant 372 Bloor St W ☎416/513-0077. **Subway: Spadina.** A wonderful addition to an already great strip of restaurants, *Goldfish* manages to be sleek and chic without attitude – and that goes double for the food. The vegetable Napoleon is a case in point: thin planes of shaved veggies layer upwards in a tower of alternating tastes, colours and textures. The foie gras is another crowd-pleaser, as are the fish dishes, which have a discernible Middle Eastern accent. Meat mains are hearty and perhaps less playful. The desserts are as well thought-out as the rest of the meal; first-timers should be sure to sample the home-made ice creams. Moderate to expensive.

Gus 1033 Bay St ☏416/923-8159. **Subway: Wellesley.** This huge space – with only a banner bearing a lone "G" for signage – offers a menu that borrows from the Greek tradition of listing categories of foods (meats, seafood, vegetables, etc) that can be combined in any number of ways. This method of meal-making immediately gets people sharing, talking, laughing and, in general, thoroughly enjoying themselves. Moderate to expensive.

Joya 577 College St, ☏416/588-6458. **Streetcar: College (#506).** This long, skinny addition to hipster heaven on the College strip has garnered a solid fan base, which means the joint can get crowded on a weekend. Food-wise, the most discernible accent is Italian, with a good grill for meaty mains. Pastas are always a sure bet, as they feature seasonal, market-fresh ingredients. Prices are very reasonable, even though the decor is cutting-edge and the staff look like models. The patio presents a great opportunity for people-watching. Moderate to expensive.

The Town Grill 243 Carlton St ☏416/963-9433. **Streetcar: Carlton (#506).** A genuine neighbourhood bistro, the *Town Grill* is constantly being "discovered" by jaded foodies searching for uncomplicated but well-prepared food in a quiet, comfortable setting. Beef is king in this Cabbagetown favourite, and the signature dish is the tenderloin served with mushrooms and roasted garlic mashed potatoes. Moderate.

Italian

Bar Italia 584 College St ☏416/535-3621. **Streetcar: College (#506).** *Bar Italia* is a tradition in a neighbourhood that often seems fixated on the moment. The food is reliably delicious: antipasti, risotto, pasta and panini

are dished up amid the clatter of wine glasses by a solicitous staff. One of their best buys is a huge antipasti platter – you can view the daily selections in a luncheon counter near the front – that is meant to be shared and perfect for a light meal. The chic little patio out front makes prime people-watching theatre. Moderate.

Bar Mercurio 270 Bloor St W ☏416/960-3877. **Subway: St George.** *Bar Mercurio*'s small opening onto Bloor Street means that this great little restaurant is often overlooked – but not by those who care about good, inexpensive Italian food in pleasant surroundings. The mostly Northern Italian approach to the range of antipasti, salads, pastas, fish and meat dishes relies on an understanding of the (very fresh) ingredients, so that the natural flavours come through first and foremost. Here, it's all about high-quality virgin olive oil, shaved curls of Parmesan-Reggiano and paper-thin carpaccio. The desserts are a world unto themselves, and everything takes place in a quiet, intimate space with fine service, all for a very reasonable price. Moderate.

Café Diplomatico 594 College St ☏416/534-4637. **Streetcar: College (#506).** This restaurant vestige of an earlier time has managed to hold its own among new, chi-chi neighbours. Substantial, no-nonsense pizzas (with a selection of market-fresh toppings) and pastas served inside or on the packed patio. Inexpensive.

Café Nervosa 75 Yorkville Ave ☏416/961-4642. **Subway: Bay.** One of the few reasonably priced restaurants left in Yorkville, *Café Nervosa* is a great spot for people (aka, celebrity) watching. The open kitchen can't handle anything too complicated, so salads, pastas and pizzas dominate the menu selection – which, limited though it may be, is excellent: don't miss the two-person, regionally named pizzas with thin, crispy crusts and an authentic variety of toppings. *Nervosa*'s also one of the few places in town that offers a pizza blanca: thin slices of Yukon Gold potatoes, Parmesan cheese, onions, rosemary and olive oil. The daily pastas are substantial meals, so if you have something lighter in mind, choose a la carte. The dinner menu offers grilled striploin prepared with a mushroom risotto or as a bisteca alla fiorentina (steak and potatoes), grilled sea bass or, more interestingly, grilled chicken breast stuffed with goat's cheese and sun-dried tomatoes. Service is unfailingly pleasant. Moderate.

Giovanna 637 College St ☎416/538-2098. **Streetcar: College (#506).** Deceptively simple Northern Italian cooking is *Giovanna*'s claim to fame. Velvet cream and mushroom sauces on home-made pasta, coupled with light, tender vegetable dishes, are elegant triumphs. Perfectly baked chicken falls from the bone, while a wood-burning oven turns out light, crisp pizzas, with lots of toppings to choose from. Patio tables are available, but the clattering of the passing streetcar makes conversation difficult. Otherwise, the ambience is pleasant and the staff are friendly, prompt and knowledgeable. Moderate to expensive.

Grano 2035 Yonge St ☎416/ 440-1986. **Subway: Davisville.** Many Italian restaurants go to a great deal of trouble and expense to make their place look and feel like home. In the case of *Grano*, this is no illusion: the family lives upstairs and works downstairs, and when you step into the restaurant you know you're a real guest, and not just a customer. Family photographs adorn the walls; family recipes make the pastas, seafood and meat dishes a personal slice of Tuscany; and the brilliant antipasti is positively addictive: the fried zucchini blossoms, golden rice balls with a mozzarella centre or the perfectly grilled eggplant are incomparable. The charming back patio is closed only during the depths of winter. Moderate to expensive.

Japanese

Mariko 348 Danforth Ave ☎416/463-8231. **Subway: Chester.** This Japanese bistro and sushi bar is a favourite neighbourhood haunt amongst Riverdalers, due to its health-conscious, vegetarian-friendly menu, the attractive East/West decor, and the unfailing courtesy of its staff. The bento boxes can be on the pricey side, but the udon and soba noodle soups are a bargain. Moderate.

Rikishi Japanese Restaurant 833 Bloor St W ☎416/538-0760. **Subway: Christie.** Stuck out among Portuguese, Cuban and Somalian sports bars, this little gem not only serves well-prepared traditional Japanese dishes – either individually or in bento boxes as a

prix fixe – but also offers over thirty makki options, plus a variety of veggie bento boxes. Dishes, decor and service are all very Japanese, but Western cutlery is available upon request. Waitstaff are extremely helpful and attentive. Moderate.

Latin American and Spanish

Boulevard Café 161 Harbord St ☎416/961-7676. **Streetcar: Spadina (#510). Bus: Wellesley (#94).** The menu at this popular South Annex eatery draws from the entire South American continent. There's seafood from Peru (shrimp, sea bass, oysters), steak from Argentina and Latin staples like corn, beans and avocados, prepared with a light touch, a little heat and plenty of citrus. Cosy surroundings in a converted house, with dining rooms upstairs, downstairs and on a long sidewalk terrace. Moderate to expensive.

La Carreta 469 Danforth Ave ☎416/461-7718. **Subway: Chester.** This jazzy Cuban joint offers a pleasing alternative to the souvlaki palaces that cram Danforth Avenue. The food is an intriguing mix of African, Spanish and Caribbean influences. Huge grazing platters, including a vegetarian selection, make great introductions to the different dishes. Sangria, potent Cuban rum cocktails, and liquor-laced coffees take pride of place on the drinks menu. Moderate.

Segovia 5 St Nicholas St ☎416/960-1010. **Subway: Wellesley.** Cavernous and darkly discreet, this old-time favourite has become a hot uptown venue for power lunches. The paella is somewhat staid, but the cod brandine is a classic. There is also a tapas bar upstairs. Moderate to expensive.

Middle Eastern

Jerusalem 955 Eglinton Ave W ☎416/783-6494. **Moderate. Subway: Eglinton West.** This Israeli restaurant has been delighting diners for more than two decades now. The combination platters for two are an excellent bargain, and give the best example of this establishment's fusion of Middle Eastern and traditional Jewish dishes. The service is quick, friendly and helpful.

Kensington Kitchen 124 Harbord St ☎416/961-3404. **Streetcar: Spadina (#510) or Bus: Wellesley (#94).** Another Toronto favourite, this airy, converted house offers upstairs and downstairs dining amid carefully selected knick-knacks and crimson-ochre carpets. The menu is pan-Mediterranean, with Lebanese, Greek and Moroccan classics. Plenty of choices for vegetarians. Moderate.

Seafood

Joso's 202 Davenport Ave ☎416/925-1930. **Inconvenient public transport; best to take a taxi.** This much-loved restaurant, described at length by Margaret Atwood in her novel *Robber Bride*, is famous for three things: its squid-ink risotto, the plethora of breasts and buttocks in owner Joso Spralja's paintings and statues that decorate the place – along with the odd Dali and Picasso – and the celebrities who can't get enough of *Joso's* signature Adriatic treatment of seafood. Expensive.
La Pecherie Mövenpick 133 Yorkville Ave ☎416/926-9545. **Subway: Bay.** *La Pecherie*

offers first-rate selections of ocean-fresh seafood, expertly prepared. Mounds of fresh fish are on display, but apart from that the decor is demure and restrained. Staff are attentive and handy with a fish knife, de-boning patrons' fish filets at the table upon request. Pastas, chicken dishes and salads are also featured, as is an excellent wine list. Expensive.

Steakhouses

George Bigliardi's 463 Church St ☎416/922-9594. **Streetcar: Carlton/College (#506).** Smack in the middle of the rainbow-coloured world of Toronto's Gay Village is this monument to granite-jawed manhood. *Bigliardi's* is particularly well-known for its chateaubriand, but seafood is also available. The staff has been here for eons, so expect the most respectful of traditional service, which means that casual dress and manners are literally frowned on. Expensive.

Bars

For a city that didn't serve mixed drinks until 1948, and is still subject to Canada's often puzzling liquor regulations, Toronto has managed to eke out a remarkably vital **bar scene**. You'll find everything from grizzled taverns, some of which still maintain a separate entrance for women, to sleek cocktail bars. People are huddled inside during the cold winter months, but in the summer many bars spread out **open patios** for all-day carousing.

Most bars and lounges featuring entertainment have a weekend **cover charge** after 9pm ranging between $5 and $10. Cover charges may apply during the week if there is a special act, performance, or top guest DJ. The legal drinking age throughout Ontario is nineteen, and **last call** at all establishments is 2am. This doesn't, however, necessarily herald an end to the night's festivities: after-hours bars riddle the city, and the people who will generally be able to guide you to them are the very bartenders serving your last orders. Be aware, though, that speakeasies (known locally as **booze cans**), roughly defined as unlicensed, after-hours clubs serving alcohol, are flat-out illegal and can be raided.

All Toronto bars are required to serve **food**, presumably to soak up all that booze – though the quality and service of this can often be sorely lacking. Let observation be your guide; if you don't see anyone eating, the food probably isn't worth ordering. At the moment, **smoking** is permitted in Toronto bars – but don't be surprised if this changes, as the city is definitely moving in a smoke-free direction.

Laws pertaining to **drinking and driving** are strict, so if you end up getting sloshed, leave your car in a car park, or better yet, don't take it along in the first place. **Taxicabs** are far easier to find than parking spots, and **public transportation** roams the city's main arteries 24 hours a day.

Downtown

Academy of Spherical Arts 38 Hanna St ☎416/532-2782. Streetcar: Queen (#501). Located in a former billiard table factory, this splendid pool and billiards hall offers an array of antique tables to play on, along with over one hundred varieties of single malt scotch.

The Amsterdam 600 King St W ☎416/504-1040. Streetcar: King (#504). This venerable brew pub located in an spacious Victorian building is a reminder of the days when this stretch of King Street West was a desert of empty warehouses. The strip's current trendiness has not afflicted the 'Dam. There are eight home brews to sample at the long bar and, for the curious, tours of the facility on weekends.

Apothecary 340 Adelaide St W ☎416/595-6333. Streetcar: King (#504). Effortlessly cool as a sheet of ice, *Apothecary* is the neighbourhood bar that every hipster wants close by, with its good crowd, attentive staff, and a trance/hip-hop DJ who can raise the roof after the sun goes down.

Black Bull 298 Queen St W ☎416/593-2766. **Streetcar: Queen (#501).** The line of gleaming motorcycles parked outside give an idea of who the regular patrons are at this popular spot, one of the oldest taverns in Toronto. The *Black Bull* also has an excellent summer patio, plus a grill menu heavy on the burgers.

Bouchon 38 Wellington St E (downstairs) ☎416/862-26750. **Subway: Union Station.** This recent addition to the theatre strip in the St Lawrence Market area became an instant favourite. The staff knows its wines and share their knowledge without being snobbish, and the dining area serves hearty French bistro fare, though filling snacks such as *croque monsieur* can be ordered at the curvy oak bar and the imported grill perfectly broils cheese toppings.

Bovine Sex Club 542 Queen St W ☎416/504-4239. **Streetcar: Queen (#501).** Despite its comically evocative name, the *Bovine* doesn't proclaim its existence with a sign nor does it have anything to do with cows or sex. The exterior is encrusted with layers of industrial scrap and bicycle parts, offering no glimpse of the playground within, which is filled with kinetic sculptures built from old portable record players, and has a couple of bars and pool tables.

Brassaaii 461 King St W ☎416-5938-4730. **Streetcar: King (#501).** Go through the wrought-iron gates and into the courtyard to find this smart establishment on the up-and-coming King West strip. The cavernous space holds a lounge, bar and dining area, with photographs by Brassaï hanging on the whitewashed walls. The main dishes on the menu draw their inspiration from Eastern Europe, and surprisingly, breakfast is also served, starting at 8am.

C'est What? 67 Front St E ☎416/867-9499. **Subway: Union Station.** Located in the dark, low-ceilinged basement in the St Lawrence Market area, *C'est What* has over twenty microbrews on tap – including the popular house brand, hemp beer – plus an impressive selection of single malt scotches and hearty pub food. The performance space here has seen the likes of Bare Naked Ladies and Jeff Buckley, to name just a few.

The Cameron House 408 Queen St W ☎416/703-0811. **Streetcar: Queen (#501).** This

old tap house has been a performance space and refuge for members of Toronto's alternative arts scene for two decades, and includes its own vibrant cabaret. The beautiful interior is covered with tromp l'oeil skies and angels and gilt plaster, while outside, artists have been rearranging the facade for twenty years now, the only constant being the huge, red metal ants marching up the side of the building.

Eau 609 King St W ☎416/203-9399. **Streetcar: King (#504).** This glamour bar's *raison d'être* is its proximity to the celebrated Asian fusion restaurant *Susur* (see review p.132) – after dinner, patrons retire to this chic spot for a cocktail. Food is also served here but who cares?

Element Bar 553 Queen St W ☎416/359-1919. **Streetcar: Queen (#501).** Despite concerns that this trendy bar was simply too cool and too good to last, *Element* continues apace with its winning Retro-Mod interior and progressive DJs, drawing a youngish but sophisticated crowd. The only downside is the line to get in on Saturday night, which can be daunting to the casual clubgoer.

Fez Batik 129 Peter St ☎416/204-9660. **Streetcar: Queen (#501).** This barn-like space features a quasi-Moroccan restaurant on the ground floor but the real attractions are the dance floors, the patio and a little upstairs club called *B-Side*.

Fluid Lounge 217 Richmond St W ☎416/593-6116. **Streetcar: Queen (#501).** One of the few Clubland establishments on the Richmond Street strip that doesn't curl up and die in the middle of the week, this youngish dance bar is also a prime spot to mingle with the locals.

The Gladstone Arts Bar 1214 Queen St W ☎416/531-4635. **Streetcar: Queen (#501).** The bar in this landmark Edwardian hotel is as grotty as it was before plans to refurbish the hotel went awry. Virtually nothing is new or improved and the draught is still cheap. The big change is the neighbourhood. Parkdale, once in the city's outer reaches, is now convenient to galleries, lofts and restaurants on Queen West, making the bar's over-the-top karaoke nights on Wednesdays and Saturdays more popular than ever.

Healy's 178 Bathurst St ☎416/703-5882. **Streetcar: Queen (#501).** Blues guitarist Jeff Healy opened up this tight little space and assured himself and the Jazz Wizards a permanent gig as the house band. Like many other bars these days, Wednesday is a karaoke night and occasionally Jeff shares the stage with another act, but generally speaking he is holding court here.

The Last Temptation 12 Kensington Ave ☎416/599-2551. **Streetcar: Dundas (#505).** A change of ownership and the attendant renovation saved this well-located Kensington Market dive from sheer nastiness. Now, it has a neighbourhood club ambiance, helped out by the generous patio out front. There's a Middle Eastern/Mediterranean menu as well, but the main reason to pop in is to have a drink and watch the lively street life go by.

Left Bank 567 Queen St W ☎416/504-1626. **Streetcar: Queen (#501).** This gorgeously decorated restaurant-cum-dance hall re-imagines Paris circa 1880. The dining room, spacious dance floor, pool room and remarkable *salon privée* are all still intact, and the youngish crowd is mainly local. A good place to start the night while you can still make out the interior.

Library Bar in the *Fairmont Royal York Hotel*, **100 Front St W** ☎416/368-2511. **Subway: Union.** One of the few places left in town where bar staff knows how to make a good martini and, better still, brings a little flask holding the other ounce of your drink. The bar also sports huge leather wing-back chairs, racks of newspapers, and it never plays loud music.

The Paddock 176 Bathurst ☎416/504-9997. **Streetcar: Queen (#501).** Rising phoenix-like from a grotty recent past to reclaim its original, authentic Deco glory, *The Paddock* boasts the world's longest Bakelite-topped bar. The crowd is mainly smart young filmmakers and TV types, and there's a kitchen that produces straightforward, meat-and-potatoes-type fare.

Rain 19 Mercer St ☎416/599-7246. **Streetcar: King (#504).** A former women's prison transformed into an ultra-stylish temple to Asian minimalism. The waitstaff here is as chic and good-looking as their surroundings and are mercifully without attitude. There's also an excellent restaurant here specializing in Asian fusion cuisine.

Reservoir Lounge 52 Wellington St E ☎416/955-0887. **Subway: Union Station.** An intimate subterranean club with a good selection of wines by the glass, microbrews on tap and a friendly bar staff. Live jazz on the weekends.

The Rivoli 332 Queen St W ☎416/504-1320. **Streetcar: Queen (#501).** High-backed booths line either side of Queen Street West's venerable temple to fusion cooking. Wookie balls, Asian noodle soups, and a global selection of appetizers are some of the offerings on the ever-changing menu. There is a long bar beside the dining room, a cabaret space in the back, and a pool-and-billiards room upstairs.

Toad in the Hole 525 King St W ☎416/593-8623. **Streetcar: King (#504).** Once an outpost of sorts for cheap suds and pub grub, these days the *Toad* offers much the same but amid the fancy lounges and restaurants that now line King West.

The Wheat Sheaf 667 King St W ☎416/504-9912. **Streetcar: King (#504).** Toronto's oldest public house served its first pint in 1849 and in the ensuing century and a half the *Wheat Sheaf* has embraced three innovations: indoor plumbing, refrigeration and a television permanently tuned to sporting events. Other than that things haven't changed much: there are jars of pickled eggs, anything worth drinking is in a keg, and of course there's a pool table.

Uptown

Artful Dodger 10 Isabella St ☎416/964-9511. **Subway: Wellesley.** An English-style pub that looks and feels authentic. A home away from home for locals, the *Dodger* also sees any number of social clubs and dart teams hanging out amid its red velvet banquettes and flocked wallpaper.

The Brunswick House 481 Bloor St W, Uptown ☎416/964-2242. **Subway: Spadina.** This old public house and neighbourhood fixture has been pulling pints and serving pitchers of cheap draught to poets, students and working stiffs since the 1880s. Despite a recent clean-up, the *Brunswick* has remained steadfastly downscale. There is always some community event or other going on in one of the taprooms and weekends usually see some live music. Thursday's cheap pitcher night is the best time to stop by.

Ciao Edie 489 College St ☏416/927-7774.
Streetcar: College (#506). Warhol muse Edie
Sedgwick was a source of inspiration for
this deliberately kitchy but cool lounge,
which is unselfconsciously decorated in
original Seventies garage finds. DJs spin
acid jazz and trip-hop, and Sundays feature
the ever-popular singles' night.

Eat My Martini 649 College St ☏416/516-
2549. **Streetcar: College (#506).** While it is possible to eat here, the main attraction, not
surprisingly, is the extensive martini list,
which boasts over eighty concoctions to
put you over the top at the end of a long
day.

Lava Lounge 507 College St ☏416/966-5282.
Streetcar: College (#506). Lava lamps and
slick red banquettes and booths give the
place a Sixties feel, while the good bar
menu features Middle Eastern, Asian fusion
and grill items to sop up the martinis, beer
and wine. DJs usually reign although the
odd live act has been known to perform.

The Madison 14 Madison Ave ☏416/927-1722.
Subway: St. George. The *Madison* was once
three joined Annex houses and is now a
massive multi-floor pub, with two pool
rooms, a piano bar and a dance floor.
Popular with students, especially fraternity
types, from the University of Toronto.

Myth 417 Danforth Ave ☏416/461-8383.
Subway: Chester. A cavernous space with a
huge suspended TV screen that silently
plays Hollywood films with Greek mythological themes, like *Jason and the Argonauts*.
Although you'll find better Hellenic fare elsewhere on the Danforth, *Myth's* lively late-
night crowd is a major draw, as are the
massive chandeliers hanging from 20-foot
ceilings, exposed beams and pillars burned
with runic symbols, and the classically beautiful blonde wood bar.

Pauper's 539 Bloor St W ☏416/530-1331.
Subway: Bathurst. This former bank has been
performing a far more useful function as a
two-story beer hall for about a decade now.
Pauper's is rightly esteemed for its rooftop

patio, which can tend toward loud boister-
ousness on the weekend evenings.

Roof Lounge in the *Park Hyatt Hotel*, 4 Avenue
Rd ☏416/924-5471. **Subway: Bay or Museum.**
Long a retreat for establishment literati, the
Roof Lounge offers a spectacular view of
the city and hands down the very best martinis in Toronto. The bartender has been
perfecting his method for almost four
decades. Sofas, a fireplace and silken
smooth service make this spot a treasured
oasis.

Souz Dal 636 College St ☏416/537-1883.
Streetcar: College (#506). This cocktail bar on
Toronto's College Street strip is famous for
its extensive, frequently goofy, cocktail list
and its dark ambience. The backroom is
really a walled patio, open to the stars and
lit exclusively by banks of votive candles.
Waitstaff drop by with little dishes of pista-
chios and keep the drinks coming. A great
place to end an evening out.

Ted's Collision 573 College St ☏416/533-2430.
Streetcar: College (#506). The image that
Ted's likes to project is all grunge and beer-
swilling but the space itself has something
of a Piranesi look going for it, thanks to
fake Roman ruins and a whiff of decay. The
bar also hosts assorted arts events.

Wish 3 Charles St E ☏416/935-0240. **Subway:**
Yonge/Bloor. *Wish* works equally well as a
bar or café. The intriguing "smoking" fountain (it looks like dry ice, but it isn't) on the
patio is only one of the many visual delights
that combine with attentive service and
good food to make this attractive little
establishment an inviting option just off
busy Yonge Street.

Yammy the Cat 1108 Yonge St ☏416/515-
1729. **Subway: Rosedale.** An appealing neighbourhood hangout whose zebra-print
booths, flea market sofas and tiny bar brim
with genuine cool. The two people who
operate the bar, hot plate and CD player
run the place like a 1950s rec room, where
it's fine to get a little tipsy and (if there's
room) start a samba line.

Clubs and live music

oronto's **nightlife**, like its restaurant scene, has blossomed in recent decades, and the city's reputation for rolling up its sidewalks after 10pm is no longer true. Today, there are **clubs**, **lounges** and **discos** for every taste and disposition. During the winter, nightlife is decidedly an indoor phenomena, but the explosion of pent-up energies during those first warm spring nights fill the club-lined streets of Downtown until dawn.

Most of the disco-type dance clubs are located on the Richmond Street strip, just south of Queen West, which is home to a number of **live-band venues**. The College Street strip, west of Palmerston, is also a likely spot to look for an up-and-coming dance bar amid all the cafés and bistros (although the emphasis here is more lounge-oriented). Also in the mix are venues that are staunchly **jazz**, **blues** or **R&B**, and that vigorously eschew trends, preferring a classic night-owl, smoke-filled ambience.

Most clubs and all lounges serve **alcohol** and, like in Toronto's bars, last call is at 2am. That means that all drinks have to be consumed and bottles taken away by 3am. Most clubs, however, will stay open until 4am on weekends, though live music spots tend to wind down earlier. The **rave scene** of the mid-nineties continues in various floating venues throughout the club district, although their main constituents are the kids under 19 who can't get into bars. This technicality has led to table signs reading "No minors served until after 3am."

For **venue listings**, consult *NOW*, *eye*, or *TRIBE*, three free weekly newspapers which are available in stores, restaurants and in newsboxes on the street. The most comprehensive listings are in *NOW*, which puts the emphasis on live music, while *TRIBE* specializes in dance/rave/house discos, and *eye* does a bit of both.

A good nightlife alternative to hearing some music or dancing is a **comedy club**. Toronto has a proven track record when it comes to showcasing emerging comedic talent, and several venues around town are specifically dedicated to stand-up or improv, with comedy cabarets finding a regular slot in some of the more varied venues.

Live music

Toronto's **live music scene** boasts a long and venerable tradition. Guitar guru Neil Young is a local boy who got his start in Toronto bars, as did Robbie Robertson and Joan Anderson, who later morphed into Joni Mitchell. Current artists like Holly Cole, Ron Sexsmith, Molly Johnston and Sarah Harmer keep the live performance torch burning, along with local bands like Jake and the Blue Midnights, Our Lady Peace, Do Make Say Think, Barenaked Ladies and The Rheostatics.

The city goes well beyond just guitar-based rock. In the late 1970s and early 1980s British New Wave bands established a solid fan base in Toronto, and consequently many Anglo performers tend to show up. **Blues** and **R&B** may be on the wane, but **jazz** has made a strong comeback in all its bebop, acid and classical varieties. **Latin dance** continues to hold a firm place near the top of the trend list in all its permutations: salsa, mambo, tango and merengue bands are tapping into the dance revival in a big way. And, of course, the city's large Afro-Caribbean population ensures a fairly consistent offering of dancehall **reggae** and **socca**.

Venues

The 360 326 Queen St W, Downtown ☏416/593-0840. Streetcar: Queen (#501). This venue hasn't expended much extra effort to spruce up its grungy appearance, but the place is nevertheless an extremely hot venue to see rock musicians and innovative cabaret acts.

Big Bop 651 Queen St W, Downtown ☏416/504-6699. Streetcar: Queen (#501). This vast space is filled with urban rockers and contains several different stages, all of which cater to the live alternative rock scene. The main stage was recently decorated with sumptuous mural-sized reproductions of famous nineteenth-century paintings – making the walls the best-dressed thing in the joint.

Black Swan 154 Danforth Ave, Uptown ☏416/469-0537. Subway: Broadview. One of the few remaining R&B outposts, this Riverdale neighbourhood institution also has folk on Sundays.

College Street Bar 574 College St, Uptown ☏416/533-2417. Streetcar: College (#506). A laid-back jazz bar that often dips into the realm of R&B. An excellent alternative to some of the over-hyped, trendier establishments in the area. Open until 2am seven days a week.

El Mocambo 464 Spadina Ave, Downtown ☏416/968-2001. Streetcar: Carlton/College (#506) or Spadina (#510). The stuff of legends insofar as live acts are concerned, having had visits from luminaries like the Rolling Stones, B.B. King, Blondie, and hometown faves like Nash the Slash. The tables are sticky and the carpet is scary, but the bands are (usually) great.

Government Queens Quay E, the waterfront ☏416/869-0045. Subway: Union Station. Down on the shores of Lake Ontario, this huge barn of a dance club books live bands for its downstairs cavern and has a multitude of DJs spinning in the two discos upstairs.

Horseshoe Tavern 368 Queen St W, Downtown ☏416/598-4753. Streetcar: Queen (#501). Lots of Toronto bands got their start here, and it's still a favourite place for the now-famous to sit in for a set or stage a special one-off concert. The interior is relentlessly unglamorous, but the phenomenal bar staff is a major compensation.

Lee's Palace 529 Bloor St W, Uptown ☏416/532-1598. Subway: Bathurst. Lee's continued popularity has nothing to do with the decor, the food or even the draft beer. Its reputation is entirely based on the outre bands it consistently books. Patrons can also check out the DJ dance action upstairs at the aptly named Dance Cave.

Matador 466 Dovercourt, Uptown ☏416/533-9311. Streetcar: College (#506). This noble institution has been memorialized in song by none other than Leonard Cohen in "Closing Time". When everyone else starts to shut down, the Matador opens. Don't think about showing up before 1.30am. A good place to star-watch and catch great bands trying out new material.

Opera 735 Queen St E, Downtown ☏416/466-0313. Streetcar: Queen (#501). This former vaudeville theatre is the chosen outpost for hard-core rock acts who like to thrash the night away. It's also a popular venue for the S&M/leather crowd, and is home to Toronto's annual Leather Ball.

Phoenix Concert Theatre 410 Sherbourne St, Downtown ☏416/323-1251. Streetcar: Dundas (#505). An imaginative renovation – and equally imaginative booking agents – makes this venue a popular place to catch a concert. Big-name acts looking for intimate venues, guitar legends and world music divas perform on the main stage space, which looks lie a cross between a Wild West saloon and an old vaudeville theatre.

The Rex Hotel Jazz Bar and Grill 194 Queen St W, Downtown ☏416/598-2475. In fierce arguments about which is the best jazz club in town, this one is consistently near the top of the list. A well-primped crowd lounges in the spiffed-up interior, but any reservations about pretensions evaporate once the music – which is always top-notch – begins.

Savage Garden 550 Queen St W, Uptown ☎416/504-2178. Streetcar: Queen (#501). It's official: this is the last real Goth in town. Industrial sound with lots of cages, metal sculptures and live thrash bands. Not for the timid.

Sneaky Dees 431 College St, Uptown ☎416/603-3090. Streetcar: College (#506). This no-attitude slacker palace has live rock bands, pinball, pool and Tex-Mex grub until 5am seven days a week.

Top O' The Senator 249 Victoria St, Downtown ☎416/364-7517. Subway: Dundas. Right near the groovy new Yonge/Dundas Square, this upstairs bar to the *Senator* restaurant serves light entrees and snacks along with a good line in scotch and beer. Its main claim to fame, however, is the superior jazz: when the big names play a Toronto club, it's usually this one.

Clubs and lounges

New strains of **clubs** are springing up in Toronto like never before, assuring a quality night out whatever your tastes. Weekends tend to be busy, and the more popular clubs can have long lines in the winter or summer. On weekends especially, be prepared to pay a **cover charge**, usually between $8 and $15. Some clubs book live bands on occasion, but most stick to the DJ formula. **Lounges** rarely have live music – space being at more of a premium – but they generally don't have cover charges, either. Check the listings in the free *NOW* or *eye* papers (see p.149) to see which DJs are playing where.

2 Cats 569 King St W, Downtown ☎416/204-6261. Streetcar: King (#504). A cosy little hipster refuge, with a lounge in the front and a stand-up long bar in the back.

606 606 King St W, Downtown ☎416/504-8740. Streetcar: King (#504). One of the early lounges on this increasingly trendy strip, the front area is a garage-doored restaurant and the back is a clubhouse-like space with intimate corners.

The Airport Lounge 492 College St, Uptown ☎416/921-3047. Streetcar: Carlton (#506). Stylish yet comfortable; filled with great-looking people but not snobbish; fun but not expensive. Who could ask for more? There are clever little snack-type things to order from the menu in case your martinis make you peckish.

Bambu by the Lake 245 Queens Quay W, the waterfront ☎416/214-6000. Streetcar: Harbourfront (#509). When the *Bamboo* shut its doors on Queen West, many said that an era had passed. Now, the same owners, staff and chef have reopened one of Toronto's best-loved clubs as *Bambu by the Lake*, in the former Pier Museum. Like its predecessor, the space is cavernous, needing a happy, dancing crowd to warm it up. It's a good thing, then, that the bookings – mostly salsa and reggae – are usually hot, keeping the big dance floor moving.

Bauhaus 31 Mercer St, Downtown ☎416/977-9813. Streetcar: King (#504). *Bauhaus*, a split-level club, is as much about the display of its patrons as it is the actual dancing. Dress special or you won't make it past the doorman.

Betty Ford Temple 469 King St W, Downtown ☎416/598-4050. Streetcar: King (#504). The *BFT* proves that the spirit of the booze can (speakeasy) will never fade, even when the club is legit. Exceptionally popular among those youthful souls who never ducked an after-hours drink. Ear plug-decibel level sound system. The upstairs lounge makes a nice hideaway.

Charlotte Room 19 Charlotte St at Adelaide, Downtown ☎416/598-2882. Streetcar: King (#504). Considered one of the top pool halls in North America, this club-like space is as close as most will come to a British gentlemen's club – but without the inbred attitude and with an abundance of cachet.

The Docks 11 Polson St, the waterfront ☎416/461-DOCK. Cab only, south of the Gardiner expressway on the Toronto Harbour. This massive complex – the lakefront patio is 41,000 sq ft – is like a theme park for clubbers. The music veers from old school disco and

R&B to Top 40 and dance, just to make sure no one gets left out. If you get tired of the nightclub, disco or restaurant, you can watch double and triple features at the drive-in.

Easy and the Fifth 225 Richmond St W, Downtown ☎416/979-3000. Streetcar: Queen (#501). Movie stars and supermodels are fond of this expensive, well-appointed nightclub, which is also known for its very fine restaurant. Great rooftop patio.

El Convento Rico 750 College St, Uptown ☎416/588-7800. Streetcar: College (#506). Walking into this lively joint, replete with red velvet, flocked wallpaper and baroque spot welding, makes you feel like you've stumbled on the best party in town – and you may well have. The crowd ranges from earnest suburbanites to dishy Latino drag queens, and the DJs spin Latin and disco classics until 4am six nights a week (until 10pm on Sunday).

Hush 457 Adelaide St W at Spadina, Uptown ☎416/366-4874. Streetcar: King (#504). *Hush*'s old, rough exterior gives way to a high-toned, mahogany-stained bar and lounge that is part Rat Pack and part *2001: A Space Odyssey*. If you've nothing else to do in this swank space, you can amuse yourself and an acquaintance with a game of chess played on one of the upright chessboard "pods".

Joker 318 Richmond St W, Downtown ☎416/598-1313. Streetcar: Queen (#501). A stylish behemoth of a club whose weekend patrons are willing to line up around the block. The music is generally heavy-handed techno, with smatterings of hip-hop and R&B in the third-floor disco.

Kubo DX 234 Bay St at King, Downtown ☎416/368-5826. Subway: King. *Kubo* was a popular restaurant and DX refers to the Design Exchange (see p.44). Put the two together in the glacially perfect Mies van der Rohe Toronto Dominion Tower and you

have a totally unexpected delight. Really nice staff, a good selection of brews and cocktails and a youthful, post-work crowd.

Red Drink Boutique 225 Richmond St W at Duncan, Downtown ☎416/351-0408. Streetcar: Queen (#501). This is where you take the relatives when you want to impress on them that they are not in Kansas anymore. Apparently, there is a functional entrance off Richmond, but the doorway with the bouncer and velvet rope is down an alley beside *Easy and the Fifth* (see above). The waitstaff all appear to be models in Victoria's Secret ads and their decorousness tends to blur the fact that the service is slow and inaccurate. Never mind. Movie stars, rock stars and other celebs swan through this teak-and-steel interior and, if you like that sort of thing, the overpriced drinks are a bargain.

This Is London 364 Richmond St, Downtown ☎416/351-1100. Streetcar: Queen (#501). Yet another club you have to enter off an alleyway (and up a flight of stairs). When it opened, people were appreciative of its stylish interior, DJ selections of disco, soul and good old Top 40, but the real buzz was about the women's washrooms: they take up the whole top floor, and hairdressers and make-up artists are on hand for touch-ups. Not a good choice of clubs if your date already spends too much time powdering her nose.

YYZ 345 Adelaide St W, Downtown ☎416/599-3399. Streetcar: King (#504). Look at your airplane ticket and you'll see where the name comes from. This sort of cleverness – plus the seamless James Bond perfection of *YYZ*'s bachelor pad interior, and the flights of champagne on offer, for big bucks – makes you want to dislike the place, but you can't. The staff are great, the decor is beautiful, and the wine list deserves to be seriously considered.

Comedy clubs

Alt.Comedy Lounge at the Rivoli 332 Queen St W, Downtown ☎416/332-1908, Streetcar: Queen (#506). The cabaret space in the back of the Rivoli hosts an alternative comedy night on Mondays at 9pm. Acts vary from wobbly stand-up routines to truly inspired nuttiness.

The Laugh Resort 370 King St W, Downtown ☎416/364-5233, Streetcar: King (#504). A comedy club with nightly bookings; consult *NOW* or call ahead to see who's on and when.

Second City 56 Blue Jay Way, Downtown ☏ 416/343-0011, Streetcar: King (#504). This is the Toronto-based company that spawned John Candy, Martin Short, Catherine O'Hara and the SCTV crowd. Time has not dulled the troupe's taste for political satire. A good place to learn all you need to know about local as well as global affairs.

The Tim Sims Playhouse 56 Blue Jay Way, Downtown ☏ 416/343-0011, Streetcar: King (#504). A co-tenant with Second City, TTSP specializes in staging an amorphous, improvisational comedy matrix. It could be about a mob wedding, it could be based on a 1950s game show, it could morph into who knows what.

Yuk-Yuks Downtown 224 Richmond St W, Downtown ☏ 416/967-6425, Streetcar: Queen (#501). This is the place where stand-ups have to make it to cash out their chips and move on up the food chain. Everyone has played Yuk-Yuks at some point or another. Catch them on the way up or in the opposite direction.

11

Performing arts and film

PERFORMING ARTS AND FILM · Theatre

oronto is one of North America's most vibrant centres for the **performing arts**. The city's strength is its **theatre scene**, which is the third-largest in the English-speaking world (after London and New York). **Dance**, **opera**, **classical music** and **film** are also well represented, and the city is justifiably proud of the many performance-oriented **festivals** it sponsors throughout the year. The most renowned is the **Toronto International Film Festival**, which has become not only one of the world's best, but also one of the most attended. The high season for most of the performing arts begins in late September and runs through May, adding vibrancy to Toronto's long winter months. Summer is ruled by a plethora of outdoor festivals and events; see Chapter 16 for more information.

Theatre

Home to more than six hundred opening nights a year, Toronto offers an exceptionally varied array of **theatre** productions, from opulent international hits to idiosyncratic fringe affairs. Classical drama rubs shoulders with edgy improvisational comedy, and big, Broadway-bound musicals co-exist with Baroque period pieces.

As if the wealth of choice during peak season were not enough, Toronto also boasts a number of **summer festivals**. The biannual Du Maurier Limited World Stage, held in April (☎416/973-3000), is a major international event, hosting alternative theatre companies from more than twenty countries; and the annual Fringe Festival of Toronto showcases approximately eighty workshops and alternative performances in ten days in early July. Finally, although they aren't within the confines of Toronto proper, the Stratford Festival and the Shaw Festival, both located two hours from Toronto in the towns of Stratford and Niagara-on-the-Lake, respectively, are two of the largest and most respected theatre festivals in North America; see the boxes on pp.156 and 157, respectively, for full details.

Prices for all theatrical endeavours – which range from $17 for smaller companies to $90 for prime seats at major stages – can be cut in half for same-day performances at **T.O. TIX office** (Tues–Sat noon–7.30pm; ☎416/536-6468 ext 40, ⓦtotix.edionysus.com), located on the southeast corner of the newly finished Dundas Square, right across from the Toronto Eaton Centre. Tickets go on sale at noon, so it's a good idea to get in line a half-hour before. Cash, Visa, MasterCard and Interac are accepted, and no reservations are made by phone. When deciding on seats in an unfamiliar venue, check the front section of Toronto's *Yellow Pages*, which thoughtfully includes the seating charts for the Hummingbird Centre, Roy Thompson Hall and Massey Hall.

Should half-price tickets still exceed your means, look for performances listed as PWYC ("Pay What You Can"). These have a suggested ticket price of about $10, but the boldest or poorest can get away with offering a few bucks (or maybe even nothing at all).

There are three main **theatre districts** in Toronto. The **Downtown** district, encompassing the area around Yonge, Front, King Street West and John streets, is the oldest, and includes some of the most established companies; the **East End** district, which occupies the southeast corner of the city, features primarily small, fringe companies; and **the Annex** neighbourhood, east of Bathurst between Dupont and Bloor, holds some of the best alternative companies.

Downtown

12 Alexander Street Theatre 12 Alexander St ☎416/975-8555. Subway: Wellesley. Tucked away on one of the tree-shaded side streets comprising Toronto's gay and lesbian quarter, 12 Alexander is home to the gay-specialist "Buddies in Bad Times" company. When not spouting the best in original queer-culture performance, the theatre is landlord to visiting alternative theatre companies and home-base for the annual Rhubarb! Theatre Festival (see pp.166 & 189 for more).

Artworld Theatre 75 Portland St ☎416/366-7723. Streetcar: King (#504). At only 150 seats, this intimate stage and gallery space features consistently innovative programming that reflects Toronto's many diverse communities.

Cameron House Backroom 408 Queen St W ☎416/703-0811. Streetcar: Queen (#501). The Backroom is a 50-seat cabaret space behind the much-loved, well-used and ever-popular *Cameron House* (which hosts live bands and DJs). The Backroom has bookings for innovative performances throughout the year, but is best-known for its twice-yearly performances by the Video Cabaret troupe of Michael Hollingsworth's amazingly innovative play cycle about Canadian history, *The Village of the Small Huts*.

Canon Theatre 265 Yonge St ☎416/872-1212; box office 244 Victoria St, ☎416/593-1962. Subway: Dundas. Just up the street from the Elgin Theatre and Winter Garden (see opposite), the Canon, formerly the Pantages, was saved from demolition and restored to its former vaudeville glory by impresario Garth Drabinsky, for his Toronto production of *Phantom of the Opera*. These days, the Canon is used for visiting companies and special guest acts.

Elgin Theatre and Winter Garden 189 Yonge St ☎416/314-2901. Subway: Queen. The Elgin and Winter Garden are the last functioning double-decker theatres in the world, with the latter built on top of the former in a highly economical use of one city lot. The theatres were given a full restoration by the Ontario Heritage Foundation to their exact, original specifications. While the downstairs Elgin is a treat, with its plush, red upholstery and gilt-plaster ornaments, it is the upstairs Winter Garden that really takes your breath away. This tiny gem was constructed to look like a garden, its ceiling replete with real leaves and its pillars clad to look like tree trunks. Tours are given on Thursdays at 5pm, and on Saturday and Sunday at 11am. Today, the Elgin specializes in visiting dramatic and musical productions, while the Winter Garden uses its more intimate setting to stage special events.

Hummingbird Centre 1 Front St E ☎416/872-2262. Subway: Union Station. Formerly known as the O'Keefe Centre, the Hummingbird kick-started the then-moribund Toronto theatre scene when it opened its neo-Expressionist doors in 1960. At 3200 seats, it is too large for intimate drama; rather, it's Downtown's venue of choice for family-oriented musicals and visiting artistes. It has also been the home of the Canadian Opera Company and the National Ballet for the past four decades (see pp.158 and 159, respectively, for more).

Princess of Wales Theatre 300 King St W ☎416/872-1212. Subway: St Andrew. Built in 1993 to accommodate the helicopter in

Miss Saigon, and currently home to the blockbuster musical *The Lion King*, this beautiful addition to Toronto's more traditional playhouses has a deceptively intimate feel, despite its 2000 seats. The murals and loge reliefs by artist Frank Stella are an added visual bonus.

Royal Alexandra Theatre 260 Yonge St ☎416/872-1212. Subway: St Andrew. The dowager of Toronto theatres, the "Royal Alex", as she is known to residents, was saved from demolition in 1963 by local businessman Ed Mirvish. Designed in 1906 by architech John Lyle, this graceful Beaux Arts building has been fully restored to its Edwardian splendour, and puts on everything from classical repertory theatre to exuberant musicals like *Mamma Mia*. The dramatically cantilevered balcony ensures clear sightlines from every seat.

St Lawrence Centre for the Arts 27 Front St E ☎416/386-3100. Subway: Union Station. The St Lawrence Centre is home to the Canadian Stage Company, and contains two stages: the Bluma Appel Theatre specializes in presenting new works by contemporary artists, and, upstairs, the studio-sized Jane Mallett Theatre not only presents experimental and workshop productions. but is also the performing home of the Toronto Operetta Theatre (see p.159).

The East End

Alumnae Theatre 70 Berkeley St ☎416/962-1948. Streetcar: King (#504). Original theatre with low-budget charm has long been the Alumnae Theatre's mandate. Low on frills, high on fringe.

Canadian Stage 26 Berkeley St ☎416/368-3110. Streetcar:King (#504). In addition to being the second stage of the Canadian Stage Company, which presents its more experimental pieces here, this location often houses avant-garde or workshop performances, and is an excellent place to see young talent.

Lorraine Kisma Young People's Theatre 165 Front St E ☎416/862-2222. Streetcar:King (#504). Originally a stable, this muscular, Romanesque-style building was saved from the wrecking ball in 1977. The innovative productions are geared towards a young audience, but are often as intriguing as (if not better than) many of the city's more mainstream offerings (see also Kids' Toronto, p.186).

The Annex

Factory Theatre 125 Bathurst St ☎416/504-9971. Streetcar: King (#504). Originally an auditorium for factory workers (hence the name), this spot, with its pressed-tin

The Stratford Festival

For more than half a century now, the **Stratford Festival** – held in the eponymous town, two hours southwest of Toronto on the banks of the Avon River – has been thrilling audiences with remarkable productions that have revamped some old favourites. Each season, North America's largest classical repertory company puts on two of Shakespeare's tragedies and two of his comedies; this programme is augmented by other classical staples (Moliere, Sheridan, Johnson), as well as the best of modern and musical theatre. The festival also hosts a lecture series, various tours (of backstage and a costume warehouse, for example), music concerts, an author reading series and meet-and-greet sessions with the actors.

The festival runs from mid-May to early November. Regular **tickets** start at $49 for dramas or $61 for musicals, though prices can drop substantially for preview performances, same-day performances, and for early spring or fall performances. Contact the box office for more information at ☎1-800/567-1600, or consult their website at ⊛www.stratfordfestival.ca.

As for **getting to Stratford**, the most direct route by car (from Toronto) is to take Hwy-401 West to Interchange 278 in Kitchener. From Kitchener, you should then take Hwy-8 West, switching to Hwy-7/8 West to Stratford. The town also boasts a small municipal **airport** (☎519/271-2040), and there are two **trains** daily from Toronto (☎416/366-8411). Return train tickets from the city start at around $45 for an adult fare. Further reductions are available to seniors, students and children.

The Shaw Festival

The second-largest repertory theatre company in North America – after the Stratford Festival (see box, p.156) – is the **Shaw Festival**, held in Niagara-on-the-Lake, a genteel Upper Canadian town nestled among the vineyards and fruit orchards of the Niagara Peninsula (see "Day-trips," p.97, for a full account of the town).

The Shaw Festival is the only festival in the world devoted solely to the works of George Bernard Shaw and his contemporaries. Indeed, it is mandated to produce only plays written in the playwright's lifetime (1856–1950), which the company refer to as "plays about the beginning of the modern world". The Shaw, like the Stratford Festival, has a generous selection of backstage activities, including tours, concerts, fairs, and a number of free programmes that introduce the company to its audience. **Ticket prices** are $22–65, and substantial discounts are available for previews, matinees, lunchtime and Sunday-night performances. Contact the box office (☎1-800/511-SHAW) for information.

As for **getting to Niagara-on-the-Lake**, it's two hours by car from Toronto. Drive towards Niagara along the Queen Elizabeth Way (QEW) and, once across the Garden City Skyway at St Catherines, take the Niagara-on-the-Lake exit (38B). A left onto York Road and a right onto Hwy-55 East (Niagara Stone Road) will take you to downtown Niagara-on-the-Lake. Unfortunately, as of right now there's really **no easy public transportation** way to reach Niagara-on-the-Lake. You can take a Greyhound bus to Niagara Falls ($40 / return trip), but then you have to get into a taxi to finish your journey. If you choose to go this route, 5-0 Taxis (☎905/358-3232; roughly $10 one-way, or $15 return) is probably the best company to use.

decorative ornaments and seemingly fragile balcony, has a special charm. Since opening in 1970, the Factory has staged more then 400 Canadian plays; while its downstairs sister, the Factory Studio Café, has nurtured a reputation for innovative contemporary theatre.

Poor Alex 296 Brunswick St ☎416/923-1644. Subway: Spadina. The Poor Alex Theatre has been the launching pad for many a career, and is the alternative/bohemian alter-ego of Mirvish Productions (better-known for Broadway brava). As likely to house productions by Albey and Pinter as original plays by talented unknowns, this Annex institution creates an inviting atmosphere for audiences.

Tarragon Theatre 30 Bridgman St ☎416/531-1827. Subway: Dupont. A renovated factory space, the Tarragon has contributed much to Toronto's thriving theatrical community, by consistently presenting challenging, innovative performances.

Theatre Gargantua 365 College St ☎416/260-4660. Streetcar: College (#506). On Sundays, this charming little Gothic Revival church is home to the St Stephens-in-the-Field Anglican congregation – but from Monday to Saturday it houses the Theatre Gargantua troupe, whose richly textured play cylces have been performed here since the early 1990s.

Theatre Passe Muraille 16 Ryerson Ave ☎416/504-7529. Streetcar: Queen (#501). The unusual configuration of this former factory allows set designers a broad scope for dramatic possibilities. One of the best alternative theatres in the city.

Classical music, opera and dance

Thanks to strong moral and fiscal support from a dedicated fanbase, Toronto maintains a wide-ranging, diverse programme of **opera**, **dance** and **classical music**. The biggest news, however, is that the city's ongoing attempts to build a permanent opera house have finally paid off: in April 2003 the groundbreaking ceremony for the **Four Seasons Centre for the Performing Arts** paved the way for the Canadian Opera company's new home – and its planned 2006 landmark production of Wagner's Ring Cycle.

Single adult **ticket prices** for opera, dance and classical music performances range from $35 to well over $165 – but, as with theatre tickets, **T.O. Tix**, at the southeast corner of Dundas Square (Tues–Sat noon–7.30pm; ☎416/536-6468 ext 40, ⊛totix.edionysus.com), sells spare day-of-show seats at half-price.

You should also check the music listings in *NOW* for **smaller venues**, that nevertheless feature wonderful performers such as the Orpheus Choir (☎416/530-4428), the Music Umbrella concerts series (☎416/461-6681) and the free lunchtime recitals given in different churches throughout the city.

Classical music

Glenn Gould Studio 250 Front St W, Downtown ☎416/205-5555. Streetcar: King (#504). Named for the great pianist and composer (see p.53), this small, boxy hall in the Canadian Broadcasting Centre (see p.44) is so sprung for sound that enthusiastic performances leave audiences literally vibrating. The programming is first-rate, generally showcasing Canadian talent (particularly since most performances are later broadcast on CBC Radio).

Massey Hall 178 Victoria St, Downtown ☎416/872-4255. Subway: Dundas. A turn-of-the-century recital hall that boasts great acoustics, and has hosted a wide variety of performers – everyone from Enrico Caruso and Maria Callas to Jarvis Cocker. The austere architecture is offset by Moorish details, like the fanciful moulding along the balconies.

The Music Gallery Centre for New and Unusual Music 197 John St, Downtown ☎416/204-1080, ⊛www.musicgallery.org. Streetcar: Queen (#501) When the original Music Gallery space closed due to a proposed development, a collective wail was heard city-wide. Thankfully, the new, ecclesiastical space in St George the Martyr has kept one of the most intense, tantalizing performance centres in the city open and ready for experimentation. A great place to see Toronto originals such as diva Fides Kruker, pianist Eve Egoyan or the Glass Orchestra, whose musical instruments are made entirely of glass. Guest artists come from around the world, and performances are linked with lectures and workshops.

Roy Thompson Hall 60 Simcoe St, Downtown ☎416/593-4828. Subway: St Andrew. Roy Thompson Hall is home primarily to the Toronto Symphony Orchestra (☎416/593-4828), though it also hosts the Toronto Mendelssohn Choir (☎416/872-4255). The

building, finished in 1982 to a design by Arthur Erickson, looks by day like an upturned café au lait bowl – but at night, the place is transformed, as the glass-panelled walls glow transparently, casting light over the reflecting ponds and a public square outside. Inside, the circular hall has excellent sightlines, and its acoustics have been recently tweaked to rave reviews.

Toronto Centre for the Arts 5040 Yonge St, North York ☎416/872-2222. Subway: North York Centre. The classical wing of the Toronto Centre for the Arts, the George Weston Recital Hall, is an acoustically precise performance hall that competes with the Roy Thompson Hall (see below) for top-name classical acts.

Trinity-St Paul's Centre 427 Bloor St W, Uptown ☎416/964-9562 or 964-6337, ⊛www.tafelmusik.org. Subway: Spadina. Toronto's riveting Tafelmusik Baroque Orchestra, renowned worldwide for historical performances on period instruments, marks its 25th season in 2003/2004. And, far from being subjected to academic, bloodless exercises in musical historicism, audiences are constantly dazzled by the new insight they're offered into the Baroque repertoire. Under first violin and musical director Jean Lamon's leadership, Tafelmusik (German for table music) performs over fifty concerts a year in Toronto.

Opera

Autumn Leaf Performance various venues ☎416/535-9998, ⊛www.autumnleaf.com. This company bills itself as practitioners of the "x-treme art of opera". Autumn Leaf goes for the jugular with its sometimes Dadaist sensibilities and daring approach to performance.

Canadian Opera Company The Hummingbird Centre, 1 Front St E, Downtown ☎416/363-6671, ⊛www.coc.ca. Canada's national opera troupe, the COC has dazzled international audiences for years with its ambitious productions, devotion to young talent and the musical erudition of its director, Richard Bradshaw. Seats are often scarce, particularly for the eagerly anticipated season premieres, so reserve as far in advance as possible – ticket prices vary widely, from $35 to $165. Rush tickets are only available to seniors and students, and are not released until two hours before a performance.

Opera Atelier various venues ☎416/25-3767, ⊛www.operaatelier.com. A Baroque opera/ballet company known for sumptuous productions loved by opera buffs and first-timers alike. There are only a handful of productions each year, but their daring and artistic merits have attracted a devoted following. Ticket prices range from $45 to $90.

Tapestry Music Theatre 55 Mill St, The Cannery, Studio 315, Downtown ☎416/537-6066, ⊛www.tapestrynewopera.com. This company is dedicated to supporting and producing new operas by Canadian composers, such as Chan Ka Nin's *Iron Road*, which is about the Chinese migrant labour that built the Canadian Pacific Railway, or, more recently, Linda Catlin Smith's *Facing South*, about Peary's ambitious Arctic adventure. Performances are staged in a variety of venues.

Toronto Operetta Jane Malette Theatre, St Lawrence Centre for the Arts, 27 Front St E, Downtown ☎416/465-2912, ⊛www.torontooperetta.com. Just in case you thought Toronto was only interested in the avant-garde or the exotically historical, this company specializes in accessible theatrical renditions of meringue-light operettas, including Franz Lehar's confections as well as rousing renditions of Gilbert and Sullivan.

Dance

du Maurier Theatre 231 Queens Quay W, the waterfront ☎416/973-4000. LRT (from Union Station): Queens Quay. Part of the Harbourfront Centre (see p.75), this modern theatre stages primarily dance recitals, but also the occasional theatrical or musical performance.

National Ballet Company Hummingbird Centre, 1 Front St E ☎3416/45-9595. Subway: Union Station. The NBC's prima ballerinas, notably Karen Kain and Veronica Tennant, are revered as national treasures. This company has proven that it is one of the most accomplished corps anywhere, performing classical ballet and contemporary dance with equal artistry.

Premier Dance Theatre 207 Queen's Quay W, the waterfront ☎416/973-4921. LRT (from Union Station): Queens Quay. A beautiful new facility built specifically for dance performances, this space also hosts a number of dramatic events, including Toronto's exciting classical repertory troupe, the Soul Pepper Theatre.

Toronto Dance Theatre 80 Winchester St, Cabbagetown ☎416/967-1365. Streetcar: Carlton (#506). In a city once infamous for its repressive "Sunday Blue Laws" – which, among other things, forbade theatrical performances on Sunday – it is fitting irony that this, like many of Toronto's contemporary theatres, is housed in a former church. Tucked deep in the heart of the historic Cabbagetown neighbourhood, the Toronto Dance Theatre and its affiliated school create and stage daring, original productions.

Film

Toronto is one of North America's most active film sets, with huge production trailers, miles of cable and laconic film crews trawling the urban landscape all year long. The city is also one of the film world's busiest body doubles, passing for New York in *Moonstruck*, Boston in *Good Will Hunting*, Tangiers in *Naked Lunch,* and Chicago in *Chicago*, *My Big Fat Greek Wedding* and *John Q. Public*, to name but a few. Toronto has also contributed plenty of big names to the movie industry: on the acting side, there's Mary Pickford, Mike Myers and Jim Carrey, while on the directing side there's Atom Egoyan, David Cronenberg, Deepa Mehta and Norman Jewison. The city also hosts a number of **film festivals**, the premier event being the Toronto International Film Festival; see the box on p.161.

Moviemaking in Toronto

In less than 25 years, filmmaking, animation and television production in Toronto has developed into a billion-dollar industry. Apart from the obvious fact that the Canadian dollar gives an advantage to producers working in US currency, few cities have such a diversity of landscape and architecture to use as a backdrop. Of equal significance is Toronto's status as a theatre haven: it already owns a large pool of talented theatre workers to draw on for costumes, sets and lighting, and there is the abundance of classically trained actors. Add to these resources a home-grown genius for film animation and high-grade post-production facilities, and you have all the ingredients for a filmmaking centre of international stature.

First-run cinemas in Toronto range from multiplex shoeboxes (invented by Torontonian Garth Drabinsky) to old-fashioned picture palaces – although, as elsewhere, the latter are regrettably dwindling in number. To combat the impact of home video on the cinema trade, Toronto instituted "Half Price Tuesdays", cutting the usual price of $12 for a first-run evening performance to $6 (consequently, Tuesday-night seats are hard to come by if you arrive late). Matinee performances are reduced to half-price on weekdays, as well.

Most of the city's **second-run or repertory cinemas** are operated under the umbrella of the Festival Group, a coalition of independent theatres that screen film favourites and whatever else might strike its members' fancy. Memberships cost just $3, so if you plan on seeing two or more Festival Group movies, there's really no reason not to join: adult admission to a film for members is $6, or $8 for non-members. Matinees and Tuesdays are $4 for members. For more information, check their website at ⓦ www.festivalcinemas.com.

First-run cinemas

Beach Cinemas 1651 Queen St E, The Beaches ⓣ416/699-5971. Streetcar: Queen (#501). A plump suburban multiplex serving the cinema needs of the growing number of young families in this East End neighbourhood.

Canada Square 2200 Yonge St, Uptown ⓣ416/483-9428. Subway: Eglinton. A sprawling thirteen-screen cineplex offering a mix of foreign, independent and mainstream films.

Carlton 20 Carlton St, Uptown ⓣ416/598-2309. Subway: College. When Garth Drabinsky's Cineplex chain muscled in on the Toronto scene, a number of arthouse cinemas closed. To compensate for this, Drabinsky set aside the Carlton to show first-run art films, and its eleven screens are still doing just that. The café and espresso bar make a nice change from standard concessions fare, although that too is available. The smaller cinemas here can feel cramped.

Cumberland 4 159 Cumberland St, Uptown ⓣ416/964-5971. Subway: Bay. This multiplex (contrary to its name, it actually has five screens) in the heart of Yorkville is an uptown version of the Carlton, catering to arthouse film fans. Larger screens and more leg room make for more comfortable viewing than at the Carlton.

Paramount 259 Richmond St W, Downtown ⓣ416/444-3456. Streetcar: Queen (#501). Perfect venue for filmgoers who want to feel like extras in *Blade Runner*. Half the spectacle is in the theatre itself, with a mammoth pixel-board cube showing film clips to the club-hoppers outside, an almost verticle ride up the escalator to the cinemas and, of course, a sound system that will blast you out of your seat.

Regent 551 Mount Pleasant St ⓣ416/480-9884, Uptown. Subway: Davisville. Wonderful single-screen Art Deco cinema with a great chrome box office and illuminated marquee. Features mainstream fare.

Silvercity Yonge 2300 Yonge St, Uptown ⓣ416/544-1236. Subway: Eglinton. Another premium-priced movie venue that attempts to be an entertainment complex unto itself, this one aimed squarely at the youth market.

Uptown 764 Yonge St, Uptown ☎416/922-6361. Subway: Bloor/Yonge. One of the last cinema palaces left in the city. The main theatre upstairs has a huge curved screen left over from the panorama days, opulent gold curtains, plush red upholstery and plenty of plaster ornamentation. Its 921 seats ensure that this is where the biggest blockbusters open; during the Toronto International Film Festival it's always packed to capacity.

Varsity 55 Bloor St W, Uptown ☎416/961-6303. Subway: Yonge-Bloor. A recent expansion has turned this two-screener into an eleven-cinema behemoth, replete with displays of Hollywood costumes, premium prices and full-service (drinks and snacks delivered to your seat) screening rooms. The cinemas are well-appointed with deep, comfortable seats.

Second-run cinemas

Bloor Cinema 506 Bloor St W, Uptown ☎416/532-6677. Subway: Bathurst. Though this cinema won't win any beauty contests, it's still a great place to view films. Frequently plays host to the numerous film festivals in Toronto (see box below).

Cineforum 463 Bathurst, Uptown ☎416/603-6643. Streetcar/Subway: Bathurst. An inde-pendent among independents, Cineforum is indispensible to film students and buffs who want to catch up on the history of film without resorting to cropped video and DVD versions.

Cinematheque Jackman Hall, Art Gallery of Ontario, 317 Dundas St W, Downtown ☎416/968-FILM. Streetcar: Dundas #505. Cinematheque is a year-round extension of the Toronto International Film Festival; its programmer, James Quandt, is so respected that the French awarded him with a Legion d'Honneur. The quality of prints he finds are beyond compare.

The Fox 2236 Queen St E, The Beaches ☎416/691-7330. Streetcar: Carlton (#506). This former vaudeville theatre, mentioned several times in Michael Ondaatje's *In the Skin of the Lion*, is an alternative to its multiplex cousin, Beach Cinemas, up the road. There's no glitzy marquee and the popcorn is best avoided – just comfortable seats and a good selection of films.

Kingsway Theatre 3030 Bloor St W, Uptown ☎416/236-1411. Subway: Royal York. Small and a bit worn at the heels, this theatre makes up for its lacklustre interior by offering a top-notch selection of films.

The Music Hall 147 Danforth Ave, Uptown ☎416/778-8272. Subway: Broadview. Though this space is still used for live performances and musical concerts, this – perhaps the

---

The Toronto International Film Festival

At any given point in the year, someone is sure to be holding a film festival in Toronto. The most famous is the **Toronto International Film Festival** (or TIFF; ☎416/968-3456, ⊛www.e.bell.ca/filmfest/2003), which in two decades has gone from being an obscure celluloid celebration for hard-core film fans to being one of the most respected festivals in the world – and the largest in North America. A ten-day affair, the festival begins on the first Thursday in September. Single, same-day **tickets** are available from the Film Festival's box offices – or as **rush tickets** immediately before screenings – for $13.75, or $24.50 for Gala screenings – usually the big, star-studded Hollywood efforts. **Lines** to get in to the films can be fearsome, but once you do, the directors and stars introduce their pictures and then make themselves available for question-and-answer periods after a film's first showing (all films screen twice).

Many regular TIFF attendees plan their holidays around the Festival, buying **books of tickets** in advance – a somewhat more economical method. There are a variety of plans to choose from, and if you purchase before July 21st there is a modest discount: the least expensive of these is a book of ten tickets which can be used for all but Gala screenings. There's also the **Daytime Pass**, which gets you into 25 screenings, though only for those held between the hours of 8am and 6pm. All of these passes can be purchased from the TIFF website (see above for the address). For **other film festivals** throughout the year, see Chapter 16, "Festivals and events".

last working-class music hall in Toronto – has recently been converted for use as a cinema as well.

Ontario Place Cinesphere 955 Lakeshore Rd W, the waterfront ☏416/314-9900. Streetcar: Harbourfront #509 or free shuttle (May–Sept) from Union Station. Located inside Ontario Place (see p.78) and open year-round, the Cinesphere plays both 35mm and IMAX films. Admission is separate from admission to Ontario Place.

Paradise Cinema 1006 Bloor St W, Uptown ☏416/537-7040. Subway: Ossington. Another neighbourhood cinema saved by the Festival Cinemas group, the Paradise tends toward the edgier, downtown programming, and is a draw for cineasts across the city.

Revue Cinema 400 Roncesvalles Ave, High Park ☏416/531-9959. Subway: Dundas West. This cinema has long had a reputation for some of the finest programming outside of the festival circuit. Well worth the trip.

The Royal 606 College St, Uptown ☏416/516-4845. Streetcar: Carlton (#506). Situated on the hippest block in the city, the Royal has recently had new seats installed and its 1940s interior touched up.

Gay Toronto

Over the past 25 years, Toronto's relationship with **gays and lesbians** has evolved from blunt intolerance to enthusiastic celebration. In addition to hosting one of the largest Pride celebrations in the world, the lesbian and gay community now has significant economic, political and social clout. Toronto boasts the largest "out" population of any city in Canada. The neighbourhood at the centre of the activity – known commonly as the Gay Village – is focused on the intersection of Church and Wellesley streets, about one block east of Yonge Street.

Although gay establishments are not exclusive to this neighbourhood, it is where the lion's share of lesbian/gay/bisexual (LGB) community services, bars, clubs and restaurants are located. As is the case in many cities, the gay scene is far more conspicuous than its lesbian counterpart – though this neighbourhood is nothing if not inclusive. Even if the bars seem to be specifically for gay men, lesbian and bi women should call for info on dyke nights, women-only events and mixed theme nights.

One of the more interesting developments over the past decade has been the addition of a **family element** to the neighbourhood. For those who remember the monogenerational lesbian and gay communities of decades past, it is a joy to watch supportive parents of LGB children, along with out parents and their children, sort through the minutiae of day-to-day life in a tolerant, open environment. There is also strong community recognition of **transsexual** and **transgendered people**, whose place in the LGB community is growing and evolving.

Throughout the city, look for the **free gay weeklies** *fab* and *Xtra!*, distributed in newsboxes and in many Downtown bars and restaurants. The lesbian magazine *Siren* is a bit harder to find, but the user-friendly website can be found at Ⓦwww.siren.ca. Besides *Siren*'s site, several other **websites** cater to the LGB community: Ⓦwww.gaycanada.com has extensive listings of what's going on in Toronto; Ⓦwww.outintoronto.com has a basic overview of the gay community; and Ⓦwww.gaytoronto.com is an excellent online resource for the city. The Canadian Lesbian and Gay Archives website, Ⓦwww.clga.ca/archives, focuses primarily on doctrines of gay rights and advocacy.

Contacts

The 519 Community Centre 519 Church St, Uptown ☎416/392-6874, Ⓦwww.the519.org. **Subway: Wellesley.** Once a private club, this solid building in the heart of the gay quarter is now the hub for the city's LGB and transsexual outreach and awareness programmes. Over 300 groups, mostly part of the LGBT communities, utilize this space.

Gay pride

In 1971, Toronto's first gay pride celebration was held at Hanlan's Point in the Toronto Islands – a paltry one hundred people showed up. Today, the celebration stretches over an entire week at the end of June, and attracts an annual attendance of over 700,000. Festivities promoting gay awareness fill the week and culminate with the Gay Pride Parade, which begins at the intersection of Church and Wellesley and trucks down Yonge Street before terminating at Church Street. To show solidarity with Toronto's gay population, the mayor rides at the front of the parade, and the premier of Ontario writes warm letters of support in the publications like *Canada's Gay Guide*, which is available in bookstores throughout the city.

Pride Committee of Toronto 65 Wellesley St E, suite 304, Uptown ☎416/927-7433, ⓦwww.torontopride.com. Subway: Wellesley. This is Mission Control for the annual Gay Pride celebrations, an organizational feat that requires eleven months of planning and fundraising events. A great place to find out about upcoming events in the gay community.

Accommodation

Maps, with the accommodations below keyed to them, can be found in the main part of the Guide: see p.36 for Downtown and p.62 for Uptown. For an explanation of the price codes used below – ❻, etc – see the box on p.117.

Amazing Space 246 Sherbourne St, Downtown ☎416/925-3799 or 1-800/205-3694, ⓦwww.amazingspacebb.com. Streetcar: Dundas (#505). The actual location isn't the prettiest, but it is central, with the Eaton Centre's Downtown nexus and the Gay Village an easy 10 minute walk away. In addition to location, this B&B is clean and quiet. En-suite and shared baths available. ❹

Banting House 73 Homewood Ave, Uptown ☎416/924-1458, ⓦwww.bantinghouse.com. Subway: Wellesley. A sensitively restored Edwardian house with cosy furnishings. The nine guest rooms have either en-suite or shared baths, and several have their own entrances. Buffet-style continental breakfast is included. ❹

the bearfoot inn 30A Dundonald St, Uptown ☎416/922-1658 or 1-888/871-BEAR, ⓦwww.bearfootinn.com. Subway: Wellesley. All rooms to this central bear boy inn have en-suite three-piece baths, mini fridges, TVs and safes. Pets are welcome and clothing is optional. ❹

Cawthra Square Bed & Breakfast Inns 10 Cawthra Square, 512 Jarvis St, and 111 Gloucester St, Uptown ☎416/966-3074 or 1-800/259-5474, ⓦwww.cawthrasquare.com.

Subway: Wellesley. These three very well-run, fabulously furnished Victorian mansions-turned-B&Bs are in the heart of the Gay Village. They feature upscale amenities including PC access, fax, voicemail, and afternoon tea. ❹

Immaculate Reception Bed and Breakfast 34 Monteith St, Uptown ☎416/925-4202 or 1-800/335-9190. Gracious 1880s townhouse overlooks the central action on Cawthra Square, in the heart of the Gay Village. Full hot breakfasts included. ❹

Muther's Guest House 508 Eastern Ave, Downtown ☎416/466-8616. Streetcar: Queen (#501). Upstairs from *The Toolbox* (see p.165), *Muther's* has seven guest rooms, both en-suite and shared bath, with amenities like refrigerators, microwaves and a private rooftop patio for sunbathing in the buff. ❹

Victoria's Mansion 68 Gloucester, Uptown ☎416/921-4625. Subway: Wellesley. The rainbow flag flies proudly over this Victorian mansion, whose rooms are all equipped with fridges, microwaves and coffeemakers – and Victoria herself is on hand to make her guests feel at home. ❹

Bars, clubs and restaurants

Bar 501 501 Church St ☎416/944-3272, Uptown. Subway: Wellesley. Famed for its Sunday evening "Window Show" drag promenade and the ever popular "Hags on Heels" review, *Bar 501* has gone beyond being a neighbourhood institution, and has earned its place as a Toronto icon.

Bar Babylon 553 Church St, Uptown ☎416/923-2626. Subway: Wellesley. Three floors of frenetic fun keep this youth-oriented bar/lounge fresh with locals and fun for visitors. The martini menu has over 200 concoctions to choose from, and the kitchen features delicious innovations like a renowned lentil and couscous soup.

The Barn/Stables 418 Church St, Uptown ☎416/977-4684. Subway: Wellesley. Another three-floor party house (see *Bar Babylon*, above), this one draws an all-ages leather and denim crowd. Both live music and DJs are featured.

Black Eagle 459 Church St, Uptown ☎416/413-1219. Subway: Wellesley. A popular leather and denim cruise spot, with multiple bars and a rooftop patio where you can cool off when things get too hot. Strict fetish dress code in effect on Fridays and Saturdays, with an emphasis on leather. Every third Sunday of the month is Women's Night Out.

Byzantium 499 Church St, Uptown ☎416/922-3859. Subway: Wellesley. A stylish place that's divided into equal parts martini bar and restaurant. The extremely long, narrow space promotes mixing and mingling.

Fly 8 Gloucester St, Uptown ☎416/410-5426. Subway: Wellesley. Recognizable to fans of the *Queer as Folk* TV programme, *Fly* is the neighbourhood's – and the city's – number one hot gay dance club. Special events are held on Fridays, while the party on Saturday lasts until 7.00am Sunday morning.

Hair of the Dog 425 Church St, Uptown ☎416/964-2708. Subway: Wellesley. A popular neighbourhood watering hole, *Hair of the Dog* is a two-storey bar and restaurant that leans toward the upscale side. A nice place to go on a date.

Pope Joan 547 Parliament St ☎416/925-6662, Uptown. Streetcar: Carlton (#506). A cavernous space, this is one of the few lesbian-specific bars in town. On the weekends, DJs play disco and dance tracks for an appreciative crowd.

Red Spot 559 Church St, Uptown ☎416/967-7768. Subway: Wellesley. *Red Spot* features live music, DJs and comedy nights. Mostly, though not exclusively, for Grrrls.

Remington's Men of Steel 379 Yonge St, Downtown ☎416/977-2160. Subway: Dundas. A cheesy gay strip bar that took over this location from a former cheesy straight strip bar. Predictably garish.

Slack Alice Bar & Grill 562 Church St ☎416/969-8742. Subway: Wellesley. As laid-back and poseur-free as its name suggests. Does a nice line of martinis and has an international menu that ambles between continental and Middle Eastern. Delicious daily specials.

Tallulah's Cabaret 12 Alexander St, Uptown ☎416/975-8555. Subway: Wellesley. The very popular bar/cabaret space attached to the Buddies in Bad Times theatre. Hosts a youngish LGB and transsexual crowd, in addition to straight thesbian-lovers.

Tango 508 Church St, Uptown ☎416/972-1662. Subway: Wellesley. *Tango*, a lesbian pick-up bar, pitches to a younger crowd, but welcomes women of all ages.

The Toolbox 508 Eastern Ave, Downtown ☎416/466-8616. Streetcar: Queen (#501). Lots of leathery dominants here, not to mention nudists and bikers. Summertime brings an active patio which features an excellent Sunday brunch for those who make it through the weekend. If you go, bring a sense of adventure.

Wilde Oscar's 518 Church St, Uptown ☎416/921-8142. Subway: Wellesley. The expansive patio here grudgingly shuts down in winter, but the two floors worth of bistro and bar inside are perfectly comfortable during the chilly months.

Woody's/Sailor 467 Church St, Uptown ☎416/972-0887. Subway: Wellesley. This place has an excellent selection of microbrews and draught ales, daily specials and a popular weekend brunch – not that anyone comes here for the food: there's a men's bare-chest competition at midnight on weekends, and a Sunday tea dance with drag performers, singers and outlandish themes.

Zelda's Bar and Restaurant 542 Church St, Uptown ☎416/922-2526. Subway: Wellesley. *Zelda's* patio is *the* place to have a ringside seat during the Gay Pride celebrations. The

food in general, and the Sunday Brunch in particular, are fabulous, as is the bar. A new party room addition adds to the general sense of excitement. On occasion, Zelda herself whooshes in to hold court.
Zipperz 72 Carlton St, Uptown ☎ **416/921-0066. Streetcar: Carlton (#506).** Across the street

from Maple Leaf Gardens, Toronto's former temple to hockey, *Zipperz*' exterior looks rather like a sports bar for beer-swilling mullet-heads. Fortunately, times change, and these days it's a rather good piano and dance bar for an out clientele – though beer is still served in abundance.

Theatre

Gay theatre in Toronto makes its home at the 12 Alexander Street Theatre (see p.155), where the Buddies in Bad Times company puts on a repertoire of queer-culture performances of original works. Prized by all Toronto theatre-goers, Buddies in Bad Times also puts on the annual Rhubarb! Festival (see p.189 for more).

Shops

Body Bodywear 500 Church St, Uptown ☎ **416/929-2639. Subway: Wellesley.** The International Male-style of clothing here at Body Bodywear features pec-hugging shirts and trousers that would make a codpiece blush. Perfect for gym bunnies and weekend warriors.
Come as You Are 701 Queen St W, Downtown ☎ **416/504-7934. Streetcar: Queen (# 501).** A wonderfully matter-of-fact sex-toy shop and bookstore that caters primarily, though not exclusively, to lesbians and bisexual women.
Glad Day Bookstore 598A Yonge St, Uptown ☎ **416/961-4161. Subway: Wellesley.** Information central for the LGB community for over two decades, this bookstore was

once the only overt sign that a gay community existed in Toronto.
He & She Clothing Gallery 263 Queen St E, Downtown ☎ **416/594-0171. Streetcar: Queen (#501).** For work or play, these exuberantly sleazy outfits are deliberately provocative and loads of fun. There's a full range of stiletto pumps in sizes big enough to accommodate both sexes.
Priape 465 Church St, Uptown ☎ **416/586-9914. Subway: Wellesley.** Wittily described as Toronto's "gay insight centre", this is more than a boy-toy emporium: books, magazines, costumes and a knowledgeable staff guide customers towards the realizations of their secret and not-so-secret desires.

Gay baths and spas

The Barracks 56 Widmer St, Downtown ☎ **416/593-0499.** A venerable institution, this is Toronto's oldest gay baths, and the city's Stonewall: it used to be raided all the time, and one of these raids resulted in a court case that hugely changed the gay community's relations (for the better) with city hall and the police.

Bijou 64 Gerrard St E, Uptown ☎ **416/971-9985. Subway: Wellesley.** Bijou is not your average skanky place. Rather, it's clean and comfortable, with plenty of steam and porn, and there's little chance of being raided.
Excess 105 Carlton St, ☎ **416/260-2363, ⊛ www.spaexcess.com. Streetcar: Carlton (#504).** A safe environment for casual encounters.

Shopping

W hether you're after computers or couture, antiques or the avant-garde, Toronto is a terrific place to **shop** for your wares. The city is Canada's biggest and most cosmopolitan, and the wealth of shopping possibilities spans the whole of the metropolitan area. **Business hours** are fairly consistent: most stores are open seven days a week from 10am to 7pm, with somewhat longer hours on Thursday and Friday and somewhat shorter hours on Saturday and Sunday. One exception to this rule is the large Downtown music stores, which stay open until 10pm on weekdays and midnight on Friday and Saturday.

Toronto can be broken down into numerous distinct **shopping districts**. The intersection at **Yonge and Dundas** is a magnet for youth and teems with teenagers who flock here from the suburbs and beyond. With the Eaton Centre stretching a full city block to the southwest, The Gap's flagship store to the north, and most of the city's major music vendors to the east, anything a young person could want is within easy reach.

Trekking north from here – on Yonge, to Bloor Street West – takes you to the cusp of **Yorkville**, a nest of streets including Cumberland Avenue, Yorkville Avenue and Scollard Street. Although Yorkville was the Flower Power epicentre in Toronto during the 1960s, the area is now filled with costly boutiques and a large percentage of Toronto's beautiful people. Even if you can't afford to buy anything here, though, it still makes for a pleasant stroll.

Back down on the lower west side of the city, the expanse of **Queen Street West** between University and Bathurst is an eclectic jumble of shops, galleries and street-side stands. This used to be the place for trend-setting designer duds, though an incursion of chain stores is slowly gentrifying the area. Now, the best of the independent shopping scene has been pushed west of Spadina into an area known as **West Queen West**, which runs to Ossington. In addition to having the flea market ambiance Queen Street West used to posses, this stretch has become known for its galleries, featuring up-and-coming artists and photographers.

On a final note, visitors from outside Canada are entitled to claim a **refund** of the seven percent federal Goods and Service Tax (GST) on accumulated purchases of a minimum of $200, as long as each receipt is for at least $50 (before tax) and that the goods were taken out of Canada within sixty days of purchase. Submit your receipts along with a GST Refund form, which is readily available in hotels, major stores, airports or Ontario Travel Information Centres. If you're Canadian, but not an Ontario resident, you can apply for a refund on the eight percent Ontario Sales Tax – but the accumulated purchases must add up to a minimum of $625, and the form isn't as commonly found as the GST form. Call ☏1–800/263-7965 and ask for one to be mailed to you.

Antiques and vintage furniture

507 Antiques 50 Carroll St, Downtown ☏416/462-9989. Streetcar: Queen (#501). A mammoth cache of architectural salvage, large wrought-iron pieces and garden statuary. Most of the stock isn't particularly portable, but there are rooms of smaller furniture at the back and downstairs in a cavernous basement. Custom and antique wrought iron also available. Little decorative accessories are scattered throughout.

Absolutely 1132 Yonge St, Uptown ☏416/324-8351. Subway: Rosedale. The narrowness of this store is accentuated by the stacks of wonderful finds piled high along the walls and in every possible nook and cranny. Huge sea sponges perch atop delicate Victorian pedestals, antique hat forms adorn Georgian desks, and huge Belle Epoch gilt mirrors reflect everything, doubling the sense of wondrous clutter.

Horsefeathers 1212 Yonge St, Uptown ☏416/934-1771. Subway: Summerhill. A well laid-out jumble of nineteenth- and twentieth-century pieces with some amusing accents (try a life-size Buddha head candle for a coffee table ornament). Tasteful but not stultifying. Prices can be bracing but quality is never in doubt.

L'Atelier 1224 Yonge St, Uptown ☏416/966-0200. Subway: Summerhill. Small and elegant, L'Atelier specializes in twentieth-century French furniture and decorative objects with a somewhat masculine flair.

The Paisley Shoppe 77 Yorkville Ave, Uptown ☏416/923-5830. Subway: Bay. Housed in the last of Yorkville's Regency cottages, this Toronto institution specializes in furniture, decorative accessories and tableware items from the eighteenth and nineteenth centuries.

Phil'z 792 Queen St W, Downtown ☏416/461-9913. Streetcar: Queen (#501). A very good source for twentieth-century design. A Geo Ponti chair was recently spotted here, and the hanging 1960s bubble chairs still excite covetousness.

Prince of Serendip 1073 Yonge St, Uptown ☏416/925-3760. Subway: Rosedale. Patrons are treated with warmth and attentiveness at this aptly named store. Wares in the huge bay window at the front include substantial Victorian furniture and gigantic chandeliers, and the intriguing, dim interior extends back into a garden, where you can find a selection of outdoor statuary.

Putti Fine Furnishings 1104 Yonge St, Uptown ☏416/972-7652. Subway: Rosedale. A genuine treasure-trove of beautiful objects, some old and some new, from antique boudoir tables and Venetian glass mirrors to fine perfumes, soaps and scented emollients. Jewellery, Limoge pill boxes and fine writing paper are artfully arrayed to tempt. Putti is also the lone North American representative for several French and Italian houses (try coffee and chocolates from Venice's *Café Florian*). The Christmas tree ornaments are so clever and/or splendid that even people who don't celebrate the season end up buying the stuff.

Red Indian Art Deco 536 Queen St W, Downtown ☏416/504-7706. Streetcar: Queen (#501). You never know what you'll find crammed into this narrow, deep store, but it's always worth a look. Finds have included matching Eames chairs, rare Fornasetti pieces, and a series of ceramics by Jean Cocteau.

Wilde P.S. Antiques 86 Parliament St, Downtown ☏416/368-8128. Streetcar: King (#504). A particularly pleasing antique store for the serious collector who has scant resources. Finds recently spotted include a Biedermier secretary, extraordinary twin Italian armoires, and all manner of quirky footstools. Very high quality for sane prices. The owners are unfailingly helpful and easy-going.

Books

Toronto is a highly literate city. It hosts the world's largest literary festival (see p.193), has a year–round authors' reading series at the waterfront, and is home to a large population of authors. Reflecting this bibliophilic disposition are a number of excellent bookstores, both specialist and general.

New

Bookcity 348 Danforth Ave, Uptown ☏416/469-9997. Subway: Chester. A solid neighbourhood bookstore with a good range of new-release literature, magazines and children's selections. If you can't find what you're looking for, the knowledgeable and highly literate staff will make special orders.

Chapters 110 Bloor St W, Uptown ☏416/920-9299. Subway: Bay. One of the big-box book emporia that waddled into Toronto in the mid-1990s. Despite a heavy-handed start, Chapters currently maintains a benign presence. Browsers are encouraged to linger in a cosy atmosphere that includes deep couches, skylights, a fireplace and a café on the ground level. Also has Internet access.

Indigo Books, Music & Café 55 Bloor St W, Uptown ☏416/925-3536, ☜www.indigo.ca. Subway: Bay. This Canadian chain of large bookstores decks out its many locations (including this one) in bleached wood and buffed aluminium. Has the de rigeur cafés, comfy seating areas and CD, software and gift sections. High marks for its children's book selection and its championship of Canadian authors.

Nicholas Hoare 45 Front St E, Downtown ☏416/777-2665. Subway: Union Station. A beautifully appointed store replete with Gothic folly flourishes, this bibliophile refuge provides comfy chairs and sofas in front of a working fireplace. Their large selection runs the gamut, but the collection of books on all aspects of design is particularly stunning. Intelligent, friendly staff on hand to answer your questions.

Pages 265 Queen St W, Downtown ☏416/598-1447. Streetcar: Queen (#501). The bookstore of choice for the sophisticated reader, this place has the edgiest and most compre-

hensive collection of contemporary literature and art and social criticism in town. There are also good travel, film, music, art and architecture sections, as well as an extensive range of magazines and small-press publications. The erudite owner and his staff answer even the most arcane questions with grace and ease.

This Ain't the Rosedale Library 483 Church St, Uptown ☏416/929-9912. Subway: Wellesely. A funky neighbourhood bookstore offering lots of magazines, contemporary literature, and an excellent resource/research section with an emphasis on gay and lesbian culture. The easy-going owners are usually available to discuss their twin passions: Canadian literature and baseball.

World's Biggest Bookstore 20 Edward St, Downtown ☏416/977-7009. Subway: Dundas. When giant bookstore chains collide (Smith's, Coles and Chapters, in this case) they spawn entities like the World's Biggest Bookstore. With over 150,000 titles, it's easy to spend the better part of a day combing through this barn-like structure. If you can't find what you want elsewhere, you're sure to find it here.

Used and antiquarian

Acadia Art and Rare Books 232 Queen St E, Downtown ☏416/364-7638. Streetcar: Queen (#501). The neighbourhood is a tad scary, but it's worth stepping over a few winos to find this place. Really low prices for high-quality antiquarian books and prints. This is where other dealers shop for stock, and the owner appreciates a knowledgeable customer.

D & E Lake 237 King St E, Downtown ☏416/863-9930. Streetcar: King (#504). This is what an antiquarian bookstore and print gallery should look like: a Dickensian brick building with paned windows and creaky floors. The owner can spellbind you with the length of cigarette ash he'll allow to dangle over a precious first edition. This is a collector's first stop: the wide selection includes military, art, architecture and medical books, all in excellent condition.

Eliot's Bookstore 584 Yonge St, Uptown ☎416/925-0268. Subway: Wellesley. A good general and scholastic collection. Also has a used magazine selection that is particularly strong on arts and music.

Specialist

Bakka Books 598 Yonge St, Downtown ☎416/963-9993. Subway: Wellesley. Founded in 1972, Bakka is the world's oldest science fiction specialises bookstore. Here, one can find a huge selection of SF, fantasy and speculative fiction, with a solid representation of horror. In its more than thirty years of business, Bakka has nourished its share of authors: Tanya Huff, Robert J. Sawyer and Michelle Sagara West all made change here while penning their novels.

Ballenford Books on Architecture 600 Markham Ave, Uptown ☎416/588-0800 or 1-888/588-0806, ⊛www.ballenford.com. Subway: Bathurst. One of the best specialist bookstores on architecture in the world. For over twenty years, owners Susan Ford and Barbara Ballentine have been supplying professionals and enthusiasts from around the globe with beautiful and frequently rare books about all things architectural. The beautiful store is also a gallery; its walls have been graced with the original drawings by such luminaries as Aldo Rossi and Steven Holl.

The Beguiling 601 Markham St, Uptown ☎416/533-9168. Subway: Bathurst. A compre-hensive selection of 'zines, illustrated novels and comics (both underground and mainstream), with some quirky postcards and ephemera thrown in.

The Cookbook Store 850 Yonge St, Uptown ☎416/920-2660, ⊛www.cook-book.com. This place is fun. There are cooking classes, cooking demonstrations, cooking superstars (it's Julia Child's favourite Toronto hangout) and sometimes elaborate celebrations of cookbooks. For example, when the Elvis cookbook appeared, the store hired drag king Elvis impersonators to serenade shoppers.

David Mirvish Books on Art 596 Markham, Uptown ☎416/531-9975. Subway: Bathurst. A browser-friendly art bookstore with exceptional sections on contemporary and Canadian art as well as some terrific bargains. The Mirvish's connection with American artist Frank Stella is apparent: his remarkable, fifty-foot painting *Damascus Stretch Variation* adorns the back wall. A must-stop shop for serious collectors.

TheatreBooks 11 St Thomas St, Uptown ☎416/922-7175, ⊛www.theatrebooks.com.☎416/922-7175, ⊛www.theatrebooks.com. Subway: Bay. This bookstore specializes in the performing arts: theatre, film, opera, dance and media. An excellent resource centre and a beautiful shop, housed on a quirky, tiny street in a quirky, old house.

Toronto Women's Bookstore 73 Harbord St, Uptown ☎416/922-8744. Streetcar: Spadina (#510). Housed comfortably in a Victorian row house, this hub of Toronto feminist literature has an extensive bulletin board with listings for women's health services, community issues and upcoming rallies and events.

Cigars and tobacco

Groucho and Company 150 Bloor St W, Uptown ☎416/922-4817. Subway: Museum. In addition to a full line of quality cigars, Groucho's is also notable for its excellent selection of fine cigarettes, including all the Shermans varieties.

Le Casa del Habano Toronto 170 Bloor St W, Uptown ☎416/926-9066. Subway: Museum. The Toronto location of this international chain carries a select range of Cuban cigars for the connoisseur.

Clothing

Independent designers

Comrages 654 Queen St W, Downtown ☎416/360-7249. Streetcar: Queen (#501). Toronto fashion pioneers Judy Cornish and Joyce Gunhouse are famed for their ongoing reinterpretations of the little dress. Their retail space shows off a full range of creations, from casual to formalwear, all beautifully crafted.

Delphic 706 Queen St W, Downtown ☎416/603-3334. Streetcar: Queen (#501). Delphic proffers very clean-line clothing for Mod types, male or female. Also has Danish design home accessories.

Fashion Crimes 395 Queen St W, Downtown ☎416/592-9001. Streetcar: Queen (#501). Designer Pam Chorley has held her own on the trendy Queen St West strip for almost two decades with a fashion philosophy that denies rules and revels in the notion that opulent beauty is a head space, not a price tag. Her romantic designs have been described as the most beautiful dresses in Toronto, ranging from form-flattering, bias-cut dresses to theatrically Baroque bridal frocks. There is also a full range of idiosyncratic accessories to complete the look.

Flavour Hall 500 College St, Uptown ☎416/839-9943. Streetcar: College (#506). Bright orange plexiglass doors swing open into a tiny space crammed from top to bottom with the most experimental, whimsical clothing and accessories of Toronto's up-and-coming designers, including the owner herself. For example, a "memory skirt" is stiched with twelve clear plastic pockets, into which one can put personal mementos.

Hoax Couture 176 John St, suite 401, Downtown ☎416/597-8924. Streetcar: Queen (#501). In recent years, Chris Tyrell and Jim Searle's designs have focused on sleek, innovative eveningwear for both men and women, with an emphasis on superb craftsmanship. Lately they have been producing men's silk brocade shirts for tuxedo-replacing formal occasions. Ask about custom-made fits and flourishes.

LuluLemon Athletica 734 Queen St W, Downtown ☎416/703-1399. Streetcar: Queen (#501). A recent addition to the local designers of the West Queen West strip, LuluLemon was an instant hit. Whereas all other exercise wear looks like a dingy bag, LuluLemon's has curves, fit and colour. Yoga pants, warm-ups, hoodies, fleeces, and lots of T-shirts in a wide range of seasonal palettes. Comparable to the big chains in price but light years ahead in quality and design.

Mothership 670 Queen St W, Downtown ☎416/535-8618. Streetcar: Queen (#501). Techno-duds for chicks and dudes with lots of Velcro straps and plenty of fabric play. You get the feeling the designer/owners watch a lot of anime and read *Giant Robot*.

Wenches & Rogues 610 Queen St W, Downtown ☎416/536-2172. Streetcar: Queen (#501). This new address consolidated the two uptown locations into one big store. Seasonal collections from Canada's top independent designers for men and women's clothing, including David Dixon, Misura and Crystal Siemens. Prices are excellent.

Y5 5 Yorkville Ave, Uptown ☎416/920-9173. Subway: Yonge/Bloor. Architectonic, futuristic designer Ula Zukowska has finally opened her own place on Yorkville, meaning that fans of her inspirational approach to textiles, form and cut now have a regular outlet for their UZ fix. Be prepared to buy if something fits and you want it: items move fast and lines are not repeated.

Designer/haute couture

Chanel Boutique 131 Bloor St W, Uptown ☎416/925-2577. Subway: Bay. Purveyors of the ultimate power suit for Ladies Who Lunch, Chanel offers dependable excellence at astronomical prices.

I-cii 99 Yorkville Ave, Uptown ☎416/925-3380. Subway: Bay. A gallery-like space that displays clothes like cloth sculptures. Regulars really know their stuff and appreciate the selection of Comme des Garcons, Junya Watanabe and Issy Miyake.

Prada 131 Bloor St W, Uptown ☎416/513-0400. Subway: Bay. Prada's Toronto outlet is comparable to the company's other North American stores, stocking a fairly decent range of the latest lines of pricey clothes, accessories, shoes and handbags.

TNT Woman and TNT Man in the Hazelton Lanes mall (see p.173), 87 Avenue Rd, Uptown ☎416/975-1810. Subway: Bay. The femme store has been accurately described as one-stop shopping for "It Girls", as labels from Teenflo to Betsy Johnson and Barbara Bui are racked out row on row with great shoes and accessories. Flirty little items and techno-power suits don't come cheap here, and a teensy bit of label obsession is probably necessary to pay full price. The men's version carries Zenga Sport, Diesel, Iceberg Jean and the like; the place is pretty laid-back about looking good, but expensive nonetheless.

Vintage

Courage My Love 14 Kensington Ave, Downtown ☎416/979-1992. Streetcar: Dundas (#505). Vintage clothing for men and women augmented with an eclectic selection of beads, amulets and buttons. The clientele here ranges from high school girls looking for funky prom dresses to fashion-magazine editors looking for cheap chic. The most venerable of the Kensington Market schmatta shops.

Divine Decadence 136 Cumberland Ave, 2nd floor, Uptown ☎416/324-9759. Subway: Bay (Cumberland exit). With a stunning collection of vintage haute couture, this Toronto favourite carries Chanel from the 1930s, Dior from the 1950s, Pucci from the 1960s, and museum-quality accessories. An absolute must for connoisseurs.

Preloved 613 Queen St W, Downtown ☎416/504-8704. Streetcar: Queen(#501). In addition to the vintage pieces on display, the owners started a huge trend a few years back when they cut up and reconfig-

ured their by-the-pound rags and turned them into purses, dresses, and patched-together jeans. Thrifty divas like Alanis Morrisette and Amanda Marshall are patrons, and Preloved pieces are now carried by hipster stores in the US and Hong Kong.

So Hip It Hurts 323 Queen St W, Downtown ☎416/971-6901. Subway: Osgoode. A good source for party glad rags and costume jewellery. The name alone pulls the curious in off the street.

Thrift

Honest Ed's 581 Bloor St W, Uptown ☎416/537-1574. Subway: Bathurst. Toronto's ultimate discount store. Three carnival-like floors graced with goofy jokes and pictures of owner Ed Mirvish with showbiz personalities ranging from Claire Bloom to Peter Tosh. The signs exhort shoppers to lighten up and buy something cheap, and there are some amazing finds if you have the time to rummage through the troves of clothes and accessories.

Tom's Place 190 Baldwin Ave, Downtown ☎416/596-0297. Streetcar: Spadina (#510) or Dundas (#505). A Kensington Market institution, Tom's Place offers a huge selection of men's and women's designer clothes at discount prices. The actual price tags are more or less suggestions for bartering with the deeply courteous Tom: the more he likes you, the better the deal. The staff is top-notch and alterations are speedily performed on-site.

Crafts

Arts on King 169 King St E, Downtown ☎416/777-9617. Streetcar: King (#504). Local, regional and national crafts people display their wares in this cavernous old warehouse space. Downstairs there's jewellery, glass, ceramics and assorted knick-knacks; upstairs features art exhibitions. A good spot to search for a unique gift.

Bounty 235 York Quay Centre, the waterfront ☎416/973-4993. Streetcar: Harbourfront/Spadina LRT (#509/#510). This consignment shop features the output of visiting and resident artisans who produce

beautiful stained and blown glass, jewellery, baskets, fired clay, ironware, turned wood and much more.

The Guild Shop 118 Cumberland, Uptown ☎416/921-1721. Subway: Bay. A Canadian institution, the Guild Shop has been representing Canadian artists and artisans for seven decades. They mix newcomers with collectible veterans and carry glass, ceramics and turned wood; they also have a very good gallery of First Nations and Inuit art at entry-level prices.

Department stores and malls

Department Stores

The Bay 176 Queen St, Downtown ☎416/861-9111, Subway: Queen; also intersection of Bloor and Yonge, Uptown ☎416/972-3333, Subway: Yonge/Bloor. With two locations (each takes up a full city block), The Bay has become a formidable retail presence. The name is taken from the Hudson Bay Company, the world's oldest corporate entity and former owner of most of the Canadian North. You can still purchase the Hudson's Bay Blanket here (a must-have item during the fur trade), but the rest of the basic department-store stock is decidedly contemporary.

Holt Renfrew 50 Bloor St W, Uptown ☎416/922-2333. Subway: Bay. Toronto's premier one-stop shopping destination for both men and women. Specializes in signature collections from the likes of Jean-Paul Gaultier, Gucci, Sonia Rykiel and Armani, as well as upper-echelon Canadian designers such as Catherine Regehr and Lida Baday. Holt aims to wrap its customers in full-service, and hence provides a concierge desk by the main entrance, two cafés, a full day spa and a great staff to help you out.

Sears 290 Yonge St, Downtown ☎416/343-2111. Subway: Dundas. Once the flagship of Canada's oldest department store chain (Eaton's), this former haughty beauty is now a Sears, carrying fashion, perfume, cosmetics and housewares that one won't find in the average outlet of the utilitarian American department store chain.

Malls

BCE Place 181 Bay St, Downtown Subway: Union Station. One of the most dramatic complexes in the city, the BCE was designed by Spanish architect Santiago Calatrava, who found a way to incorporate rather than bulldoze the walls of the Commerce Bank of the Midland District (Toronto's oldest stone building) and a block of Victorian shops into the development. A galleria of shops and office space, the BCE has a vaulted ceiling that allows sunlight to pour in – a welcome antidote to the subterranean fluorescent lighting of the Underground City (see box below).

Eaton Centre 290 Yonge St, Downtown Subway: Queen or Dundas. Anchored at its northern boundary by the Sears department store (see above), this enormous mall covers the distance between two subway stops, contains hundreds of stores on five levels and takes the better part of an afternoon just to walk from one end to the other. This is perhaps the best place to shop if you have limited time, simply because every chain store of any significance is here. The layout follows one general rule: high-end shops are on the third level, mid-price shops on the second, and the cheap stuff is on the bottom.

Hazelton Lanes 55 Avenue Rd, Uptown Subway: Bay. This mall is almost too classy to be so labelled. It has high-end clothing, home decor and food stores – both chains and independents – mixed in with a few restaurants and cafés. A wonderful spot through which to browse if the weather outside is too cold, too hot or too wet.

The Underground City

The largest mall in Toronto is invisible from the surface, buried beneath the streets in eleven kilometres of tunnels known as the **Underground City**, which stretches north/south from Front to Dundas, and east/west between Yonge and Richmond. The entrances to the Underground City are brightly marked with the coloured **PATH** logo. This subterranean network of plazas co-evolved with the banking towers that dominate the street level, when their developers had the idea of creating shopping environments for the hundreds of thousands of workers who pour into the city's core daily. As a result, today, no matter how bad the weather, you can always go shopping, visit a gallery or find something to eat in the well-planned labyrinths beneath Toronto.

Food and drink

Gourmet

Alex Farm Products 377 Danforth Ave, Uptown
☎416/465-9500, Subway: Chester; also at the St
Lawrence Market, Downtown ☎416/368-2415,
Subway: Union Station. A cheese fanatic's
dream, this place's specialities include a
large selection of sheeps-milk cheeses, a
remarkable array of goat cheeses (regularly
flown in from France) and a Trappist raw-
milk cheese made by Canadian monks that
is delicious.

Caviar Direct at the St Lawrence Market,
Downtown ☎416/361-3422 or 1-800/74-CAVIAR.
Subway: Union Station. An emporium for
Beluga and Persian caviars, this place also
touts the Canadian variety, a golden caviar
from the sturgeon of Lake Huron. Be sure
to try a piece of "Indian candy" – smoked
salmon cured in maple syrup.

Holt Renfrew Gourmet 50 Bloor St W, Uptown
☎416/922-2333. Subway: Bay. One side of
this shop is a lunch counter and take-away
deli, and the other is filled with a wide
range of condiments and prettily packaged
herbs. Especially good for its range of
sweets.

Pusateri's 1539 Avenue Rd ☎416/785-9100,
ⓦwww.pusiteris.com. Subway: Lawrence.
Serious food critics have proclaimed this
family-run operation as what New
York's Balducci's used to be: foodie heaven.
Every item is absolutely top-quality, and
special features include an olive oil tasting
bar, cooking demonstrations by the city's
leading chefs, and unique outside of Italy,
an entire wall of Italian Parmigian Reggiano
cheese wheels. The Internet has made
home deliveries possible throughout North
America.

Summerhill Station LCBO 10 Scrivner Sq,
Uptown ☎416/922-0403, ⓦwww.lcbo.com.
Subway: Summerhill. Probably the coolest,
best-stocked liquor store in Canada, this
30,000 square foot outlet was once a
railway station, complete with marble walls
and a Venetian clock tower. Today it carries
more than 5000 wines, spirits and beers
from around the world, with a vintages section, tasting sections and a demonstration
kitchen. A proud booster of Ontario wines,
Summerhill Station also features Ontario
microbreweries that are otherwise hard to
find.

Bakeries and patisseries

Carousel Bakery at the St Lawrence Market,
Downtown ☎416/363-4247. Subway: Union
Station. Absolutely the best place for
brioche, Carousel also gets high marks for
its speciality breads, focaccia and its
famous peameal bacon sandwiches.

Daniel et Daniel 248 Carlton St, Uptown
☎416/968-9275. Streetcar: Carlton (#506).
Classically French, Daniel et Daniel creates
superb cakes, jewel-like fruit tarts and
dainty pastries. Be on the look-out for traditional French confections.

Rahier Patisserie 1717 Bayview Ave
☎416/482-0917. Bus: 11 Bayview from
Davisville. Torontonians had just about every
kind of food in the world – but until Rahier
arrived in town a few years back they
lacked a really good croissant. His patisserie's location proves that if you bake it
people will come. Arrive early though, as
there's nothing left but crumbs by 3pm.

Yung Sing Pastry 22 Baldwin St, Downtown
☎416/979-2832. Subway: Queens Park.
Lunchtime crowds throng to this tiny take-
out-only bakery, which features spicy beef-
stuffed buns, pork or veggie spring rolls,
lotus-nut shortcake and the richest egg
custard tarts you've ever tasted. A complete lunch here won't cost more than $3.

Health food

Big Carrot 348 Danforth Ave, Uptown
☎416/466-2129. Subway: Chester. This holistic
supermarket collective provides one-stop
shopping for people who don't want chemi-
cals in their food or toxins in their personal
hygiene items. Although there are many
vegetarian-friendly choices, the Big Carrot
also stocks organic meat, poultry and fish.
It has a very good vegetarian deli
counter/café and has branched out into so
many areas that it is rapidly engulfing the
little neighbourhood square named for it,
The Carrot Common.

The House of Spice 190 August Ave, Uptown
☎416/593-9724. Streetcar: College (#506).
Cherished in Toronto for its breathtaking
range of products – spices, coffees, teas,
oils, condiments and exotic tinned foods –
as well as for its exceptional prices. The
owner keeps a stack of photocopied

recipes from her own collection at the register for curious customers. Worth a visit just to savour the sights and smells.
Whole Foods 87 Avenue Rd, Uptown ℡416/944-0500, ⊚www.wholefood s.com.℡416/944-0500, ⊚www.wholefoods.com. **Subway: Bay.** The Toronto outlet of the US health food supermarket chain, this place has a full selection of organic produce, fish and meat, bulk foods and a vegetarian deli counter. Because of its chi-chi location there are also very fine chocolates, baked goods and cheeses.

Inuit/First Nations galleries

In Canada, all aboriginal peoples are known as **First Nations**, and within the First Nations are the **Inuit**, or, "The People". Most Europeans and Americans know them as Eskimos, but this is a name the Inuit abhor. The divirsity of First Nations and Inuit **art** is staggering, particularly so in the case of the Inuit. The vast space of the Canadian Arctic engendered many distinct styles and techniques among these artists, who have long had a tradition of working in relative isolation. The shops and galleries below can provide a good introduction to this intriguing art and culture.

Fehley Fine Arts 14 Hazelton Ave, Uptown ℡416/323-1373. **Subway: Bay.** Fehley's is an international leader in the complex and diverse area of Inuit art, representing artists and sculptors from across the enormous expanse of the Canadian Arctic to serious collectors. Although the sculptures here tend to be the star attractions, don't miss the graphic-art pieces, either.
The Guild Shop 118 Cumberland St, Uptown ℡416/921-1721. **Subway: Bay.** Long distinguished as an outlet for Canadian artists and crafts people, the Guild is also the city's oldest dealer of Inuit and native art. Its Inuit statuary is exceptional, often very affordable, and the curator is more than happy to expound on the pieces' significance. An excellent place for collectors who are just starting out.
Isaacs Inuit Gallery 9 Prince Arthur Ave, Uptown ℡416/921-9985. **Subway: St George.** Serious collectors have long patronized Isaacs, which carries Inuit sculpture, prints, drawings and wall hangings.
Maslak-McLeod Gallery 25 Prince Arthur Ave, Uptown ℡416/944-2577. **Subway: St George.** This gallery carries some of the most important names in First Nations and Inuit painting, including masters like Norval Morrisseau and Abraham Aghik.

Markets

The Farmers Market 92 Front St E, Downtown ℡416/392-7219. **Subway: Union Station.** Also known as North Market, the vendors here produce what they sell, offering up fresh honey, pots of herbs, home-baked goods, fresh cheeses and fruits and vegetables straight off the farm. Open Saturday only, from 5am to 5pm.
Kensington Market Dundas St W and Kensington Ave, Downtown. **Streetcar: Dundas (#505).** This is a United Nations of food: one street is stuffed with Ethiopian, Vietnamese, Trinidadian, Bahamian, Chinese, Portuguese and Jewish food shops, while around the corner merchants from throughout Latin America congregate with vendors from the Middle East, the Mediterranean and Central Europe. If you can't find it here, the odds are you won't find it anywhere. In addition to the edibles there are vintage clothing stores, over-the-edge designers, pubs, cafés and patios. Closed Sunday.
St Lawrence Market Front and Church streets, Downtown ℡-416/392-7219. **Subway: Union Station.** On the site of Toronto's first city hall, this market boasts two levels of stalls, shops and bins filled with tantalizing international goods. The busiest and most festive day to visit is Saturday, when buskers

of every description play to the crowds. Apart from the array of international items, you can sample treats specific to Canada, like peameal bacon sandwiches (back bacon coated in a cornmeal crust), fiddle-

head ferns, salmon cured in maple syrup and an astonishing variety of mustards. The lower level also has a crafts market, where vendors sell hats, scarves, jewellery and wooden toys. Closed Sunday.

Museum shops

The Art Gallery of Ontario Gallery Shop 317 Dundas St W, Downtown ☎ 416/979-6610. Subway: St Patrick. In addition to items themed around current exhibits, the AGO's shop stocks work by local potters, glass blowers and silversmiths. There's also an excellent selection of children's toys, posters, books, cards and multimedia teaching aids.

Gardiner Museum Shop 111 Queen's Park, Uptown ☎ 416/586-5699. Subway: Museum. Perhaps the best place in town to find innovative, one-off ceramics, the Gardiner's gift shop carries consignment items from some of the best ceramicists working in Canada today. An excellent place to start one's own collection.

The ROM Shops 100 Queen's Park, Uptown ☎ 416/586-5775. Subway: Museum. The gift shops at the Royal Ontario Museum carry scarves, jewelry, and charming what-nots themed to major exhibits; reproduction items based on the permanent collection; and emphatically Canadian works by local artists on consignment, including raku, porcelain, textiles and native crafts. The book selection has an excellent range of titles dealing with Canadian and First Nations history and culture, while the children's shop, located downstairs, is chock-full of educational books and toys themed to the museum's collections, particularly – and predictably – the dinosaurs.

Music

Because many entertainment corporations use Toronto's diverse, cosmopolitan population as a test market for North America, Toronto has some of the **best prices** for new-release compact discs in the world – frequently half of what they cost in Europe. The standard CD price is $15, up to $21–23 for expensive imports and specialist labels.

New

HMV 333 Yonge St, Downtown ☎ 416/586-9668. Subway: Dundas. The four comprehensively stocked floors here are packed with nearly all musical genres. Listening posts play selections from Top-40 tracks, and if the staff isn't familiar with a title they will consult their computers to find it for you. There are five other central locations around town, too.

L'Atelier Grigorian 70 Yorkville Ave, Uptown ☎ 416/922-6477. Subway: Bay. The comprehensive selection of classical and ancient music here includes many imported labels and hard-to-find titles. Nothing comes cheap, but if you really need that four-disc set of Byzantine liturgical music, this is the place to shop.

Metropolis Records 162A Spadina Ave, Downtown ☎ 416/364-0230. Streetcar: Spadina

(#510). This modest walk-up carries only trip-hop, drum 'n' bass and other electronic club sounds, on both DJ vinyl and CD. A handy spot to pick up fliers on clubs, lounges and the odd after-hours joint.

Rotate This 620 Queen St W, Downtown ☎ 416/504-8447. Streetcar: Queen (#501). A bit further down the Queen West strip than Kop's (see below), and therefore less likely to be filled with young things from the suburbs on a Saturday afternoon. Diverse selection of many genres.

Sam the Record Man 347 Yonge St, Downtown ☎ 416/646-2775. Subway: Dundas. Rumours of this store's death-by-bankruptcy were apparently inaccurate: this Yonge Street landmark still sells an extensive collection of rock, jazz, classical and world music.

Soundscapes 572 College St, Uptown ☎416/537 -1620. Streetcar: College (#505). Alternative indie labels like Merge and Thrill Jockey, and imports at commiserate prices. No Top-40 here.

Used

Kop's 229 Queen St W, Downtown ☎416/593-8523. Subway: Osgoode. A highly popular fixture on the Queen West strip, this boxy store is crammed with new and used CDs, some cassettes, and a collection of vinyl upstairs. The stock is rock-heavy, but there are some interesting finds in the jazz and blues sections.

Second Vinyl 2 McCaul St, Downtown ☎416/977-3737. Subway: Osgoode. Despite the name, this store carries only a limited selection of records. One side of the store is devoted to used jazz and classical CDs, and the other is filled with rock and alternative titles.

She Said Boom 372 College St, Uptown ☎416/944-3224. Streetcar: Carlton (#506). An emporium devoted to popular culture and sounds, filled with new and used CDs and books.

Vortex 2309 Yonge St, Uptown ☎416/483-7437. Subway: Eglinton. One of the oldest used-CD stores in the city, this second-storey walk-up has a sprawling collection that will delight browsers.

Wild East 360 Danforth Ave, Uptown ☎416/469-8371. Subway: Chester. This Riverdale walk-up specializes in unusual titles and musical curiosities, ranging from electronica to vintage recordings. New and used CDs are available, and customers are encouraged to listen to titles before buying. The selection is large and varied, and the owner is famous for his encyclopedic knowledge of music.

Speciality shops

Kidding Around 91 Cumberland Ave, Uptown ☎416/926-8996. Subway: Bay. A large turning key over the door warms you up for this delightfully goofy store, where you can buy quality rubber chickens, punching nuns, metal lunch boxes decorated with Hindu gods, huge dragon puppets or a variety of keychains.

Northbound Leather 7 St Nicholas St, Uptown ☎416/972-1037. Subway: Wellesley. Spiffy duds in latex, leather and PVC, with a full complement of masks, whips and other props for erotic home theatre. Beautiful workmanship, high-quality materials and a broad-minded, attentive staff willing to answer questions or take special orders.

Spytech Spy Store 2028 Yonge St, Uptown ☎416/482-8588. Subway: Davisville. Spytech is dedicated to electronic surveillance gadgets like bugging or anti-bugging devices, teensy cameras and night-vision goggles. A handy place if you're into espionage or just plain paranoid.

Sporting goods

Curbside Cycle and Inline Skate Centre 412 Bloor St W, Uptown ☎416/920-4933. Subway: Spadina. Large selection of urban mobility items plus bike accessories, clothing and skateboards. They even do ice-skate sharpening in the winter.

Hogtown Extreme Sports 401 King W, Downtown ☎416/598-4192. Streetcar: King (#504). Hogtown specializes in skateboarding equipment, baggy clothes and snowboards, though they also do a nice line in bike gear.

Mountain Equipment Co-op 400 King St W, Downtown ☎416/340-2667. Streetcar: King (#504). An annual membership (for a nominal fee) gets you access to the city's most extensive range of top-flight sports equipment. If you're planning to dog-sled in the Arctic, bike across China, climb mountains or go deep-sea diving, you can buy everything you need here at better-than-average prices. Mountain Co-op also does daily rentals of bicycles, cross-country skis, canoes and kayaks for the urban outdoors person. The building itself is even interesting: it's made from recycled materials and has a wildflower garden on the roof.

Nike Toronto 110 Bloor W, Uptown ☎416/921-6453. Subway: Bay. A superstore devoted to all things Nike. Fans of the swoosh will find all the latest lines and models here under one roof.

Sports and outdoor activities

There is no shortage of **spectator sports** and **outdoor activities** in Toronto. Ice hockey, basketball, baseball and Canadian football provide a calendar year's worth of excitement in both the professional and amateur ranks. Historic rivalries between regional and city teams are no longer the political allegories they once were, but partisan sentiment for the home team can make being in the stands almost as exciting as the action on the field.

In the early stages of its urban development Toronto was on the vanguard of the Victorian-era parks movement, and High Park is the result of that time. Over a century later the city has continued to build on its creative approach to providing excellent recreational facilities, courses and activities for all its citizens.

Toronto is an exception among large cities the world over for the amount of parkland and green space it maintains within the city limits. At 8000 hectares of green space, more than 12 percent of the entire city land mass is a park of one type or another. Within those parameters are some three million trees, 1500 named parks, 97 community centres, more than 200 swimming pools (including 90 indoor pools and 60 wading pools), and 372 tennis courts. There are also all-night baseball diamonds, soccer pitches, hiking and cross-country skiing trails, greenhouses and gardens and wildlife sanctuaries. To find a facility or to check on opening hours and fees, call the Toronto Parks Hotline (☎416/338-0338); Metropolitan Toronto Parks and Recreation (☎416/392-8000, ⓦwww.city .toronto.on.ca/depts/parksdiv1.htm); or check the Municipal Blue Pages in the phone book.

Major sporting venues

There are currently two main **venues** for spectator sports in Toronto, both located right downtown:

Air Canada Centre 40 Bay St ☎416/815-5500. Home of the Toronto Maple Leafs hockey team and the Toronto Raptors basketball squad.

SkyDome 277 Front St W ☎416/341-3110. Plays host to the Toronto Blue Jays baseball team and the Toronto Argonauts football team. See p.38 for much more on the building and tours.

Ice hockey

Hockey is Canada's national pastime, and with players hurtling around at nearly 50kph and the puck clocking speeds of over 160kph, this would be a high-adrenaline sport even without its relaxed attitude to combat on the ice. As an old Canadian adage has it, "I went to see a fight and an ice-hockey game broke out".

Once upon a time, the **Toronto Maple Leafs** were the only professional sports team in Toronto; they were also the best team in the National Hockey League (NHL), and were deified by Toronto's citizens. To this day they maintain a strong hold on the locals, who have a pronounced taste for a rough and tumble game style colloquially known as lunch-bucket hockey. The Maple Leafs' old home, the fabled Maple Leaf Gardens was, like the team, beginning to get a little worn around the edges, and in February of 1999 the squad moved to the **Air Canada Centre** (☎416/815-5500). This state-of-the-art complex, replete with all the pixelboard gadgetry and sound systems any modern arena demands, also hosts Toronto's professional basketball team, the Toronto Raptors (see p.180). The ACC is connected to Union Station by an underground walkway and is therefore very easy to reach by public transport.

The regular **season**, which lasts from October to May and sometimes June is composed of approximately ninety games. **Ticket prices** range from $20 and can exceed $300 if there is the merest chance of the Maple Leafs making it to the playoffs and contention for the Stanley Cup, the Holy Grail of professional hockey. In those years when the Leafs do make the playoffs, tickets are virtually impossible to obtain. Leaf fans are notoriously faithful, even though the last time Toronto won the Stanley Cup was in 1967.

Canadian football

Professional **Canadian football**, played under the aegis of the Canadian Football League (CFL), is overshadowed by the United States' National Football League (NFL). The best Canadian homegrown talents move south in search of more money, and the NFL's castoffs tend to come north to fill the ranks. The two countries' football games vary only slightly. In Canada the playing field is longer, wider and has a deeper end zone, and there are twelve rather than eleven players on each team. There is also one fewer "down" in each series of the game, meaning that after kickoff the offensive team has three, rather than four, chances to advance the ball ten yards and regain a first down. The limited time allowed between plays results in a more fast-paced and high-scoring sport, in which ties are often decided in overtime or in a dramatic final-minute surge.

Toronto's team, the Argonauts (or "Argos"), share the 63,000-seat **SkyDome** (☎416/595-0077) with the Toronto Blue Jays baseball team. The **season** takes place between August and November, and culminates in playoffs for the Grey Cup, Canadian Football's championship trophy. The Grey Cup weekend is an excuse for large house parties and general revelry, **Tickets** for games range from $6 to $35 for a regular series and as much as $100 for a Grey Cup match.

Baseball

When the **Toronto Blue Jays** won their first World Series in 1992, more than a million people jammed downtown to celebrate the victory. When the Jays repeated the feat the following year, Toronto's newfound love for baseball was sealed. Some people consider **baseball** to be on a par with chess as an intellectually challenging game of strategy. Others consider its entertainment value to be marginally shy of watching paint dry. Somewhere in between are people who simply enjoy the relaxed pace of the game while sipping beer and snacking on hot dogs on a warm summer day.

The Blue Jays (affiliated with Major League Baseball's American League) play 81 home games a **season**, which lasts from April to October. Games are generally played in the afternoon or at night and can last anywhere from two to four hours. **Tickets** for a match at the Blue Jays' splendid home, SkyDome (see above), start at around $20 and are usually easy to obtain.

Basketball

Canadians are fond of annoying Americans with the fact that **basketball** was invented by a Canadian, James Naismith. It is with less enthusiasm, though, that they acknowledge that it was not until Naismith took his game south of the border in 1891 that it actually took off.

Toronto had a professional basketball team in the Thirties and Forties, but when the American divisions reorganized themselves into the National Basketball Association (NBA) in the Fifties, the Toronto franchise was dropped. Toronto didn't rejoin the professional ranks until 1995, when the **Toronto Raptors**, named for the dinosaurs made famous by Michael Crichton's *Jurassic Park*, joined the NBA.

The Raptors play home games during the November through May **season** at the ultramodern **Air Canada Centre** (see above). **Ticket prices** range from $11 to $500, although the upper range prices are rare and indicate the best seats for an all-star game. At the time of writing the Raptors are far from being a top NBA team. However it is worth attending a game to marvel at the sheer athleticism of professional basketball players.

Lacrosse

Although Canada's national sport is now ice hockey, the first and perhaps most truly Canadian sport is **lacrosse**, which is currently enjoying a vigorous resurgence in popularity. This fast, rugged game was invented by the Iroquois peoples of the Six Nation Confederacy, whose games would include hundreds of players on both sides and were mistaken by the first European sports spectators for battles. The rules of play, simplified and codified in the mid-nineteenth century, state that the game's objective is simply to send the ball through the opponent's goal as many times as possible while preventing the opposing team from scoring. There are ten players to a team and the long-handled, racket-like implement, called the crosse, used to toss and catch the ball, is the most distinctive feature of the game. As in hockey, players face off in midfield, their crosses touching the ground and the referee drops the ball between them. Other similarities lacrosse shares with hockey are body checks and penalties for slashing, tripping and fist-fights. The local National Lacrosse League team, the **Toronto Rock**, are back-to-back series champions. From January to April the Rock play at the **Air Canada Centre** (see above). **Tickets** are around the $10 mark.

△ Vince Carter, of the Toronto Raptors basketball team

Soccer

One of the few things almost all the diverse cultures who have settled in Toronto have in common is a passionate love of **soccer**. The years when World Cup championships are played turn virtually everyone into a soccer expert as restaurants, coffee houses and bars stay open straight through the night so fans can watch live broadcasts from around the world. Global alliances are made, unmade and then made again as different communities play off and then root for other communities. Victories are celebrated with much flag waving, toasting and car horn blowing. Locally, the game remains largely an amateur sport, although a national amateur team exists. Parks with baseball diamonds also have soccer pitches chalked out for the use of local teams or for neighbourhood pickup matches. Access to the parks is free but it may be necessary to book ahead for organized matches through the Metropolitan Toronto Parks and Recreation department (see p.178). A spot of footie on a vacant pitch is, of course, the sort of exercise the whole parks system was built for.

Bicycling

Bicycles have proliferated in Toronto, both as a means of transportation and for recreation. Indeed, the municipal government even has a Cycling Committee, which devotes itself to protecting the interests of cyclists in the city. The committee also sponsors a variety of group rides and bike-friendly activities; for more information call ☎416/392-7592. Bike lanes have made an appearance on the main traffic arteries throughout the city, and there are over 85 kilometres of cycling paths in Toronto's parklands. **Map**s of the various cycling routes are available free of charge at bike shops, Toronto Information kiosks and through Metro Parks and Culture (☎416/392-8186); one of the best of these maps is put out by the Green Tourism Association (seep.184).

Because bicycles are considered vehicles, cyclists are subject to the same rules of the road as car drivers with one addition: cyclists under the age of eighteen must wear a protective helmet. Bicycles are allowed on streetcars, subways and buses except during weekday rush hours: 6.30–9.30am and 3.30–6.30pm.

Bicycles can be **rented** on the Toronto Islands (see p.81) at Hanlan's Point and on Centre Island; onshore, your best bet is McBride Cycle, 180 Queen's Quay W (☎416/203-5651), which charges $12 for the first hour, and $2 for every hour thereafter. Other competitively priced rental locations for bicycles include Wheel Excitement, 5 Rees St (☎260-9000), Bathurst Cycle at 913 Bathurst St (☎416/533-7510), and The Cyclepath at 2106 Yonge St (☎416/487-1717) and three other locations.

Skateboarding, snowboarding and skiing

Although the modernist plazas surrounding the downtown skyscrapers are a serious temptation for **skateboard** enthusiasts, boarding downtown is not always looked kindly upon by authorities – not to mention the locals. There are, however, plenty of skateboarding parks ringing the city. A popular downtown skatepark is Shred Central, 19 St Nicolas St, near Yonge and Wellesley (☎416/923-9842 or 924-2589). Skateboarding's winter twin, **snowboarding**, as well as **cross-country skiing**, can be experienced without leaving the city limits. In the hilly northern bounds of Toronto, try the Raven Ski Snowboard

Club, 206 Lord Seaton Rd, Willowdale (☎416/225-1551); lessons are available for beginners. Two municipal centres that rent **equipment** and provide **lessons** are the North York Ski Centre (☎416/395-7931), located in Earl Bales Park at Sheppard and Bathurst streets, and the Centennial Park Ski Hill at Renforth and Rathburn streets (☎416/394-8754). Some city parks also have steep banks and cliffs suitable for beginner snowboarding. In particular, try the Broadview side of Riverdale Park (take the #504 or #505 streetcar to the Broadview station), although on a snowy Sunday you may have to make way for young tobogganers. Rentals, equipment and local skatepark tips can be had at Hogtown Skateboard & Snowboard Shop, 401 King St W (☎416/598-4192).

Ice skating

More than 120 indoor and outdoor iced surfaces operate day and night in the city's parks, suitable for **ice skating** and "shinny" (informal ice hockey). One of the most popular rinks is right out front of the New City Hall in Nathan Phillips Square (see p.49), which also has a skate rental facility. There is no charge to use any of the various park skating facilities, but if you don't have your own skates, a rental pair will set you back $5–7. For information on the various locations, hours of operation and ice conditions call the parks service number at ☎416/392-1111 (Mon–Fri 8.30am–4.30pm).

Hiking and walking

There are nine walking trails – referred to by the city as **Discovery Walks** – winding through the city's parklands, ravines and neighbourhoods (for more information call ☎416/392-1111). The meandering routes are perfect for families, and are peppered with signs that explain the flora, fauna and historical significance of the trails. The Central Ravines, Belt Line and Gardens Discovery Walk winds through the Don River's wooded ravines, following an old rail line north to the pastoral setting of Mount Pleasant Cemetery. Another favourite is the Don Valley Hills and Dales Discovery Walk, which is particularly popular with young families, and weaves through a bird sanctuary before crossing the Don River and heading up into Riverdale Park, whose hills are a tobogganers dream in the winter. Perhaps suprisingly, the Downtown Toronto Discovery Walk is the most informative because much of the natural landscape features continue to exist beneath the concrete surface. The best coastal paths are the Western and Eastern Ravines and Beaches Discovery Walks, which lead to a shoreline boardwalk through natural ponds, marshes and lakeshore parks. From here – or any of the city's walking paths – it's hard to believe you're still within Toronto's city limits. Other Discovery Walks are the Northern Ravines and Gardens and the Uptown Toronto routes. There are also special walking tours organized by the city, which include bird watching, spring garden tours, fall foliage and heritage walks. For information on city-run walks call ☎416/392-8186.

Golf

More than two hundred public and semi-private eighteen-hole **golf courses** exist within an hour's drive of Toronto, some of which, like Glen Abbey (☎905/844-1800), are PGA – in essence, professional-level – courses, where a

In 2001 a movement towards environmental tourism crystallized in Toronto under the umbrella of the **Green Tourism Association** (☏www.greentourism.on.ca). The organization produces an excellent city map showing all the hiking and cycling, and public transit routes but none of the paved roads. It also maintains a website that keeps visitors up-to-date on environmentally friendly restaurants, bed and breakfast establishments, shops and walking and cycling tours. As an alternative to taking a bus tour around Toronto, professionally guided or self-guided bicycle, hiking and walking tours cannot be recommended too highly. Apart from being good exercise, they reveal the city's natural and cultural history through personal experience.

Recommended outfits

A Taste of the World ☏416/923-6813. Toronto's oldest established guided walk and bicycle tour outfit combines local lore, sneak peeks, and food, food, food. The Chinatown and Kensington Market walks are classics.

A Stroll in the Park Walking & Adventure Club ☏416/484-9255, ☏www.interlog.com/~walktalk. A mobile single's club that meets on weekends for walks, hikes and optional dinners through city parks and ravines.

ROMwalks ☏416/586-8097. Guided, volunteer-led walking tours through architecturally and historically significant Toronto neighbourhoods.

Something's Afoot ☏416/695-1838, ☏www.somethingsafoot.com. If you have explored the city's trails and byways you may want to hike a "gentle" day-trip from Toronto in the Niagara, Haliburton or Quinte regions of Ontario.

Two more private organizations offering well-organized hiking and walking tours are the **Toronto Bruce Trail Club** (☏416/690-HIKE), and **Toronto Field Naturalists** (☏416/968-6255).

full round can cost hundreds of dollars. More cost-effective options are located within the city, namely five public golf courses that offer beginners and experienced duffers alike the opportunity to whack a few balls around. They are: **Scarlett Woods Golf Course** (☏416/392-2484), a par-62 course suitable for beginners at Scarlett Road and Jane Street, south of Eglinton Avenue East; the **Humber Valley Golf Course** (☏416/392-2488), a challenging par-70 course on Beattie Avenue east of Albion Road; **Dentonia Park Golf Course** (☏416/392-2558), an excellent eighteen-hole course on Victoria Park Avenue, just off Danforth Avenue; the **Don Valley Golf Course** (☏416/392-2465), another challenging eighteen-hole, par-71 course at the intersection of Yonge Street and William Carson Crescent, a five-minute walk from the York Mills subway stop; and finally, the **Tam O'Shanter Golf Course**, the city's premier golfing facility, with eighteen holes ranked at par-70. It is located on Birchmount Road north of Sheppard Avenue East; via public transportation take either the Birchmount #17, Sheppard East #85 or Sheppard East #85A buses. Last but not least is the City Core Driving Range (☏416/640-9888), a privately owned facility which is at the foot of Spadina Ave, only a hop, skip and a jump away from the SkyDome. All of Toronto's golf courses have public washrooms, club houses and pro shops with rental equipment. Greens fees typically range from $14 to $19 for nine holes, and from $22 to $46 for eighteen holes; renting equipment is of course extra. To get up-to-the-minute course information check the following sites: ☏www.city.toronto.on.ca/parks/recreation, ☏torontogolf.com, and ☏toronto.com.

Watersports

Toronto is a port city with an active waterfront. **Sailing**, **windsurfing**, **water skiing**, and cruise **boating** are popular summer pursuits along the shores of Lake Ontario. **Swimming** in Lake Ontario is not recommended due to pollution, but the public beaches are still popular attractions for sunning and general carousing. Heading out on the lake on a sailboat, canoe or kayak is an easy proposition through the Harbourfront Canoe and Kayak Centre, 283A Queen's Quay West (℡416/203-2277), which runs classes, rentals and organized tours year-round. Another place to rent anything from canoes and kayaks to cross-country skis is Mountain Equipment Co-op, 400 King St W (℡416/340-2667).

If you happen to be visiting Toronto with your own boat in tow, the city operates four **public marinas**: Ashbridge's Bay Park (℡416/392-6095) is accessible by car from Lakeshore Boulevard East, just east of Coxwell Avenue; Bluffer's Park Marina (℡416/392-2556), with its 500-slip public marina, is reached by driving south on Brimley Road to its end; and at the city's west end, there's Humber Bay West Park (℡416/392-9715), a waterfront park with fly casting and model-boat ponds, a fishing pier, and a public boat launch and moorings. It can be reached by car via Lakeshore Boulevard near Park Lawn Road. Finally, there is also a public marina on the Toronto Islands (℡416/203-1055), which charges a nominal fee for overnight stays.

15

Kids' Toronto

Toronto does an excellent job of keeping visitors with **children** in good spirits. Its reputation as being both safe and clean goes a long way toward promoting a family-positive image, and many attractions were actually conceived with families in mind – a result of urban renewal and development coinciding with the maturing of the Baby Boom generation. In addition to this, unlike many other large North American cities, a significant portion of Toronto's population lives Downtown, meaning a **park** or **playground** is always close at hand.

Major **cultural institutions** such as the Art Gallery of Ontario and the Royal Ontario Museum (see p.55 and p.65, respectively), as well as attractions like the Ontario Science Centre (see p.88) have innovative programming specifically designed for children. Call ahead to determine seasonal availability and space. Other good ideas for families can be found in Chapter 14, "Sports and outdoor activities", as well as Chapter 16, "Festivals and events". The places and establishments that follow below are those specifically geared, at least in part, toward children.

Gardens and zoos

For an account of Toronto zoo, see p.87.

Allen Gardens Conservatory Jarvis St at Carlton St, Uptown ☎416/392-1111. Streetcar: Carlton (#506). The six greenhouses here are in bloom year-round, but the place is especially alive with children during its Victorian Christmas Flower Show, which runs from early December to early January; opening ceremonies include sleigh rides, carolling and games for children.

Far Enough Farm Centerville, Centre Island. More of a petting zoo than a farm, this petite collection of donkeys, goats and domestic fowl is a cost-free amusement for the very young. See p.81 for more.

Riverdale Farm 201 Winchester St, Uptown ☎416/392-6794. Streetcar: Carlton (#506). A slice of early twentieth century rural life lives on in the heart of Cabbagetown, in what was once the city's zoo. The old Reptile House is now flanked by a duck pond filled with turtles, while other farm residents include cows, pigs, rabbits, sheep, horses, donkeys, geese, chickens and the odd emu. Popular all year long, the spring is an especially good time for your new(ish) arrivals to see the farm's new arrivals.

Indoor activities

The Agincourt Leisure Pool 31 Glen Watford Drive, ☎416/396-8343. Subway to Sheppard Station, then bus 85 or 85A. Particularly popular in the depths of winter with locals, the

Agincourt Recreational Centre's indoor pool is a wet, tropical playground complete with water-pouring coconuts and a waterslide designed to look like a pirate ship. There is a spiralling waterslide for older children and adults. Call ahead for family and recreational swim schedules.

Amazon Indoor Playground 21 Vaughan Rd, unit 108, Uptown ☎416/656-5832, ⓦ www.amazonindoorplayground.com. Subway: St Clair West. The name says it all: this indoor playroom has a jungle theme, complete with huge Amazon tree frogs in the branches and vines covering the structural I-beams. Public playtime is Mon–Fri 10am––3pm, with weekends booked for private parties.

The Kidsway 2885 Bloor St W, Uptown ☎416/236-5437, ⓦ www.thekidsway.com. Subway: Royal York. The theme here is a storybook small town: the whole environment is designed to look like an idealized village, complete with shops and amenities.

Children can play at having their own hairdressing boutique or service station.

Lillian H. Smith Library 293 College Street, Uptown ☎416/393-5630. Streetcar: Carlton (#506). Everything here, from the vast collections to the statues of mythical beasts outside the main door, is dedicated solely to children's literature. Don't miss the Osborne Collection of Early Children's Books, which has rare and first-edition books dating from as far back as the fourteenth century.

Playground Paradise 150 Grenoble Drive, East York ☎416/395-6014, Bus: route #100 bus from Broadview Station. This former community centre was converted by Toronto Parks and Recreation into an excellent indoor playground crammed with equipment and staffed by teens. Call ahead to confirm public playtimes.

Theatre

Casa Loma 1 Austin Terrace, Uptown ☎416/923-1171. Subway: Dupont. When theatrical events take over Casa Loma, the whole castle becomes part of the stage and the experience is nothing short of wondrous. Plays and pantomimes are scheduled around predictably kid-focused times; March break, and Christmastime are the two yearly high points.

Elgin Theatre and Winter Garden 189 Yonge St, Downtown ☎416/314-2901. Subway: Queen. For eleven months of the year, the sumptuous Elgin Theatre is a very grown-up environment; December, however, is booked with the season's annual Pantomime production, featuring flashy costumes, ridiculous characters and the annual retelling of one old chestnut after another. All in all, an excellent introduction for the young ones to the magic of theatre.

Lorraine Kimsa Young People's Theatre 165 Front St, Downtown ☎416/862-2222. Streetcar: King at Sherbourne (#504). This large red-brick edifice is home to Toronto's excellent Young People's Theatre company. Although the company provides theatre that is pure entertainment, it's outstanding in scheduling playbills that assume their young audiences can think for themselves. Some productions are pitched towards early teen age groups. Call ahead for seasons and schedules.

Solar Stage Children's Theatre Madison Center, lower level, 4950 Yonge St, North York ☎416/368-8031, ⓦ www.solarstage.on.ca. Subway: Sheppard-Yonge. Although many Toronto troupes offer productions for children, Solar Stage actually carved out a dedicated company, with its goal to provide excellent theatrical entertainment for children ages six through twelve. Call for seasonal offerings or check the website.

Shops

Clothing

Floriane 38 Avenue Rd, Uptown ☎416/920-6367. Subway: Bay or Museum. Some children exibit extremely well-defined, possibly expensive taste at an early age. Others simply have parents who can afford to

dress them that way. Whichever the case, this boutique is based on the notion that one is never too young for sartorial sophistication.

Get Outside 437 Queen St W, Downtown ☎416/593-5598. Streetcar: King (#504). At the very sharp point of cutting edge, this 'tween-to-teen emporium has shoes, clothes and accessories for both genders of today's youth. This is the best place in town for Paul Frank lines as well as Emily the Strange stuff. Stay tuned for future trends.

Jacadi in the Hazleton Lanes mall, 87 Avenue Rd, Uptown ☎416/923-1717. Subway: Bay. A branch of the haute couture Parisian chain that introduces kids to fashion's foibles at a very young age. The clothes are very well made, very nice and very expensive.

Misdemeanours 322 Queen St W, Downtown ☎416/351-8758. Streetcar: Queen (#506). Everyone who walks into this store immediately tries to think of any little girl they can shop for, so desirable are the items here. The ultimate in imaginative, girly-girl dresses, forward accessories and playwear for girls aged newborn to fourteen, Misdemeanours is the offspring of Fashion Crimes across the street (see p.171 for a review), and exhibits the same commitment to confident whimsy and slightly skewed style.

Roots Kids at the Eaton Centre, 220 Yonge St, Downtown ☎416/542-1618. Subway:Queen. No age is missed out from this all-Canadian line of high-quality, casual clothing. The beaver logo is much in evidence on hats, fleeces, hoodies and, of course, the signature leather jackets.

Books and toys

The Lion, The Witch and the Wardrobe in the Bayview Village Mall, 2901 Bayview Ave, Uptown ☎416/223-0044. Subway: Bayview. A children's bookstore with a big Narnia theme, The Lion carries educational children's books, games and tapes as well as an adults' section of bestselling books about children.

Mastermind 3350 Yonge St, Downtown ☎416/487-7177. Subway:Lawrence. One-stop shopping for toys that have stood the test of time: Lego, Play Doh, Plasticine and the like. An excellent resource for puzzle games and other intellectual amusements for children.

Science City 50 Bloor St W, Uptown ☎416/968-2627. Subway: Bay. Various branches of scientific inquiry inform the games, toys and puzzles for all skills and age levels in this underground store, which is part of the Holt Renfrew Centre (see p.173).

The Toy Shop 62 Cumberland St, Uptown ☎416/961-4870. Subway: Bay. The creative, well-crafted toys sold here come from around the world and are geared toward infants through teens. At least four generations of Canadians have bought their teddy bears here.

Family restaurants

Mövenpick Marche 42 Yonge St, Downtown ☎416/366-8986. Subway: Union Station. To get your food, diners visit a variety of food stations, where their orders are prepared before their eyes. Select from choices like pasta, Belgian waffles, stir-fries, pizza, omelettes and mounds of fresh fruit and fruit smoothies – all of which get high marks for variety, freshness and quality. Young patrons can eat their meals seated at diminutive tables on tiny chairs, and there is a play area for toddlers who can't sit still while their elders finish up. Sunday from 10am–3pm is family day, where a clown does face-painting, makes balloon animals and performs magic tricks.

Old Spaghetti Factory 54 The Esplanade, Downtown ☎416/864-9761. Subway: Union Station. Several generations of birthday parties have been held in this cavernous restaurant, which includes a section made from an old streetcar. The food is what is the name suggests: spaghetti and other pasta dishes, with lots of menu choices and treats for kids.

Shopsy's TV City 284 King St W, Downtown ☎416/599-5464. Streetcar: King (#504). Not the place for parents who hope to converse with their offspring over dinner. The booths are equipped with Sony Playstations hooked up to dazzling monitors – and if that isn't enough, over thirty TV monitors scattered throughout the place play endless rounds of cartoons. The menu is (obviously) kid-oriented, with deli and grill favourites.

Festivals and events

Toronto boasts a large number of **festivals** and **annual events**, particularly in the summer months. From June to September there is something big going on every weekend; even better, most of these events are free, or have free components. Though things slow down come deep winter, Toronto's historical homes, such as Spadina House, MacKenzie House, and Colborne Lodge in High Park, observe holiday dates and special occasions with music, food and open house activities; check Ⓦ www.toronto.ca for details. Meanwhile, places like the Harbourfront Centre host various **music festivals** throughout the summer, as well as rosters of touring bands; see Ⓦ www. harbourfront.on.ca for more. For **further information** about various festivals and events, contact Tourism Toronto at ☎ 416/203-2600, or visit their website at Ⓦ www.torontotousism.com. You can also call Ontario Tourism at ☎ 1-800-ONTARIO (also Ⓦ www.ontariotravel.net) for a seasonal guide.

January

International Boat Show third week of the month Considered by the ever-hopeful to be the first sign of summer, this boat show has become hugely popular among mariners and landlubbers alike. ☎ 416/591-6772.

Robbie Burns Day the 25th Traditional Scottish ceilidh (house party) on the Caledonian Bard's birthday, held at MacKenzie House and featuring poetry readings, Scottish music and dancing and a haggis ushered in to the sound of the bagpipes. ☎ 416/392-6915.

Metro Home Show last week of the month Dream home fantasies are one step closer to realization at this annual extravaganza in everything from interior decorating to double glazing. ☎ 416/385-1880.

February

Lunar Chinese New Year The exact date of the New Year depends on the Chinese lunar calendar, so celebrations can take place in the last week of January or the first week of February. Cultural institutions like the Harbourfront Centre hold special events featuring Chinese and Southeast Asian arts and feasts. The daily newspapers will keep you up to date on the most auspicious things to say, do, wear and eat on any given day of the festival.

African Heritage Month all month long The African Diaspora celebrates its different cultures and histories throughout February. Activities and events, including the Kuumba: Jambalaya Jump Up festival, take place at the Harbourfront Centre. Open to all ages, the events include special guest performers, storytelling, arts and craft exhibits, film screenings and culinary events. ☎ 416/973-3000.

Rhubarb! Theatre Festival beginning on the first weekend For over two decades the Rhubarb! has been the first theatre festival of the year, as well as the largest new works festival curated by a Canadian company. It has been both a theatre lab and launching pad for the best and brightest in new Toronto stage. Takes place over three weeks at the Buddies in Bad Times Theatre (see p.155 for more).

Listen Up! Annual Toronto Festival of Storytelling second week of the month A hugely popular week-long festival of storytelling events, held in various venues throughout the city. Workshops and concerts round out the main event. Mostly free of charge. ☎416/656-2445, ⊛www.storytelling.org.

North York Winter Fair mid-month A free community event designed to chase away the winter blues, featuring live performances, ice sculptures, ice skating and children's amusements. It takes place at the North York City Hall and Mel Lastman Square, 5100 Yonge St. ☎416/395-7350.

March

Canada Blooms Flower Show usually the second weekend Massively popular event among spring-hungry, garden-loving Torontonians. Landscape artists, architects and horticulturalists of every description descend on the Metro Convention Centre and transform it into an oasis of herbacious wonders. Hundreds of exhibitors and thousands of square feet make this a must-see show. ☎1-888/256-6677.

St Patrick's Day Parade the Sunday closest to the 17th This is the day when all Torontonians – no matter their heritage – claim to be Irish; it's a good excuse to indulge in Irish step-dancing, music, food, poetry, history and, of course, Guinness. ☎416/487-1566.

April

du Maurier World Stage Festival all month long A biannual festival of the best contemporary theatre from around the world, including lectures, workshops and special events. Many productions – which take place in theatres and less conventional spaces throughout the city – are world premieres, which play Glynbourne later in the season. ☎416/973-3000.

Sprockets International Children's Film Festival third weekend The people who put on the Toronto International Film Festival are behind this cultivation of future supporters: children's films from around the

world screen over two weekends along with behind-the-scenes events for children ages four and up. ☎416/967-7371, ⊛www.e.bell.ca/filmfest.

May

Mother's Day Cream Tea, Spadina House second Sunday Another seasonal event at one of Toronto's heritage houses, the Mother's Day Cream Tea is not only a slice of Toronto's past, when virtually all special events were teas of one sort or another, but it is also a nice thing to do with your mum on Mother's Day. There are two sittings and a $10 charge, plus tax. ☎416/392-6910, ⊛www.toronto.ca.

Milk International Children's Festival second and third weekends One of the largest children's and family events in North America, this annual festival of the performing arts features theatre, dance, music and a guest lecture series, all geared to kids ages four and up. Exceptional programming never patronizes the audience. Takes place at the Harbourfront Centre and many events are free. ☎416/973-3000, ⊛www.harbourfront.on.ca/milk.

Doors Open Toronto last two weekends This is the insider event everyone can get into: Toronto's historical buildings of note, many of which are normally closed to the public, open their doors for guided tours. A great opportunity to really get deep into the history of Toronto. ☎416/338-3888, ⊛www.toronto.com.

June

Toronto International Dragon Boat Race third week of the month Two full days of ongoing cultural performances from Toronto's Asian communities, as well as more than 160 drum-pounding races with national and international competitions, all free at Toronto's Centre Islands.

du Maurier Downtown Jazz Festival last week of the month International jazz headliners representing all the genre's disciplines play venues throughout the city, including free lunchtime concerts and midnight shows for low admission prices. The latter have evolved into some of the Festival's most exciting events. ☎416/363-8717, ⊛www.tojazz.com.

Gay & Lesbian Pride Celebration and Parade last week of the month The city cele-

△ A peacock dancer at Caribana, the Toronto International Carnival

brates gay pride for a full week with festive cultural celebrations, memorials and events, all culminating in a massive parade the last weekend of the month, in what is rapidly becoming the largest Pride Celebration anywhere. ☎416/92-PRIDE.

July

Canada Day Celebrations the 1st On this, Canada's birthday and national holiday, celebrations are held throughout the city, with a full roster of concerts and fun events in Queen's Park outside the Ontario Legislature buildings. ☎416/314-7524.

Toronto Harbour Parade of Lights the 1st Part of the city's Canada Day celebrations at the Harbourfront Centre, the Parade includes illusionists, storytelling, music and children's performers. It concludes with all the boats in the harbour putting on their lights, and a fireworks display. ☎416/973-3000.

Outdoor Art Exhibition second weekend During this exhibition, Nathan Philips Square, outside of Toronto's graceful city hall, is filled with the works of over 500 artists exhibiting their works in fifteen categories, for juried awards of more than $20,000 in cash prizes. One of the major annual art shows and an excellent opportunity to acquire a new piece. ☎416/408-2754, ⓦwww.torontooutdoorart.org.

Molson Indy Car Racing second weekend Formula One fanciers line Lakeshore Blvd to watch the top drivers compete in this annual race on the Indy circuit. ☎416/922-7477.

Beaches International Jazz Festival fourth weekend Jazz artists from Canada and around the world perform free in the parks, patios and street corners of Toronto's Beaches neighbourhood. ☎416/698-2152.

Toronto International Carnival (Caribana) last week of the month Toronto is home to the largest Caribbean festival outside Trinidad, a week-long festival that features music, dance, fabulous food and fashion. Check for a daily schedule of events at ⓦwww.toronto.com.

Toronto International Carnival (Caribana) Parade end of the month The apex of the International Carnival Festival is the parade. Hundreds of floats, steel bands, eye-popping costumes and jaw-dropping dancing make this parade a blast. The 1.5km

parade route goes along Lakeshore Blvd. See ⓦwww.toronto.com for route details.

August

Rogers AT&T Cup second week of the month See international tennis champions slash, slice, and pound their way through a game at the York University courts. Men's and women's championships are held on alternating years. ☎416/665-9777, ⓦwww.rogersattcup.com.

Canadian National Exhibition (CNE) second week of the month, until Labour Day An annual ritual signalling the beginning of the end of summer for generations of Toronto youth, the CNE is pure carny, love it or leave it. Kids will always enjoy the noise, rides, shell games and junk food, and the Midway at night can still be a thrill. There are many special events such as the air show and the concert series, and permanent on-site pavilions are filled with agricultural and industrial exhibits. ☎416/393-6000, ⓦwww.theex.com.

September

Toronto International Film Festival ten days following the first weekend The Toronto Film Festival is the only major film festival open to the public, which is why it remains phenomenally successful. Stars, living legend directors, big-time producers and thousands of film nuts take over the city's Downtown cinemas for ten days, making this one of the biggest parties of the year. Passes go on sale towards the end of July and are snapped up quickly, although rush tickets are available fifteen minutes before scheduled screenings. ☎416/967-7371, ⓦwww.e.bell.ca/filmfest.

Cabbagetown Festival second weekend The oldest and largest of Toronto's many neighbourhood festivals, the Cabbagetown one includes its own film festival, pub crawl, arts-and-crafts fair, tour of homes, folk dancing, musical performances and a slew of children's events. The epicentre of activities is the Riverdale Park and its little farm. ☎416/921-0857, ⓦwww.oldcabbagetown.com.

Annual Vegetarian Food Fair second weekend Held at the Harbourfront Centre, this is North America's largest vegetarian celebration, and proof positive that every foodie in this city gets their own festival. Cooking demos, activist booths and lots of free food to sample. ☎416/973-3000, ⓦwww.harbourfront.on.ca.

October

World Moves Dance Season October to May An international dance festival comparable in calibre to the du Maurier World Stage festival (see p.190), weekly shows are held at the Premier Dance Theatre at the Waterfront throughout the fall and spring (though there's less going on from November to January). If you ever wished you knew more about the art of the dance, this assembly of talent is a great place to start. Devotees, meanwhile, have an opportunity to see some of the world's most exciting troupes. ☎416/973-3000, ⓦwww.harbourfront.on.ca.

Thanksgiving second Sunday Brits may know this fall celebration as Harvest Sunday and Americans don't think it takes place until the end of November, but this is different – this is the Canadian Thanksgiving (though it entails the same family gatherings and food).

International Festival of Authors third week of the month One of the world's largest, most prestigious literary events, held at the Harbourfront Centre, features on-stage interviews, special events, a lecture series and a full roster of readings of fiction, poetry, drama and biography, by over eighty of the finest writers in the world. ☎416/973-3000, ⓦwww.harbourfront.on.ca.

Hallow'een the 31st As is perhaps fitting for a town very fond of its Gothic elements, Hallow'een is a holiday everyone likes to indulge in. Private residences outdo one another in constructing chilling lawn tableaux, children are escorted from house to house to trick-or-treat, and the closest Saturday to the 31st is an occasion for costumed adult revelry and impromptu parades up and down the Yonge Street strip. The warmer the weather the bigger the parade.

November

Santa Claus Parade first weekend of the month The original department store parade and the unofficial beginning of the Christmas shopping season, this parade features clowns, brass bands, animated floats, hundreds of costumed paraders and, of course, the jolly old elf himself. Held along a traditional route stretching from Bloor and Christie down Yonge Street to Front. Check ⓦwww.toronto.com for route specifics and dates.

Royal Agricultural Winter Fair from the first weekend, for two weeks The Royal has promoted agricultural and equestrian excellence for more than seven decades. City folk flock to see languorous bovines, exotic poultry, giant vegetables and butter sculptures, while the horsey set thrills to events like the Royal Horse Show and the National Showcase of Champions. ☎416/393-6400.

Remembrance Day the 11th Canada's day to honour the men and women of her armed services. On the eleventh day of the eleventh month at the eleventh hour – the day the Armistice was signed to end World War I – traffic stops, bells toll and citizens are silent. The symbol of Remembrance Day is a red poppy lapel pin, which refers to Canadian officer John McCrea's great poem about the burial fields of Flanders during the Great War.

Canadian Aboriginal Festival last weekend of the month Held at the SkyDome, this major event features the Toronto International Pow-Wow, film, theatre, music, arts-and-crafts, dancing competitions and a marketplace for First Nations peoples from across North America. ☎416/751-0040.

One of a Kind Craft Show and Sale end of the month What started as a neat idea for craftspeople and artisans has blossomed into a remarkable celebration of creativity, innovation and idiosyncrasy. A great place to look for a Christmas gift for that hard-to-shop-for friend. Held at the National Trade Centre. ☎416/960-3680, ⓦwww.ontariotravel.net.

December

Victorian Christmas all month long At Colborne Lodge, Spadina House and MacKenzie House, the sights, sounds and tastes of nineteenth-century Toronto Christmases past are recreated in the city's heritage properties. Yuletide concerts, activites and baked goodies are all part of the historically accurate festivities. Check the different properties for specifics. ☎416/392-6916, ⓦwww.toronto.ca.

The Christmas Story every weekend until **Christmas** This nativity pageant has been a tradition since 1938. Held in the charming Church of the Holy Trinity in Trinity Square, behind the Eaton Centre, the Biblical Christmas story is told through mime, narration, organ music and carols sung by an unseen choir. ☎416/598-8979.

Kensington Festival of Light on the winter solstice Founded as a neighbourhood event that would celebrate the diversity of Kensington's residents, this lantern-lit neighbourhood pageant begins at dusk on the solstice and encompasses images and traditions from Hanukkah, Christmas and other winter solstice celebrations from around the world. ☎416/598-2829.

Hogmanay! Happy New Year! the 31st A New Year's Eve Party at historic MacKenzie House at 82 Bond Street, with traditional Scottish music, holiday food and gaslit tours of the house. ☎416/392-6915, ⊛www.toronto.ca.

First Night Toronto the 31st A nonalcoholic, family-oriented New Year's Eve celebration held in Nathan Philips Square at Toronto's city hall, with musical concerts, singing, children's activities and a huge fireworks display to start off the New Year properly. ☎416/362-3692, ⊛www.toronto.com.

Directory

Airlines The best place to get face-to-face service from any of the large airlines is within the airport itself. Two major carriers that have a Downtown presence are Air Canada and United Airlines, which have offices in the *Royal York Hotel*, 100 Front St W ☎416/368-2511. For airline contact information, see Basics p.10.

Airport car services Airline Limousine ☎416/675-3638; Air Flight Limousine Services ☎416/445-1999; Airport Taxi Service ☎416/445-1999 or 1-800/268-6843; Share-A-Limo ☎416/310-5466.

ATMs Automated Teller Machines are everywhere. US and overseas visitors can use their ATM cards at most of them, if their cards are linked to the Cirrus or Plus systems.

Banks Bank of America, 200 Front St W ☎416/349-4100; Bank of China, 130 King St W ☎416/362-2991; Bank of Montreal, 55 Bloor St W ☎416/927-6000; Bank of Nova Scotia/Scotiabank, Scotia Plaza, 40 King St W ☎416/866-6777; Bank of Tokyo-Mitsubishi, Royal Bank Plaza, 200 Bay St ☎416/865-0220; Canadian Imperial Bank of Commerce CIBC, Commerce Court, King St W at Bay ☎416/980-2211; Chase Mutual Investment, 2 Bloor St W ☎416/922-4273; Citibank, 123 Front St ☎416/947-4100 or 1-800/387-9292; Deutsche Bank, 222 Bay St ☎416/682-8400; Royal Bank, Royal Bank Plaza, 200 Bay St ☎416/974-3940; TD Bank Financial Group (main branch), 55 King W ☎416/982-2322, foreign exchange ☎416/308-1396.

Car rental Budget, 150 Cumberland St ☎416/927-8300; Discount, 595 Bay St ☎416/597-2222, or 416/310-CARS for thirty-three other Toronto locations; Dollar, 1108 Bay St ☎416/515-8800, or 1-800/800-400 for thirteen other Toronto locations; National, Union Station, 65 Front St E ☎416/364-4191 or 1-800/227-7368; Rent for Less, 102 Gerrard St E, ☎416/599-1230; Thrifty, in the *Royal York Hotel*, 100 Front St W ☎416/947-1385 or 1-800/847-4389.

Consulates Australia,175 Bloor St E ☎416/323-1155; New Zealand, 225 MacPherson Ave, suite 2A West ☎416/947-000; Republic of Ireland, 20 Toronto St, suite 1210 ☎416/366-9300; United Kingdom, 777 Bay St ☎416/593-1267; United States, 360 University Ave ☎416/595-1700.

Currency exchange Most large Downtown banks will change currency and traveller's cheques. American Express cheques should be cashed at their Downtown office, 50 Bloor St W (Mon–Wed & Sat 10am–6pm, Thurs & Fri 10am–7pm, closed Sun; ☎416/967-3411). Other currency exchange offices include Thomas Cook, 10 King St E (Mon–Fri 9am–5pm; ☎416/863-1611), and Cafforex, whose main branch is at 170 Bloor St W (daily 8.30am–7pm; ☎416/921-4872).

Dentist For emergencies, call the Academy of Dentistry hotline (daily 9am–11pm; ☎416/967-5649).

Emergencies ☎911 for fire, police and ambulance. Other emergency numbers include the Assaulted Women's Helpline (☎416/863-0511), the Child Abuse Hotline (☎416/395-1500), and the Rape Crisis Hotline (☎416/597-8808).

Film and photography Henry's, 119 Church St ☎416/868-0872; Japan Camera, 777 Bay St, College Park ☎416/598-1133; Korner Color, 1200 Bloor St W ☎416/928-1008; Vistek, 496 Queen St E ☎416/365-1777.

Hospitals and clinics Toronto General Hospital, 200 Elizabeth St ☎416/340-3111;

Women's College Hospital, 76 Grenville Ave ☎416/966-7111; Hospital for Sick Children, 555 University Ave ☎416/813-1500. For minor medical injuries and illness visit Bay College Medical Centre, 777 Bay St ☎416/977-8878; First Canadian Medical Centre, 100 King St W ☎416/368-6787 or the Walk-In Medical Clinic, 1910 Yonge St ☎416/483-2000. Please note that Canadian citizens are covered by a national health plan. Foreign visitors will require health insurance to cover direct fees for medical services. Emergency health care cannot be refused for lack of funds.

Internet access Cyber Orbits, 1 Gloucester St ☎416/920-5912; Geocity Net, 30 Eglinton Ave E ☎416/483-8288; Ground Zero Network, 211 Yonge St ☎416/328-2133; Internet Café, 370 Yonge St ☎416/408-0400; Net Space, 275 Queen St W ☎416/597-2005; Netropolis Internet Lounge, 721 Yonge St ☎416/961-7707; SX Gaming, 752 Yonge ☎416/963-5000.

Laundromats The Laundry Lounge, 531 Yonge St ☎416/975-4747; 24-hour Coin Laundry, 566 Mt Pleasant Ave ☎416/487-0233; Splish Splash Cleaning Centre, 590 College St ☎416/532-6499.

Left luggage Union Station, 65 Front St, has lockers (24-hour maximum), as does the Toronto Coach Terminal, 610 Bay St (at Dundas), the Bloor-Yonge St subway station or the Metro Reference Library, 789 Yonge St. Most lockers cost a mere 25 cents.

Library The main Downtown branch is the Toronto Reference Library, 789 Yonge St (Mon–Thurs 10am–8pm, Fri & Sat 10am–5pm, Sun during winter 1.30–5pm, closed Sun during summer; ☎416/393-7131).

Parking Public parking lots are identified by a large "P" in a green circle. The rates vary upwards the closer you are to the Downtown centre. Payment at both public lots and street parking is made at meters.

Older street meters require coins, but the newer, solar-powered meters accept both change and credit cards. Time limits will apply in busy areas.

Pharmacies Shopper's Drug Mart, 700 Bay St ☎416/979-2424; also 722 Yonge St ☎416/920-0098. For a holistic pharmacy, including herbal and traditional treatments, try the Big Carrot Wholistic Dispensary, 348 Danforth Ave ☎416/466-8432.

Police stations Main precinct, 40 College St at Yonge ☎416/808-2222. For emergencies call ☎911.

Public restrooms Try the lobbies of Downtown hotels, any shopping centre, subway stations (particularly Union Station) or the Toronto Reference Library.

Taxis Beck Taxi ☎416/751-5555; Co-op Cabs ☎416/504-2667; Diamond Cabs ☎416/366-6868; Maple Leaf Taxi ☎416/465-5555; Metro Cab ☎416/504-8294; Yellow Cab ☎416/504-4141.

Time Toronto is on Eastern Standard Time (EST), the same time zone as New York, which is five hours behind Greenwich Mean Time. Daylight Savings Time runs from the first Sunday in April to the last Sunday in October.

Travel agents The Flight Centre has four Downtown locations: 382 Bay St ☎416/934-0670; 335 Bay St ☎416/363-9004; 130 King St W ☎416/865-1616 and 1560 Yonge St ☎416/932-1899. For full-service assistance for cruises, air, rail and tours, try Carlson Wagonlit at 1220 Yonge St ☎416/224-0867.

Traveller's aid Downtown, go to Union Station, room B23 (☎416/366-7788) or the bus terminal at Bay and Dundas (☎416/596-8647); both are open daily 9.30am–9.30pm. At Pearson International Airport there are kiosks at terminal 1 (☎905-676-2868), terminal 2 (☎905-676-2869) and terminal 3 (☎905-612-5890); these are open daily 9am–10pm.

Contexts

Contexts

A brief history of Toronto

Toronto only emerged as a major international city in the 1950s. Before then, like much of Canada, the squeeze of the British Empire had dimmed its urban lights – even though both sides were happy with the arrangement. Since then, Toronto has made up for lost time, and is now one of North America's most invigorating cities.

Beginnings

In prehistoric times, the densely forested northern shore of Lake Ontario was occupied by nomadic **hunter-gatherers**, who roamed in search of elk, bears, caribou and perhaps mammoths, supplementing their meaty diet with berries and roots. Around 1000 BC, these nomads were displaced by **Iroquois-speaking peoples**, who gained a controlling foothold in what is now modern-day southern Ontario, upper New York and Québec. The settlers of this period (usually called the **Initial Woodland** period – 1000 BC to 900 AD) differed from their predecessors only in so far as they constructed burial mounds and used pottery. In the **Terminal Woodland** period (900–1600 AD), however, these same Iroquois-speakers developed a comparatively sophisticated culture, based on the cultivation of corn (maize), beans and squash. This agricultural system enabled them to lead a fairly settled life, and the first Europeans to sail up the St Lawrence River stumbled across large communities, often several hundred strong. Iroquois villages were invariably located on well-drained ground with a reliable water supply. They comprised a series of elongated longhouses, up to 50m long, built of saplings covered in bark and heated by several open hearths situated in a line down the middle. Pits were dug around the longhouses for food storage and each village was encircled by a timber palisade. Archeologists have discovered the remains of over 190 Iroquois villages in the Toronto area alone and the restored settlement of Sainte-Marie among the Hurons (see p.106) illustrates all these features.

Iroquois society was divided into matriarchal clans, which were governed by a female elder. The clan shared a longhouse, and when a man married (always outside his own clan), he moved to the longhouse of his wife. Tribal chiefs (*sachems*) were male, but they were selected by the female elders of the tribe and they also had to belong to a lineage through which the rank of *sachem* descended. Once selected, a *sachem* had to have his rank confirmed by the federal council of the inter-tribal league – or confederacy – to which his clan belonged. These **tribal confederacies**, of which there were just a handful, also served as military alliances, and warfare between them was endemic. In particular, the Five Nations confederacy, which lived to the south of Lake Ontario, was almost always at war with the Hurons to the north.

The coming of the Europeans

In the sixteenth century, **British and French fur traders** began to inch their way inland from the Atlantic seaboard. The French focused on the St Lawrence

River, establishing Québec City in 1608. From their new headquarters, it was a fairly easy canoe trip southwest to **Toronto** (the Huron word for "place of meeting"), which was on an early portage route between Lake Ontario and Georgian Bay. The French allied themselves with the Hurons, and in 1615 **Samuel de Champlain** led a full-scale expedition to southern Ontario to cement the Huron alliance and boost French control of the fur trade. When he arrived, Champlain handed out muskets to his Huron allies, encouraging them to attack their ancient enemies, the Five Nations. He also sent **Étienne Brulé**, one of his interpreters, down to Toronto with a Huron war party, the first recorded visit of a European to Toronto.

In the short term, Champlain's actions bolstered France's position, but the Five Nations never forgave the French for their Huron alliance, and thirty years later they took their revenge. In 1648, Dutch traders began selling muskets to the Five Nations to enhance their own position. The Five Nations were duly grateful and the following year they launched a full-scale invasion of Huron territory, massacring their enemies and razing the settlement of Sainte-Marie among the Hurons to the ground.

The rise of the British

The destruction of Sainte-Marie was a grisly setback for the French, but it didn't affect their desire to control southern Ontario. In the second half of the seventeenth century, they rushed to encircle Lake Ontario with a ring of forts-cum-trading posts. The British did the same. Initially, the French out-colonized the British and they also crushed the Five Nations confederacy in the 1690s, forcing them deep into New York state. Furthermore, in 1720, the French established a tiny fur-trading post at Toronto, the first European settlement on the site, and although it was soon abandoned, the French returned thirty years later to build a settlement and a stockade, **Fort Rouillé**, on the lakeshore. This was to be the high-water mark of French success. During the Seven Years' War (1756–63), the British conquered New France (present-day Quebec) and over-ran the French outposts dotted around the Great Lakes. The Fort Rouillé garrison didn't actually wait for the British, but prudently burnt their own fort down and high-tailed into the woods before the Redcoats arrived. The site lay abandoned for almost forty years until hundreds of Loyalist settlers arrived following the American Revolution.

Early Toronto (1793–1812)

In the aftermath of the American Revolution (1775–83), thousands of Americans fled north to Canada determined to remain under British jurisdiction. These migrants were the **United Empire Loyalists**, and several hundred of them settled along the northern shore of Lake Ontario. The British parliament responded to this sudden influx by passing the **Canada Act** of 1791, which divided the remaining British-American territories in two: Upper and Lower Canada, each with its own legislative councils. Lower Canada was broadly equivalent to today's Québec, and Upper Canada to modern-day Ontario. The first capital of Upper Canada was Niagara-on-the-Lake (see p.97), but this was much too near the American border for comfort, and the province's new lieutenant-governor, the energetic **John Graves Simcoe**, moved his administration to the relative safety of Toronto in 1793. He called the new settlement **York** in honour of Frederick, the Duke of York and a son of George III, and he began his residence with an elaborate imperial ceremony, complete with a 21-gun salute from the warship on which he had arrived. Eton- and Oxford-educated, Simcoe was a man of style and vim, who brought his home with him in the form of the large tent that had originally been made for Captain Cook's Pacific trips. Actually, the term "tent" hardly does it justice – the structure had wooden walls, insulating boards and proper doors and windows; Simcoe's soldiers were much impressed. Simcoe's wife, Elizabeth, also made a marked impression on the area: her witty diaries remain a valuable source of information on colonial life, and her watercolours are among the first visual records of Native American life along the Lake Ontario shoreline.

The lieutenant-governor promptly arranged for the surrounding area to be surveyed, but his enthusiasm was skin-deep. Simcoe had wanted the new capital to be established further inland in a much more benign location, but his headlong approach had irritated his superior, Governor Dorchester, who vetoed his choice with the wry comment that the only way of getting to Simcoe's chosen site was by hot-air balloon. Simcoe had decided to make a go of things, and he certainly thought York's harbour was first-rate, but he became increasingly exasperated by the marshy conditions, writing, "the city's site was better calculated for a frog pond ... than for the residence of human beings". Three years later, Simcoe had had enough and sailed off back to England, leaving control in the hands of **Peter Russell**, a one-time British soldier, slave owner and compulsive gambler. Despite his chequered history and his relatively advanced age – Russell was 63 when Simcoe left – Russell proved a good administrator, improving Toronto's roads and setting land aside for a church, a court house and a market. Nonetheless, nicknamed "**Muddy York**", the capital failed to attract many settlers, and twenty years later it had just seven hundred inhabitants. The main deterrent to settlement, however, was the festering relationship between Britain and the US, which culminated in the **War of 1812**, whereby the Americans hoped to eject the British from Canada. The Americans thought this would be a fairly straightforward proposition and expected to be greeted as liberators. In both respects, they were quite wrong, but they did capture York without too much difficulty in 1813. Most of the American casualties came when the garrison of Fort York (see p.39) blew up their own munitions and accidentally pulverized the approaching US army. The Americans stayed for just twelve days, and returned for an even shorter period three months later. Neither occupation was especially rigorous, with the Americans content to do a bit of minor burning and looting. Even this, however, was too much for the redoubtable **Reverend John Strachan**, who bombarded the Americans with demands about the treatment of prisoners and the need for the occupiers to respect private property. The **Treaty of Ghent** ended the war in 1814, and under its terms the US recognized the legitimacy of British North America.

The Family Compact

The Canada Act had established an Upper Canada government based on a Legislative Assembly, whose power was shared with an appointed assembly, an executive council and an appointed governor. This convoluted arrangement ultimately condemned the assembly to impotence. At the same time, a colonial elite built up chains of influence around several high-level officials, and by the 1830s economic and political power had fallen into the hands of an anglophile oligarchy christened the **Family Compact**. This group's most vociferous opponent was a radical Scot, **William Lyon Mackenzie** (see p.54), who promulgated his views both in his newspaper, the *Colonial Advocate*, and as a member of the Legislative Assembly. Mackenzie became the first mayor of Toronto, as the town was renamed in 1834, but the radicals were defeated in the elections two years later, and a frustrated Mackenzie drifted towards the idea of armed revolt. In 1837, he staged the **Upper Canadian Rebellion**, a badly organized uprising of a few hundred farmers, who marched down Yonge Street, fought a couple of half-hearted skirmishes and then melted away. Mackenzie escaped across the border and two of the other ringleaders were executed, but the British parliament, mindful of their earlier experiences in New England, took the hint, quickly liberalizing Upper Canada's administration instead of taking reprisals. In 1841, they granted Canada responsible government, reuniting the two provinces in a loose confederation that pre-figured the final union of 1867 when Upper Canada was re-designated Ontario as part of the British **Dominion of Canada**. Even Mackenzie was pardoned and allowed to return. His pardon seemed to fly in the face of his portrayal of the oligarchs as hard-faced reactionaries - indeed, this same privileged group pushed through a range of comparatively progressive social measures.

Victorian Toronto

Toronto boomed in the second half of the nineteenth century, consuming and exporting the products of its agricultural hinterland and benefiting from its good harbour and excellent maritime connections. During this time, the city sprouted scores of factories, mostly secondary manufacture like textiles and ship repair. Soon, Toronto had become a major manufacturing centre and, as a result, a railway terminus as well.

Politically, the city was dominated by a conservative mercantile elite, which was exceedingly loyal to the British interest and maintained a strong Protestant tradition. This elite was sustained by the working-class **Orange Lodges**, whose reactionary influence was a key feature of municipal politics – spurring Charles Dickens, for one, to write disparagingly of the city's "rabid Toryism" when he visited in the 1840s. That said, the Protestant working class was enthusiastic about public education as were the Methodist-leaning middle classes, who also spearheaded social reform movements, specifically Suffrage and Temperance. Like every industrial city of the period, Toronto was characterized by a discordant mixture of slums and leafy residential areas, its centre dotted with proud Victorian churches, offices and colleges.

The Victorian period came to an appropriate close with a grand visit by the future **King George V**, who toured Toronto in 1901 with his extravagantly dressed entourage – all bustles and parasols, bearskins and pith helmets.

The early twentieth century

In the early twentieth century, Toronto's economic successes attracted immigrants by the thousands: in 1850, the city had 30,000 inhabitants, 81,000 in 1882, and 230,000 in 1910. Most of these immigrants came from Britain, and when **World War I** broke out in 1914 the citizens of loyalist Toronto poured into the streets to sing "Rule Britannia". Thousands of volunteers subsequently thronged the recruiting stations – an enthusiasm which cost many their lives: no fewer than seventy thousand Torontonians fought in the war, and casualties amounted to around fifteen percent.

Immediately after the war, Canada hit the economic buffers and just when it appeared that matters were on the mend, the economy was hit by the stock market crash of 1929. During the **Great Depression** unemployment reached astronomical levels – between thirty and thirty-five percent – and economic problems were compounded by the lack of a decent welfare system. The hastily established Department of Welfare was only able to issue food and clothing vouchers, meaning that thousands slept in the streets. Fate was cruel too: Toronto experienced some of the severest weather it had ever had, with perishing winters followed by boiling hot summers.

At the start of **World War II**, thousands of Torontonians rushed to join the armed forces once again. The British were extremely grateful and Churchill visited Canada on several occasions, making a series of famous speeches here (see p.50). The war also resuscitated the Canadian economy – as well as that of the United States – and Toronto's factories were speedily converted to war production. Boatloads of British kids were also shipped to Toronto to escape the attentions of Hitler's Luftwaffe. After the war, Toronto set about the process of reconstruction in earnest. There was a lot to do. The city's infrastructure had not kept pace with the increase in population, and the water, transportation and sewage systems were desperately in need of improvement. Political change was also needed. A jumble of politically independent municipalities now surrounded a burgeoning core, with industries strung along the lakeshore and residential districts spreading beyond. The need for an overall system of authority was self-evident. Vigorous horse-trading resulted in the creation of **Metropolitan Toronto** in 1953, its governing body an elected council comprising 24 representatives, 12 apiece from the city and suburbs. The dominant figure of Metro politics for the first ten years was the dynamic **Frederick G. Gardiner**, aka "Big Daddy", who authorized the construction of the Gardiner Expressway.

The latter twentieth century

Nevertheless, for all its status as the capital of Ontario, Toronto remained strikingly provincial in comparison to Montréal until well into the 1950s. It was then that things began to change, the most conspicuous sign being the 1955 defeat of the incumbent mayor, Leslie Saunders, by **Nathan Phillips**, who became the city's first Jewish mayor. Something of a bon viveur, Phillips was often criticized for neglecting city business in favour of banquets and festivals, but he was very popular, being elected no less than four times between 1955 and 1962. Other pointers were the opening of the city's first cocktail bars in 1947 (there'd been taverns before, but none that sold liquor), and, three years later, a closely fought referendum whose result meant that public sporting events could be held on Sundays. Up until then, Sundays had been preserved as a "day of rest" and even Eaton's department store drew its curtains to prevent Sabbath-day window-shopping. The opening of the **St Lawrence Seaway** in 1959 also stimulated the city's economy, though not quite as much as had been anticipated – only after its completion did it become obvious that road transport would render much waterborne traffic obsolete.

In the 1960s the economy exploded, and the city's appearance was transformed by the construction of a series of mighty, modernistic **skyscrapers**. This helter-skelter development was further boosted by the troubles in Québec, where the clamour for fair treatment by the Francophones prompted many of Montréal's Anglophone-dominated financial institutions and big businesses to up-sticks and transfer to Toronto. Much to the glee of Torontonians, the census of 1976 showed that Toronto had become **Canada's biggest city**, edging Montréal by just one thousand inhabitants, and the gap has grown wider by the year. Meanwhile, Toronto's **ethnic complexion** was changing too, and by the early 1970s Canadians of British extraction were in the minority for the first time.

In the last twenty years, Toronto's economy has followed the cycles of boom and retrenchment common to the rest of the country, though real estate speculation was especially frenzied in the 1980s until the bottom fell out of the property market in 1988. In the mid-1990s, the **Progressive Conservatives** took control of Ontario, and their hard-nosed leader, **Mike Harris**, pushed through another governmental reorganization, combining the city of Toronto with its surrounding suburbs. This **"Mega City"**, as it has come to be known, has a population of around 4.5 million and covers no less than 10,000 square kilometres.

Toronto today

The change in status to megalopolis was deeply unpopular in the city itself, but Harris still managed to get himself re-elected in 2000 with the large-scale support of small-town and suburban Ontario. A hated figure amongst the province's liberals and socialists, Harris's conservative social policies are often blamed for the dramatic increase in the number of homeless people on the city's streets.

In 2002, Harris passed the premiership over to another Progressive Conservative, **Ernie Eves**, the province's 23rd premier, a less divisive figure perhaps, but one who has maintained his predecessor's conservative policies, albeit in a rather less confrontational – some would say decisive – fashion. At the time of going to press, Eves is sitting on his hands hoping that his party's poll ratings will improve so that he can go for a provincial election – the mayoralty of the mega-city in modern times being largely titular.

With or without the Progressive Conservatives, Toronto has become one of the world's favourite capitals, sporting a flamboyance, self-confidence and vibrancy that would have amazed earlier generations. It is also a thoroughly cosmopolitan metropolis, with a strong environmental lobby that trains a beady eye on developers – often serving to stave off hare-brained schemes that might otherwise pulverize their surroundings.

Literary Toronto

Although there has been a literary scene in Toronto since the mid-nineteenth century, Toronto as a theme in Canadian literature has emerged only in modern decades. From the diaries of Elizabeth Simcoe in the late eighteenth century to the fiery editorials of William Lyon Mackenzie and the fond sketches of Henry Scadding at the turn of the twentieth century, early writings about Toronto were almost entirely non-fiction. When writers did delve into fiction, their subjects were often lofty discussions on matters of church and state, not the pastoral aspects of Toronto life. As early Canadian novelist Sara Jeanette Duncan (1861–1922) wrote of the fictional Ontario town of Elgin in *The Imperialist*, "Nothing compared with religion but politics, and nothing compared with politics but religion." These were the topics worthy of serious discussion.

Social realism

Social realism became a popular literary theme in the aftermath of World War I, but this gritty real-world writing style was slow to take off in Canada, where people preferred historical romances and small-town settings. Two important exceptions were **Morley Callaghan** (1903–1990) and **Hugh Garner** (1913–1979), who wrote about their native Toronto from a class perspective, focusing on aspects of life that had none of the high moral tones or Gothic romance associated with nineteenth-century novelists. Garner and Morley also tended to hover on the left of the political spectrum, far from the peculiarly Canadian Red Tory brand of social satire best captured by humorist **Stephen Leacock** (1869-1944). The overwhelming emphasis was on small-town Ontario, which obscured the fact that the urban population of Toronto was awash in a sea of change. In Callaghan's *Such is My Beloved* (1934), a description of the demographic shift in a Toronto parish between World Wars has a contemporary ring, even though it describes a social construct that no longer exists:

The Cathedral was an old, soot-covered, imitation Gothic church that never aroused the enthusiasm of a visitor to the city. It had been in that neighbourhood for so long it now seemed just a part of an old city block. The parish was no longer a rich one. Wealthy old families moved away to new and more pretentious sections of the city, and poor foreigners kept coming in and turning the homes into rooming houses. These Europeans were usually Catholics, so the congregation at the Cathedral kept getting larger and poorer. Father Anglin really belonged to the finer, more prosperous days, and it made him sad to see how many of his own people had gone away, how small the collections were on Sunday and how few social organisations there were for the women. He was often bitter about the matter, although he should have seen that it was really a Protestant city, that all around his own Cathedral were handsome Protestant Churches, which were crowded on Sunday with well-dressed people, and that the majority of the citizens could hardly have told a stranger where the Catholic Cathedral was.

The Hugh Garner co-operative housing development on Ontario Street is named in testament to Garner's novel *Cabbagetown*. The book is set in the Depression and takes its name from the Toronto neighbourhood that Garner famously described as the largest Anglo-Saxon Slum in North America. An unexpurgated version of the novel did not appear until 1968, by which time the streets he described had either been turned into tracts of sanitized public housing or refurbished as upscale Victorian residences for moneyed professionals. The improbable transformation of the Cabbagetown neighbourhood (see p.71) is documented in Garner's 1976 novel *The Intruders*.

The 1950s and 1960s

In the late 1950s and early 1960s, Toronto was the home base for a remarkable flowering of prose, poetry, painting and theatre. Many of Canada's leading poets, essayists and novelists, most notably **Margaret Atwood**, emerged from the milieu that crowded into the all-night poetry readings at the Bohemian Embassy on St Nicholas Street. Other major talents from that era were **Milton Acorn**, known across Canada as "The People's Poet", **Gwendolyn MacEwen**, and **b.p. nichol** and **Paul Dutton**, both of whom belonged to the Four Horsemen, a poetry performance group. These artists and their contemporaries set up awards to encourage new writers and sustain established ones; they mentored one another at every opportunity, and took many newcomers under their wings. They encouraged a school of writing that considered place, in this case Toronto, to be fundamental to storytelling. For them, Toronto was not, as Robert Fulford said, "a place to graduate from", it was a place to stay. In this passage from **Michael Ondaatje's** (who came later, though the passage still applies) *In the Skin of a Lion* (1987), Commissioner Harris, who built Toronto engineering feats like the Bloor Street Viaduct and the Water Filtration Plant (see p.86), describes a vision:

One night, I had a dream. I got off the bus at College – it was when we were moving College Street so it would hook up to Carlton – and I came to this area I had never been to. I saw fountains where there used to be an intersection. What was strange was that I knew my way around. I knew that soon I should turn and see a garden and more fountains. When I awoke from the dream the sense of familiarity kept tugging me all day. In my dream the next night I was walking in a mysterious park off Spadina Avenue. The following day I was lunching with the architect John Lyle. I told him of these landscapes and he began to laugh. "These are real," he said. "Where?" I asked. "In Toronto?" It turned out I was dreaming about projects for the city that had been rejected over the years. Wonderful things that were said to be too vulgar or too expensive, too this, too that. And I was walking through these places, beside the traffic circle at Yonge and Bloor, down the proposed Federal Avenue to Union Station. Lyle was right. These were real places. They could have existed. I mean, the Bloor Street viaduct and this building here are just a hint of what could have been done here.

In 1965 Stan Bevington and Wayne Clifford took over a back-lane carriage house space where Marshall Mcluhan had lectured and founded **Coach House Press**, which became the incubator for all that was new and adventurous in Canadian literature. In addition to publishing the early works of Atwood and Ondaatje, whose *In the Skin of a Lion* is perhaps the definitive Toronto novel – Coach House began a tradition of giving talented new writers their first break: Paul Quarrington, Susan Swan and anthologist Alberto Manguel are just three examples. The company continued to expand its interests, putting out textbooks and a Québec translation series featuring emerging Québecois authors like Jacques Ferron, Nichole Brossard and Victor-Levy Beaulieu. A turbulent period of conflict on the editorial board and financial difficulties caused the press to be dissolved in 1996, but in 1997 Bevington announced the birth of Coach House Press Books, an establishment devoted to beautiful, handmade limited editions and, way at the other end of the publishing spectrum, online novels for the Internet.

The 1970s and 1980s

More prominent Toronto-based authors followed in the wake of this particularly fertile period, including **Timothy Findley** and **Robertson Davies**. Findley's third novel, *The Wars* (1977), established him as a major literary talent, and more recent novels such as *Headhunter* (1993) and *The Piano Man's Daughter* (1995), both set in Toronto, make great use of local history, lore and settings.

Robertson Davies, one of the most significant novelists of the postwar era, uses quirky, thinly veiled descriptions of Toronto institutions like the University of Toronto in novels like *The Rebel Angels* (1981), which is imbued with a strong sense of place. Both Davies and Findley have a knack for recognizing the rich stories that have yet to be told about the people and the city of Toronto. Rather than portraying Toronto as a stuffy, provincial town, the characters of a Findley or Davies novel are flamboyant, mystical, and are often based on obscure mementos of Canadian history.

In the Seventies and Eighties, new voices continued to find their way into Canadian literature. The **immigrant experience** in Toronto has been covered since the early nineteenth century, but early writers usually saw themselves as importing values and mores, and they shared similar cultural backgrounds and religions. Writers like **Austin Clarke**, who was born in Barbados, **Michael Ondaatje**, who was born in Ceylon, and **M.G.Vassanji**, who is originally from Kenya, contributed a different perspective of immigrant life in Toronto. In Vassanji's *No New Land*, customary activities become strange, and the landmarks native Torontonians see as everyday landmarks become exotic:

What would immigrants in Toronto do without Honest Ed's, the block-wide carnival that's also a store, the brilliant kaaba to which people flock even from the suburbs? A centre of attraction whose energy never ebbs, simply transmutes, at night its thousands of dazzling lights splash the sidewalk in flashes of yellow and green and red, and the air sizzles with catchy fluorescent messages circled by running lights. The dazzle and sparkle that's seen as far away as Asia and Africa in the bosoms of bourgeois homes where they dream of foreign goods and emigration. The Lalanis and other Dar immigrants would go there on Sundays, entire families getting off at the Bathurst station to join the droves crossing Bloor Street West on their way to that shopping paradise.

Toronto also has an ambiguity about it that has long made capturing the city's essence difficult. Poet-turned-novelist **Anne Michaels**, however, beautifully explored the city's many faces in *Fugitive Pieces* (1996):

Like Athens, Toronto is an active port. It's a city of derelict warehouses and docks, of waterfront silos and freight yards, coal yards and a sugar refinery; of distilleries, the cloying smell of malt rising from the lake on humid summer nights.

It's a city where almost everyone has come from elsewhere – a market, a caravansary – bringing with them their different ways of dying and marrying, their kitchens and songs. A city of forsaken worlds; a language a kind of farewell.

It's a city of ravines. Remnants of wilderness have been left behind. Through these great sunken gardens you can traverse the city beneath the streets, look up to the floating neighbourhoods, houses built in the treetops.

It's a city of valleys spanned by bridges. A railway runs through back yards. A city of hidden lanes, of clapboard garages with corrugated tin roofs, of wooden fences sagging where children have made shortcuts. In April, the thickly treed streets are flooded with samara, a green tide. Forgotten rivers, abandoned quarries, the remains of an Iroquois fortress. Public parks hazy with subtropical memory, a city built in the bowl of a prehistoric lake.

The above description would have confounded earlier generations of the city's writers, who lived in Toronto but uniformly placed their poems and novels elsewhere. Likewise, the perspective of outsiders who came to Toronto in the nineteenth and early twentieth centuries almost always stressed the city's perceived rigidities. From Charles Dickens to Ernest Hemingway and Wyndham Lewis, literary visitors often took Toronto's social and political milieu to be narrow and provincial. With the city's social and cultural maturation in the latter half of the twentieth century, however, the city has come to recognize a new literary pride; one that has allowed Toronto's artists to describe the city with passion, compassion and lyricism.

Books

T
hough all the books below have something to recommend them by, we've marked titles we highly recommend with a ⊡. Wherever possible, books are listed by their most recent edition and most accessible imprint. If unavailable in bookstores, most can be ordered directly from the publisher. Out-of-print titles are indicated by o/p.

Impressions and memoirs

John Bently-Mays *Emerald City: Toronto Visited* (Viking Press). Thoughtful critical essays about the city, its architecture and its inhabitants.

C.S. Clark *On Toronto the Good: A Social Study* (Coles Canadiana Collection, o/p). Originally published in 1898, this is one of the city's earliest urban studies, exploring the evolution of the many aspects of city life that have made Toronto what it is today.

John Robert Colombo *Haunted Toronto* (Houslow Press). Colombo is a poet, novelist and indefatigable anthologist of Canadiana. This collection of Toronto hauntings highlights the city's interest in the weird and fantastic.

Wayne Grady *Toronto in the Wild: Field Notes of an Urban Naturalist* (Macfarlane, Walter & Ross). Toronto has a wide assortment of flora and fauna living in its ravines, parks, empty lots and rooftops. Grady chronicles them all in this picture-filled book.

William Kilbourn (ed) *The Toronto Book: An Anthology of Writings Past and Present* (Macmillan of Canada, o/p). A collection of over a century of informed, uninformed and imaginative descriptions of Toronto.

David McFadden *Trip Around Lake Ontario* (Coach House Press, 1988; reprinted in Great Lakes Suite, Talon Books). Part of a trilogy detailing the author's circumnavigation of lakes Ontario, Erie and Huron written in a deceptively simple style.

⊡ **George Rust D'Eye** *Cabbagetown Remembered* (Stoddart and Company). An intimate portrait and historical account of this popular Toronto neighbourhood (see p.71), its people and its landmarks. Wonderful photographs.

William White (ed) *The Complete Toronto Dispatches, 1920–1924* (Charles Scribners Sons). Ernest Hemingway's first professional writing job was with the *Toronto Star* as both a local reporter and as a European correspondent. This is a collection of his dispatches for the paper.

History

Carl Benn *The Iroquois in the War of 1812* (University of Toronto Press). In 1812 the United States, at war with Canada, invaded and briefly occupied York (Toronto). The role played by the Five Nations and Iroquois peoples in the war was pivotal in Canada's survival, and the ramifications of the War of 1812 affected the aboriginal people of Ontario for years to come.

William Dendy *Lost Toronto* (Oxford University Press). This book documents the unfortunate loss of countless historically important Toronto buildings to the wrecking ball, fire and neglect. An eye-opener for those who can only think of Toronto's urban landscape as modern.

★ **Harold Innis** *The Fur Trade in Canada: An Introduction to Canadian Economic History* (University of Toronto Press). Words like dramatic, sweeping and engaging are not usually associated with books on economic history, but in this case they fit the bill. Innis's study is invaluable for the insight it gives to pre-European Canada, and its trading customs with Ontario's native peoples.

Anna Jameson *Winter Studies and Summer Rambles in Canada* (Coles Publishing Company). Originally published in 1839, these tart observations of early Toronto's colonial society are marked by a sense of wonderment at the vastness of Canada's untamed land.

Kenneth McNaught *The Penguin History of Canada* (Penguin). A concise, annotated analysis of Canada's economic, social and political history.

Henry Scadding *Toronto of Old* (Oxford University Press, o/p). Originally published in 1873, and written by a member of one of Toronto's founding families, these sketches and pen-and-ink illustrations have an immediacy and charm that give insight to Toronto's early years.

★ **Elizabeth Simcoe** *Mrs. Simcoe's Diary*, Mary Innis, editor (Macmillan of Canada). The wife of Upper Canada's first lieutenant-governor and an early resident of York (Toronto), not only did Simcoe give detailed observations of the landscape and the city's way of life, but she was also an astute political observer, offering portraits of major historical figures like Chief Joseph Brant.

Randall White *Toronto The Good: Toronto in the 1920s* (Dundurn Press). A detailed portrait of the evolution of a modern city and its people. Stuffed with intriguing facts, observations and photographs.

George Woodcock *A Social History of Canada* (Penguin). An erudite and very readable book about the peoples of Canada and the country's development. Woodcock is the most perceptive of Canada's historians.

Architecture and arts

★ **Eric Arthur** *Toronto: No Mean City* (University of Toronto Press). One of the earliest and best-known studies of Toronto's architectural heritage, written by the father of the city's architectural conservancy movement.

Robert Fulford *Accidental City* (Macfarlane, Walter & Ross, o/p). This entertaining book on the vagaries of the city's development pokes around in some unlikely nooks and crannies. The central thesis is somewhat bogus (almost all

cities develop haphazardly), but it's a good read all the same.

Greg Gatenby *Toronto, A Literary Guide* (McArthur). This walking-tour guide of Toronto is a wonderful way to get to know the city. Gatenby is the director and moving spirit behind the marvellous International Festival of Authors (see p.193).

Glenn Gould *The Glenn Gould Reader*, Tim Page, editor (Lester & Orpen Dennys, o/p). Sometimes chatty, sometimes pompous, Gould's voice and erudition shine through this collection of essays, articles and letters written from early adulthood to the end of his short life.

Liz Lundell *The Estates of Old Toronto* (Boston Mills Press). A pictorial study of nineteenth-century domestic architecture in Toronto, as well as a social history. Most of the buildings, unfortunately, have been lost to time.

Patricia McHugh *Toronto Architecture: A City Guide* (McClelland and Stewart o/p). A comprehensive guide to Toronto architecture and neighbourhoods. Each photo-rich chapter functions as a walking tour through different sections of the city.

Dennis Reid *A Concise History of Canadian Painting* (Oxford University Press). Not especially concise, this book is a thorough trawl through Canada's leading artists, with bags of biographical detail and lots of black-and-white (and a few colour) illustrations of major works.

Harold Towne and David P. Silcox *Tom Thomson: The Silence in the Storm* (McClelland and Stewart). A study of the career and inspirations of Tom Thomson, one of Toronto's best-known artists. Towne, the co-writer, was also a major Canadian artist.

Travel and specific guides

Katherine Ashenburg *Going to Town: Six Southern Ontario Towns* (Macfarlane, Walter & Ross). A terrific day-trip guide to a variety of towns within driving distance of Toronto.

Green Tourism Association of Toronto *The Other Guide to Toronto: Opening the Door to Green Tourism* (Green Tourism Association). This is

a perfect guide book: it imparts useful and intriguing information Toronto's green spaces. Sure to contain surprises even for life-long Torontonians.

Elliott Katz *The Great Toronto Bicycling Guide* (Great North Books). A useful guide to Toronto area bike paths as well as background information about the region itself.

Fiction

Margaret Atwood *The Robber Bride* (McClelland and Stewart). Toronto readers had a field day with the thinly veiled descriptions of famous and infamous Torontonians. A snap-shot of time and place, this book lives up to Atwood's high storytelling standards.

Austin Clarke *The Origin of Waves* (McClelland and Stewart). Two Barbadians meet in a Toronto blizzard after a separation of almost fifty years. A warm novel of two lives and the journeys each has made.

★ **Robertson Davies** *The Cunning Man* (McClelland and Stewart). Jonathan Hullah is a

Toronto doctor befuddled by the death of one Father Hobbes, some twenty years earlier. As he recalls the circumstances surrounding the priest's death, Hullah also finds time to ruminate on theatre, art, God and the strange secrets of a doctor's consulting room.

★ **Timothy Findley** *Headhunter* (Harper Collins). A sombre, futuristic novel that brings aspects of Conrad's Heart of Darkness to contemporary Rosedale, an haute bourgeois Toronto neighbourhood.

Lawrence Hill *Any Known Blood* (Harper Collins and William Morrow & Co). Canadian novelists and their readers love books about dynasties, and *Any known Blood* is an exceptional addition to the multi-generational novel. Five generations of Langston Canes seek, find, lose and refind freedom and redemption. Extremely valuable in giving a portrait of African-Canadian, as opposed to African-American, history.

Gwendolyn MacEwen *Norman's Land* (Coach House Press, o/p). MacEwen once called Canada the most exotic place in the world, and she defends this thesis admirably in this enormously creative novel about a character she first introduced in her short-story collection *Norman*.

★ **Michael Ondaatje** *In the Skin of a Lion* (Vintage Books). This is the novel that introduces readers to the charcters in the more famous *The English Patient*. It spans a period between the end of World War I and the Great Depression in East End Toronto.

Nino Ricci *Where Has She Gone?* (McClelland and Stewart). The third in a trilogy that began with *Lives of the Saints*, this book is about an Italian-Canadian family's sometimes tragic attempts to find its identity.

Robert J. Sawyer *Calculating God* (Tor Books). Hollus, an alien scientist, comes to earth, specifically Toronto, believing that the fossil collection at the Royal Ontario Museum (see p.65) will prove the existence of God. Hollus enlists the assistance of the ROM's human palaeontologist, a life-long atheist dying of cancer. Nominated for a coveted Hugo Award.

Susan Swan *The Wives of Bath* (Alfred J. Knopf). At a Toronto girls' school in the Sixties, the protagonist, Mouse, struggles with notions of feminine beauty as her best friend struggles with gender identity. A wry novel written in a genre the author describes as "sexual Gothic".

Index

+ small print

Index

Map entries are in colour

INDEX

O

O

Y

Z

A Rough Guide to Rough Guides

In the summer of 1981, Mark Ellingham, a recent graduate from Bristol University, was travelling 'round Greece and couldn't find a guidebook that really met his needs. On the one hand there were the student guides, insistent on saving every last cent, and on the other the heavyweight cultural tomes whose authors seemed to have spent more time in a research library than lounging away the afternoon at a taverna or on the beach.

In a bid to avoid getting a job, Mark and a small group of writers set about creating their own guidebook. It was a guide to Greece that aimed to combine a journalistic approach to description with a thoroughly practical approach to travellers' needs – a guide that would incorporate culture, history and contemporary insights with a critical edge, together with up-to-date, value-for-money listings. Back in London, Mark and the team finished their Rough Guide, as they called it, and talked Routledge into publishing the book.

That first *Rough Guide to Greece*, published in 1982, was a student scheme that became a publishing phenomenon. The immediate success of the book – with numerous reprints and a Thomas Cook prize shortlisting – spawned a series that rapidly covered dozens of destinations. Rough Guides had a ready market among low-budget backpackers, but soon also acquired a much broader and older readership that relished Rough Guides' wit and inquisitiveness as much as their enthusiastic, critical approach. Everyone wants value for money, but not at any price.

Rough Guides soon began supplementing the "rougher" information about hostels and low-budget listings with the kind of detail on restaurants and quality hotels that independent-minded visitors on any budget might expect, whether on business in New York or trekking in Thailand.

These days the guides – distributed worldwide by the Penguin group – offer recommendations from shoestring to luxury and cover more than 200 destinations around the globe, including almost every country in the Americas and Europe, more than half of Africa and most of Asia and Australasia. Our ever-growing team of authors and photographers is spread all over the world, particularly in Europe, the USA and Australia.

In 1994, we published the *Rough Guide to World Music* and *Rough Guide to Classical Music*; and a year later the *Rough Guide to the Internet*. All three books have become benchmark titles in their fields – which encouraged us to expand into other areas of publishing, mainly around popular culture. Rough Guides now publish:

- Travel guides to more than 200 worldwide destinations
- Dictionary phrasebooks to 22 major languages
- History guides ranging from Ireland to Islam
- Maps printed on rip-proof and waterproof Polyart™ paper
- Music guides running the gamut from Opera to Elvis
- Restaurant guides to London, New York and San Francisco
- Reference books on topics as diverse as the Weather and Shakespeare
- Sports guides from Formula 1 to Man Utd
- Pop culture books from Lord of the Rings to Cult TV
- World Music CDs in association with World Music Network.

Visit ⊛ **www.roughguides.com** to see our latest publications.

Rough Guide Credits

Text editor: Hunter Slaton
Managing Director: Kevin Fitzgerald
Series editor: Mark Ellingham
Editorial: Martin Dunford, Jonathan Buckley, Kate Berens, Ann-Marie Shaw, Helena Smith, Olivia Swift, Ruth Blackmore, Geoff Howard, Claire Saunders, Gavin Thomas, Alexander Mark Rogers, Duncan Clark, Peter Buckley, Lucy Ratcliffe, Clifton Wilkinson, Alison Murchie, Matthew Teller, Andrew Dickson, Fran Sandham, Sally Schafer, Andy Turner, Matthew Milton, Karoline Densley (UK); Andrew Rosenberg, Yuki Takagaki, Richard Koss, Hunter Slaton, Thomas Kohnstamm, Chris Barsanti (US)
Design & Layout: Helen Prior, Julia Bovis, Dan May, John McKay, Sophie Hewat,

Diana Jarvis (UK); Madhulita Mohapatra, Umesh Aggarwal, Sunil Sharma (India)
Cartography: Maxine Repath, Ed Wright, Katie Lloyd-Jones (UK); Manish Chandra, Rajesh Chhibber, Jai Prakesh Mishra (India)
Cover art direction: Louise Boulton
Picture research: Sharon Martins, Mark Thomas
Online: Kelly Martinez, Anja Mutic-Blessing, Jennifer Gold, Audra Epstein, Suzanne Welles, Cree Lawson (US); Manik Chauhan, Amarjyoti Dutta, Narender Kumar (India)
Finance: Gary Singh
Marketing & Publicity: Richard Trillo, Niki Smith, David Wearn, Chloë Roberts, Demelza Dallow, Claire Southern (UK); Geoff Colquitt, David Wechsler, Megan Kennedy (US)
Administration: Julie Sanderson
RG India: Punita Singh

Publishing Information

This 3rd edition published Nov 2003 by **Rough Guides Ltd,**
80 Strand, London WC2R 0RL.
345 Hudson St, 4th Floor,
New York, NY 10014, USA.
Distributed by the Penguin Group
Penguin Books Ltd,
80 Strand, London WC2R 0RL
Penguin Putnam, Inc.
375 Hudson Street, NY 10014, USA
Penguin Books Australia Ltd,
487 Maroondah Highway, PO Box 257,
Ringwood, Victoria 3134, Australia
Penguin Books Canada Ltd,
10 Alcorn Avenue, Toronto, Ontario,
Canada M4V 1E4
Penguin Books (NZ) Ltd,
182–190 Wairau Road, Auckland 10,
New Zealand
Typeset in Bembo and Helvetica to an original design by Henry Iles.
Printed in Italy by LegoPrint S.p.A

256pp includes index
A catalogue record for this book is available from the British Library

ISBN 1-84353-087-2

The publishers and authors have done their best to ensure the accuracy and currency of all the information in **The Rough Guide to Toronto**, however, they can accept no responsibility for any loss, injury, or inconvenience sustained by any traveller as a result of information or advice contained in the guide.

Help us update

We've gone to a lot of effort to ensure that the third edition of **The Rough Guide to Toronto** is accurate and up to date. However, things change – places get "discovered", opening hours are notoriously fickle, restaurants and rooms raise prices or lower standards. If you feel we've got it wrong or left something out, we'd like to know, and if you can remember the address, the price, the time and the phone number, so much the better.

We'll credit all contributions, and send a copy of the next edition (or any other Rough Guide if you prefer) for the best letters. Everyone who writes to us and isn't already a subscriber will receive a copy of our full-colour thrice-yearly newsletter. Please mark letters: "**Rough Guide Toronto Update**" and send to: Rough Guides, 4th Floor, 345 Hudson St, New York, NY 10014, or Rough Guides, 80 Strand, London WC2R 0RL. Or send an email to ℮ **mail@roughguides.com**

Have your questions answered and tell others about your trip at

℮ **www.roughguides.atinfopop.com**

Acknowledgements

Phil Lee would like to extend a special thanks to Diane Helinski of Ontario Tourism, whose efficient assistance was, as always, invaluable. My thanks also to my co-author, Helen, who was a real pleasure to work with, and to Daniel May for typesetting and Katie Lloyd-Jones and Ed Wright for the cartography.

Helen Lovekin would like to offer many, many thanks to the legion of friends, colleagues, store owners, restaurateurs, artists and impresarios whose creativity and hard work have given Toronto all the wonderful facilities detailed here. Also a word of gratitude to our editor, Hunter Slaton, whose gentle persuasiveness brought this edition to a successful conclusion, and to my dear friend and co-author Phil Lee. Finally, deepest thanks to John Harnden, whose support, advice and love makes all things possible.

The editor would like to thank the authors for their hard work and good humour, Daniel May for his skilled typesetting, Veneta Bullen and Sharon Martins for the picture research, Jennifer Bailey at PC Graphics, Katie Lloyd-Jones and Ed Wright for their detailed cartography, Amanda Jones for her proofreading, Julia Bovis for overseeing the production, Yuki Takagaki for her invaluable editorial assistance, and Richard Koss and Andrew Rosenberg for their astute editorial guidance.

Readers' letters

Thanks to all the readers who took the trouble to write in with their comments and suggestions (and apologies to anyone whose name we've misspelt or omitted):

Chris Clayton, Brad Darch, Jamie from Ireland, Simone Meixner, Nicole & Kai Sauerbier, Andrew Young

SMALL PRINT

Photo credits

Cover pictures

Main front picture: Chinatown © Ontario Tourism Marketing Partnership Co.
Small front top picture: City Hall © Getty
Small front lower picture: Red Rocket Street Car © Ontario Tourism Marketing Partnership Co.
Back top picture: Toronto skyline © Getty
Back lower picture: Hockey Hall of Fame Ontario © Tourism Marketing Partnership Co.

Colour introduction

Painted storefronts & signs © Corbis/Jan Butchofsky-Houser
Flatiron Building & towers © Neil Setchfield
Cape Dorset Inuit art by Mary Oshutsiaq © Trip/Helene Rogers
Fireworks over Ontario Place © Ontario Tourism
A Northern Canadian Lake by Tom Thomson © Bridgeman Art Library
Yorkville Avenue street scene © Trip/T. Bognar
The Distillery District © Toronto Star/Bernard Weil
Air Canada Centre © Ontario Tourism

Things not to miss

1. Food advertisements, Kensington Market © Corbis/Dave G Houser
2. The Mulberry Tree B & B © Paul Buer, The Mulberry Tree B & B
3. Hockey Hall of Fame © Ontario Tourism
4. Interior view of Art Gallery of Ontario © Art Gallery of Ontario
5. Walking along the boardwalk © Ontario Tourism
6. CN Tower, street scene © Trip/Bob Turner
7. Victorian houses, Cabbagetown © Corbis/Dave G Houser
8. Shoes, Bata Shoe Museum © Bata Shoe Museum

9. Market in Chinatown © Corbis/Dave G. Houser
10. Pedestrian walking past mural in the St Lawrence Market © Corbis/Dave G Houser
11. Dinosaurs, Royal Ontario Museum © Ontario Tourism
12. Yorkville district © Trip/N. Cull
13. Poster for the Toronto Film Festival, Echo Advertising & Marketing Inc. © Toronto International Film Festival
14. Toronto Symphony Orchestra © Ontario Tourism
15. Shakespeare performance, High Park © Corbis/Bob Krist
16. An aerial view of the Toronto Islands & Lake Ontario © Corbis/Layne Kennedy
17. Students, University of Toronto © Ontario Tourism
18. Casa Loma © Corbis/Kelly-Mooney
19. Bicycles parked by sidewalk café © Corbis/Bob Krist
20. Ice skating at New City Hall © Corbis/Lowell Georgia
21. SkyDome © Travel Ink
22. Royal Alexandra Theatre © Ontario Tourism

Chapter photos

Henry Moore sculpture gallery, Art Gallery of Ontario © Corbis/Bob Krist (p.47)
Ming lion statue on Bloor Street © Neil Setchfield (p.69)
Niagara Falls © Corbis/Michael S Yamashita (p.101)
Dummies at table with food © Neil Setchfield (p.135)
Vince Carter, Toronto Raptors © Corbis/Duomo (p.181)
Caribana Peacock © Ontario Tourism (p.191)

stay in touch

roughnews

**Rough Guides' FREE
full-colour newsletter**

News, travel issues, music reviews,
readers' letters and the latest
dispatches from authors on the road

If you would like to receive
roughnews, please send us your
name and address:

Rough Guides, 80 Strand,
London WC2R 0RL, UK

Rough Guides, 4th Floor, 345 Hudson St,
New York NY10014, USA

newslettersubs@roughguides.co.uk

Visit us online
roughguides.com

Information on over 25,000 destinations around the world

- **Read** Rough Guides' trusted travel info
- **Share** journals, photos and travel advice with other readers
- Get exclusive Rough Guide **discounts** and travel **deals**
- Earn membership points every time you contribute to the Rough Guide **community** and get **free** books, flights and trips
- Browse thousands of CD reviews and artists in our **music** area

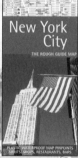

NOTES

NOTES

NOTES

NOTES

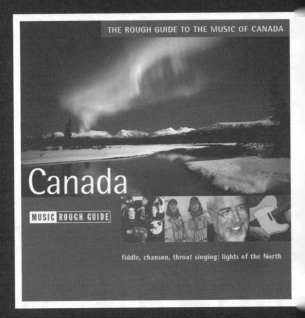

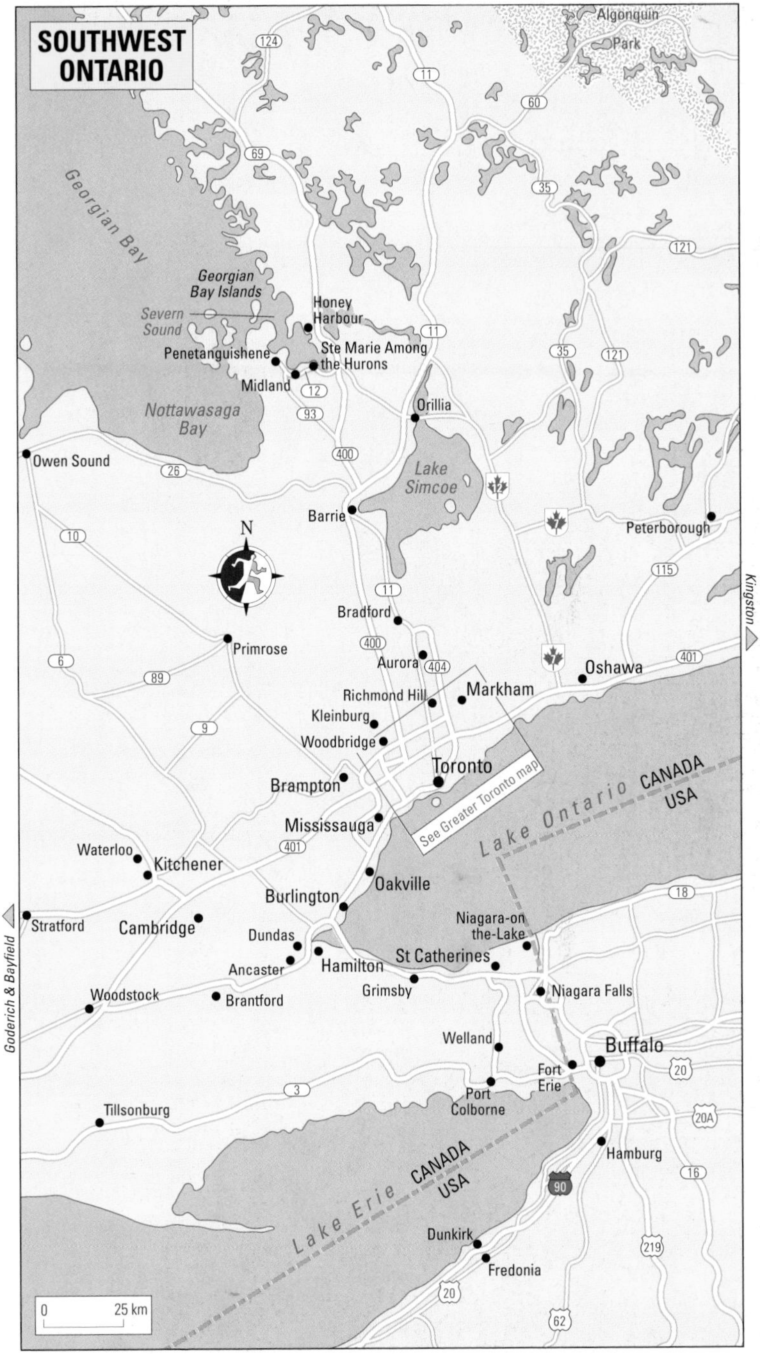

SOUTHWEST ONTARIO

Algonquin Park

Georgian Bay

Georgian Bay Islands

Severn Sound

Honey Harbour

Ste Marie Among the Hurons

Penetanguishene

Midland

Nottawasaga Bay

Orillia

Owen Sound

Lake Simcoe

Barrie

Peterborough

N

Bradford

Primrose

Aurora

Richmond Hill

Oshawa

Kleinburg

Markham

Woodbridge

Toronto

Brampton

See Greater Toronto map

Mississauga

Lake Ontario

CANADA
USA

Waterloo

Kitchener

Burlington

Oakville

Stratford

Niagara-on-the-Lake

Cambridge

Dundas

St Catherines

Ancaster

Hamilton

Woodstock

Grimsby

Brantford

Niagara Falls

Welland

Buffalo

Fort Erie

Port Colborne

Hamburg

Tillsonburg

CANADA
USA

Lake Erie

Dunkirk

Fredonia

0   25 km

Godrich & Bayfield

Kingston

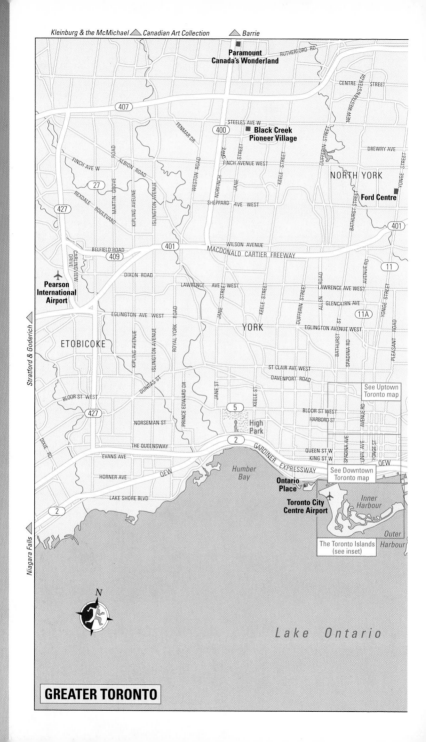

Paramount Canada's Wonderland

RUTHERFORD RD

CENTRE   STREET

NEW WESTMINSTER DR

407

FENMAR DR

STEELES AVE W

400

■ Black Creek Pioneer Village

DREWRY AVE

FINCH AVE W

ROAD

ALBION ROAD

WESTON ROAD

NORFINCH

JANE   STREET

KEELE   STREET

FINCH AVENUE WEST

DUFFERIN   STREET

NORTH YORK

27

REXDALE   BOULEVARD

MARTIN GROVE

KIPLING AVENUE

ISLINGTON AVENUE

SHEPPARD   AVE WEST

BATHURST   STREET

YONGE   STREET

Ford Centre ■

427

401

CARLINGVIEW DRIVE

BELFIELD ROAD

401

WILSON   AVENUE

MACDONALD CARTIER FREEWAY

AVENUE RD

11

409

DIXON ROAD

LAWRENCE   AVE   WEST

JANE

STREET

KEELE   STREET

DUFFERIN   STREET

LAWRENCE AVE WEST

ALLEN   GLENCAIRN AVE

YONGE   STREET

PLEASANT   ROAD

Pearson International Airport

EGLINGTON AVE WEST

ROYAL YORK   ROAD

11A

ST

EGLINTON AVENUE WEST

ETOBICOKE

KIPLING AVENUE

ISLINGTON AVENUE

DUNDAS ST

YORK

BATHURST   ST

SPADINA RD

ST CLAIR AVE WEST

DAVENPORT ROAD

See Uptown Toronto map

BLOOR ST WEST

PRINCE EDWARD DR

JANE   ST

KEELE ST

BLOOR ST WEST

HARBORD ST

AVENUE RD E

SPADINA AVE

427

NORSEMAN ST

5

High Park

THE QUEENSWAY

2

QUEEN ST W

KING ST W

UNIV AVE

YONGE ST

See Downtown Toronto map

QEW

EVANS AVE

GARDINER   EXPRESSWAY

Humber Bay

Ontario Place

Inner Harbour

DIXIE RD

HORNER AVE

QEW

Toronto City Centre Airport

LAKE SHORE BLVD

2

Outer Harbour

The Toronto Islands (see inset)

N

Stratford & Goderich ◁

Niagara Falls ◁

Lake Ontario

GREATER TORONTO

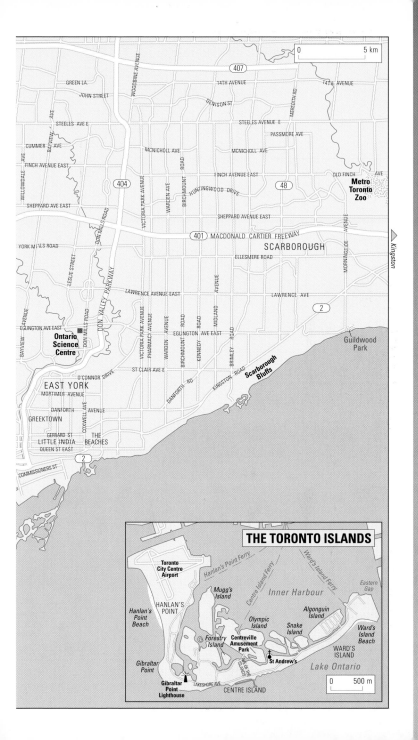

THE TORONTO ISLANDS

Toronto City Centre Airport

Hanlan's Point Ferry

Centre Island Ferry

Ward's Island Ferry

Inner Harbour

Eastern Gap

Mugg's Island

HANLAN'S POINT

Hanlan's Point Beach

Olympic Island

Algonquin Island

Snake Island

Ward's Island Beach

WARD'S ISLAND

Forestry Island

Centreville Amusement Park

St Andrew's

Gibraltar Point

AVENUE OF THE ISLANDS

LAKESHORE AVE

Lake Ontario

Gibraltar Point Lighthouse

CENTRE ISLAND

0   500 m

0   5 km

407

14TH AVENUE   14TH AVENUE

GREEN LA.

JOHN STREET

DENISON ST.

WOODBINE AVENUE

MEREDITH RD

STEELES AVE E   STEELES AVENUE E

PASSMORE AVE

CUMMER

BAYVIEW AVE

AVE

FINCH AVENUE EAST

WILLOWDALE

MCNICHOLL AVE   MCNICHOLL AVE

FINCH AVENUE EAST   48

OLD FINCH   AVE

Metro Toronto Zoo

404

VICTORIA PARK AVENUE

WARDEN AVE

BIRCHMOUNT   ROAD

HUNTINGWOOD DRIVE

SHEPPARD AVE EAST   SHEPPARD AVENUE EAST

DON MILLS ROAD

LESLIE STREET

YORK MILLS ROAD

401   MACDONALD CARTIER FREEWAY   SCARBOROUGH

ELLESMERE ROAD

▷ Kingston

BAYVIEW AVENUE

EGLINTON AVE EAST

Ontario Science Centre

DON VALLEY PARKWAY

VICTORIA PARK AVENUE

PHARMACY AVENUE

WARDEN   AVENUE

BIRCHMOUNT   ROAD

KENNEDY   ROAD

MIDLAND   AVENUE

BRIMLEY   ROAD

KINGSTON ROAD

LAWRENCE AVENUE EAST   LAWRENCE AVE.

2

Guildwood Park

EGLINTON AVE EAST

ST CLAIR AVE E

Scarborough Bluffs

O'CONNOR DRIVE

EAST YORK

MORTIMER AVENUE

DANFORTH   AVENUE

COXWELL AVE

DANFORTH RD

GREEKTOWN

GERRARD ST

LITTLE INDIA   **THE BEACHES**

QUEEN ST EAST

2

COMMISSIONERS ST

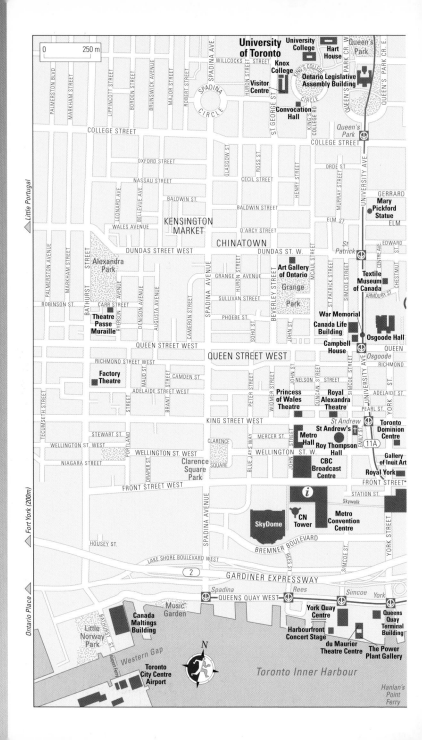

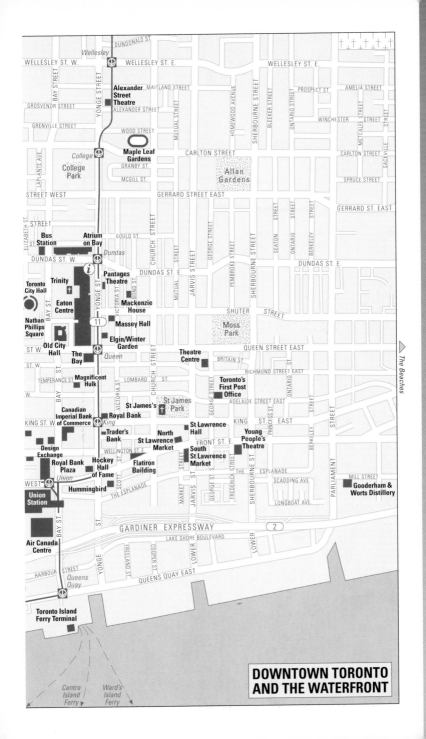

WELLESLEY ST. W. WELLESLEY ST. E. WELLESLEY ST. E.

Wellesley

DUNDONALD ST.

BAY STREET

YONGE STREET

MAITLAND STREET

Alexander Street Theatre

ALEXANDER STREET

WOOD STREET

GROSVENOR STREET

GRENVILLE STREET

HOMEWOOD AVENUE

SHERBOURNE STREET

BLEEKER STREET

ONTARIO STREET

PROSPECT ST

AMELIA STREET

METCALFE STREET

WINCHESTER STREET

College

Maple Leaf Gardens

CARLTON STREET

College Park

GRANBY ST.

MCGILL ST.

Allan Gardens

CARLTON STREET

SPRUCE STREET

SACKVILLE

LAPLANTE AVE

STREET WEST

GERRARD STREET EAST

GERRARD ST. EAST

ELIZABETH ST

STREET

Bus Station

Atrium on Bay

GOULD ST.

CHURCH STREET

STREET

GEORGE STREET

JARVIS STREET

PEMBROKE STREET

SHERBOURNE STREET

SEATON STREET

ONTARIO STREET

BERKELEY STREET

DUNDAS ST. W.

Dundas

DUNDAS ST. E.

DUNDAS ST. E.

i

Trinity

Pantages Theatre

Toronto City Hall

Eaton Centre

VICTORIA ST.

BOND ST.

Mackenzie House

MUTUAL STREET

SHUTER STREET

11

Massey Hall

Nathan Phillips Square

Old City Hall

Elgin/Winter Garden

Moss Park

ST W.

The Bay

Queen

Theatre Centre

QUEEN STREET EAST

ST. W.

BRITAIN ST.

TEMPERANCE ST.

Magnificent Hulk

LOMBARD ST.

RICHMOND STREET EAST

Toronto's First Post Office

ONTARIO

STREET

W.

BAY

Canadian Imperial Bank of Commerce

Royal Bank

St James's

St James Park

ADELAIDE STREET EAST

KING ST. W.

KING ST. EAST

PRINCESS STREET

Trader's Bank

North St Lawrence Market

St Lawrence Hall

Young People's Theatre

Design Exchange

WELLINGTON ST. E.

FRONT ST. E

Royal Bank Plaza

Hockey Hall of Fame

Flatiron Building

South St Lawrence Market

MARKET STREET

JARVIS STREET

GEORGE ST.

FREDERICK STREET

SHERBOURNE ST.

THE ESPLANADE

Union

Hummingbird

SCOTT ST.

THE ESPLANADE

SCADDING AVE

PARLIAMENT STREET

MILL STREET

Gooderham & Worts Distillery

WEST

BAY ST.

Union Station

LONGBOAT AVE

GARDINER   EXPRESSWAY

2

Air Canada Centre

LAKE SHORE BOULEVARD

YONGE STREET

FREELAND ST.

COOPER ST.

LOWER

LOWER

HARBOUR STREET

Queens Quay

QUEENS QUAY EAST

Toronto Island Ferry Terminal

Centre Island Ferry

Ward's Island Ferry

▷ *The Beaches*

DOWNTOWN TORONTO AND THE WATERFRONT

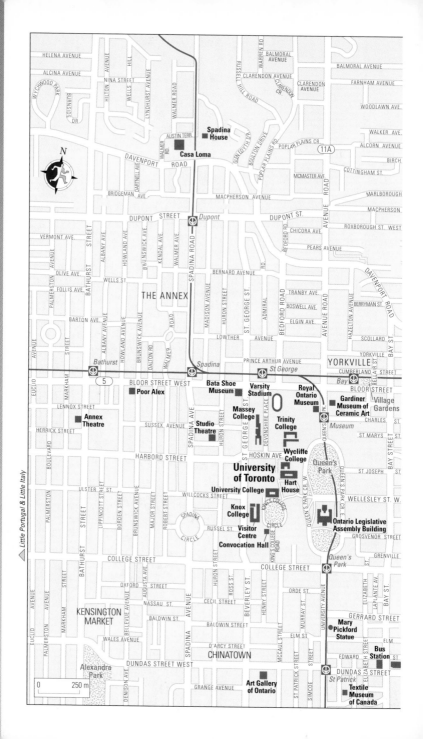

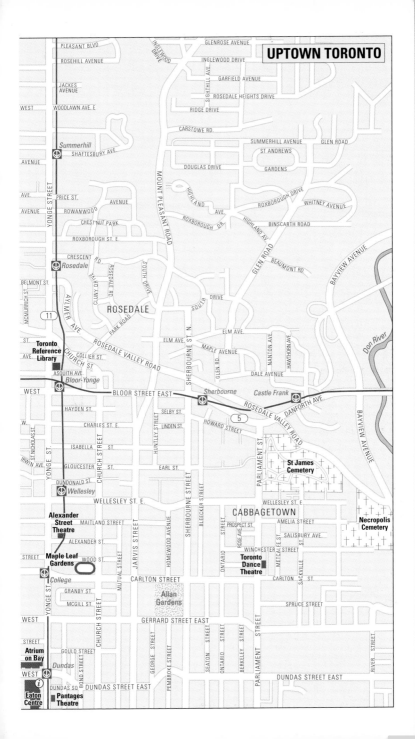

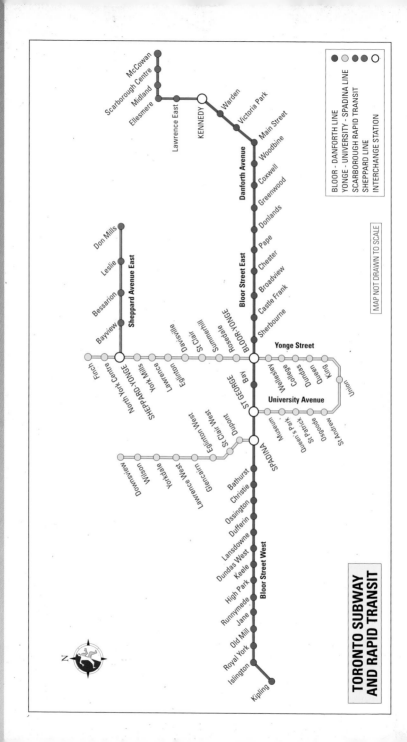

TORONTO SUBWAY
AND RAPID TRANSIT